STRAIN OF VIOLENCE

Strain
of Violence

HISTORICAL STUDIES OF AMERICAN
VIOLENCE AND VIGILANTISM

Richard Maxwell Brown

New York   Oxford University Press   1975

To Brooks and Laura

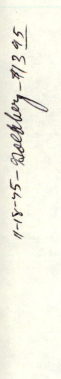

Constructive and peaceable processes have dominated human relations in American history, but the fact remains that violence, and nonviolence as well, has been a major aspect of our nation's past, just as extremism has coexisted with moderation; and the lawless and the law-abiding, both, have been significant models for Americans. The eve of our national bicentennial should be a thoughtful, reflective time for us and not merely one of complacent self-congratulation: Why, then, have we had such a violent past, and why, today, are we such a violent people? The answer is not simply that our history has been riddled with conflict. Conflict in itself is not an unhealthy state of society.[1] Conflict only reveals that people—and particularly so in the case of Americans—are disagreeing among themselves on specific issues or problems. The key question is this: Why have we resorted so frequently to violence as a way of resolving conflict? The answer emerging from this book is that repeated episodes of violence, going far back into our colonial past, have imprinted upon our citizenry a propensity to violence. Our history has produced and reinforced a strain of violence, which has strongly tinctured our national experience.

The historical process of imprinting began in the early American period, with the insurgencies, riots, and slave rebellions and conspiracies of the colonial period, with the violent resistance to the mother country in the revolutionary period, with the rise of vigilantism and lynch law on the frontiers of South Carolina and Virginia, and with the emergence of the revolutionary-era concept of popular sovereignty as a powerful philosophical rationale for civil violence.

Much American violence has been devoted to preserving the status quo. The typical frontier vigilante movement was socially conservative. It was dedicated to the defense of traditional structure and values of the local community against the threatening presence of the criminal and the disorderly. But not all American violence has defended established power and privilege. The black ghetto riots of the 1960's climaxed centuries of black insurgency against white domination. Among whites, dissident farmers and workers reacted violently against their oppressors.

In recent years, American historians have turned more and more to the states and the localities to seek an explanation of national trends and to probe their underlying causes; this method has been basic to my approach to both violence and vigilantism. Aside from the many local manifestations of the national institution of vigilantism explored at length in this book, consideration is given to a significant aspect of American violence: the violence-prone region. Smaller than a state but larger than a county, the violence-prone region is a geographical entity with a unique history of turmoil and with an impact far beyond its own boundaries. Two violence-prone regions are studied here: the Back Country of South Carolina and central Texas. In South Carolina's Back Country, the crucial period of violence was from 1760 to 1785, whereas, in central Texas, the crucial period was the middle and late nineteenth century; but, in each case, the heritage of these turbulent regions is still felt in our own time.

As suggested by the study of both South Carolina and Texas, the complex historical backgrounds of the violent events of the present generation must not be overlooked. The black ghetto riots of the 1960's comprised not only the latest and largest chapter in the long-term history of black-white violence but were the result, too, of revolutionary changes in black demography and consciousness extending back into the early twentieth century. And, for an increased understanding of Lyndon B. Johnson's role as the protagonist of America's violent intervention in Vietnam, it is instructive to consider his central Texas homeland where the ethic of violent self-defense—so notable in Johnson's foreign affairs leadership—had become a behavioral norm.

The collusion of public officials in illegal activity, emplified by the recent Watergate and related crimes, is an old story. The Watergate mentality, which justified burglary and other felonies in the interest of national security, and that of President Richard M. Nixon (whose political survival was deemed essential for the nation's welfare), was a throwback to the vigilante attitude that encouraged taking the law into one's own hands for "the public good." In a similar vein are the alleged improper domestic and foreign activity by the Central Intelligence Agency. If the allegations are true, the C.I.A.'s conduct resembled vigilantism on a worldwide scale: conduct similar to the early imperialist behavior of the great powers (Great Britain, France, Germany, Russia, and the United States), which, in 1915, Theodore Roosevelt (see Chapter 6) approvingly compared to vigilantism.[2]

Finally, there are two questions that, although not within the scope of this book, readily come to mind when the subject of violence in American history is confronted. I want to state my position on them. The first question is, Is violence justified?[3] My belief is that, in the long run, violence is a poor tactic for conflict resolution. One can settle a dispute with a neighbor by hitting him over the head, but such an action is likely to result in a series of undesirable consequences, such as entanglement with the authorities, jail, or a lawsuit for damages. In short, violence is apt, over the long term, to create more problems than it solves. Whether or not this insight is correct, men, so far, have not been guided by it, for, as Mihailo Marković notes, "Violence has always been present in human history both in individual behavior and in social life, in both the 'legitimate' form [i. e., violence legally employed by the state] and as a means to promote social change."[4] Yet, our noblest moral precepts enjoin violence, and the profound wisdom thus embodied in our ethical tradition should not be dismissed lightly.

That violence has always been with us in American history does not necessarily mean that it always must be. This suggests the second question: What are the prospects for a significant reduction of American violence in the foreseeable future? An attack on the contemporary root causes of violence plus improved public control of crime and disorder, the program recently advocated by the National Commission on the Causes and Prevention of Violence[5] would surely lower the amount of violence in our country. For example, the simple, relatively inexpensive expedient of a comprehensive system of gun control not incompatible with civil liberty and constitutional freedom would almost certainly reduce our soaring homicide rate, while the reform and rationalization of our criminal justice system advocated by President Ford in his speech of April 25, 1975, would quite possibly have a similar effect on violent crime in general.[6]

Yet, an ambitious anti-violence agenda, such as that proposed by the Violence Commission and President Ford, would still have to counteract the inertia of history, for the burden of this book is that America has a historical tradition of violence—a tradition not to be dissolved easily or quickly, a tradition to be ended (as it was created) only in the historical process. We are not, however, condemned for all time to the travail of violence we have thus far undergone. As a free people desiring to control our own destiny, we have it in our power to take stock of our violent past, to reflect on our violent present, to give thought to the future, and, as willful participants in the historical process, to mitigate our affliction of violence.

R. M. B.

Williamsburg, Virginia
June, 1975

ACKNOWLEDGMENTS

I am grateful to the following organizations for generously providing assistance for research and writing: the Committee on Faculty Research of the College of William and Mary, the Rutgers Research Council, the Harvard University Center for the Study of the History of Liberty in America, the Newberry Library, the Henry E. Huntington Library and Art Gallery, the American Council of Learned Societies, and the Social Science Research Council.

It is a pleasure to acknowledge the many individuals who helped me in various ways. It is not possible to mention all such persons, but those who were especially helpful are cited in the paragraphs below. My debt of gratitude to these persons is great, but the responsibility for the interpretations in this book and for any flaws in it is entirely my own.

Most generous with their encouragement and support were Bernard Bailyn, Ray A. Billington, Donald Fleming, Harold L. Fowler, Oscar Handlin, Lawrence W. Towner, Ludwell H. Johnson III, and Hugh Davis Graham. Also rendering valuable aid for various aspects of my work were William W. Abbot, Robert M. Calhoon, Mark Carroll, Lester J. Cappon, William J. Crotty, Ted Robert Gurr, James H. Hutson, James F. Kirkham, Stephen G. Kurtz, Sheldon G. Levy, Richard P. McCormick, W. Warner Moss, Jr., Joseph Sahid, and Richard Walsh.

C. L. Sonnichsen was extremely kind; he allowed me to consult his extracts from Texas newspapers and his notes on Texas feuds and violence, and they are cited in the notes to Chapter 8 as the Sonnichsen papers. Paul D. Riley went far beyond normal expectations in his help to me. Others who eased my way with encouragement, advice, suggestions, or help were Leonardo Andrea, Dane Archer, P. T. Artman, Geoffrey T. Blodgett, Robert V. Bruce, Robert Canady, Donald F. Carmony, Boyd Coyner, Scott Donaldson, Brother Stephen Donlon, Herbert A. Johnson, Stanley N. Katz, Stanley I. Kutler, Howard R. Lamar, Barnes F. Lathrop,

Paris Legrow, Virgil W. McKenna, Charles V. Macune, Jr., Gary T. Marx, Anthony S. Nicolosi, Doyce B. Nunis, Jr., Stephen W. Salsbury, Thomas F. Sheppard, Warren I. Susman, Cam Walker, Edward L. Wright, and Peter B. Young.

I am indeed grateful for the aid given me by the expert, knowledgeable staffs of the many libraries, archives, and historical societies where I did research. Heading a long list are my own university libraries: those of the College of William and Mary and of Rutgers University (where I taught before coming to William and Mary in 1967). I note those persons who were particularly helpful: Earl Gregg Swem Library of the College of William and Mary (William C. Pollard, Suzanne Foley Brown, Betsy Smith, Marcia A. Bush, Cynthia H. Ward, Charles Reeder); Marshall-Wythe Law Library of the College of William and Mary; Central Library of Rutgers University (Donald F. Cameron, Francis A. Johns, Gertrude Higgins, H. Gilbert Kelley, Lillian B. Goodhart, Oliver K. Westling, Donald A. Sinclair, F-X. Grondin); Newberry Library (L. W. Towner, Colton Storm, Frederick Hall, James Wells, Charles Ellsworth, Joseph C. Wolf); Henry E. Huntington Library and Art Gallery (John E. Pomfret, Ray A. Billington, Mary Isabel Fry, Haydée Noya, Anne Hyder, John M. Steadman); Library of Congress; New York Public Library; and Firestone Library of Princeton University.

Also, the University of Arkansas Library; Bancroft Library of the University of California, Berkeley; Charleston Library Society (Virginia Rugheimer); Chicago Historical Society (James E. Morris); State Historical Society of Colorado; Filson Club (James R. Bentley); Illinois State Historical Library (Margaret A. Flint, S. A. Wetherbee); Indiana State Library (Hazel Hopper); Indiana Historical Bureau and Indiana Historical Society (Hubert H. Hawkins, Caroline Dunn); Lilly Library of Indiana University (David A. Randall); Kansas State Historical Society (Nyle H. Miller, Robert W. Richmond, Joseph Snell, Forrest R. Blackburn, Elsie Beine); University of Kentucky Library (Jacqueline Bull); State Historical Society of Missouri (Richard S. Brownlee, Elizabeth Comfort); Nebraska State Historical Society (Marvin F. Kivett, Donald F. Danker, Paul D. Riley, Paul Bakkan); New Mexico State Records Center and Archives (Myra E. Jenkins); New Mexico State Library (Dorothy J. Watkins); Museum of New Mexico (Ruth Rambo);

University of New Mexico Library; Ohio Historical Society; University of Oklahoma Library (Jack D. Haley, Alice M. Timmons); Oklahoma State Library and Archives (Ralph Hudson); Oklahoma Historical Society (Elmer L. Fraker); South Carolina Archives Department (J. H. Easterby, Charles Lee, Francis M. Hutson, William L. McDowell, Wylma Wates, Ruth S. Green, Mary B. Crawford); South Caroliniana Library of the University of South Carolina (Robert L. Meriwether, E. L. Inabinett, Clara Mae Jacobs); South Carolina Historical Society (Mary B. Prior); University of Texas main library; Barker Texas History Center of the University of Texas (Llerena Friend, Mary Fleischer); University of Texas Archives (Chester Kielman); Texas State Library and Texas State Archives (Dorman H. Winfrey, James M. Day, Mary Osburn); Texas State Historical Association (C. A. Barr, Jr., Frances Parker); Western Reserve Historical Society (Judith Reynolds); and Western Americana Collection of the Beinecke Rare Book and Manuscript Library of Yale University (Archibald Hanna, Jr.).

Sheldon Meyer of Oxford University Press was an inspiration with his encouragement, sound advice, and patience, and Carol Miller was a skillful editor. Diane Nesley and Carol E. Radford typed portions of the manuscript, and Ms. Radford also provided expert secretarial assistance during the final stages of work.

My wife, Estella Dee Brown, was far too busy with her own important tasks to serve as a co-worker or an assistant, but her contribution as a critic, and as a constant source of encouragement, was enormous. The dedication is to our children, Brooks and Laura.

Chapter 1 is a completely revised version (both in conception and content) of an essay first published in Hugh Davis Graham and Ted Robert Gurr, eds., *Violence in America: Historical and Comparative Perspectives* (U.S. Government Printing Office; Washington, 1969), and Chapter 4 (incorporating major revisions) was also first published in the same work; for the initial publication of both essays, I wish to thank Professors Graham and Gurr and the National Commission on the Causes and Prevention of Violence. Chapters 3, 7, and 8 appear here for the first time.

CONTENTS

Part I

INTRODUCTION

Chapter 1

PATTERNS OF AMERICAN VIOLENCE

. . . there is even now something of ill omen amongst us. I mean the increasing disregard for law which pervades the country—the growing disposition to substitute the wild and furious passions in lieu of the sober judgment of courts, and the worse than savage mobs for the executive ministers of justice. This disposition is awfully fearful in any community; and that it now exists in ours, though grating to our feelings to admit it, it would be a violation of truth and an insult to our intelligence to deny. Accounts of outrages committed by mobs form the every-day news of the times. They have pervaded the country from New England to Louisiana; they are neither peculiar to the eternal snows of the former nor the burning suns of the latter; they are not the creatures of climate, neither are they confined to the slaveholding or the non-slaveholding states. Alike they spring up among the pleasure-hunting masters of Southern slaves, and the order-loving citizens of the land of steady habits. Whatever then their cause may be, it is common to the whole country.

Abraham Lincoln, *The Perpetuation of Our Political Institutions* (1837)

Violence has accompanied virtually every stage and aspect of our national existence. Our most heroic episode, the Revolution, was shot through with domestic violence in both its origins and its progress. During the Civil War, when the slave gained freedom and the unity of our country was preserved, internal violence flared behind the lines of the bloodily contending Northern and Southern armies. Nor did the violence pale in the postwar period, which turned out to be one of the most turbulent epochs in American history.

One significant feature of the Revolution is that the example of violent resistance to the mother country, and all the acts of violence associated with that great event, served as a grand model for later violent actions by Americans in behalf of any cause—law and order, for example—deemed good and proper, for a salient fact of American violence is that, time and again, it has been the instrument not merely of the criminal and disorderly but of the most upright and honorable. Thus, in our two great national crises—the Revolution and the Civil War—we called on violence to found and to preserve the nation.

Apart from its role in the formation and preservation of the nation, violence has been a determinant of both the form and the substance of American life. The threat to the structure of society mounted by the criminal and the disorderly has been met energetically by the official and unofficial violence of the forces of law and order. Often perceiving a grave menace to social stability in the unsettled conditions of frontier life and racial, ethnic, urban, and industrial unrest, solid citizens rallied to the cause of community order. They did this indirectly by granting to the police and other duly constituted agents of the community the power to commit violence to preserve order. Not confining themselves to passive approval of police action, these upright citizens revealed their deep commitment to community order by their own violent participation in lynch mobs and vigilante movements and related extralegal bodies. Violence, thus employed, has been socially conservative. Whether employed legally or extralegally, it has been used to support the cohesive, three-tiered structure of the American community with its upper, middle, and lower classes and its underlying social values of law and order and the sanctity of property. The second part of this overview, then, deals broadly with the challenge to the respectable community posed by the criminal, murderous, turbulent, depressed elements of American life and the violent response to this challenge by the established order.

Much American violence has related not only to the structure of the community but to the substance of the American experience— the nature and content of our society. In this connection, violence has characterized the struggle of American groups in conflict from the colonial period to the present. Group hostility has often escalated to the level of violence in white-Indian wars, white-black confrontations, ethnic rivalries, religious vendettas, agrarian uprisings, and the struggles of laborers against industrialists. Here, too, the violence has been tinctured with social conservatism. Established groups have been quick to resort to violence in defense of the *status quo* they dominate.

In one way or another, much of our nineteenth- and twentieth-century violence has represented the attempt of established Americans to preserve their favored position in the social, economic, and political order. This seems to be the true significance of much of the urban rioting of the nineteenth century, of the industrial violence down to the 1930's, and of the twentieth-century race riots. Conversely, the unsympathetic and unyielding stance of established power in the face of rightly aggrieved groups has frequently incited insurgent violence that stretches from the afflicted yeomanry and lower gentry, who enlisted in Bacon's Rebellion in late seventeenth-century Virginia, to the distressed urban black rioters of our own generation.[1]

I

Our nation was conceived and born in violence—in the violence of the Sons of Liberty and the patriots of the American port cities of the 1760's and 1770's. Such was the Boston Massacre of 1770 in which five defiant Americans were killed by British officers and troops who were goaded by patriotic roughnecks. The whole episode was a natural continuation of nearly a century of organized mob violence in Boston. The same was true of the Boston Tea Party, wherein the ancient, organized South End Mob of Boston was enlisted in the tea-dumping work. During the long years of resistance to British policy in the 1760's and 1770's, the North End and South End Mobs, under the leadership of Henry Swift and Ebenezer Mackintosh, had been more or less at the beck and call of

Samuel Adams, the mastermind of patriot agitation, and of the middle-class patriots who made up the "Loyal Nine." [2]

With the decision in 1774 to resist the British by military means, the second round of revolutionary violence began. The main goal of revolutionary violence, in the transitional period from 1774 to 1777, was to intimidate the Tories who lived in fairly large numbers in seaport cities and the hinterland. The country-wide Continental Association of 1774 was drawn up to interrupt all trade between the colonies and the mother country, but a related purpose was to ferret out Tories, expose them to public contumely and intimidation, and bring them to heel or to silence.[3] When exposure in the newspapers was not enough, strong-arm tactics were used against the Tories. The old American custom of tarring and feathering was mainly a product of the patriotic campaign to root out Toryism.[4]

Aside from the regular clash of the Continental and British armies, the third and final phase of revolutionary violence was the guerrilla activity all the way from the Hudson to the Savannah. Wherever strong British occupying forces were to be found—as in New York City, Philadelphia, and Charleston—in opposition to an American-dominated hinterland, the result was the polarization of the population and the outbreak of savage guerrilla warfare, desperate hit-and-run forays, and the thrust and counterthrust of pillage and mayhem. Thus, the lower Hudson Valley of New York was the theater of rival bushwhacking parties of Whigs and Tories. The Hackensack Valley of North Jersey, opposite the British bastion on Manhattan Island, was a sort of no man's land across which bands of Whigs and Tories fought and ravaged.[5] South Jersey's bleak and trackless pine barrens furnished ideal cover for the "land pirates" of both Whig and Tory persuasion, who appeared as the result of the British and American competition for the allegiance of New Jersey and the Philadelphia area.[6]

South Carolina emerged as the great battlefield of the war after 1780. North Carolina and Georgia suffered at the same time from the scourge of guerrilla warfare, but casualties were light compared to those incurred as a result of the dreadful cut-and-thrust of the Whig and Tory forces in the Palmetto state, where Andrew Pickens, Thomas Sumter, and Francis Marion led Whig-partisan bands in their own sectors of the Back Country. Negro slaves were stolen back and forth, and baleful figures, like the half-crazed Tory leader Bloody Bill Cunningham, emerged from the shadows to wreak their special brand of murder and massacre. Neither side showed any mercy. Prisoners were tortured and hanged.[7] Virginians felt the destruction of Benedict Arnold's vengeful campaign in 1781 but experienced nothing like the sufferings in South Carolina. Still, it was characteristic of the rising passions of the time that strife among Whigs and Tories in the Virginia Piedmont gave rise to an early manifestation of lynch law.

Two things stand out about the Revolution. The first, of course, is that it was successful and immediately became enshrined in our tradition and history. The second is that the meanest and most squalid sort of violence was from the very beginning to the very end put to the service of revolutionary ideals and objectives. The operational philosophy that the end justifies the means became the keynote of revolutionary violence. Thus, given sanctification by the Revolution, Americans have never been loath to employ the most unremitting violence in the interest of any cause deemed a good one.

Violence was interwoven with the creation of the American nation. By the same token, it became the handmaiden of American salvation in the era of Civil War and Reconstruction, for the Civil War was not only a time of pervasive violence in its own right but had an almost incalculable effect in the following decades. The latter part of the nineteenth century was one of the most violent periods of American history—an era of Ku Kluxers, lynch mobs, White Caps, Bald Knobbers, night riders, feudists, and outlaws— and much of that violence is traceable to the Civil War and to the earlier legitimizing effect of the revolutionary war.

The years before the Civil War were years of mounting violence in both North and South. Feeling against the Fugitive Slave Law in the North gave rise to vigilance committees concerned with protecting runaway slaves and to increasingly fervent abolitionism. Below the Mason-Dixon Line, abolitionists had long since ceased to exist in anything save the minds of slaveholders and Southern nationalists, but from this delusion were formed vigilante movements to deal with nonexistent abolitionists. Violence of the most tangible sort was far from absent. Bleeding Kansas was truly just that as marauding bands of slaveholder and antislaveholder sympathizers surged through the territory.

In the East, John Brown's raid on Harper's Ferry sent a tremor of fear through those who genuinely wished to forestall a bloody civil war. For the more sanguinary in the North, John Brown was an inspiration for holy war against slavery; to the war-minded in the South, the John Brown raid was seen as proof that the South could never rest easy in a union that included free states and harbored abolitionists. The nation sensed that it was on the verge of a grand Armageddon.[8] The general nervousness came to a height in the South in the summer of 1860 as Southerners gloomily awaited the almost certain election of Lincoln. Forebodings of violence, never far from the surface, were suddenly realized in the Great Fear that swept across the South in the summer of 1860. From the Rio Grande to the Atlantic plot after plot by secret abolitionists and unionists for the raising-up of slaves in bloody rebellion were exposed.[9] At this distance it seems that the fears of slave uprisings were groundless, but parts of the South were in the grips of a hysteria that was real enough. Vigilante groups and self-styled committees of safety sprung up.[10] The Great Fear of the South in the summer of 1860 seems to have been as baseless in fact as the remarkably similar *grande peur* (Great Fear) that gripped the French peasantry in the first year of the French Revolution.[11] Both the Great Fear in the American South and the *grande peur* in France revealed the profound anxieties that lacerated the white Southerners and the French peasants in the summers of 1860 and 1789, respectively.

Symbolically, the Great Fear on the eve of the Civil War was altogether fitting as a prelude to the decade and more of violence and mischief that would follow. The struggle between the armies of the North and the South still stands as the most massive military bloodletting in American history, but almost forgotten is the irregular underwar of violence and guerrilla conflict that paralleled military action by the regulars. In numerous localities throughout the North, resistance to the military draft was continuous and violent. The apogee of resistance to the draft occurred in New York City with the massive riots of 1863, when the city suffered through three days of fierce rioting.[12] Related troubles occurred throughout the war years in southern Indiana, southern Illinois, and southern Iowa, where widespread Copperhead feeling caused large-scale disaffection, antidraft riots, and guerrilla fighting between Union soldiers and deserters and Copperhead sympathizers.[13] The guerrilla war along the Kansas-Missouri border has seldom been equaled for unmitigated savagery. The Kansas Jayhawkers traded brutal blows with Missouri's Confederate guerrillas, headed by William Quantrill's band, which also included Frank and Jesse James and the Younger boys.[14] Kentucky, too, was the scene of frequent ambushes and affrays.[15]

The Confederate South was bedeviled by pockets of resistance to official policy. The mountain regions of north Arkansas, north Alabama, and eastern Tennessee contained important centers of Unionist sentiment, where the people had never become reconciled to the war effort.[16] Even Mississippi had one county (Jones) where there was widespread disloyalty to the Confederate cause—as did Alabama (Winston).[17] The frontier areas of northern and central Texas were liberally dotted with Unionist sympathizers and antislavery Germans. At best the German-Americans never gave more than grudging support to the war and sometimes resorted to sabotage. The result was brutal retaliation by the "Heel Flies" (Confederate home guards) who were often quite careless of whom they injured.[18]

Among legacies of the Civil War was a surge of domestic violence. Racial strife and Ku Klux Klan activity became routine in the old Confederate states. Regulator troubles broke out in central Kentucky and the Blue Grass region. Outlaw and vigilante activity blazed up in Texas, Kansas, and Missouri. As late as the closing years of the century, white capping, bald knobbing, and night riding, while spurred by particular social and economic conditions, remained as legacies of the violent emotions and methods bred by the Civil War.[19] Especially prominent, too, in the violent heritage of the Civil War was the surge of local feuding in southern Appalachia and in Texas during the postwar period.

The family blood feud was virtually nonexistent in this country before the Civil War. The feud appears on the scene quite dramatically in the decades following the war. The era between the Civil War and World War I is the great era of the southern mountain feud in Kentucky, West Virginia, and Virginia. This is the period that produced the Hatfield-McCoy feud (1873–1888) of the Kentucky-West Virginia border,[20] the Martin-Tolliver (1884–1887) and Hargis-Cockrell (1902–1903) feuds of eastern Kentucky,[21] and the Allen family outburst at Hillsville in the Virginia Blue Ridge in 1912.[22]

The evidence is convincing that southern mountain feuding was triggered by animosities generated by the Civil War. The mountains were divided country, where Confederate and Union sympathizers fought in rival armies and slew each other in marauding guerrilla bands. After the war, old hatreds did not die out but, fueled anew by political partisanship and moonshine whiskey in a region bedeviled by isolation, poverty, and minimal education, burned on as never before. The formal law barely operated; its power was manipulated for selfish purposes by close-knit political and family factions. Since regular law and order was such a frail reed, families and individuals came increasingly to depend upon their own strong arms. Each feuding family, in self-defense, had its own clan leader: a man who best combined in the highest degree the qualities of physical strength, bravery, wealth, and family leadership. Such men were "Devil Anse" Hatfield and Judge James Hargis. In the absence of an effective system of law and order, these men functioned as family "enforcers," around whom the feuding families rallied for protection.[23]

The great feuds of Texas and the Southwest were strikingly similar to those of the southern Appalachians, were about as well known in their own day, and had similar origins. As in the Appalachians, the main era of feuds in Texas was between the Civil War and World War I. The Texas feuds took place principally in the central portion of the state, which, like the southern mountains, was a region of conflicting Civil War loyalties and mordant Reconstruction hatreds. The war-spawned turbulence of central Texas was heightened by a combination of other factors: the extremely rapid development of the cattle industry with its accompanying frantic competition, rustling, and disorder; the fact that the western margins of the central Texas region were seared repeatedly by one of the cruelest of all American-Indian wars, that of the Comanches and Kiowas with the white settlers; and, finally, by the ethnic hostility between antislavery, pro-Union German settlers and native Southern inhabitants. The result was a series of deadly feuds that were every bit as terrible as their Appalachian counterparts.[24] Not even the Hatfield-McCoy feud exceeded for length, casualties, and bitterness the great Sutton-Taylor feud

(1869–1877) of DeWitt and other counties in Texas.[25] Among the major feuds of central Texas were the Horrell-Higgins feud of Lampasas County (1876–1877), the Jaybird-Woodpecker feud of Fort Bend County (1888–1890), and the Townsend-Stafford/Reese feuds of Colorado County (1890–1906).[26]

In New Mexico Territory, the family and factional feud was built into the political system.[27] New Mexico before World War I was probably the only American state where assassination became a routine political tactic.[28] The most deadly of all American feuds was fought in neighboring Arizona from 1886 to 1892. This was the "Pleasant Valley War" between the Graham and Tewksbury families, a conflict that was exacerbated by the Grahams being cattlemen and the Tewksburys sheepmen. The bitter feud was fought, like the title phrase of Zane Grey's novel of the vendetta, "to the last man." Only with the lone survivor of the two families did it come to an end.[29]

As in so many other instances of American violence, the Civil War forms the "great divide" in regard to the phenomenon of political assassination. Not one important American assassination occurred before the Civil War (an 1835 attempt on Andrew Jackson's life by a crazed individual failed). The role of the Civil War vis-à-vis political assassination is partly cause and partly coincidence. Some of the assassinations noted below are traceable directly to the Civil War (Lincoln by John Wilkes Booth and his accomplices; John W. Stephens and others, who were felled in Reconstruction-era assassinations), or indirectly (President Garfield by a deluded stalwart Republican factionist; John M. Clayton of Arkansas, undoubtedly a victim of unreconstructed Democrats; William Goebel of Kentucky, almost certainly killed by hotheaded mountain Republicans from eastern Kentucky's feud region, and there were the series of New Mexican assassination plots, in which Republicans and Democrats, inflamed partly by old Civil War animosities, killed or sought to kill each other). But our twentieth-century assassinations clearly spring from the problems of modern America. Even the assassinations of our time refer back, ultimately, to the example of the acts of assassination so prevalent in the post-Civil War era.

The Civil War marked the replacement of the two-man personal duel by assassination as the main mortal hazard to the American politician and statesman. The duel, involving nonpolitical as well as political gentlemen, was common before the Civil War. Most famous of all was Alexander Hamilton's death in a duel with Aaron Burr but, among other leading instances of noted politicos who fought duels, were Andrew Jackson (who in two pre-presidential duels killed one man); Senator Thomas Hart Benton of Missouri, one of the political giants of the ante-bellum period, who killed a man in a duel early in his career; the eminent Virginia political journalist, Thomas Ritchie, Jr., who slew a rival editor in an 1845 duel; and, in 1857, on the eve of the Civil War, Judge David S. Terry of California, who killed Senator David C. Broderick of the same state in a duel. Dueling faded after the Civil War, as state antidueling laws began to be obeyed rather than ignored and as leading men came to see no dishonor in rejecting challenges to participate in what public opinion had come to view as an outmoded, barbarous practice.[30]

With the lapse of dueling, political assassination came to the fore. In quantitative terms, assassination has not been conspicuous in the history of American violence, but, at the highest level of our political system, the presidency, it has had a heavy impact. In a hundred-year span (1865–1965) four presidents (Lincoln, Garfield, McKinley, and Kennedy) fell to assassins' bullets, and others were the intended objects of assassination. One of the victims, Lincoln, was the target of an assassination conspiracy. The other three victims—Garfield, McKinley, and Kennedy—were the prey of freelance assassins in varying states of mental instability. Charles Guiteau, the slayer of Garfield, was a disappointed office seeker, but mental derangement seems to have been at the bottom of his action.[31] Both Leon Czolgosz, the assassin of McKinley, and Lee Harvey Oswald, Kennedy's assassin, appear to have had strong ideological commitments. Czolgosz was an anarchist, and Oswald was a self-styled Marxist. Both, however, were independent operatives. Czolgosz was rejected by the organized anarchist movement of his day, and Oswald was not a member of the Communist organization in America or of any of the American-Marxist splinter groups. Czolgosz seems to have been in the early stages of insanity.[32] Evidence amassed by the Warren Commission strongly suggests that Oswald was psychotic, but the Commission itself cautiously refrained from reaching that conclusion—saying only that Oswald was "profoundly alienated from the world in which he lived." [33]

Although the mortality rate of American presidents in the last century has been a high one at the hands of assassins, some comfort can be taken in the fact that assassination has not become a part of the American political system as it has elsewhere in the world, in the Middle East, for example.[34] None of the major political parties have resorted—even indirectly—to assassination at the national level. Notable, also, is the immunity other high political officials—vice-presidents, Supreme Court justices, and cabinet officers—have enjoyed from assassination.

Despite some prominent cases, assassinations at the state and local level have, on the whole, been few and far between with the exceptions of the New Mexico Territory (discussed below) and the South during Reconstruction. In the often chaotic Reconstruction period in the South, the assassination of John W. Stephens was typical. Stephens, a native white Southerner and a rising radical Republican politician of Caswell County, North Carolina, was in 1870 the victim of an assassination plot by a local faction of the Ku Klux Klan–oriented conservative political opposition.[35] Stephens's killers certainly wanted him out of the way because of his political effectiveness, and the killing was just one of many, many examples of the terrorist impulse of the Klan movement throughout vast areas of the South. Similar to the assassination of Stephens was the killing—years later—of John M. Clayton, Republican congressional candidate in Arkansas, by "parties unknown." Although defeated in the fall election of 1888, Clayton was contesting the result when he was killed in January 1889 while visiting Plummerville, Arkansas.[36]

In our own time, two notable political assassination attempts below the presidential level were successfully aimed at Senator Robert F. Kennedy of New York in 1968, and unsuccessfully at Governor George C. Wallace of Alabama in 1972. In the 1960's, three outstanding black leaders—Martin Luther King, Malcolm X, and Medgar Evers—perished at the hands of assassins as did the white leader of the American Nazi Party, George Lincoln Rockwell. More recently, Joseph Yablonski, insurgent leader, was assassinated in the course of a struggle for the control of the United Mine Workers union. Much earlier, one of the most famous assassinations in American history took the life of Senator Huey Long of Louisiana at the height of his flourishing national political career on September 8, 1935. Long's assassin was slain on the spot, and, to this day, considerable mystery surrounds his motives. Authorities differ, and it is not clear whether Long's killer acted from strictly personal emotion and grievance or whether he was part of an assassination conspiracy.[37] An earlier famous (but now forgotten) assassination of a leading state figure definitely stemmed from the context of a political conflict. This was the fatal wounding of the governor-elect of Kentucky, William Goebel, at Frankfort on January 30, 1900.[38] The charismatic leader of the Democratic party in Kentucky, Goebel had been waging a hot battle against the Republicans and the railroad interests of his state at the time of his death. His assassination occurred during an infusion into Frankfort of thousands of anti-Goebel Republicans from the hot-blooded mountain region of eastern Kentucky. Mortal feuds had often been linked with local political rivalries in the Kentucky mountains in previous decades (see the section above on feud violence), and it is not surprising that Goebel's assassins seem to have sprung from that background.[39]

Apparently the only place in America where assassination became an integral part of the political system was the New Mexico Territory from the end of the Civil War down to about 1900. Many assassinations occurred there, among the most prominent being that of Colonel Albert J. Fountain, a leading Republican of southern New Mexico, in 1896.[40] Other leading New Mexican politicians narrowly missed being killed, and many New Mexicans were convinced that the two chieftains of the Republican and Democratic parties, respectively, had been involved in assassination plots. Thomas B. Catron, the autocratic Republican boss, was thought by many to have been a party to one of the notable assassinations of the era; Catron himself seems to have been the target of an unsuccessful assassination attempt.[41] The recent biographer of Colonel Fountain has brought forth strong evidence to support his charge that Albert Bacon Fall, the incisive Democratic leader, was guilty of leading complicity in the plot against Fountain.[42] The most important point is that virtually all political factions in New Mexico accepted and used assassination as a way of eliminating troublesome opponents.[43]

The frightening phenomenon of assassination in territorial New Mexico still awaits searching study by the historian. In the absence of such a study, it is hard to say just why assassination became such a prominent political feature only in New Mexico. The territory was indeed a violent one at the time; it was scarred by a savage Indian war (with the Apaches), numerous vigilante movements and lynch mobs, a host of criminal outlaws (Billy the Kid, Clay Allison, and others), and such mordant local conflicts as the Lincoln County War and the Maxwell Land Grant troubles. This high level of violence might well have had the effect of skewing the political system in the direction of assassination as a tactic, although this did not happen in neighboring Texas, which, at the time, was every bit as violent as New Mexico. Nor does the large Latin element of the population seem to have added a measure of volatility to the political climate of New Mexico Territory, for Anglo-American politicians, such as Catron (from Missouri) and Fall (from Kentucky), were leaders in a political system that was often characterized by assassination.

A third explanation for the prevalence of political assassination in New Mexico is suggested by social scientists, who have recently posited a "contagion phenomenon" in regard to such "highly publicized and dramatic acts of deviant behavior" as prison riots, bomb scares, slum uprisings, mass murder, and psychopathic sexual acts.[44] Beginning with the first assassination in New Mexico (that of the territorial chief justice, John P. Slough, in 1867), it is possible that something like a "contagion phenomenon" set in to perpetuate assassination until it became a part of the political system itself. After 1900 the level of general turbulence in New Mexico life subsided. It may have been no coincidence that the politics of assassination faded, too. Students of the "contagion phenomenon" have seen it as a short-run phenomenon characterized by an accelerating pace followed by an abrupt end, which might, in long-run terms, be analogous to the experience in New Mexico and in America from 1963 to 1968 when John F. Kennedy, Robert F. Kennedy, Martin Luther King, Medgar Evers, and Malcolm X were all cut down by assassins.

II

An examination of American criminal violence reveals four noteworthy facts: (1) Organized interstate (or, earlier, intercolonial) gangs of criminals are an old story, going well back into the eighteenth century. (2) Before the Civil War, the most prevalent type of criminal activity—especially in frontier areas—was horse theft and the counterfeiting of the myriad number of private banknotes then in circulation. (3) After the Civil War, a new era of crime began with the popularization of train robbery by the Reno brothers of Indiana and bank robbery by the James-Younger gang of Missouri. (4) The modern era of big-city organized crime with its police and political connections began to emerge in the early twentieth century.

America has long been ambiguous about crime. Official condemnation of the outlaw has been matched by social adulation. The ambiguity is not restricted to America, for the British historian, E. J. Hobsbawm, has shown the existence in European history of the "social bandit." By social bandit, Hobsbawm means largely what we have come to denote by a "Robin Hood," i.e., an outlaw whom society views as its hero rather than its enemy, an outlook that reflects widespread social alienation.[45]

There have indeed been American social bandits. Jesse and Frank James gained a strong popular following in Mid-America after the Civil War. To the many Southern sympathizers in Missouri, the James brothers, who were former Confederate guerrillas, could do no wrong, and, to many Grange-minded farmers, the Jameses' repeated robberies of banks and railroads were no more than these unpopular economic institutions deserved.[46] Other social bandits have been Henry Berry Lowry (a hero to his people—the Lumber River Indians of southeast North Carolina—during a period of harassment by the dominant white faction during the Reconstruction era), Billy the Kid (the idol of the poor Mexican herdsmen and villagers of the Southwest),[47] Pretty Boy Floyd (Public Enemy No. 1 of the 1930's, who retained the admiration of the sharecroppers of eastern Oklahoma from which stock he sprang),[48] and John Dillinger (the premier bank robber of the Depression Era). Modeling himself on an earlier social bandit, Jesse James, John Dillinger by freehanded generosity cultivated the Robin Hood image while robbing a series of Midwestern banks. The rural–small-town era of American crime came largely to an end with the demise of John Dillinger, Pretty Boy Floyd, Clyde Barrow and Bonnie Parker, and other "public enemies" of the 1930's.[49] With them the American tradition of the social bandit declined.

While the tradition of the rural American social bandit was waxing and waning, urban crime was increasing in importance. The first urban criminal gangs arose in New York and other cities in the pre–Civil War decades, but these gangs were limited in significance and restricted to such ethnic "slum" neighborhoods as Five Points and the Bowery in New York City.[50] Murder, mayhem, and gang vendettas were a feature of the proliferation of these gangs. Meanwhile, in the early decades of the twentieth century the present pattern of centralized, city-wide criminal operations under the control of a single "syndicate" or "organization" began to take shape in New York under Arnold Rothstein.[51] Converging with this trend was, apparently, the Mafia tradition of criminal organization, which Sicilian immigrants seem to have brought into East Coast port cities in the decades around 1900.[52] During the 1920's and 1930's, the two trends merged into the predominant pattern of centralized operations under Mafia control, which the Kefauver crime investigation highlighted in 1951.[53] Systematic killing to settle internal feuds and the use of investment capital (gained from illicit activities), threats, and extortion to infiltrate the world of legitimate business have been the characteristics of contemporary urban organized crime.[54]

In contrast to the relatively impersonal, well-organized criminal gangs and the widely admired exploits of the American social bandits has been a type of personalized violence, historically, that has aroused deep emotions of horror in the populace: freelance multiple murder. The vendettas of criminal combines have produced some notable killings (for example, the St. Valentine's Day massacre of Chicago, 1929, and New York City's so-called Castellammarese War, 1930–1931, involving competing Italian-American crime factions), but to be considered here is the murder of many persons by one or two individuals—freelance multiple murders—unconnected with any gang. It was the summer of 1966 that made Americans wonder whether the freelance multiple murder was becoming the characteristic American crime, for, in the space of a few weeks, two shocking mass murders occurred. First, in Chicago, Richard F. Speck murdered, one by one, eight student nurses.[55] Then, less than a month later, Charles Whitman ascended to the top of the tower of the University of Texas library in Austin and left tower and campus strewn with 13 dead or dying and 31 wounded as a result of his unerring marksmanship. The utter horror of these two killing rampages attracted world-wide attention, but not a year goes by without the appearance of one or more multiple murderers.[56] Speck, the hapless product of a blighted personal background, saw himself as "Born to Raise Hell." Whitman came from an upright and respectable middle-class background that was allegedly, on closer examination, a veritable witches' cauldron of tensions and hatreds.

Neither Speck nor Whitman were normal in the usual sense of the word, and the freelance multiple murderer is often a fit subject for the abnormal psychologist. (Recently it has been suggested that male killers, such as Speck, have a genetic abnormality arising from a doubling of the male sex chromosome.) But some observers have wondered whether the anxieties and neuroses of contemporary life in America have not led to a rise in the abnormal behavior exemplified by multiple (or mass) murder.[57] Crime statistics are not sufficiently available to answer the question, but there have been many examples of freelance multiple murderers in American history. The annals of crime in the United States abound with them. Among the earliest were the brutal Harpe brothers, Micajah (Big Harpe) and Wiley (Little Harpe), who during the years 1798 and 1799 accounted for anywhere from about 20 to 38 victims in the frontier states of Kentucky and Tennessee. Dashing out babies' brains against tree trunks in sudden frenzies was a practice that they may have learned from the Indians. Finally, in August, 1798, a party of Kentucky settlers ended the career of Micajah. Wiley escaped but was captured, tried, and hanged in Mississippi in 1804. So feared and hated were the Harpes that, following death, the head of each was cut off and displayed as a trophy of triumphant pioneer justice.[58]

Numerous freelance multiple murderers crop up in the nineteenth century. Among them was the evil Bender family of southeastern Kansas. The Benders, from 1871 to 1873, did away with at least 12 unwary travelers who had the bad judgment to choose the Bender roadside house for a meal or lodging. Eventually the Benders were detected, but they seem to have escaped into anonymity one jump ahead of a posse.[59] Another mass murderer was H. H. Holmes (the alias of Hermann Webster Mudgett) of Englewood (near Chicago), Illinois. He confessed to killing 27 people from about 1890 to 1894—many of whom he had lured to their death in his bizarre castlelike house while they were attending the Chicago World's Fair in the summer of 1893.[60] Although example after example can be named, such questions as the actual number of multiple murderers and their relationship to social conditions still await the deeper study of the historian.[61]

The threatening presence of the criminal and disorderly in American life has incurred the violent riposte of the forces of law and order, ranging from the police and associated legal bodies to lynch mobs, vigilantes, and related extralegal groups.

Law enforcement in colonial America was quite simple, consisting mainly of sheriffs for the counties and constables for the cities and towns. With the tremendous expansion of population and territory in the nineteenth century, the system took on a much greater complexity. Added to the county sheriffs and local constables were municipal police organizations, state police (including such special and elite forces as the rangers of Texas and Arizona) and federal marshals and Treasury agents.[62] The most important development of the century was the rise of the modern urban police system in the mid-century years from 1844 to 1877. The new system was a direct response to the great urban riots of the 1830's, 1840's, and 1850's. The antiquated watch-and-ward system (daytime constables and nighttime watchmen) was simply inadequate to cope with large-scale rioting and increasing urban disorder. The reform in the police system came first in New York, Philadelphia, Boston, and other cities that had acute problems of criminal violence and rioting.[63] (Thus, the Riot Era, from the 1830's through the 1850's, produced the present urban police system. The riots of the 1960's have, similarly, spurred a trend toward the professionalization of the police as the obverse of another result of the 1960's riots: increasing hostility between the predominantly white police and black ghetto militants.)

Scarcely less important than the development of the urban police system was the creation of the National Guard to replace the obsolete state militia system that dated back to the eighteenth century. The rapid development of the National Guard system in the 1880's was largely a response to the great urban labor riots of 1877. The National Guard was established first and most rapidly in the industrial states of the North that were highly vulnerable to labor unrest: Massachusetts, Connecticut, New York, Pennsylvania, Ohio, and Illinois. By 1892, the system was complete throughout the nation.[64] Officered primarily by businessmen and professionals, and sometimes the recipients of large subsidies from wealthy industrialists,[65] National Guard contingents were often called out to suppress labor violence from the late nineteenth century down to the time of World War II.

In the latter half of the nineteenth century there also grew up a sort of parapolice system with the founding of numerous private detective agencies (headed by the famed Pinkerton National Detective Agency)[66] and the burgeoning of thousands of local anti-horse thief associations or detecting societies, which were often authorized by state laws and invested with limited law enforcement powers.[67] After the Civil War, industrial corporations frequently set up their own police forces. Most notable in this category were the private coal and iron police that the state of Pennsylvania authorized to deal with labor unrest in mines and mills.[68] It was during the nineteenth century, as well, that the science of crime detection was inaugurated.[69]

Undue violence in the course of enforcing the law has long been a matter of concern. In an earlier generation, the public worried about the employment of the "third degree" to obtain criminal confessions. In our own time, the concern is with "police brutality," often against Negroes.[70] The use of violence by police in the pursuit of their regular duties has been related to the large measure of violence associated with the incarceration of prisoners in jails and prisons. For over a century and a half we have gone through bursts of prison reform only to have the system as a whole lapse back into (if indeed it ever really transcended) its normal brutality and sadism. As time has passed, many of the most well-meaning reforms (such as the early-nineteenth-century system of solitary confinement) have proved to be ill-conceived.[71] Even as our knowledge and expertise have increased, prison reform has foundered again and again on the rock of inadequate financial support from an uncaring society.

Police brutality, police riots (in which large numbers of police rage out of control in a law-enforcement situation, as happened in Chicago at the 1968 Democratic National Convention),[72] and the violence in penal institutions all illustrate the paradoxical but intimate and all too common connection between lawfulness and lawlessness. Heightening the paradox is the contradictory coupling of lawlessness in behalf of lawfulness to be found, historically, in lynch law and vigilantism.

Lynch law has been defined as "the practice or custom by which persons are punished for real or alleged crimes without due process of law." The first organized movement of lynch law in America occurred in the South Carolina back country in 1767–1769.[73] It appeared again in the Virginia Piedmont near the present city of Lynchburg during the latter years of the Revolution. The Virginia movement was initiated by Colonel Charles Lynch (from whom "lynch law" gained its name) and was employed against Tory miscreants.[74] Well into the nineteenth century, lynch law meant merely the infliction of corporal punishment—usually 39 lashes or more well laid on with hickory withes, whips or any readily available frontier instrument. By the middle of the nineteenth century, lynch law had come to be synonymous, mainly, with hanging or killing by illegal group action. The term lynch mob refers to an organized, spontaneous, ephemeral mob that comes together briefly to do its work and then breaks up. The more regular vigilante (or regulator) movements engaged in a systematic usurpation of the functions of law and order.

Lynch-mob violence (in contrast to vigilante violence) was often resorted to in trans-Appalachian frontier areas before the Civil War, but it became even more common after the Civil War. In the postwar period (down to World War I), lynch-mob violence was employed frequently in all sections of the country and against whites as well as against blacks, but in this period it was pre-eminently directed against the Southern Negro. From 1882 to 1903 the staggering total of 1,985 Negroes were killed by Southern lynch mobs.[75] Supposedly the lynch-mob hanging (or, too often, a ghastly burning alive) was saved for the Negro murderer or rapist, but statistics show that Negroes were frequently lynched for lesser crimes or in cases where there was no offense at all or the mere suspicion of one.[76] Lynch-mob violence became an integral part of the post-Reconstruction system of white supremacy.[77]

Although predominant in the South, lynch-mob violence was far from being restricted to that section. In the West, the ephemeral "necktie party" was often foregathered for the summary disposal of thief, rapist, rustler, murderer, or all-around desperado. Frenzied mobs also worked their will in the North and East, where (as in the West) villainous white men were the usual victims.[78]

The phenomenon of vigilantism appears to be native to America. The British Isles—especially Scotland and Ireland—were violent enough in the seventeenth and eighteenth centuries, but a tradition of vigilantism was unknown there. The taking of the law into one's own hands, the classic definition of vigilantism, was repugnant to the British approach to law and order. Vigilantism arose in response to a typical American problem: the absence of effective law and order in a frontier region. It was a problem that occurred again and again beyond the Appalachian Mountains. It stimulated the formation of hundreds of frontier vigilante movements.[79]

The first phase of American vigilantism occurred mainly before the Civil War and dealt largely with the threat of frontier horse thieves and counterfeiters. Virtually every state or territory west of the Appalachians possessed well-organized, relentless vigilante movements. We have tended to think of the vigilante movement as being typical of the Western plains and mountains, but, in actuality, there was much vigilantism east of the Missouri and Mississippi rivers. The main thrust of vigilantism was to re-establish in each newly settled frontier area the community structure of the old settled areas along with the values of the sanctity of property and law and order. Vigilante movements were characteristically in the control of the frontier elite and represented the elite's social values and preferences. This was true of the first vigilante movement, which was in South Carolina during 1767–1769, with members known as "Regulators"—the original, but now obsolete term for vigilantes, and it was also true of the greatest of all American vigilante movements, that of San Francisco in 1856. The San Francisco vigilance committee of 1856 was dominated lock, stock, and barrel by the leading merchants of the city, who organized to stamp out crime and political corruption.[80]

Although the typical vigilante movements were dominated by social conservatives who desired to establish order and stability in newly settled areas, there were disconcertingly numerous departures from the norm. Many vigilante movements led not to order but to increasing disorder and anarchy. In such cases, vigilantism left things in a worse condition than had existed before. Frequently the strife between vigilantes and their opponents (exacerbated by individual, family, and political hatreds) became so bitter and untrammeled that order could be restored only by the governor calling out the militia. Such was the case when the Bald Knobbers of the Missouri Ozarks rose in 1885–1886 to curb the evils of theft, liquor, gambling, and prostitution in Taney and Christian counties. Intervention by outside authorities was finally needed.[81]

The elite nature of nineteenth-century vigilante leadership is revealed by the prominent men who figured in vigilante movements; they included U.S. senators and congressmen, governors, lawyers, and capitalists.[82] Even presidents of the United States were attracted to vigilantism. President Andrew Jackson once approved the resort of Iowa pioneers to vigilante methods pending the clarification of their territorial status.[83] As a young cattle rancher in North Dakota, Theodore Roosevelt begged to be admitted to a vigilante band that was being formed to deal with rustlers and horse thieves. The cattlemen rebuffed the impetuous young Harvard blueblood and went on with their vigilante movement.[84] Today, among educated men of standing, vigilantism is viewed with disapproval, but it was not always so in the nineteenth century. In those days, the leaders of the community were often prominent members of vigilante movements and proud of it.

America changed from the basically rural nation it had been in the ante-bellum era to an urban, industrial nation after the Civil War. The institution of vigilantism changed to match the altering character of the nation. From a generally narrow concern with the classic frontier problems of horse thieves and counterfeiters, vigilantism broadened its scope to include a variety of targets connected with the tensions of the new America: Catholics, Jews, Negroes, immigrants, laboring men and labor leaders, political radicals, advocates of civil liberties, and nonconformists in general. This new vigilantism, or neovigilantism, flourished as a symptom of the growing pains of post-Civil War industrial and urban America but utterly failed to solve the complex social problems of the era.[85]

The post–Civil War era also saw the climax of two movements that had strong affinities with vigilantism. One was the anti-horse thief association, which had its greatest growth in the rural Midwest and Southwest after the Civil War, although its roots were to be found in the Northeastern United States as early as the 1790's. The anti-horse thief association pattern involved state charter of local associations that were often vested with constabulary power. By 1900, the movement's associations numbered hundreds of thousands of members in its belt of greatest strength, which stretched from the Great Lakes to the Rio Grande. Forming a flexible and inexpensive (the members shared costs whenever they arose) supplement to immobile, expensive, and inefficient local law enforcement, the associations afforded the farmer insurance against the threat of horse and other types of theft. With the rapid development of the automobile around the time of World War I the anti-horse thief associations lost their *raison d'être*.[86]

Quite different in character was the White Cap[87] movement. White Caps first appeared in southern Indiana in 1887,[88] but, in short order, the phenomenon had spread to the four corners of the nation. The White Cap movement copied the vigilante movements of the late eighteenth and early nineteenth centuries in its preference for flogging as a mode of punishment. White capping varied greatly from locality to locality and region to region. In northern Texas and southern Mississippi the White Caps were anti-Negro,[89] in southern Texas they were anti-Mexican,[90] and in northern New Mexico the White Caps were a movement of poor Mexican herders and ranchers against land-enclosing rich Mexicans and Americans. In the late 1960's, Reies Tijerina's sometimes violent *Alianza* movement to regain land (originally held in ancient ancestral Spanish land grants) for the poor Mexican-Americans of New Mexico and the Southwest was in some respects a revival of the late nineteenth-century White Cap movement of New Mexico.[91]

In general, however, white capping was most prevalent as a sort of spontaneous movement for the moral regulation of the poor whites and ne'er-do-wells of the rural American countryside. Thus, drunken, shiftless whites who often abused their families were typical targets of White Cap violence.[92] Loose women frequently became the victims of White Caps.[93] Vigilantism as far back as the South Carolina Regulators of 1767–1769 had often been concerned with the moral regulation of incorrigible whites, hence white capping was, in part, a throwback to the early era of frontier vigilantism. At the same time, white capping seems to have been an important link between the first and second Ku Klux Klans. White Cap methods, in regard to punishment and costume, seem to have been influenced by the first Klan, whereas White Cap attacks on immoral and shiftless whites foreshadowed the main thrust of the second Klan of the 1920's. Chronologically, white capping began in the 1880's, about two decades after the first Klan, and, by the turn of the century, it had become such a generic term for local American violence that Booth Tarkington made White Cap violence the pivot of his popular novel *The Gentleman from Indiana* (1899).[94] At the time of World War I, white capping was fading from view; shortly thereafter the second Ku Klux Klan rose to take its place.

III

Unquestionably the longest and most remorseless war in American history was the one between whites and Indians that began in tidewater Virginia in 1607 and continued, with intermittent truces, for nearly 300 years down to the final event, the massacre of the Sioux by U.S. troops at Wounded Knee, South Dakota, in 1890. Nor has white-Indian conflict disappeared. Such conflict is ordinarily nonviolent, but that was not the case in early 1973 when a violent confrontation between militant members of the American Indian Movement (AIM) and white federal agents, which took place, again, at Wounded Knee, led to fatalities.

Bitter, implacable white-Indian hostility was by no means inevitable. The small Indian population that existed in the continental United States allowed plenty of room for white settlement. The economic resources of the white settlers were such that the Indians could have been easily and fairly reimbursed for the land needed for occupation by the whites. In fact, a model of peaceful white-Indian relations was developed in seventeenth-century New England by John Eliot, Roger Williams, and other Puritan statesmen. The same was true in eighteenth-century Pennsylvania, where William Penn's humane and equitable policy toward the Indians brought that colony decades of white-Indian amity.[95] Racial prejudice and greed in the mass of New England whites finally reaped the whirlwind in King Philip's War of 1675–1676, which shattered the peaceful New England model.[96] The same sort of thing happened in Pennsylvania in 1763, when Pontiac's Rebellion (preceded by increasing tensions) ended an era of amicable white-Indian relations in the Keystone colony.

Other Indian wars proliferated during the seventeenth and eighteenth centuries, nor did the pace of the conflict slacken in the nineteenth century. It is possible that no other factor has exercised a more brutalizing influence on the American character than the Indian wars. The struggles with the Indians have sometimes been represented as being "just" wars in the interest of promoting superior Western civilization at the expense of the crude stone-age culture of the Indians. The recent ethnohistorical approach to the interpretation of white-Indian relations has given us a more balanced understanding of the relative merits of white and Indian civilizations. The norms of Indian warfare were, however, more barbaric than those of early modern Western Europe. Among the Indians of eastern America, torture was an accepted and customary part of war-making.[97] In their violent encounters with Indians, the white settlers adopted the cruel practices of Indian conflict. Scalping had not been prevalent in Europe since the Dark Ages, but in the new world white men—responding to the Indians' widely (but not universally) practiced habit of scalping—reverted to this savage form of warfare. Down to the battle at Wounded Knee, lifting the hair of an Indian opponent was the usual tactic among experienced white fighters. Broken treaties, unkept promises, and the slaughter of defenseless women and children all, along with brutal warfare, continued to characterize the white American's dealings with the Indian.[98] The effect on our national character has not been a healthy one; it has done much to further our proclivity to violence.

In the realm of intergroup conflict, racial violence between whites and blacks, extending far back into the eighteenth century, is unequaled in persistence as a factor in the history of American violence. The first slave uprising occurred in New York City in

1712 and was put down with great ruthlessness. In 1739, there was the Stono Rebellion in South Carolina, and, in 1741, New York City was again wracked with fears (apparently justified) of a slave conspiracy. The result was that New York white men went on a hysterical rampage in which scores of blacks were burned, hanged, or expelled.[99] The demographic situation in what is now the United States (in contrast to that of the West Indies and South America where the black-white population ratio, more favorable to blacks, enhanced slave insurgency) was such as to inhibit slave rebellions.[100] There were, however, two major aborted plots for slave uprisings by Gabriel Prosser in Richmond, 1800, and by Denmark Vesey in Charleston, 1822,[101] as well as two major actual rebellions by Louisiana slaves in St. Charles and St. John the Baptist parishes in 1811 and by slaves in Southampton County, Virginia, in 1831 under the leadership of Nat Turner.[102] The rebellion of Nat Turner, although a failure, is better known than the single successful instance of large-scale violent resistance to slavery by American blacks: the case of the Florida Maroons, who, in coalition with the Seminole Indians, successfully fought down to 1838 to maintain their status as freed men or escapees from white servitude.[103] Lesser instances of maroon resistance to slavery abounded in the South during the nineteenth century, while countless blacks resisted slavery, too, by such acts of low-level violence as assault, murder, arson, and running away.[104]

With the end of slavery and its conjoined slave patrols and black codes, the white people of the South developed a special organization for dealing with the blacks: the Ku Klux Klan. The latter has been one of the most consistent features in the last 100 years of American violence. There have been three Ku Klux Klans: the first Ku Klux Klan of Reconstruction times, the second Ku Klux Klan of the 1920's, and the third, current, Ku Klux Klan of the 1950's to 1970's. The first Ku Klux Klan was employed to intimidate the Radical Republicans of the Reconstruction Era and, by violence and threats, to force the freedman to accept the renewed rule of Southern whites.[105] The second Ku Klux Klan differed significantly from both its predecessor and successor. Although the second Ku Klux Klan was founded in Atlanta in 1915, its greatest growth and strength actually took place beyond the borders of the old Confederacy. During the early 1920's it became a truly national organization. For a time it enjoyed great strength in the Southwest, West, North, and East. The strongest state Klan was in Indiana, and such wholly un-Southern states as Oregon and Colorado felt its vigor. The second Ku Klux Klan surely belongs to the violent history of America, but, unlike either the first or the third Klans, the Negro was only a secondary target for it. Although denunciation of Catholics and Jews ranked one-two in the rhetoric of the second Klan, recent students of the movement have shown that Klan violence—whippings, torture, and murder—were directed less against Catholics, Jews, and Negroes than against ne'er-do-wells and the allegedly immoral of the very same background as the Klansmen: white, Anglo-Saxon Protestant. The Klan, thus, attacked Americans of similar background and extraction who refused to conform to the Bible Belt morality that was the deepest passion of the Klan movement of the 1920's.[106] The Ku Klux Klan resurgence of the last fifteen years has been largely restricted to the South; it is only too well known for acts of violence against the civil rights movement and against desegregation.

Paralleling the Ku Klux Klan has been a host of other movements of racial, ethnic, and religious malice. Before the Civil War, the Northeastern United States was marked by convent burnings and anti-Catholic riots.[107] This "Protestant Crusade" eventually bred the political Know Nothing movement. Anti-Chinese agitation that often burst into violence became a familiar feature in California and the West as the nineteenth century wore on.[108] In 1891, eleven Italian immigrants were the victims of a murderous mob in New Orleans.[109] The fear and loathing of Catholics (especially Irish and Italians), which often took a violent form, was organized in the nonviolent but bigoted American Protective Association (A.P.A.) of 1887.[110] Labor clashes of the late nineteenth century and early twentieth century were in reality, often, ethnic clashes with native, old stock Americans ranged on one side as owners, foremen, and skilled workers against growing numbers of unskilled immigrants—chiefly Jews, Slavs, Italians, and others from Southern and Eastern Europe.[111]

The arena of violent racial, ethnic, religious, political, economic, and industrial group conflict in American history has frequently been the urban riot. The situation seemed at its worst in the late 1960's when the country was widely believed to be on the verge of some sort of urban apocalypse, but the fact is that our cities have been in a state of more or less continuous turmoil since the colonial period.[112] As early as the latter part of the seventeenth century the cores of the organized North End and South End Mobs that dominated Boston in the eighteenth century had already formed. Maritime riots occurred in Boston during the middle eighteenth century and were frequent in the colonies in the 1760's.[113] Leading colonial cities of the revolutionary era—Charleston, New York, Boston, and Newport, Rhode Island—were all rocked by the Liberty Boy troubles, which embodied an alliance of unskilled maritime workers, skilled artisans, and middle-class businessmen and professionals in riotous dissent against toughening British colonial policy as exemplified by the Stamp Act and Townshend Acts.[114]

Economic and political conditions brought more urban turmoil in the post-revolutionary period of the 1780's and 1790's, and, by the mid-nineteenth century, with industrial and urban expansion occurring by leaps and bounds, the cities of America found themselves in the grips of a new era of violence. The pattern of the urban immigrant slum as a matrix of poverty, vice, crime, and violence was set by Five Points in lower Manhattan before the Civil War.[115] Ulcerating slums along the lines of Five Points and severe ethnic and religious strife stemming from the confrontation between burgeoning immigrant groups and the native American element made the 1830's, 1840's, and 1850's decades of sustained urban rioting, particularly in the great cities of the Northeast. It may have been the era of the greatest urban violence America has ever experienced. During this period, at least 35 major riots occurred in Baltimore, Philadelphia, New York, and Boston. Baltimore had twelve,[116] Philadelphia eleven,[117] New York eight,[118] and Boston four.[119] The violence also extended into the growing cities of the Midwest and the lower Mississippi Valley; Cincinnati had four major riots during this period. But the urban violence of the 1830's to 1850's was not restricted to the greatest and best-known cities. In a recent thorough study, John C. Schneider announced that "at least seventy per cent of American cities with a population of twenty thousand or more by 1850 experienced some degree of major disorder in the 1830–1865 period." Specifically, Schneider found that the American cities of 20,000 or more in size suffered eighty major riots from 1830 to 1865.[120] Among the most important types of riots were labor riots,[121] election riots,[122] antiabolitionist riots,[123] anti-Negro riots,[124] anti-Catholic riots,[125] and riots of various sorts involving the turbulent volunteer firemen's units.[126]

Except for Civil War draft riots, the urban violence subsided in the 1860's and 1870's until the year of 1877 produced a tremendous nationwide railroad strike that began along the Baltimore and Ohio Railroad and spread to the Far West. Violent rioting shook Baltimore, and great stretches of Pittsburgh were left in smoking ruins.[127] (The similarity of what befell Baltimore and Pittsburgh in 1877 and what befell Los Angeles, Chicago, Newark, Detroit, Washington, and other cities from 1965 to 1968 is striking.) Many other cities suffered less serious damage.

The forces of law and order responded strongly to the nineteenth-century urban violence. The modern urban police system was created in response to the riots of the 1830's, 1840's, and 1850's, and the present National Guard system to the uprisings of 1877.[128] To deal with urban tumult, vigilantism was also used frequently in the nineteenth century. The greatest of all American vigilante movements occurred in the newly settled (by Americans) but thoroughly urban and up-to-date San Francisco of 1856; other nineteenth-century urban vigilante movements occurred in Los Angeles, New Orleans, San Antonio, St. Louis, Cincinnati, Rochester, and Natchez.[129]

The prototype of the anti-Negro urban race riot was established in the North as far back as the 1820's and 1830's, and after the Civil War it was replicated in such major Southern outbreaks as the riots in Wilmington, North Carolina (1898) and Atlanta (1906). These earliest riots were, in effect, pogroms—one-sided attacks on urban blacks by whites.[130] By the era of World War I, however, the pogrom-type race riot was eclipsed by the appearance of the "communal" riot in which, with whites still usually dominant, mobs of counter-rioting blacks and whites raged through city streets. Among a number of communal riots from 1917 to the 1940's, the greatest were those of Washington, D.C. and Chicago in 1919 and Detroit in 1943.[131] In the 1960's, two long-term trends combined to reverse the typical pattern of white primacy in rioting: one was a demographic revolution in which, during the course of the twentieth century, American blacks made the transition from being a predominantly rural, Southern people to a predominantly urban people heavily concentrated in Negro ghetto areas of Northern and Western cities; the other was a comparable revolution in black consciousness, resulting in a mood of black pride and aggressiveness that became stunningly evident in Los Angeles's Watts riot of 1964, the first of the black super-riots of the 1960's.[132]

Violent American group conflict has by no means been restricted to the urban sector with its manifold racial, ethnic, and economic antagonisms. The countryside, too, has been the domain of relentless violence growing out of our agrarian history. The tree of liberty in America has been nurtured by a series of movements in behalf of the ever-suffering farmer or yeoman. Often these movements—generally considered to be liberal in their political character—have been formed for the purpose of redressing the economic grievances of the farmer; at times they have been land-reform movements. The dissident farmer movements have been deemed among the most heroic of all American movements of political insurgence; they have been the especial favorites of historians who, with love and sympathy, have chronicled their ups and downs. There have been many agrarian uprisings, and they have been equally prevalent in both the colonial and national periods of our history. The initial agrarian uprising was that led by Nathaniel Bacon in late-seventeenth-century Virginia, followed by the New Jersey land rioters of the eighteenth century. Similarly, in the 1760's, were the Paxton Boys' movement of Pennsylvania,[133] the North Carolina Regulators (not a vigilante movement but one for reform of local government),[134] and the New York antirent movement (which stretched on into the nineteenth century).[135] With independence, there appeared Shays' Rebellion in Massachusetts (1786–1787),[136] the Whiskey Rebellion in western Pennsylvania (1794),[137] and Fries' Rebellion in eastern Pennsylvania (1798–1799).[138] Further West—in the Mississippi Valley before the Civil War—there appeared the Claim Clubs to defend the land occupancy of squatters.[139]

After the Civil War, a plethora of economic problems for the farmer gave rise to the Grangers, the Greenbackers, the Farmers' Alliance (which originally began in central Texas as a quasi-vigilante movement),[140] and the Populist party.[141] About the same time there appeared a land reform movement in California against the monopolistic landholdings of the Southern Pacific Railroad,[142] and, in New Mexico, there appeared a White Cap movement of poor Mexicans against the land-enclosing tactics of well-to-do Mexicans and Americans, as mentioned earlier. Western Kentucky, and the Ohio-Mississippi Valley area, generally, was the scene in the early 1900's of a tobacco farmer's cooperative movement to end the control of the American Tobacco Company and foreign companies over the marketing system.[143] Farmers became increasingly attracted to the Socialist party, and the nonindustrial state of Oklahoma soon led the nation in Socialist party members. Connected with the rise of socialism among Oklahoma farmers was the appearance there during World War I of the Working Class Union, which developed into a pacifist, antidraft movement of sharecroppers and small farmers.[144] In the upper Great Plains of North Dakota during 1915 there rose the radical Nonpartisan League, which enacted many reforms in that state and inspired similar progressive farm movements in other states of the Northwest.[145] The Farm Bloc emerged in Congress in the 1920's to promote legislation for easing the agricultural depression. When conditions worsened in the 1930's, the Farmers' Holiday Association, formed in the Midwest, led farmer strikes and boycotts in protest against the economic system.[146] In the 1960's, the National Farmers' Organization adopted similar tactics.

The insurgent farmer movements have thus formed one of the longest and most enduring chronicles in the history of American reform but one that has been blighted again and again with violence. Nathaniel Bacon's movement became a full-fledged rebellion that resulted in the burning of Jamestown. The New Jersey land rioters used violence to press their claims against Jersey land companies. The New York antirent movement frequently used force against dominant landlords. The North Carolina Regulators rioted against the courthouse rings that ground them down under the burden of heavy taxes and rapacious fees. The Paxton Boys of Pennsylvania followed their massacre of Indians with a march on Philadelphia. The followers of Daniel Shays in Massachusetts broke up court sessions in order to forestall land foreclosures. The farmers of Pennsylvania rebelled against taxes on liquor and land in the Whiskey and Fries uprisings. The Western

Claim Clubs (which, paradoxically, were sometimes dominated by land speculators pursuing their own interests) used intimidation to protect "squatters' rights." The land reform movement in California spawned a night-rider league in Tulare County (1878–1880) to resist railroad land agents. The tobacco farmer cooperative movement in Kentucky did not succeed in breaking monopoly domination of the marketing system until it utilized a night-rider organization and raided several western Kentucky towns, destroyed tobacco warehouses, and abused noncooperating farmers. The New Mexican White Caps fought the land-enclosure movement with a reign of terror. The Working Class Union of Oklahoma fomented the Green Corn Rebellion; the "rebels" contemplated only a peaceful march on Washington but did arm themselves and commit a few acts of violence before being rooted out of the hills and breaks along the South Canadian River by sheriffs and posses. The Farmers' Holiday Association dumped milk cans, blocked roads, and roughed up opponents. Farmer grievances were serious, and, repeatedly, farmers used a higher law—the need to right insufferable wrongs, the very justification of the American Revolution—to justify the use of violence in uprising after uprising.

The labor movement in American history—like the farmers'—has been bathed in the same sort of glory that anointed the agrarian uprisings. Most would agree that by raising the health and living standards of the working man the American labor movement has been a significant factor in advancing the social well-being of the nation. But the labor movement reveals the same mixture of glorious ends with inglorious means—violence—that has characterized the agrarian movement. (Ironically, the white backlash against the black uprisings in the cities of our time has been strongest in the rural countryside and the blue-color metropolitan wards, i.e., among the inheritors of the violent agrarian and labor movements.)

A rudimentary labor movement was to be found in the port cities of the colonial period. Although there was no organization of laborers as such, sailors, longshoremen, and other workers of the maritime industry occasionally rioted—stirred up by impressment gangs and sporadic economic stringency.[147] The unskilled workers and skilled artisans who contributed the force to the violent Liberty Boy movement of the 1760's were made especially restless by the economic depression that followed the end of the Great War for the Empire.[148]

It is with the coming of the Industrial Revolution to America in the nineteenth century that the labor movement really gets underway, concomitantly with the tremendous growth of American industry after the Civil War. Various labor organizations mushroomed: the Knights of Labor, American Railway Union, American Federation of Labor, Western Federation of Miners (W.F.M.), and the Industrial Workers of the World (I.W.W.). All made the strike a major weapon, and, in case after case, violence broke out during the strike. The blame was certainly not on the side of labor alone. The unyielding attitude of capitalists in regard to wages, hours, and working conditions gave impetus to the desire to unionize that led to the calling of strikes. The violent attempts by capital to suppress unions and break up strikes frequently incited the workers to violence. But laborers, too, were often more than ready to resort to violence, as many of the great upheavals after the Civil War indicate. The great railroad strike of 1877 triggered massive riots, which, in Pittsburgh, reached the level of insurrection. About the same time, the decade-long Molly Maguire[149] troubles in the hard-coal field of eastern Pennsylvania came to a climax. The Molly Maguires were a secret organization of Irish miners who fought their employers with assassination and mayhem.[150] Such events as the Haymarket Riot in Chicago (1886),[151] the Homestead strike (1892),[152] the Coeur d'Alene, Idaho, silver mining troubles (1892 and after), and the 1910 dynamiting of the Los Angeles *Times* building (by the McNamara brothers of the supposedly conservative American Federation of Labor)[153] led Louis Adamic correctly to label the period from the late 1800's to the early 1900's as the "dynamite era" in American labor relations.

The Western mining state of Colorado affords a paridigm of the dynamite era of labor violence. From 1884 to 1914, Colorado had its own "Thirty Years' War" of strikes and violence, which typified the economic, class, and ethnic tensions of the period.[154] Colorado's 30-year period of acute labor violence came to a climax with what may have been the most violent upheaval in American labor history: the coal miners' strike against the Colorado Fuel and Iron Company (1913–1914). During the first 5 weeks of the strike (which took place in southern Colorado) there were 38 armed skirmishes in which 18 persons were killed. The final horror took place on April 20, 1914, at Ludlow, Colorado. A 15-hour battle between strikers and militiamen ended in the burning of the strikers' tent city during which 2 mothers and 11 children suffocated to death in the "Black Hole of Ludlow." Following this tragedy, maddened miners erupted in a 10-day rebellion that brought anarchy and unrestrained class warfare to a 250-mile area of southern Colorado before federal troops ended the violence.[155] The Ludlow conflict was, in truth, an actualization of the apocalyptic visions of class warfare of Jack London (in *The Iron Heel*)[156] and other writers of the period.

The last great spasm of violence in the history of American labor, to date, came in the 1930's, with the sit-down strike movement that accompanied the successful drive to unionize the automobile and other great mass production industries. A tendency to labor violence survives, however, as the case of the national strike of independent truck drivers in early 1974 shows. The strikers had been a part of the so-called "middle American" element that had most strongly opposed black riots and campus violence in the 1960's and had responded positively to Governor George Wallace's national political campaigns in behalf of law and order, but when the independent truckers found themselves fighting for economic survival against a combination of fuel shortages and high fuel prices they did not hesitate to use violence against non-striking truck drivers in their effort to make their strike effective and bring about a change in the federal government's policy on the allocation and pricing of diesel truck fuel. As a result of the strikers' violence, men were killed and injured, and, in eight states, it was necessary to call out the National Guard to keep the main highways open until the strike ended.[157]

IV

By now it is evident that, historically, American life has been characterized by continuous and often intense violence. It is not merely that violence has accompanied such negative aspects of our history as criminal activity, political assassination, and racial conflict. On the contrary, violence has formed a seamless web with some of the most positive events of U.S. history: independence (revolutionary violence), the freeing of the slaves and the preservation of the Union (Civil War violence), the occupation of the land (Indian wars), the stabilization of frontier society (vigilante violence), the elevation of the farmer and the laborer (agrarian and labor violence), and the preservation of law and order (police violence). The patriot, the humanitarian, the nationalist, the pioneer, the landholder, the farmer, and the laborer (and the capitalist) have used violence as the means to a higher end.

All too often unyielding and unsympathetic, established political and economic power has incited violence by its refusal to heed and appease just grievances. Thus, Governor Berkeley of Virginia ignored the pleas of Virginia planters, and the result was Bacon's Rebellion. The British government in 1774–1776 remained adamant in the face of patriot pleas, and the result was the American Revolution. The tobacco trust scoffed at the grievances of farmers, and the result was the Kentucky Night Rider movement. American capitalists ground workers into the dust, and the result was the violent labor movement. The possessors of power and wealth have been often arrogant in their refusal to share their advantages until it has been too late. Arrogance is indeed a quality that comes to unchecked power more readily than sympathy and forbearance.

By the same token, one can argue that the aggrieved in American history have been too quick to revolt, too hastily violent. We have resorted so often to violence that we have long since become a trigger-happy people. Violence is clearly rejected by us as a part of the American value system, but so great has been our involvement with violence over the long sweep of our history that violence has truly become a part of our unacknowledged (or underground) value structure.[158]

Part II

EARLY AMERICAN ORIGINS OF VIOLENCE AND EXTREMISM

SCIENCE AND TECHNOLOGY have created such a wide chasm between the lives of our forefathers in the eighteenth century and our own in the twentieth that we are prone to forget just how contemporary the generation of the founding fathers of the republic is to ours. The contemporaneity is not, obviously, in the realm of daily life, but in the fact that so much of the American style of behavior goes back to the colonial and revolutionary periods. Well aware of our history as a violent, turbulent people, we may be less aware that these characteristics were present far back in the colonial period and were a prelude to the tumult of the revolutionary period itself. The tendency to violence marked by a long history of insurgencies and riots in the colonial period of the seventeenth and eighteenth centuries was heightened in the revolutionary era from 1760 to 1785. Perfected during the revolutionary epoch were techniques of civil violence that Americans put to frequent use in later centuries. In the realm of ideas, the concept of popular sovereignty emerged as a powerful rationale for extralegal violence against those deemed to be enemies of the public good.

When the focus is narrowed to a particular state—South Carolina—the legacy of the revolutionary period in the growth of American violence and extremism is underscored. The case of South Carolina graphically reveals the pervasiveness of civil violence in the revolutionary period and its impact on the people. In our national history, South Carolina is best known for the movements of Nullification and Secession, but less known is the extent to which these movements (and their outcome—the Civil War) were an outgrowth of a style of extremism originating in the violent experience of the Back Country of South Carolina in the revolutionary period. The Back Country's ordeal was epitomized in the Edgefield tradition—a South Carolina tradition of extremism stemming from an old Back Country locale, Edgefield County, traumatized by revolutionary-era turbulence. Although almost unknown outside South Carolina, the Edgefield tradition has had an immense impact on the state and, indirectly, on the nation. As a source of extremism, it has had an effect on South Carolina similar to the effect of South Carolina on the South and the nation. The Edgefield tradition survived long after the Civil War, exemplified by its two most prominent representatives, Senators Benjamin R. (Pitchfork Ben) Tillman and J. Strom Thurmond. In the period between the Civil War and World War I, Tillman not only dominated the politics of his state but, at the national level, stood out as the most strident Negrophobe in American life. Following World War II, Thurmond (whose father was a protégé of Tillman) has held the nation's attention as a proponent of extreme conservatism and Old South attitudes.

Chapter 2

VIOLENCE AND THE
AMERICAN REVOLUTION

Beginning with the Revolutionary movement (but with roots deep in American history) the people came to rely more and more on their ability to organize themselves and to act "out-of-doors" whether as "mobs," as political clubs, or as conventions.

Gordon S. Wood, *The Creation of the American Republic, 1776–1787*

It has been customary for historians and statesmen to view the American Revolution from the perspective of libertarianism. From that view, our Revolution has been justly celebrated as one of the monumental landmarks in modern humanity's quest for democratic freedom. But it would be an oversimplified and unsophisticated view of the historical process to see an event as large and complex as the American Revolution in only one dimension. There is another side to the story, for the Revolution has not been an unmixed blessing in its nature or impact—which is true of most great historical events. The Revolution also contributed to the demonic side of our national history, for its origin was violent, and the concept of popular sovereignty lent itself frequently to tyranny by the majority. Long ago, Herbert Butterfield reminded us that "from the work of any historian who has concentrated his researches upon any change or transition, there emerges a truth of history which seems to combine the truth of philosophy. It is nothing less than the whole of the past, with its complexity of movement, its entanglement of issues, and its intricate interactions, which produced the whole of the complex present." [1] Violence is a part of the "complex present" of American life today, just as it was a part of the revolutionary era.

American violence owes much to the dead weight of unsolved problems from the past. The negative features of American history—abysmal relations between whites and peoples of other color and the brutal and brutalizing processes by which the frontier was extended and our economy industrialized—have long been known to us as violent chapters in the story of our development, but it has been difficult for us to accept that the grandest event in our history, the Revolution, was pursued with a civil violence that was often ignoble. Among the intellectual bequests of the American Revolution has been the precept that violence in a good cause pays, a lesson that has been well learned by Americans. In our enthusiasm, we have found many good causes, and, in emulation of the Revolution, we have turned frequently to violence in our pursuit of them.

I

The era of the American Revolution was marked by a series of violent outbreaks in town and countryside. Urban violence runs from the Stamp Act riots in 1765 through the Sons of Liberty violence, the Boston Massacre, the burning of the *Gaspee*, and the Boston Tea Party to the incident that triggered the Revolutionary War—the fighting at Lexington and Concord. Concomitant with the urban violence of the 1760's and 1770's were outbursts of violence in rural America: the Paxton Boys' uprising in Pennsylvania and the Regulator movements in North and South Carolina,[2] the emergence of the so-called "cracker" as a violent Southern prototype on the colonial frontier,[3] the rise of lynch law in Virginia,[4] and the bloody Indian wars.[5] The 1760's and 1770's—as well as the 1670's and 1680's, the 1830's through the 1850's, the 1870's through the 1890's, and the 1960's—have been among the peak periods of violence in American history. Although it is clear that the urban violence of the 1760's and 1770's merged directly into the Revolution, the connection between the rural violence of the period and the Revolution was less direct. Incidents of rural tumult were not usually connected with the controversy between England and the colonies, yet rural violence was obviously significant. Like outbreaks in the cities, rural outbreaks added to the violent ambience of the period and helped predispose and prepare Americans for the forceful overthrow of British authority.

Why was the era of the 1760's and 1770's such a violent period? Why did the colonists react so violently to British policy? Although violence was not the cause of the American Revolution,[6] two historical factors contributed to the Americans' violence in opposing British policy in the 1760's and 1770's: one was the colonial tradition of insurgency that reached back into the seventeenth century, and the other was the habitual use of the riot as a purposive weapon of protest and dissent in both Great Britain and America during the preceding two centuries.

In the period from 1645 to 1760 there were 18 insurgent movements by white Americans directed toward the overthrow of colonial governments. Among these 18 insurrections were 5 major ones: Bacon's Rebellion in Virginia (1676–1677) and Leisler's Rebellion in New York (1689), the overthrow of Governor Edmund Andros in Massachusetts (1689), Coode's Rebellion in Maryland (1689), and the overturn of the proprietary government in South Carolina (1719).[7] Less extensive uprisings were the Ingle-Claiborne insurrection in Maryland (1645–1646), Fendall's first rebellion in Maryland (1660), the New Jersey antiquitrent uprising (1672), Culpeper's Rebellion in North Carolina (1677–1678), the overthrow of Governor Seth Sothel in North Carolina (1689) and of Governor John Colleton in South Carolina (1690), and Cary's rebellion in North Carolina (1709–1711).[8] Finally, there were such minor insurgencies as the Davyes-Pate uprising in Maryland (1676), the second Fendall rebellion in Maryland (1680–1681), Gove's insurrection in New Hampshire (1682–1683), the Essex County uprising in Massachusetts (1687), the rebellion against Governor Andrew Hamilton in New Jersey (1699), and Hambright's march on the Pennsylvania government in 1755.[9] Only six of these uprisings were violent, and only one—Bacon's Rebellion in Virginia—involved major violence. More typical of these 18 colonial upheavals were the 7 armed uprisings unaccompanied by violence and the 5 nonviolent uprisings that employed neither force nor the explicit threat of force.[10]

Although bloodshed was not a predominant characteristic of these 18 colonial uprisings, they were notable examples of the pervasive antiauthoritarianism in colonial America, which came to the surface on occasion and which, in the revolutionary period, would flare into violent rebellion. Despite the relative absence of violence, these colonial insurgencies were far from ineffective: six were successful, six gained temporary success before ultimate failure, and only six were outright failures.[11] Furthermore the insurrections were widespread geographically. Nine of the thirteen colonies were affected, and insurgencies occurred in five of the most important colonies—Massachusetts, New York, Pennsylvania, Virginia, and South Carolina. Aside from the wide distribution of the uprisings, several had a deep impact upon the history of colonial America. Bacon's Rebellion in Virginia and Leisler's Rebellion in New York were among the most important events in the history of early America, for each grew out of deep-seated tensions and each had a long-lasting effect on the subsequent history of their colonies. Three other rebellions—the overthrow of Governor Andros in Massachusetts, Coode's Rebellion in Maryland, and the shattering of the proprietary regime in South Carolina—also changed the course of history in their colonies.

It is noteworthy that these insurgencies were concentrated in the last three decades of the seventeenth century. Thirteen of the eighteen uprisings took place from 1670 to 1700, among them the crucial Bacon's, Culpeper's, Leisler's, anti-Andros, and Coode's rebellions.[12] Historians have noted the turbulent character of late seventeenth-century colonial America, and one, Clarence L. Ver Steeg, interpreted the late seventeenth and early eighteenth century as a time of "transition" when "English colonies became American provinces," a period of marked social instability causing "a serious strain upon people and institutions."[13] In view of the ubiquity of insurgent activity, it would be no great exaggeration to call the years 1670 to 1700 the first American revoluntionary period.

There were seventeen black insurrectionary plots or uprisings in colonial America before 1760. Slave uprising plots were uncovered and broken to the number of twelve—with six in Virginia and in South Carolina—three.[14] The main black uprisings that did occur were far more violent than most of the white uprisings. Violent black revolts were stark in their ferocity in New York (1712) and in South Carolina (the Stono Insurrection) in 1739.[15] Eleven of the black plots or uprisings came during a period, 1712 to 1741, when, with one exception, white insurrections had run their course.[16] All the black plots or uprisings failed, and none had the impact upon their colonies that Bacon's or Leisler's rebellions, for example, had on theirs. But the violence of the main black insurrections (along with the brutality with which they were suppressed) points to a significant degree of psychic tension between whites and blacks in colonial America.[17] Although white people looked with horror and morbid fascination upon the idea of black rebellion, the black uprisings may have served to keep the idea of insurrection in the back of white consciousness long after the main period of colonial insurgency had come to an end.

Supplementing the colonial tradition of insurgency was a background of noninsurrectionary riotous activity that preceded the revolutionary period for more than a century and, in effect, came to a peak in it. One of the settled convictions of recent scholarship on the eighteenth century in Great Britain and America is that the riot was a purposive instrument of social, economic, and political protest action. George Rudé, the leading historian of early modern riots in England and France, has done much to discredit the belief, going back to Gustave Le Bon, that the riotous mob is mainly a psychological phenomenon, inchoate in purpose, uncontrolled in action, and not subject to analysis in terms of any sort of rational behavior.[18] In this country a similar view of the riot as a purposive agent of group action has been the theme of Arthur M. Schlesinger, Sr., Edmund S. Morgan and Helen M. Morgan, Lloyd I. Rudolph, Bernard Bailyn, Gordon S. Wood, William Ander Smith, Jesse Lemisch, G. B. Warden, and Pauline Maier.[19]

Writing recently of the directed and semilegitimate character of eighteenth-century American rioters, Pauline Maier has noted that "not all eighteenth-century mobs simply defied the law: some used extralegal means to implement official demands to enforce laws not otherwise enforceable, others in effect extended the law in urgent situations beyond technical limits. Since leading eighteenth-century Americans had known many occasions on which mobs took on the defense of public welfare, which was, after all, the stated purpose of government, they were less likely to deny popular upheavals all legitimacy than are modern leaders. While not advocating popular uprisings, they could still grant such incidents an established and necessary role in free societies, one that made them an integral and even respected element of the political order." [20] Similarly, William Ander Smith pointed to an eighteenth-century "mob tradition, which served Englishmen and Scots as an extralegal channel by which to make their grievances known and felt by a government which was more concerned with political brokerage and overseas empire than with internal social stresses. Since concern for English rights and liberties was a concept deeply imbedded in the society, it came to be tacitly accepted by that society that mob violence in defense of those rights or in protest against some major grievances was in itself a legitimate, if not a legal right of freeborn English subjects." [21]

Rioting was not merely a colonial phenomenon. As Smith has shown, in England, there were 159 riots from 1740 to 1775.[22] In the American colonies from 1641 to 1759 there were at least 40 riots (see Appendix 1). Since the listing in Appendix 1 is by no means definitive but is a selective list based on secondary sources, and since it lists singly several events that produced more than one riot (e.g., the boundary riots in various colonies), a round number of 75 to 100 riots would not be an excessive estimate of the total number of riots that actually occurred from 1641 to 1759.[23] In the colonies from 1760 to 1775, riot activity surged upward as the revolutionary crisis mounted. In that 16-year period, there were at least 44 riots (see Appendix 2).[24]

Furthermore, the riots were truly Anglo-American in impact, for riots on one side of the Atlantic were watched closely on the other, given the lag in time for communications to cross the ocean. In 1768, Samuel Adams, Boston's patriot agitator and something of a specialist in group violence, remarked on riot activity in England: "There, we are told, is the Weavers mob, the Seamens Mob, the Taylors mob, the Coal Miners mob . . . and in short it is to be feared the whole Kingdome, always excepting the [King] and the P[arliament], will unite in one general scene of tumult." [25] As in America, there were peak years of riot activity in England: 6 riots in 1740, 13 in the years 1749 to 1753, 31 in 1756 to 1758, and 84 in 1765 to 1770.[26] Of the 159 riots in England from 1740 to 1775, certain types—in response to social and economic dislocations in a rapidly changing economy—were predominant. There were 96 riots induced by food shortages and 20 riots by industrial and commercial stresses. Rural riots against land enclosures and turnpike management and riots against impressment and other activities of the military were common.[27]

Amidst the welter of British mob activity in the eighteenth century, there were three riots that were in themselves *cause célèbres* and models for the type of controlled urban violence that the colonists leveled against British policy in the 1760's and 1770's. These three riots were the Bushell (or Glasgow) riot of 1725, the Porteous (or Edinburgh) riot of 1736, and the London "Jew Bill" riot of 1753. In each one of these events (which were major ones not because of the casualties involved—for those were light—but because of their notoriety), violence was used or threatened to protest government action in the same way that, during the 1760's and 1770's, violence was used by urban Americans to protest and stymie British policy.

The Bushell riot of 1725 came about when Glasgow citizens rose violently in protest against a new tax on malt. They destroyed the dwelling of their member of Parliament, Daniel Campbell (believing he supported the tax), in much the same way that 40 years later an angry but controlled Boston mob wrecked the home of Lieutenant Governor Thomas Hutchinson. To quell the violence Captain Bushell was sent to Glasgow, where soldiers under his command fired into the mob and killed several citizens. Bushell was tried in court and convicted of murder but was pardoned by the crown. The city was fined by Parliament to pay for the damages to Campbell's house.[28]

The protest against the malt tax faded, but the violence of Captain Bushell's men and his pardon had not been forgotten by citizens of Edinburgh where, 11 years later, in 1736, a similar situation arose. Two smugglers had been captured, tried, and convicted in a very unpopular decision. In a courtroom scuffle, one of them escaped. The other, Alexander Wilson, became a hero, and on the day of his scheduled execution Captain John Porteous was ordered to call the entire city guard to duty to forestall disorder. After the hanging of Wilson, the mob began to harass Porteous and his men with the result that the soldiers fired into the crowd and killed six and wounded eleven. Porteous was tried and convicted of murder. When the queen gave him a six-week stay of execution, a mob (fearing that, like Captain Bushell, Porteous would go free) broke into the jail, took Porteous out, and hanged him. The murder of Porteous was a most orderly, well-controlled mob action comparable later to the well-planned and well-executed Stamp Act riots and Tea Party in Boston. Parliament responded to the disciplined protest of the Edinburgh mob by fining the city £2,000.[29]

The parallels between the Bushell and Porteous riots and the Boston Massacre of 1770 are striking, and the Scottish riots were in the minds of Americans and Englishmen in the 1760's and 1770's as colonial violence spiraled upward. Captain Thomas Preston, who commanded the British soldiers that fired on Crispus Attucks and the others in the Boston Massacre, had not forgotten the experience of Captain Porteous. His gratitude to John Adams and Josiah Quincy, Jr., who defended him successfully in court, was tempered by his fear (unjustified, as it turned out) that, like Porteous, he would be killed by a mob when released from jail.[30] In 1774, Lord North and his ministry were specifically guided by the earlier precedents of the Bushell and Porteous riots when confronted with the problem of dealing with the Boston Tea Party. Lord North sponsored the Coercive Acts in conscious emulation of Parliament's action a half century earlier in punishing the cities of Glasgow and Edinburgh.[31] Although Parliament, led by Lord North, did not fine Boston or Massachusetts, as had been the case with Glasgow and Edinburgh, the principle of municipal and provincial punishment was embodied in two of the Coercive Acts; the Boston Port Act struck a vital blow at the city by closing its port to shipping, and the Massachusetts Government Act chastised the province as a whole by substantially reducing Massachusetts's chartered privileges of self-government.

An even more striking example of the effectiveness of urban mob action in Britain—one that was a portent of similar mob protest in America against the Stamp Act—occurred in London in 1753 in connection with the so-called "Jew Bill." "The Jewish Naturalization Bill of 1753 was an innocuous enough measure," William Ander Smith has written. "It merely provided that Jews wealthy enough to do so could get private naturalization bills for themselves introduced in Parliament, so avoiding anti-semitic slights and insults that were a part of public naturalization at Magistrate's Court." In sponsoring this legislation, Henry Pelham and the duke of Newcastle hoped to "provide some token reward to [Jews] like Sampson Gideon, who had aided the government so ably in . . . the time of the Forty-Five Rebellion." But with a parliamentary election coming up, opponents of the Pelhams seized on the Jewish naturalization enactment as a potentially winning issue. With the London lower class rabidly anti-Semitic, and the middle and upper classes "frightened with stories about Jews taking over control of English trade and banking," the populace was soon agitated. As turmoil rose in the streets the cautious Pelhams beat a swift retreat and brought about repeal of the act.[32]

Paralleling and notably similar to the British mob tradition was an indigenous colonial mob tradition that, like the tradition of insurgency, stretched back into the seventeenth century. The 40 riots from 1641 to 1759 were characterized by diversity of type and by widespread geographical distribution (see Appendix 1). Economic troubles accounted for eleven riots;[33] intercolonial boundary disputes caused seven;[34] six were political or economic-political;[35] six were religious and maritime controversies;[36] elections, impressment of seamen, and social conditions caused two riots each;[37] one riot was a protest against the customs system;[38] and three riots fall under miscellaneous headings.[39] Of the forty riots, seven may be seen as being generally anti-British in character.[40] The riots were well distributed among eleven colonies: New York had eight; Massachusetts had seven; New Hampshire and Pennsylvania had five each; Rhode Island, Connecticut, and North Carolina had four each; New Jersey had three; Maryland had two; and Virginia and South Carolina had one each.[41] There was also a fairly even chronological distribution of the riots by decades, as shown in the tabulation on next page.[42]

Decade	Riots	Decade	Riots
1640's	1	1700's	8
1650's	2	1710's	12
1660's	3	1720's	7
1670's	3	1730's	10
1680's	4	1740's	7
1690's	6	1750's	12

Three riots may be briefly cited as examples of mob action in the pre-revolutionary period. First, Virginia was the scene of the tobacco plant cutters' riots of 1682. These riots, originating north of the York River in Gloucester County, arose in response to the Virginia assembly's failure to restrict tobacco cultivation in the face of an economically ruinous oversupply. Seized by deep emotions, which were near hysteria, bands of tobacco planters roamed neighboring Middlesex, New Kent, and other counties, systematically cutting down the young, growing plants. Four leaders of the movement were brought to trial, and two of them were executed.[43] This may have been the first example in American history of the technique of dealing, albeit illegally, with agricultural distress by destroying surplus crops. Crop restriction by the federal government has been familiar in our own time, but in the past—as in seventeenth-century Virginia—it has been accomplished by extralegal and violent action.[44]

A second example of the colonial riot may be seen in the New Jersey land riots of the 1740's and 1750's. The trouble grew out of an old controversy that had settlers on one side and the East Jersey proprietors on the other. The settlers claimed to hold their land by virtue of the so-called Elizabethtown titles and by purchases from the Indians, while the proprietors denied the validity of such titles. The settlers first rioted against the proprietary land policy in Newark in 1745, but, in succeeding years and well into the 1750's, the violence spread into the counties of Middlesex, Somerset, Morris, and Hunterdon. The rioters developed a large and powerful organization in northern and western Jersey. "Jails were wrecked," writes Richard P. McCormick, "sheriffs and judicial officers were threatened, and armed bands took vengeance on those who held titles from the proprietors." Law enforcement was powerless, and, states McCormick, "doubtless these lessons" of the efficacy of violent force "were remembered by the patriot leaders two decades later." [45]

Probably the most striking of the pre-1760 urban American riots was the Boston anti-impressment riot of 1747. America's earliest cities—the bustling colonial ports of Boston, Newport, New York, Philadelphia, Charleston, and Norfolk—had their share of tumult, contributed in large part by the violence-prone, lower-class population attached to the maritime industry—seamen, dock workers, laborers, and artisans. On November 17, 1747, this element of the Boston population—"armed seamen, servants, Negroes, and others"—rioted when an attempt to impress local men for service in the Royal Navy was made. For three days the rioters dominated the city, forcing the governor to flee to an island in the bay. The freeing of most of the impressed men amounted to a substantial victory for the rioters.[46] There was no attempt by the rioters to overturn the social and economic structure of Boston, and once the rioters had gained their anti-impressment objective they subsided.

With ample precedent, then, in both British and colonial experience, it is no wonder that the urban patriots of the 1760's and 1770's used the riot as an instrument of resistance to and rebellion against British policy. In the period from 1760 to 1775 there were at least 44 riots in the colonies (see Appendix 2). There was a distinct urban tenor to the rioting, for 8 of the largest American cities had more than half of the rioting—28 of 44 riots. New York City had 5; Newport had 6; Boston, Norfolk, and Providence had 11 each; New London and New Haven had 2 each; and Philadelphia was relatively calm with only 2. Rhode Island led all the colonies with 13; New York and Massachusetts had 7 each; Pennsylvania and Connecticut had 4 each; Virginia had 3; North Carolina had 2; and New Jersey, Maryland, Georgia, South Carolina, and what became Vermont had one each. There were three riots in 1760, none in 1761 and 1762, one in 1763, and from 1764 to 1775 the number of riots annually varied from two to seven with four or five per year being common. The revolutionary character of the times is illustrated by the 30 (of 44) riots that were anti-British in one way or another. The 30 anti-British riots included 17 riots directed against customs enforcement and 6 riots in protest over the impressment of Americans for service in the Royal Navy. The remaining 21 riots involved a variety of causes including politics, economics, morals offenses, Indian relations, religion, and crime.

In resistance to the Stamp Act, Edmund S. Morgan has written, "Boston showed the way." [47] This judgment of Boston's importance may be extended to the remainder of the entire pre-1776 period, for Boston violence was a major feature leading to the Revolution. Although the Stamp Act riots inaugurated Boston's violent role in the revolutionary era, there were three other significant Boston riots among the 44 riots that occurred in colonial America from 1760 to 1775: the sloop *Liberty* (anticustoms) riot of 1768, the Boston Massacre of 1770, and the Boston Tea Party of 1773. Although many cities experienced violence (especially New York and Newport), the cockpit of urban revolutionary turbulence was Boston.

Behind the violence in Boston was the city's remarkable patriot infrastructure of the 1760's and 1770's, headed by James Otis, Samuel Adams, and their colleagues. The infrastructure grew out of the convergence of a historical tradition with a contemporary situation. The historical tradition was the Cooke-Caucus heritage of popular politics in Boston, and the contemporary situation was the diversity and complexity of Boston's social, economic, and political life in the 1760's, which became a fertile seedbed for the growth of the anti-British movement.

Boston's patriot infrastructure of the 1760s was a sophisticated updating of "America's first urban political 'machine,'" whose basis was first laid in late seventeenth-century Boston by Elisha Cooke, Sr. Elisha Cooke, Jr., carried on and perfected his father's organization to the extent that the historian of the Cooke political tradition, G. B. Warden, has stated that he "contributed more than anyone else to the public life of colonial Boston." [48] In Elisha Cooke, Jr.'s, time the machine expanded from its original late seventeenth-century base among the property holders of the South End to a broader city-wide base. Following the younger Cooke's death in 1737, the machine, or "Caucus" as it came to be known, remained a vital factor in the politics of Boston. It is significant that the father of patriot Samuel Adams was a leading member of the Caucus and that the young Samuel Adams was literally raised in the Cooke-Caucus tradition. Warden has emphasized that the

Boston "political alliances" that lasted until 1776 originated in the 1730's, the era of the original Caucus Club that stemmed from the leadership of the two Cookes.

The patriot infrastructure of the 1760's was most intricately connected with Boston's vibrant associational life.[49] First, there were the patriot organizations themselves: the Loyal Nine (which has been portrayed as both the genesis and the executive committee of the Sons of Liberty) and the much broader, more inclusive Sons of Liberty. Then there were the highly political Caucus clubs: the original Caucus Club, of which Samuel Adams was a leading member, and the three area Caucus clubs—South End, North End, and Middle—that emerged during the decade of the 1760's. The tireless Sam Adams was a member of all three of the newer Caucus clubs as well as the old one. The political Caucus clubs were only four among numerous clubs, most of them social or occupational in character. Core patriot leaders were prominent members in many of these clubs, some of which were founded with political purposes in mind or were "politicized" by the activities of the patriot members. A notable example was the Saint Andrew's lodge of Freemasons, a lodge that was founded in the early 1760's and that quickly came to be, in effect, a whig political club for such rising young Bostonians as Joseph Warren and Paul Revere. This was in contrast to the established Saint John's lodge of Freemasonry, which tended to include older, wealthier men of conservative political inclinations.[50]

Closely linked to Boston's club life were the taverns where so many of the clubs met. Among the taverns of Boston—which then as now tended to attract clientele according to common political, social, and occupational interests—was the Green Dragon, which was owned by the patriot-dominated Saint Andrew's lodge and which became a favorite meeting place of the Sons of Liberty and whiggish intellectuals. The Salutation Tavern had, by custom, been a favorite of North End shipyard workers and, while not losing its original patronage, became a meeting place for patriot workingmen. There were other regular meeting places: the Liberty Tree in the South End was a popular rallying ground for outdoor meetings; the counting room of Chase and Speakman's distillery became the secret seat of the Loyal Nine, one of whose members, Thomas Chase, was a partner in the distillery; and above the *Boston Gazette* office was a long room that provided a meeting place and a name for the important Long Room Club, an elite society of 16 patriots, whose membership included James Otis, Samuel Adams, Josiah Quincy, Jr., Benjamin Church, William Molineux, and Joseph Warren.

In the realm of communications and propaganda, the infrastructure had its own printing office and paper, the *Boston Gazette*, under the co-editorship and management of Benjamin Edes, a Loyal Nine member, and John Gill. The *Gazette* became the organ for the patriot sentiments of James Otis and Samuel Adams (whom Governor Francis Bernard termed the "principal managers" of the paper) and John Hancock, Joseph Warren, and Josiah Quincy, Jr., among others. Samuel Adams regularly composed pieces and corrected the copy of other patriots in the *Gazette* office, and John Adams, who seems always to have been in the thick of the infrastructure though not a manager, recorded a visit to the *Gazette* with Otis, Samuel Adams, and Gill, who were "preparing for the next day's newspaper, a curious employment, cooking up paragraphs, articles, occurrences, etc., working the political engine." Aside from the newspaper, the *Gazette* printing office was also used for running off and selling handbills, broadsides, and the numerous political pamphlets that so effectively promoted the anti-British cause.[51]

Related to the patriot network were certain churches and ministers: the Reverend Samuel Cooper's Brattle Street Church, the Reverend Jonathan Mayhew's West Church, and the Reverend Charles Chauncy's First Church. With the probable exception of Cooper, whose parishioners included Samuel Adams, John Hancock, and James Bowdoin, these ministers confined their anti-British activities to sermons and publications. Mayhew and Chauncy were members of the patriot elite in Boston but were not apparently included in the inner circle as Cooper may have been. In the well-attended churches of late colonial Boston, the impact of a patriotic sermon could be very great, as Mayhew's anti-Stamp Act delivery of 1765 demonstrated. Another leading minister of Boston, the Reverend Andrew Eliot of the New North Church, was an intellectual exponent of the patriot ideology, although a temporizing personality ultimately prevented him from making the full commitment to the movement that distinguished Cooper, Mayhew, and Chauncy.

Crucial to the patriot cause was the nexus between the infrastructure and the formal political organizations that met in the city—the Boston town meeting, the provincial council, and the provincial assembly. The powerful town meeting named the many municipal officials, determined taxes and assessments, and adopted public service projects that were a rich source of jobs and economic largesse. For years the original Caucus and its allies in the Merchants Club had acted as the unofficial directing body of the town meeting in which Caucus stalwart Samuel Adams played a key role. Although the town meeting and its important subsidiary committees were not always under the dominance of Samuel Adams in the 1760's and 1770's, they generally were. In the provincial assembly, James Otis, John Hancock, and Samuel Adams, who as clerk turned a minor office into a powerful one, effectively advanced the patriot interest. The wealthy and aristocratic merchant James Bowdoin never joined in the operations of the patriot inner circle, but, in political and ideological terms, he was a committed Whig, and, as the dominant member of the provincial council, the General Court's upper house, he was, in the view of Clifford K. Shipton, much more important in promoting the opposition to British policy than were some of the more famous patriots.

Finally, there were the lower-class workingmen's and artisan "mobs" of the North End and South End. The two mobs were in reality social clubs organized to represent the traditional rivalry of the North and South Ends that dated back to the seventeenth century. Composed of rough men who enjoyed a good brawl, the two mobs customarily fought a pitched battle on November 5, Guy Fawkes Day, or Pope's Day as it was known in strongly anti-Catholic Boston—a street war that sometimes, as in 1764, resulted in fatalities. As long as the two mobs fought each other rather than the British and their sympathizers, the dominance the patriot leaders desired was a practical impossibility. Therefore, one of the truly crucial maneuvers the patriot chieftains managed successfully was the forging of an alliance between the North and South End mobs. It was the Loyal Nine in 1765 (probably in close cooperation

with Samuel Adams, who had Caucus connections in both the
North and South Ends) who made peace between the two mobs
and welded them together under the leadership of Ebenezer
Mackintosh, head of the South End mob. Henry Swift of the North
End mob became the second-in-command of what was virtually a
patriot militia.[52] The result was a new level of violence and
intimidation during the anti-Stamp Act riots of 1765, the *Liberty*
anticustoms riot in 1768, and the threat of mob violence that
caused the evacuation of the two British regiments in the aftermath
of the Boston Massacre.

II

In regard to techniques of social violence the revolutionary period
was one of the most creative in American history. It was the
revolutionary generation that developed, intellectually, the concept
of popular sovereignty by the majority, and it was the revolutionary generation that perfected techniques of violence to enforce
popular sovereignty. To this purpose, tarring and feathering was
levied as a weapon against the unpatriotic, and the broader
technique of vigilantism emerged by Regulator action in South
Carolina and later "lynch law" in Virginia. To climax the trend, a
shrewd organizational maneuver produced the means in the
Continental Association to intimidate the Tories in the crucial
transitional period, 1774 to 1776. The idea of the "sovereignty of
the people" gave an ideological and philosophical justification and
an awesome dignity to the brutal physical abuse or killing of men
that tarring and feathering, vigilantism, and lynching came to
embody.[53]

Tarring and feathering was a terrifying part of the vendetta that
violent patriots carried on against British sympathizers and customs officials in the 1760's and 1770's. Stripping a person naked for
the purpose of smearing him with a coat of hot tar and adding
feathers was a punishment that occurred sporadically in America
and Europe before our revolutionary period, but it was in the late
1760's that the practice emerged for the first time as the "popular
Punishment for modern delinquents." [54] In Newburyport, Massachusetts, on September 10, 1768, patriots tarred and feathered two

customs informers, and, a week later in nearby Salem a customs-house functionary was given the same treatment. There were at least five tarrings and featherings in 1769, and, in 1770, merchants were tarred and feathered for violating the patriotic policy of the nonimportation of British goods. The tarrings and featherings continued without respite from 1773 through 1775 in such cities as Boston and Charleston and were extended into the countryside of New England and the middle colonies.[55] The Tory Peter Oliver climaxed a chronicle of mob violence against Loyalists in 1774–1775 with an account of the fate of Dr. Abner Beebe of East Haddam, Connecticut, who had spoken "very freely" in favor of the crown, "for which he was assaulted by a Mob, stripped naked, and hot Pitch was poured upon him, which blistered his Skin. He was then carried to an Hog Sty and rubbed over with Hogs Dung. They threw the Hog's Dung in his Face, and rammed some of it down his Throat; and in that Condition exposed [him] to a Company of Women. His House was attacked, his Windows broke, when one of his Children was sick, and a Child of his went into Distraction upon this Treatment. His Gristmill was broke, and Persons prevented from grinding at it, and from having any Connections with him." [56]

Throughout the nineteenth century, and well into the twentieth, tarring and feathering was a favorite means of disciplining and punishing when an American mob felt itself in a vindictive but somewhat playful mood. Tarring and feathering was so common in the nineteenth century and the first half of the twentieth that it would be almost impossible to tabulate all such atrocities. Examples abound. One occurred in San Diego in 1912 when Emma Goldman and her manager-lover, Dr. Ben Reitman, visited the city in support of an Industrial Workers of the World (I.W.W.) free-speech campaign. In an event connived at by the police, Dr. Reitman was taken out into the country by vigilantes and tarred and feathered.[57] Mitford M. Mathews has cited a tarring and feathering threat as late as 1950,[58] although, during the last two decades, the practice seems to have faded out.

"It has been said," wrote sociologist James E. Cutler in 1905, "that our country's national crime is lynching." [59] From the early twentieth-century vantage point, this judgment was correct. Lynch law in the typical nineteenth-century mode by which thousands of

southern and border-state black people were extralegally executed
in mass mob spectacles has disappeared since World War II, but
vigilantism in the broad sense of the term is still very much with us
today. In fact, American vigilantism has experienced a revival in
recent years. Significant have been the avowedly self-protective and
community patrol organizations that have proliferated by the
hundreds among urban and suburban white and black Americans
since 1964. Arising chiefly in response to the turmoil in race
relations exemplified by the black ghetto riots of the 1960's and to
the steeply rising crime rate, these organizations—among them
such well-known associations as the "Maccabees" of the Crown
Heights neighborhood in Brooklyn and the North Ward Citizens'
Committee (headed by Anthony Imperiale) of Newark—have been
viewed as vigilante groups by the police, the press, the public, and
themselves. Although they have seldom taken the law into their
own hands, they have clearly emerged from the vigilante tradition
and identify with it.[60]

The more than 200-year tradition of American vigilantism began
during the revolutionary period in the South Carolina Back-Coun-
try of 1767. From then until about 1900 vigilantism—in the classic
sense of organized extralegal movements—was a constant factor in
American life. There was vigilantism in the eastern half of the
nation as well as in the western. As a frequent frontier phenomenon, vigilante movements were seen in almost all of the states
beyond the Appalachians. There were at least 326 known vigilante
movements (which took 729 lives from 1767 to 1909), but the actual
total may have reached 500.[61]

Launching the vigilante tradition was the South Carolina Regulator movement of 1767 to 1769, the prototype for hundreds of
trans-Appalachian vigilante movements of the nineteenth and
twentieth centuries. (During the nineteenth century the original
terms *regulator* and *vigilante* were synonyms for Americans who
took the law into their own hands by participating in an organized
movement; by the late nineteenth century *regulator* had faded from
general use.) Spurred into action by an outbreak of frontier crime
and violence that arose in the aftermath of an especially destructive
Indian war, and without county courts and sheriffs to combat the
banditry, respectable settlers of affluent and average means formed
as "Regulators" in late 1767 and began a two-year vigilante

campaign. Subscribing to written articles in their pledge to end the problem of crime and disorder, the Regulators attacked and broke up outlaw gangs and communities. The idle and immoral were rounded up, given trials, flogged, and expelled or subjected to forced labor on Regulator plantations. A particularly obnoxious band of outlaws was pursued northward to the North Carolina–Virginia border area, and sixteen of its members were slain.[62]

There was no direct connection between the South Carolina Regulator movement and the conditions that brought on the Revolution, but the Regulators as vigilantes were an example of the popular sovereignty impulse of the era that flared up in anti-British rioting in the cities and in tarring and feathering. (It is significant, too, that most of the South Carolina Regulators later became Whigs during the Revolution and fought on the American side against the British and Tories in South Carolina.)[63] There was a direct connection, however, between the Revolution and another phenomenon of the period that was to have an enduring legacy in the history of American social violence. This was lynching in Virginia during the Revolution.

The settlers in Bedford County, Virginia, near the Blue Ridge were plagued in 1780 by numerous Tories and by outlaws made bold by the unsettled wartime conditions on the frontier. James E. Cutler writes that

> Both Tories and desperadoes harassed the [patriots] and plundered their property with impunity. The prices paid by both armies for horses made horse-stealing a lucrative practice, and the inefficiency of the judiciary made punishment practically out of the question. The county courts were merely examining courts in all such cases, and the single court for the final trial of felonies sat at Williamsburg, more than two hundred miles away. To take the prisoners thither, and the witnesses necessary to convict them, was next to impossible. Frequently the officers in charge of the prisoners would be attacked by outlaws and forced to release their men or be captured by British troops and themselves made prisoners.

It was in response to these conditions that the leading men of Bedford County—headed by Colonel Charles Lynch, for whom the city of Lynchburg is named—"after deliberation . . . decided to take matters into their own hands, to punish lawlessness of every kind, and so far as possible to restore peace and security to their community." An extralegal organization for the capture and trial of culprits was formed. Lynch became the presiding justice of a court in which three other leading men—William Preston, Robert Adams, Jr., and James Callaway—sat as associate justices. This was literally "Lynch-law," as in time it came to be known. Like the Regulators a decade earlier in South Carolina, Lynch and his cohorts conducted regular though illegal trials. The accused "if convicted . . . was sentenced to receive thirty-nine lashes on the bare back, and if he did not then shout 'Liberty Forever' " was "hanged up by the thumbs until he did so." The punishment was immediate and was inflicted under a large and locally famous walnut tree standing in Lynch's yard. Although they had been strictly illegal at the time, the Virginia legislature later approved and pardoned the actions of Lynch and his neighbors. Among the other parts of Virginia where lynching took place during the Revolution was Washington County, where, in 1779, William Campbell, Walter Crockett, and others caught and punished Tories and outlaws.[64]

The practice of vigilantism, lynching, and tarring and feathering might have been abandoned by the American people after the turbulent revolutionary era had not the Revolution itself, with its emergent concept of popular sovereignty, furnished a powerful justification for the violent abuse of alleged enemies of the public good. In *The Creation of the American Republic, 1776–1787*, Gordon S. Wood has traced the maturation of the idea of the "sovereignty of the people" in the revolutionary period and has shown that popular sovereignty was in part the outgrowth of the colonists' "long tradition of extra-legislative action by the people, action that more often than not had taken the form of mob violence and crowd disturbance . . . . Beginning with the Revolutionary movement (but with roots deep in American history) the people came to rely more and more on their ability to organize themselves and to act 'out-of-doors' whether as 'mobs,' as political clubs, or as conventions." [65]

By the 1780's, Wood finds, the emergence of the concept of popular sovereignty was complete—and crucial. The concept was no mere intellectual construct, however. Through constitution-making, extralegal conventions, instructions to representatives, and often violent "out-of-doors action," Americans had "infused an extraordinary meaning into the idea of the sovereignty of the people." [66] The thinkers of the time upheld popular sovereignty. For example, in 1787 Samuel Chase of Maryland declared that the people's power "is like the light of the sun, native, original, inherent, and unlimited by human authority. Power in the rulers or governors of the people is like the reflected light of the moon, and is only borrowed, delegated and limited by the grant of the people." [67] About the same time James Sullivan asserted that "there is no supreme power but what the people themselves hold." [68] And John Stevens boldly announced: "All power whatever is vested in, and immediately derived from, the people only; the rulers are deputies merely, and at certain short periods are removable by them: nay, the very government itself is a creature formed by themselves, and may, whenever they think it necessary, be at any time new modelled." [69]

A historical connection may be seen between the theoretical revolutionary concept of the sovereignty of the people and the behavioral background of popular sovereignty in the local community of the colonial period. Alexis de Tocqueville's insight that "the doctrine of the sovereignty of the people came out of the townships" at the time of the American Revolution "and took possession of the state" [70] has recently gained support from Michael Zuckerman's *Peaceable Kingdoms: New England Towns in the Eighteenth Century.* Zuckerman contends that, on the basis of the New England town meeting's insistence upon harmony, "the consciousness of [the town] community, in Massachusetts, continued at least three quarters of the way through the eighteenth century as a prime value of public life" with "consolidation of consensus" as the principle and "control of conflict" as the aim.[71]

The close tie between the nascent idea of popular sovereignty and revolutionary events appears in Boston. G. B. Warden has written that "the growing unity" in revolutionary Boston "among . . . various groups" was connected to an "entity called the 'Body of the People.'" Patriots and their opponents all came to use the term "Body of the People" as a synonym for "a majority of the people" or "the greater part of the people." Soon the "Body of the People" referred to "the united will of the people" in symbolic substitution for "the Crown," and both legal and extralegal gatherings alike were characterized as the "Body of the People." In

1773 it was a meeting of the "Body"—justified as "representing all the people in the province"—that led to the Boston Tea Party.[72]

Revolutionary-period theorists of popular sovereignty probably had not intended to justify vigilantism and lynching, but to later generations of Americans—including some of the most eminent Americans, such as Andrew Jackson, Theodore Roosevelt, governors, congressmen, senators, lawyers, judges, and leading capitalists—popular sovereignty was just that: a justification for the people in all their power to take the law into their own hands and to put a miscreant to death by summary justice.[73] Typical was the attitude of an Indiana vigilante movement—the Regulators of LaGrange and Noble counties in northeast Indiana in 1858—who, to justify their successful drive on outlaws and blacklegs, stated their belief "that the people of this country are the real sovereigns, and that whenever the laws, made by those to whom they have delegated their authority, are found inadequate to their protection," it is the "right of the people" to take the law into their own hands.[74]

In the Revolution and its prelude, the Tories, of course, bore the brunt of the combination of popular sovereignty and violence. The possibilities for the harassment and oppression of the Tories were immensely increased in late 1774 by the Continental Congress's adoption of a Continental Association for a total cessation of trade with the British Isles. To enforce the Continental Association the Congress resolved

> that a committee be chosen in every county, city, and town . . . to observe the conduct of all persons touching this association; and when it shall be made to appear, to the satisfaction of a majority of any such committee, that any person within the limits of their appointment has violated this association, that such majority do forthwith cause the truth of the case to be published in the gazette; to the end, that all such foes to the rights of British-America may be publicly known, and universally contemned as the enemies of American liberty . . . .[75]

It was not really necessary to set up committees in all American communities to meet the stated purpose of the Association (cessation of trade with Great Britain), for the experience of the 1760's had shown that imports from the mother country could be stopped by merely controlling the seaports. But to create a country-wide patriotic movement in support of Samuel Adams and the other members of the Continental Congress it was necessary to establish local committees not just in the seaports but on a country-wide basis, and this may have been the main motive behind their establishment. It was particularly important to single out for intimidation the Tories, and the committees were ordered to do this to enforce the Continental Association. Congress requested only that the Tories be subjected to verbal anathema and did not mention violence. But local committees often instigated violence against the Tories, as happened in Isle of Wight County, Virginia, in August 1775, when one Anthony Warwick was tarred and feathered immediately after being called to account by the local committee.[76]

III

Long after 1776 the symbols of the Revolution continued to be used with frequency and sincerity by violent movements to enfold themselves in its sanctifying mantle. Thus, only 20 years after the first Continental Congress, the "Whiskey Rebellion" broke out in western Pennsylvania as a protest against the taxation policy of the federal government. In the summer of 1794, radical participants in the whiskey insurrection "began to revive the Revolutionary custom of erecting liberty poles" in a "call for [a] popular rising against [Federalist] tyranny."[77] In 1844–1845, another farmers' movement invoked the precedent of the American Revolution. This was the violent antirent outbreak in four upstate New York counties southwest of Albany. The roots of the antirent protest against the New York tenant system went back to the revolutionary decade of 1760's, but the movement flamed anew in the 1840's as agricultural decline in the uplands of the Hudson-Mohawk region made the renters desperate. Taking violent and sometimes fatal action against landlords and authorities, the antirenters before committing violence disguised themselves as "Mohawks" in conscious emulation of the patriotic "Indians" of the Boston Tea Party, and they denounced their opponents as "Tories."[78]

In regard to the coming of the Civil War, Charles P. Roland has

noted that Southerners "looked upon the American Revolution as
the great prototype of their own war for independence." [79] A look
at the evidence bears out Roland's statement. Robert Barnwell
Rhett, South Carolina's extremist "father of secession," as early as
the Nullification movement, made "fervent appeals . . . to the
example of the Revolution." From them until secession, Rhett, the
fire-eating editor of the Charleston *Mercury*, tirelessly promoted
Southern independence.[80] The same was true of another "fire-
eater," William L. Yancey of Alabama, who, in early 1860,
declared his aim to convince Southerners of the "mass of wrongs
committed on them" by the North and "to produce spirit enough
. . . to call forth a Lexington, to fight a Bunker's Hill," and to
"precipitate the cotton states into a revolution." [81] After Lincoln's
election and on the eve of secession the Revolutionary heritage was
again invoked in South Carolina by the organization of local
Minute Men companies whose aim was to march on Washington
and forcibly prevent Lincoln's inauguration. Nothing came of this
plan, but the action of the Minute Men was significant in whipping
up anti-Union sentiment in South Carolina, whose enthusiastic
citizens compared their secession convention of 1860 to the
Continental Congress of 1776.[82]

The spirit of '76 also flourished in Virginia, where after Lincoln's
election the hallowed tradition of the Revolution was drawn upon
to organize local companies of "minutemen" and "committees of
safety." [83] During the Civil War, Northern "Copperheads" in the
midwestern states of Ohio, Indiana, and Illinois also hearkened to
the revolutionary heritage to justify their opposition to the Union
war effort. Copperhead sentiment, and the vociferous Unionist and
Republican opposition it encountered, led to frequent episodes of
violence in the southern Midwest—riots and raids, in particular.
When Copperheads wanted to escalate their insurgency, they, too,
called from the past a revolutionary symbol. This time it was the
"Sons of Liberty," which, in the Copperhead incarnation, was a
secret organization with grandiose plans but which, according to its
historian, Frank L. Klement, had power more in the fears and
imaginations of Copperhead-hating Republicans than in actuality.[84]

The Civil War was not the last example of Americans legitimizing violence in terms of the Revolution, for the practice has

survived to our own time. A generation ago, in 1932–1933, the Farmers' Holiday Association movement blazed up in Iowa and other corn-belt states. This movement, led by Milo Reno, was a protest against adverse economic conditions stemming from the Great Depression but with a background of farm grievances that went back to the Grangers, Greenbackers, and Populists of the late nineteenth century. Violent, direct action was a principal feature of the movement. The farmers defied legal processes, blocked highways, dumped milk from trucks, forcibly halted farm foreclosure sales, and, on one occasion, assaulted a county judge. The example of the American Revolution was much in the minds of observers, supporters, and members of the Farmers' Holiday movement. Henry A. Wallace compared the movement to that of the Boston Tea Party, and a sympathizer compared the spirit of the organization to the "spirit of 1776." The farmers themselves drew on the heritage of the Revolution when they enlisted in a violent subgroup of the movement in northwest Iowa whose members called themselves the "Modern Seventy-Sixers." [85]

In our own day, talk of revolution is common. We think, correctly, of the current revolutionary fervor as being on the left side of the political spectrum, but the right wing in American history has ever been quick to adopt the symbols of the Revolution, and the present is no exception. It seems that when violence-prone Americans see a crisis approaching their first thought, often, is to organize as "minutemen." An example is the secret, right-wing paramilitary organization of 8,000 to 10,000 "Minutemen" founded in 1961 as an anti-Communist movement. During their peak period in the 1960's violence was central to the Minutemen's approach to the alleged Communist threat. They trained themselves in guerrilla warfare against the day when the Communists might attempt a total take-over of the nation. Violent activity of the Minutemen included a try at bank robbery, dynamite attacks on police and power stations near Seattle, and a raid on a peace group in Connecticut.[86]

More recently, the violence of the Minutemen was eclipsed by the violence of extremist elements among the white New Left and the black militant movements. The contemporary white and black revolutionaries used violent "know-how" gained from the training manuals of the Minutemen in accomplishing some of the 1,391 "guerrilla acts of sabotage in the U.S., 1965–1970" recorded in the January 1971 issue of *Scanlan's Monthly* on "Guerrilla War in the U.S.A." But, unlike the Minutemen, the current revolutionaries do not identify with the American Revolution. Instead, white and black American revolutionaries of today seek their models, not in Samuel Adams, Thomas Jefferson, and George Washington, but in a galaxy of present-day heroes including Mao Tse-Tung, Ché Guevara, Malcolm X, George Jackson, and the slain members of the Symbionese Liberation Army. That current revolutionaries, unlike previous American dissidents, no longer identify with the American Revolution may be one of the most important developments in our contemporary intellectual history. It may suggest that the long-range era of the American Revolution has at last come to an end, for, despite the bicentennial observance, it seems that our Revolution now has little impact as an inspiration for dissent and reform whether peaceable or violent.[87]

Chapter 3

SOUTH CAROLINA EXTREMISM AND ITS VIOLENT ORIGINS: FROM THE REGULATOR MOVEMENT TO THE EDGEFIELD TRADITION, 1760–1960

Edgefield . . . has had more dashing, brilliant, romantic figures, statesmen, orators, soldiers, adventurers, daredevils, than any county of South Carolina, if not any rural county in America . . . . The Brookses, Simkinses, Pickenses, Butlers, were Edgefield families. All of these were kin, by blood or marriage, and they and other related families gave to their . . . county a character that was more South Carolinian, intense, more fiery, than was found elsewhere.

William Watts Ball, *The State that Forgot*

. . . to hell with the Constitution.

Senator Benjamin R. (Pitchfork Ben) Tillman of Edgefield County

Among all Southern states before the Civil War, South Carolina was the leader in sectional extremism. Various explanations have been offered. One is the economic decline of South Carolina in the decades before the Civil War, a decline that saw the Palmetto State caught in a squeeze between the high tariff imposed by the North and the competition of lush new cotton fields developed by South Carolina's sister states of the Southwest.[1]

Another reason cited is the presence of a tremendous black slave population in South Carolina, with South Carolina whites banding together to form a harsh and rigorous police state to keep down the slaves and extremism the consequence in state and national politics.[2] Still another often-mentioned factor is the majesty and brilliance of John C. Calhoun's intellectual and political leadership, which saw him emerge as the philosopher of Nullification and the patron saint of secession.[3]

All of these explanations are helpful, but they do not take into consideration the fact that other southern states were subject to such factors, and yet none equaled the extremism of South Carolina. Virginia, North Carolina, and, to an extent, Georgia were other old South Atlantic states that experienced economic decline for the same reasons. Alabama, Mississippi, and Louisiana similarly had huge slave populations and police-state conditions, but they, too, lagged behind South Carolina in extremism. We are prone to distinguish the moderation of Jefferson, Madison, and the old Virginia school on the issue of slavery and the staunch proslavery doctrine of Calhoun of South Carolina, but, before the war between the states, Virginia produced a thinker, George Fitzhugh, who, surpassed Calhoun as a social philosopher and defender of slavery.[4] And yet, Virginia lagged far behind South Carolina in the passion of its allegiance to the cause of Dixie.

Restricted to South Carolina alone was a factor that goes far to explain why that state was the leader in secession. In South Carolina, itself, the main source of political extremism was the "Up Country." The Up Country was the nineteenth-century outgrowth of the revolutionary period's "Back Country" section—the interior district above the "Low Country" region along the coast. The extremism of the ante-bellum Up Country had its origins in an entire generation of violence and civil strife that sundered the old Back Country of South Carolina from 1760 to 1785. The excessive violence in the Back Country, 1760–1785, traumatized the area's inhabitants and bred a tendency to extremism that formed the background of Calhoun's leadership and came to be best exemplified by the Edgefield tradition—an extremist syndrome emanating from turbulent Edgefield County of the old Back Country. Having an impact on South Carolina analogous to that of South Carolina on the nation, the Edgefield tradition has been most saliently represented by Benjamin R. (Pitchfork Ben) Tillman of the post-Civil War generation and by Senator J. Strom Thurmond of our own time.[5]

I

Before the American Revolution, society and politics in South Carolina were dominated by the old Low Country aristocratic families, frequently of Barbadian or Huguenot origin, who had established a culture of affluence and elegance on the basis of notable success in planting and commerce.[6] But, in the second and third decades of the nineteenth century, the old names—the Pinckneys, Rutledges, Smiths, Brewtons, Manigaults, Izards, Mazycks, Draytons, Guerards, Middletons, and Lowndeses—began to lose their primacy in South Carolina politics. As William R. Taylor and George C. Rogers, Jr., have shown, the old families were being shouldered aside by upstart politicos—often of Scotch-Irish stock —hailing from the Piedmont and the Up Country.[7] The "new men" were "vigorous newcomers from the county courts" who, in the view of such Charleston aristocrats and intellectuals as Hugh Swinton Legaré and William Elliott, were upsetting the "stable social world of the South." The "new men" were ambitious, able, unscrupulous, and insensitive. Many of them were, of course, lawyers, and the "lawyers of the old school" quailed before their "rude assault." [8] The change became apparent to conservative, nonviolent, moderate, Unionist men like Legaré, Elliott, and James L. Petigru about the time of the Nullification controversy. "The day has really come when passion is openly preferred to reason," said Petigru in an 1831 denunciation of the Nullification movement.[9] To Legaré, the Nullification crisis was "another revolution in which the canaille were rising to overthrow the old planter leadership." Labeling the Nullifiers "Jacobin" insurgents, and viewing them as social upstarts and opportunists, Legaré spoke as a member of the old Lowland aristocracy in 1832 when he lamented: "We are (I am quite sure) the *last* of the *race* of South-Carolina. I see nothing before us but decay and downfall." [10]

Although his rise to political leadership in South Carolina came long before the Nullification controversy, no one better represented the "new men" than John C. Calhoun. John C. Calhoun's father, Patrick, joined the stream of Scotch-Irish immigrants who were diverted to the South from Pennsylvania after Braddock's defeat in 1755. Pausing briefly in the Waxhaws district, Patrick moved into South Carolina's Long Canes section (in what was later to be old Abbeville County) between the Saluda and Savannah rivers, where he survived one Back Country crisis after another: a Cherokee massacre in 1760, the Regulator troubles of the late 1760's, the outbreak of the Revolution in 1775 and 1776, followed by the mordant Whig-Tory vendettas of the early 1780's.[11] Patrick Calhoun was a remarkable man, and he prospered to the extent that young John was given a Yale education. But what really established the young man was marriage to a Low Country heiress—and that, too, was part of the classic pattern for an aggressive Back Country youth. Is it any surprise that John C. Calhoun's legacy for South Carolina was a doctrine and a politics that, despite its surface rationalism, in Petigru's language preferred "passion" to "reason"? For John C. Calhoun's heritage was truly a heritage of violence. His grandmother, the mother of Patrick, was slain with dozens of other Scotch-Irish refugees in a Cherokee ambush on February 1, 1760. The son, Patrick, later returned to the site of the massacre to bury the scalped and butchered bodies.[12] Although there is no documentary evidence that Patrick Calhoun was a Regulator, he certainly sympathized with them and may have been a party to Regulator activity. In the Revolution, all the Calhouns were exposed to Tory outrages, as the great Nullifier recalled in later life. John Caldwell Calhoun himself was named after an uncle, Captain John Caldwell, who was murdered by Back Country Tories.[13]

The tales and traditions of the Back Country's generation of violence from 1760 to 1785 were a part of the formative years of John C. Calhoun, and so it was for the other "new men" of the Up Country who stamped upon South Carolina the doctrines of Nullification and secession. The psychic roots of the "new men" were in the Back Country generation of violence from which they were only one or two generations removed. Not only did the Back Country's generation of violence form a direct part of the heritage of extremists like Calhoun, but, in a general way, it had a crucial influence on the Up Country, which, by the second quarter of the nineteenth century, had supplanted the Low Country as the socially and politically significant section of the state.

II

The Back Country's generation of violence began with the brutal Cherokee War of 1760–1761 and continued with a wave of crime and mayhem that led to the Regulator-Moderator conflict of 1767–1769. A short period of comparative calm in the early 1770's was shattered by an outbreak of fighting between Back Country Whigs and Tories in 1775 and 1776. Another short breathing spell was ended in 1780 by a renewal of the Whig-Tory war, and, for three years, the Back Country was wracked by some of the most cruel and devastating civil strife that has ever beset an American community. The war officially ended in 1783, but some of the Whig-Tory feuds were fought on into the middle of the decade. Seldom has an American community gone through the sustained violence and strife that was the South Carolina Back Country's fate from 1760 to 1785. Georgia had its own bitter Whig-Tory war in the 1780's but was spared the calamities that fell to South Carolina in the 1760's. North Carolina had a Regulator war that ended much more disastrously than South Carolina's, but the Tarheels escaped the Cherokee War and had a far less serious civil war between the Whigs and the Tories.

The brutalizing effects of the generation of violence are seen at the outset in the Cherokee War of 1760–1761. The Indians began the war with a mass onslaught on the Back Country that killed scores of settlers and set others running toward the safety of such Middle Country centers as Augusta and Orangeburg. Those that remained in the Back Country congregated in settlers' forts, where crowded conditions, disease, and the corruption of militia officers took their toll. Meanwhile, the Cherokee War continued with typical barbarity on both sides. The South Carolina Assembly raised the bounty on Indian scalps, and Back Countrymen boasted of fattening their dogs on Indian carcasses, displaying their scalps "neatly ornamented" from the top bastions of their forts. At last in mid-1761 a mixed expedition of British regulars and South Carolina militia marched into the Cherokee country and broke the back of the Indian resistance. The Back Country to within 60 miles of the coast was devastated by the war. Loss of life and property were great, and, at one time, Lieutenant Governor William Bull feared the entire area would be depopulated.[14]

The Back Country was left in chaos by the Cherokee War. So many homes were burned or broken up, and so many individuals were killed, that the orphaned and the homeless became a problem. Many of them drifted or were coerced into outlaw bands formed in the wake of the war by veterans of the fighting who were too restless or brutalized to settle down to normal, peaceful occupations. Some of the outlaws made their own communities in the Back Country where they lived undisturbed to enjoy their booty. Here and there were found settlements of runaway slaves. Some of the outlaw gangs had alliances with similar gangs to the north and the south and established Back Country way-stations in an inter-colonial network of horse thieves. "Crackers" and frontier poor whites aided and abetted the outlaws. By 1766 and 1767, the outlaws were almost supreme in the Back Country. They abducted young girls to serve as paramours in their outlaw villages and raped plantation wives or daughters who were too old, too young, or too much trouble to be carried off. When they heard of some planter or merchant with some material wealth, they set upon the hapless fellow, abused his family, and tortured him until he blurted out the whereabouts of his valuables.[15]

Maddened by these conditions, which had gone unchecked since the Cherokee War, and lacking local courts and sheriffs to enforce the law, the respectable settlers rose up in late 1767 in the first organized manifestation of the American vigilante tradition. The leaders and the small planters of the Back Country banded together as Regulators to stamp out the outlaw gangs and to discipline the disorderly and idle "lower people" who lived on what they could pilfer and plunder from their more industrious neighbors. A two-year campaign was successful. Outlaw gangs and their leaders were broken up, harried, and pursued as far away as Virginia. The idle and immoral were taken up by the Regulators, tried, whipped with 39 stripes, and, if thought hopeless, were then banished from the area. Those that were deemed "reclaimable" were given "so many acres to attend in so many days," [16] a system that the Regulators felt would keep them out of trouble and would perhaps solve the problem of the Back Country labor shortage that bothered many Regulators.

There is no doubt that the Regulator movement was a constructive one in that it did rid the Back Country of large-scale crime and did, after many years, introduce order into the chaotic Back Country life. But the Regulators were so vindictive and brutal in their punishments, that it can be argued that they introduced the strain of violence and extremism that was to be the curse of the Up Country and the nemesis of South Carolina before the Civil War. There was a strong streak of sadism in the ways and means of the Regulators. On one occasion 50 or 60 Regulators captured a "roguish and troublesome" fellow, who was alleged to be a horse thief. They stripped him down to his undershirt and bound him to a sapling with a wagon chain. Then, with drum beating and fiddle playing, the Regulators took turns beating the luckless man, each one administering 10 blows with bundles of rods and switches. Before they released him he had received 500 stripes and was left with the blood streaming down his back. Increasingly arbitrary and so extreme and violent were the Regulators in their punishments that an opposition of Moderators formed. The Moderators were sufficiently strong to gain a truce from the Regulators, and the Regulators themselves were satisfied when the provincial government provided district courts and sheriffs for them in 1769.[17]

There were echoes of the Regulator-Moderator conflict in the early 1770's, but for the first time in 10 years a calm settled over the Back Country. But it was indeed the calm before the storm, for, in 1775, the American Revolution came to the Back Country. The first phase of the Revolution in the Back Country, in 1775 and 1776, consisted of two large-scale risings by Back Country Tories, which were put down easily by Back Country Whigs when the British failed to aid their Back Country allies. In the summer of 1775, the Tory militia colonel, Thomas Fletchall, circulated a pledge of loyalty to the Crown among hundreds of Back Country Tories. This was immediately met by the propagandizing tours of Judge William Henry Drayton and the Reverend William Tennent in the Whig interest. Whig and Tory detachments began to march and countermarch until, in mid-September, 1775, an army of 1,200 Tories under Fletchall faced an army of 1,000 Whigs under Drayton at Ninety Six. But the battle was avoided when a truce between Whigs and Tories was signed on September 16th, a truce that was immediately repudiated by the Cunninghams, a leading Back Country Tory family.

The Tories had been counting on the support of Lord William Campbell, the royal governor of South Carolina, but Campbell was unable to aid them. The result was that in November, 1775, the Back Country Whig leader, Colonel Richard Richardson, Sr., led 4,000 or 5,000 Whigs (including 3,000 men from the Back Country) on a final sweep against the Back Country Tories. The Tories melted away or retreated far up country until at last, on December 22, 1,300 Whigs under the veteran Back Country Indian fighter, Colonel William Thomson, cornered what was left of the Tory band at the Great Cane Break. Only Thomson's restraint of his soldiers prevented a massacre of the Tories, but even so 130 Tories were taken prisoner and half a dozen killed or wounded. The victorious Whigs returned to their homes in a blinding snowstorm from which the event became known as the "Snow Campaign." [18]

Clinton's attack on Charleston in the summer of 1776 gave the Back Country Tories—and the Cherokees—one more chance. On July 1, 1776, the Cherokees—urged on by British Indian agents— fell on the Back Country Whigs in a surprise onslaught timed to coincide with Clinton's attack on Charleston. Many whites were massacred, including Anthony Hampton, the great grandfather of Wade Hampton, noted Civil War general and post-bellum governor. Like that of 1760 the Cherokee attack was initially successful, but retribution came fast and furious as the Back Country Whig leaders, Major William Williamson and Francis Salvador (a Jewish land developer and merchant), led an expedition against the Indians. The Tories joined the Indians, and the Whigs flocked to join Williamson and Salvador. Salvador was killed, but, in a campaign that ran from July 15 to October 11, 1776, Williamson's force—grown to 4,000 or 5,000 men and including detachments from North Carolina and Virginia—destroyed the Cherokee lower towns and middle settlements and inflicted 2,000 casualties on the Indians. The Back Country Tories were thoroughly cowed, and many Back Countrymen of Tory or neutral persuasion moved into the Whig camp in revulsion against the British employment of Indian warfare and in fear of Whig brutality.[19]

The years from 1777 to 1780, when Charleston fell, saw no

fighting in the Back Country, but Whig-Tory animosities continued. A Whig district judge, Henry Pendleton, when riding circuit in the Back Country did not hesitate to manipulate and browbeat juries to bring about the judicial murder of certain Tories. To Pendleton, Tories "were such notorious offenders that they could not possibly be objects of mercy." [20] The Back Country Tories, however, were not inactive by any means. Despite his short imprisonment by the Whigs in 1775,[21] Robert Cunningham retained great prestige among Back Countrymen. Although he acknowledged Whig rule in the state, Cunningham remained loyal to the Crown. In 1779 he defeated a staunch Whig, Colonel James Williams, for a seat in the state senate and became a part of a faction of Tories and conservative Whigs who did much to hamper a vigorous Whig defense effort.[22] And in 1778 the *Gazette of the State of South Carolina* reported,[23] in an account reminiscent of Regulator troubles, that "the most execrable outrages have been lately committed, by a desperate banditti [Tories], who have assumed the name of the East-Florida scout, and are harbored between the forks of Edisto River, they plunder houses, steal horses, abuse women, tie and whip men, and cut their ears off."

III

The second phase of the Revolution in the Back Country began in the summer of 1780 after Charleston had fallen to the British. With the fall of Charleston in May, 1780, South Carolina lay prostrate before the British. Historians are generally agreed that a wise and lenient amnesty policy on the part of the British would have consolidated South Carolina under the reinstituted British rule, but, when Clinton, on June 3, 1780, changed the neutral status of the defeated Whigs as being prisoners on parole, countless pacified Whigs were put on notice that they must "take an oath of allegiance to His Majesty's government or be considered in rebellion and treated accordingly." By this proclamation Clinton "reawakened the spirit of revolt in South Carolina." [24] The merciless warfare of Banastre Tarleton, Lord Rawdon, and other impetuous young subordinates of Cornwallis drove many quiescent Whigs once more into active armed resistance. Old Whigs like

Andrew Pickens and Wade Hampton of the Back Country, who had sought protection under the British, renounced that allegiance and returned once and for all to the Whig fold. In a matter of weeks and months, vigorous partisan warfare was under way against the British and Tories. Although Francis Marion ranged mainly through the Low Country swamps, between the Peedee and the Santee, the principal scene of partisan warfare was in the Back Country where Thomas Sumter and Andrew Pickens led the Whig militia. In 1780 and 1781 a civil war blazed in the Back Country with all the horrors usually associated with a conflict of neighbor against neighbor.

Edward McCrady, "the Gibbon of South Carolina," has minutely detailed the Back Country battles in his massive two-volume *History of South Carolina in the Revolution.* The statistics afforded by McCrady reveal that as bitter and devastating as the Cherokee war of 1760–1761 and the Regulator conflict of the late 1760's were, they pale before the Whig-Tory civil war of 1780–1781. Of a total of 137 revolutionary battles fought in South Carolina, 78 battles (or 57%) were fought in the Back Country.[25] When one considers that over one-half of the battles fought in the Low Country took place in the environs of Charleston, the concentration of the war in the Back Country is even more striking. Only four important battles of the war in South Carolina took place in the Low Country: Clinton's unsuccessful attack on Charleston in 1776, Prevost's unsuccessful siege of Charleston in 1779, the successful siege in 1780, and the Battle of Eutaw in 1781. All the other major engagements—Camden, Hobkirk's Hill, the Siege of Ninety Six, Hanging Rock, Fishing Creek, King's Mountain, Cowpens, Fishdam Ford, Blackstock's, Fort Watson, Friday's Ferry, Fort Motte and Granby, Musgrove's Mill, etc.—were Back Country battles.

Whig militia fought alongside soldiers of the Continental line but often faced British regulars and Tory militia alone. Many of the battles involved only South Carolinians, with the Tory militia being opposed by their Whig counterparts. In 1780, 28 battles were fought in the Back Country, with 18 battles involving Whig militia only. Excluding the three battles of "Buford's Defeat" (in the Waxhaws), Camden, and King's Mountain, where the forces and casualties involved were too large to be typical of the partisan warfare of that year, the total casualties on both sides in the battles were 2,331.[26] The year 1781 saw even heavier fighting. Thirty-nine battles were fought in the Back Country with twenty-two of them being fought by Whig militiamen alone, sixteen by militia and Continental soldiers together, and one (Hobkirk's Hill) by Continentals alone. Casualties in all these battles (excepting Cowpens and Hobkirk's Hill whose inclusion would skew the figures due to the large numbers involved in these two key battles) amounted to at least 1,448.[27] These casualty figures give some idea of the large number of Back Countrymen involved on both sides. Another viewpoint is given in Leah Townsend's study of South Carolina Baptists in the Revolution. She found that of 1,500 Baptists of military age—most of them Back Countrymen—about 600 men served in arms or furnished military supplies. So bloody was the strife that most Back Country Baptist churches were either broken up or failed to survive the revolutionary era.[28]

The formal statistics give an inkling of the extent of the civil war, but they do not include the many small-scale skirmishes and ambushes that lacked a chronicler. Perhaps even more important than the numbers involved was the nature of the conflict, for no conflict within the borders of the United States has surpassed the South Carolina Back Country civil war in cruelty and bitterness. Concomitant with the movements of the armies was an underwar of family and individual feuds and of neighbor against neighbor. Plunder, arson, ambush, atrocity, and death were the hallmarks of the savage underwar.

A number of the Whig and Tory militia were in the war partly for booty, and some of the combatants were motivated *only* by booty. By proclamation in August, 1780, the British headquarters in Charleston openly acknowledged that its soldiers had plundered South Carolina inhabitants and ordered that such activities immediately cease.[29] And in September, 1780, the British similarly admitted that Major Wemyss had burned the houses of the followers of Francis Marion and Peter Horry.[30]

Plundering was, however, lifted to the level of a system and made an integral part of the pay and recruitment procedures of the Whig militia in what later came to be known as "Sumter's Law." Initiated in 1781, "Sumter's Law" was used by Sumter and Pickens but not by Marion. These Whig leaders recruited for their commands on the promise that for 10 months' service each lieutenant-colonel would receive three grown blacks and one small one; each major, three grown blacks; each captain, two grown blacks; each lieutenant, one grown and one small black; each sergeant, one and one-quarter black; and each private, one grown black. In addition, officers and men would divide up two-thirds of all the goods taken from Tories. The blacks, of course, would come from defeated Tory opponents. For each Whig militia brigade a commissary was appointed to take the seized property into custody. A board of field officers was established to examine the property taken and the claims of each Whig to it. If the property was found to have been taken from a Whig, it was restored, but if taken from a Tory, it was delivered to officers and men in lieu of pay as outlined above.[31] "Sumter's Law" was effective, for under the system Sumter himself raised 1,100 men.[32] By July, 1781, the Back Country Whig colonel, Wade Hampton, noted that Whigs had been engaging in vicious plundering under "Sumter's Law," despite the efforts of Hampton and Colonel Thomas Taylor to halt it.[33]

Vicious though the plundering may have been, it was nothing compared to the mortal terror Whigs and Tories visited upon one another. The principle seems to have been that one atrocity deserved another. A case in point was one Lieutenant Fulker of the Tory militia. Many of the men who served under Marion lived near the Santee River, and their wives supposedly gave them reports of British and Tory operations. Hence, Lieutenant Fulker was ordered to move all the wives 20 miles back from the river. In the course of the removal, a Mrs. Tate, who had smallpox, was turned out of her house, caught cold, and died. Later Fulker was captured by the Whigs at Fort Motte and was forthwith stripped of his clothes and hanged without a trial.[34] Another case was that of Captain Francis Tidwell of the Tory militia, who had become involved in a feud with Samuel and John Dinkins. When the British evacuated Camden, Tidwell hid out in the swamps, only occasionally returning to his house. But one day the Dinkinses and some other Whigs caught him at home. He was winged by John Dinkins and then carried 10 miles away and without trial was hanged under most cruel circumstances:

> As his murderers never took the trouble of pinioning his arms, in his struggles, while dying, he attempted several times to take hold of the

limbs of the tree on which he was hanged; and it afforded them high amusement to beat down his hands with their whips and sticks. His body remained hanging for three days. Narbeth Corbett was the person who performed the part of executioner, and so much to the satisfaction of his friends, that they say they will find him full employment while there are any Tories in the State.[35]

Of all the atrocities inflicted on the Tories, the ones most complained of were those of the "Orangeburg Massacre." Slaying defenseless prisoners and cornered opponents was popular with both the Back Country Whigs and Tories, but the Orangeburg Massacre was one of the most horrendous examples of the practice. After Orangeburg Fort had been captured by Sumter in 1781, Captain John McCord was marching prisoners to the Congarees settlement on the morning of May 15. A few miles out of Orangeburg, McCord had 14 prisoners summarily shot. All but one, Joseph Cooper, died. The guards noticed that Cooper stirred, and one of them ran his sword through his neck and "observed that he never saw a son of a bitch bleed so much in his life." They left Cooper for dead, but, still alive, he dragged himself and a dead comrade, Millar, to whom he was handcuffed, under a shade tree where he remained until the next day when two women came by at noon and "found him in great torment from the wound, which was augmented by the stench of Millar's body, that had begun to putrify from the intense heat of the weather."[36]

In bitter reaction to the Orangeburg Massacre, the Tory *Royal Gazette*[37] published the following satirical advertisement:

Proposals
For Publishing By Subscription
The Massacre of Orangeburgh,
On the 25th Day of May, 1782   [*sic*],
With a concise Account of the conspicuous Parts acted by Col.
    Middleton and Capt. *M'Cord,*
Illustrated with Fourteen beautiful Copperplates,
Exhibiting, to the Friends of American Liberty, the most pleasing
    Views of the different Attitudes of expiring Criminals
to which is added,
A Comparison between the Methods adopted in *America* for extirpat-
    ing Tories, and those adopted in the Kingdom of our *good Ally,*
    for extirpating Hereticks, in the Reign of Charles the Ninth, by B.
    Gen. *Sumpter.*
Price to Subscribers 500 Continental Dollars, or 1 Mexican ditto

A similar catalog of crimes was laid to the British and the Tories by the Whigs. In early summer, 1780, Tarleton marked the Whig sheriff of Camden, John Wyly, for death. Sergeant Hutt and a guard of men were sent to kill Wyly, but, when they arrived at the latter's house, they mistook his brother, Samuel, for him. As Samuel bent over to unfasten his shoe buckles as demanded by the sergeant, Hutt struck at Samuel's head with his sword. Samuel parried the blow and lost some fingers and ran out the door whereupon he was struck down and killed by two concealed members of the party. The people of Camden were horrified at the killing, but it was the old Back Country motif of vengeance, because Tarleton was after John Wyly for executing some Tories under a treason statute.[38]

Numerous accounts of Tory atrocities against Whigs have survived. The wife of Captain McKoy, a Back Country Whig, was subjected to torture with thumbscrews by Tories who wanted information about her husband.[39] Major James Dunlap, a Northern Tory who served in the Back Country, was supposed to have abducted a Whig heroine and, when she resisted his advances, to have kept her imprisoned until she sickened and died.[40] A detachment of the vigorous Tory band of Major Gainey of the Peedee country surrounded the house of the Whig Colonel Kolb and set fire to it. When Kolb surrendered, the Tories executed him then and there in the presence of his wife and children.[41] So it went on both sides in the Back Country, but the goriest event in the Whig-Tory vendetta was the "Bloody Scout" of Tory militia major, William Cunningham—an incident that in South Carolina revolutionary annals, compares to the Black Hole of Calcutta, the Sicilian Vespers, or the Bataan Death March.

William Cunningham, or "Bloody Bill" as the Whigs called him, was a member of a powerful Back Country Tory family. He was a second cousin of Robert Cunningham, then a brigadier general in the Tory militia.[42] The Cunninghams lived in old Ninety Six District, an area stretching from the Savannah to the Broad River, where Whig-Tory hatreds were especially violent. Tradition has it that Bloody Bill's consuming hatred of the Whigs stemmed from a neighboring Whig militia captain's action in having Bill's lame brother whipped to death.[43] In August, 1781, Bloody Bill led a band of Tories out from Charleston into what is now Laurens

County, between the Saluda and Enoree rivers, where they killed eight Whigs.[44] Apparently promoted from Captain to Major as a reward for that exploit, Cunningham struck again in November, 1781, in the infamous "Bloody Scout." At Cloud's Creek, in what was to become old Edgefield County, Cunningham and his troop of 300 Tories cornered 30 Whigs, most of whom were in a drunken stupor, at daybreak. Only two of the thirty escaped, the other twenty-eight—including a teen-age boy—were chopped to pieces by Bloody Bill's swordsmen.[45] Cunningham and his men crossed the Saluda River and ravaged their way to Hays' Station where they massacred Colonel Hays and 17 other officers and men, putting them to the sword.[46]

Cunningham's "Bloody Scout" was the last important revolutionary action in the Back Country, but it took several years for Whig-Tory animosities to fade. Most of the top Tory militia leaders, such as Robert and William Cunningham, left the Back Country never to return. But other less important Tories were subjected to harassment and, in some cases, death. One of Bloody Bill Cunningham's most hated lieutenants, a man ironically named Love, did not leave. At the November, 1784, court at Ninety Six courthouse he was released from custody by Judge Aedanus Burke. The relatives of the Whigs who had been slaughtered on the Bloody Scout were waiting. They seized Love and hanged him from a tree in the shadow of the courthouse.[47] In another incident shortly after the war, 12 Tories returned to their homes on Fishing Creek. When they did not leave after 20 days, as ordered to do so by Whigs of the area, eight were killed and four were left alive to warn other Tories of a similar fate.[48] Dueling in South Carolina "markedly increased" after the Revolution, and, half a century later, revolutionary hatreds were not entirely forgotten: Senator William C. Preston made a general denunciation of Tories and averted a duel with a Cunningham of his day "only by explaining that he meant no reflection on the Cunninghams of the Revolution."[49]

IV

The chief aftermath of the war in the Back Country was the introduction of a strain of violence and extremism into South

Carolina politics. The Regulator movement had established the orderly organization of a Back Country society dominated by gentry and small planters. This social stability was not upset by the Revolution, which was not in any way a class struggle but a struggle for the domination of the Back Country by competing Whig and Tory leaders. But the repeated violence of the era from 1760 to 1785 produced an undercurrent of extremism below the order and stability that marked the surface of Up Country life. This barely concealed violence and extremism deeply affected the young politicians of the nineteenth century. Reaction in terms of violence and extremism even shaped the political responses of men who were, by nature, moderate and even conservative. Calhoun was perhaps an innately conservative man and, on the surface, at least, a rationalist. Yet his political theory burned with a passion for the defense of the "peculiar institution" of South Carolina and the South, heightened by the traditions of the Back Country generation of violence that were a part of his Calhoun and Caldwell heritage.

Another case in point is Preston S. Brooks, who assaulted Charles Sumner on the floor of the U. S. Senate. The revolutionary overtones of the Brooks-Sumner affair are numerous and striking. Both Congressman Brooks and Senator Andrew Pickens Butler, whose honor Brooks sought to avenge by his attack on Sumner, came from Edgefield County. Edgefield was a county of the old revolutionary Ninety Six District that had seen much Whig-Tory violence. Senator Butler was the grandson of Captain James Butler, who was one of the Whigs massacred by Bloody Bill Cunningham's men at Cloud's Creek. Captain Butler defended himself with a pitchfork until a saber stroke took off his right hand, whereupon he quickly perished. Senator Butler's father was General William Butler who, as a young man of twenty-five, was one of the vengeful Whigs who lynched Bloody Bill's lieutenant, Love, at Ninety-Six courthouse just after the war.[50] Preston Brooks had a similar background. He was the grandson of Colonel Z. S. Brooks of Big Creek, old Edgefield, who had been a brave Whig during the Revolution.[51] The Whig-Tory war was not chivalrous; any advantage was grasped for, ambush was common, and no quarter was given. In that sense, Brooks's assault on Sumner was much like a Whig-Tory affray. Brooks "ambushed" the unsuspecting Sumner in the Senate, catching the Bay Stater between desk and chair in a position from which he could not extricate himself, and took full advantage. He beat Sumner with a frenzy akin to that of his Whig ancestors in their life and death feuds with the Tories.[52]

General Wade Hampton, the dashing Confederate cavalry commander and first governor of redeemed South Carolina, was a reluctant secessionist and, for his time, a friend of the Negro.[53] Yet passion led him to undertake tasks before which his reason quailed. Thus, the reluctant secessionist became South Carolina's greatest Civil War general; the friend of the black became the figurehead of the Redshirt campaign to redeem South Carolina, end Reconstruction in South Carolina, and give the black his first push down to a system of oppression and exclusion that was completed by Ben Tillman. The heritage of Wade Hampton was the violence of the Back Country. The Hamptons emerged from obscurity in the revolutionary era. Wade Hampton's great grandfather, Anthony, the founder of the family in South Carolina, was killed in the Cherokee massacre of 1776.[54] His grandfather, the first Wade Hampton, became a Whig militia colonel under Sumter, and of him a grim tale is told. According to the *Royal Gazette* published in Charleston during the war, the revolutionary Wade Hampton bore a grudge against an old man named Dawkins. Hampton is supposed to have had a Whig named Burke shoot down Dawkins in cold blood as he marched along the road a prisoner of war.[55] Two of the revolutionary Wade Hampton's brothers served as Whig militia colonels.[56]

Calhoun, Andrew Pickens Butler, Preston Brooks, and Wade Hampton are some of the leaders whose heritage can be traced directly back to the Back Country generation of violence. Many more of the "new men" of the ante-bellum period were shaped by the generation of violence as it continued to live in the tales and traditions of Up Country land and family, but the heritage of the generation of violence came to be best exemplified in the Edgefield tradition. Little known outside the borders of South Carolina, Edgefield has always been a byword in the Palmetto State. The Edgefield tradition in South Carolina has stood for the syndrome of violence and extremism that until recent times was thought to epitomize the South Carolina spirit. Edgefield County was created from the old Back Country district of Ninety Six. No one has better expressed the essence of Edgefield than William Watts Ball, the forceful editor of the Charleston *News and Courier*; who wrote

> Edgefield . . . has had more dashing, brilliant, romantic figures, statesmen, orators, soldiers, adventurers, daredevils, than any county of South Carolina, if not any rural county in America. James Bonham and William Barrett Travis, leaders of the Texan defenders of the Alamo, the American Themopylae that "had no messenger to tell its story," were born on its soil. Edmund Bacon, the "Ned Brace" of Judge A. B. Longstreet's *Georgia Scenes*, was one of the earliest of a family of brilliant Edgefieldians. The Brookses, Simkinses, Pickenses, Butlers, were Edgefield families. All of these were kin, by blood or marriage, and they and other related families gave to their village and county a character that was *more South Carolinian, intense, more fiery, than was found elsewhere.*[57]

Relatively small in size but large in impact, Edgefield has given South Carolina ten governors and five U. S. senators.

The eastern section of old Edgefield was bitterly divided by the Revolution. The Tories were led by the Cunninghams—Robert and Bloody Bill—Ned Turner, a Stewart, and a Carghill. The Whigs were led by the Butlers, Brookses, Towleses, Corleys, Edwardses, and Smiths.[58] It was the area of Cloud's Creek, ravaged by the "Bloody Scout" of William Cunningham. Said the nineteenth-century local historian of Edgefield, "I doubt whether any part of the State, or of the United States, suffered more from the strife between Whig and Tory than did this particular section of Edgefield. . . ."[59] And, before the Revolution, old Edgefield had been the scene of Cherokee violence and a hotbed of Regulators.

Edgefield was not long in gaining its reputation for violence and extremism. A particularly garish murder came to the attention of the peripatetic Parson Weems who once passed through Edgefield, and in 1816 he began his pamphlet on the deed: "Old Edgefield again! Another murder in Edgefield!. . . . And all in Old Edge-field. For sure it must be Pandemonium itself, a very District of Devils." [60] The later history of Old Edgefield showed that the good parson was not far wrong, with Edgefield becoming a hotbed of Nullification[61] and secessionism.[62]

Preston S. Brooks and Andrew Pickens Butler, both of Edgefield, have been mentioned, but Edgefield had other leading extremists before the Civil War. Waddy Thompson lived there and was the law partner of Butler.[63] George McDuffie, although born in Georgia, moved to Edgefield, where he became active in politics and was the law partner of a leading politician, Eldred Simkins.[64] Francis W. Pickens of Edgefield, originally a moderate, was swept up in 1860 in the growing "radical persuasion" for secession and emerged as South Carolina's first Confederate governor. Pickens ran true and strong to the Back Country's violent heritage. His father, Andrew Pickens, Jr., of Edgefield had been governor of the state from 1816 to 1818. Francis W. Pickens's grandfather was Andrew Pickens, Sr., the famous Whig militia general of the Revolution. Andrew Pickens, Sr., dominated the Whig guerrilla struggle against the British and the Tories in western South Carolina in the same way that Thomas Sumter dominated the central section of the Back Country.[65]

Senator James H. Hammond, who, in the ante-bellum period gave currency to the ardent Southern concept that "cotton is king," was the son of a Massachusetts schoolmaster father and an Edgefield mother. As a poor but aggressive young lawyer-editor, typical of the Up Country, Hammond got his start in Edgefield as a hot-blooded Nullificationist politician.[66] Harking straight back to the generation of violence, Hammond once drew a significant analogy: "The Union and nullification parties bear relations to each other that have not existed since the Revolution. They have stood opposed in arms. . . . The mass of those two parties can never exist together except as the conquered and the conquerors," [67] as had been the case between Whigs and Tories in the Revolution.

The Civil War did not end the Edgefield tradition, for it was in Edgefield that the extreme policy of "intimidation and fraud as the only means of forcing blacks into subordination" was formulated as a way of overturning the legal majority of 30,000 black and white votes by which the combination of Negroes, Carpetbaggers, and Scalawags governed South Carolina in the Reconstruction era. The program of intimidation and fraud rested directly upon violence, actual and threatened; it was known as "the Straightout, the Shotgun, or the Edgefield policy." [68] Developed, also, by Edgefieldians was the Red Shirt as the uniform apparel of the members of the white paramilitary units that, on the Edgefield model, were organized statewide to capture the election of 1876 and thus redeem South Carolina for native white rule. Finally, it was the incisive Martin W. Gary of Edgefield who was the driving force behind the Red Shirt redemption that resulted in the election of Wade Hampton as governor.[69]

The Red Shirt redemption was the political nursery of a young Edgefield farmer, Benjamin R. (Pitchfork Ben) Tillman, who became one of the noted Americans of his time. On the national scene as a U. S. senator from 1895 to 1918, Tillman became the best-known and most vitriolic Negrophobe in America, while, in South Carolina, his most significant achievement was placing the keystone in the arch of post-Reconstruction white supremacy through the Negro disfranchisement accomplished under his leadership in the state constitutional convention of 1895. With countless sizzling denunciations of black people as being innately inferior to whites and the fit subjects of unrestrained white rule, Tillman not only reflected views widely held, North and South, but also shaped and sharpened such views. The distinguished Negro historian, Rayford W. Logan, has chronicled the "nadir" of black people in American life and thought in the late nineteenth century,[70] and no one better expressed the brutal white racism of that era than did Ben Tillman. Referring to the age of white supremacy in America between Reconstruction and World War II, Tillman's biographer delivered the measured, accurate judgment that "Ben Tillman fostered the modern reaction against the Negro. This achievement was one of his most significant influences on American life." [71]

Tillman burst on the South Carolina political scene in the post-Reconstruction mid-1880's at a time in which the upright, plain, white farmer of the state (Tillman's own social category) languished economically and politically under the dominance of an unsympathetic, aristocratically oriented, conservative faction of Democrats. With his ardent, uncompromising championship of the white farmer, Tillman and his quasi-Populist movement of Tillmanism—climaxed by Tillman's two-term rule as governor from 1890 to 1894—reversed the trend of South Carolina politics.[72] Although he grew more conservative later, Tillman had, once and for all, introduced the plain farmer to active political participation in South Carolina. Joined to his crusading agrarianism was Tillman's trenchant Negrophobia, a crucial aspect of his appeal to the rural white middle class and lower class of the state.

Except for a physical assault on his South Carolina colleague on the floor of the U. S. Senate—the result of a personal dispute—Tillman engaged in no direct violence after his political career began. Yet, his rhetoric was laced with violence, and the threat of it underscored his rough, bellicose oratory. Time and again he shocked the Senate with his strident speeches. On one occasion he recalled that "as governor of South Carolina I proclaimed that, although I had taken the oath of office to support the law and enforce it, I would lead a mob to lynch any man, black or white, who ravished a woman, black or white." Tillman never did lead or take part in a lynch mob, but such sentiments undoubtedly inspired many men who did. And, at another time, he shouted before the Senate, "whenever the Constitution [of the United States] comes between me and the virtue of the white women of the South, I say to hell with the Constitution!" [73] Tillman, as a politician, "openly justified violence" and "capitalized on the 'strain of violence' " that ran through South Carolina life. Nor was this merely political hyperbole, for, as Tillman's not unsympathetic biographer noted: "Violence or threat of violence underlay the crises of his career— Reconstruction; the suppression of Haskellism [an anti-Tillman faction]; the major political campaigns; the Darlington disturbance [an 1894 political riot]; the disfranchisement of the Negroes." [74]

Ben Tillman's personal appearance and manner agreed with his public image of extremism. He gained his colorful nickname, "Pitchfork Ben," when, during his 1894 campaign for the Senate, he attacked the anti-agrarian policy of President Grover Cleveland by roaring that Cleveland "is an old bag of beef and I am going to Washington with a pitchfork and prod him in his old fat ribs." [75] This was no platform pose of truculence, for even in his home surroundings Tillman was formidable. Having lost an eye in youth, Tillman was a baleful, Cyclopean figure. A big man given to violent profanity, "his enormous shock of hair, his scraggly beard, his rugged and grim features, and his single sparkling eye, made him," in the words of his biographer, "resemble a desperado." A visitor to Tillman's beloved Edgefield reported how Tillman "savagely cursed his blacks. Then looking at his hogs he uttered words which made the visitor's flesh crawl. 'I had to use the knife on those hogs, and I like to cut living flesh. . . .' " [76]

Much of this grew out of Tillman's Edgefield birth, breeding, and lifelong residency. To the end of his days, Benjamin R. Tillman was proud to boast, "I am from Edgefield." Young Ben was raised on the patriotic legends about the war between the Whigs and Tories in Old Edgefield. He heard the story of a Ryan neighbor (Ben's middle name was Ryan) who escaped from a Tory captor and then later shot the Tory from a "forest retreat." Deep in the woods Ben often saw the "Shelving Rock" where his grandmother, Annsybil Miller, nursed her brother who was ill and in hiding from the British. On Ben's mother's home plantation was the "murder field" where a Tory had been hanged.[77]

The intrepidity of Tillman's ancestors during the revolutionary phase of the Back Country generation of violence served as an example for his own dedicated and sometimes violent participation in the 1876 Red Shirt movement at the close of Reconstruction. When the "campaign of 1876" began, Ben Tillman was a hardy, excitable twenty-nine-year-old, aching to defy the Reconstruction regime and to end Negro ascendancy in South Carolina. "From actual experience in his community he knew," wrote Francis B. Simkins, "that, under a free ballot, a black majority of six hundred [in Edgefield] out of a total vote of one thousand meant Negro rule. But he also knew that this majority could be cowed by highhanded methods. Nursed in a traditon of violence and experienced in the management of Negroes, he felt no compunction on applying lawless tactics to the political situation." [78] Tillman had enthusiastically joined his township's Sweetwater Sabre Club, an illicit military-like organization of 45 white bravoes, who, by threat of arms, seized control of Edgefield County from a regiment of Negro militia in 1874–1875.[79]

Next, Tillman, as a member of the Sweetwater Sabre Club, was an active participant in the "Hamburg riot" of July 8, 1876—a successful white attack on the black militia of the Savannah River town of Hamburg located 13 miles from Tillman's home. In an aftermath of the riot, relatives of the one white man killed in the fray asked Tillman and his cohorts for a retaliatory execution of black prisoners, since only two Negroes had perished in the fight.

The request was granted, and, although Tillman did not take part directly, "an execution party, to a member of which Tillman surrendered his loaded pistol, was organized, and five 'of the meanest characters and most deserving of death'" among the prisoners were shot to death.[80]

The white victory in the Hamburg riot was the prelude to the autumn, 1876, Red Shirt election campaign, the success of which enabled Tillman and thousands of other unreconstructed whites to regain control of the state. Here, too, the young Tillman—although not yet known in the state at large—played an important part: Two months after the Hamburg riot, the Sweetwater Sabre Club went to Aiken, South Carolina, to protect the white interest at a trial of some of the participants in the riot. To awe blacks and their Radical white supporters, Tillman "induced the ladies of Aiken to make forty homespun shirts [for the Sabre Club] and . . . gathered a supply of turpentine, oil, and Venetian red with which to bedaub these garments. With two masks, a kinky chignon, and a large shirt hung upon a cross, he made the image of a giant Negro, and covered it with threatening legends and the marks of bullet holes. The parade of Tillman and his friends, wearing their bizarre shirts and bearing aloft their grotesque effigy, was a triumph of white strategy," for it made the blacks "woefully frightened" and aroused feelings of white racial solidarity. In emulation of the reddened shirts of flannel designed by Tillman, Red Shirt regiments of white activists, organized throughout the state, carried the day in the November election.[81]

Edgefield extremism continued after Tillman's death in 1918, for old Pitchfork Ben had a young protege from an old Edgefield family: J. William Thurmond. He was Tillman's personal lawyer and the local political boss of Edgefield "who had rashly killed a man in a quarrel over Tillmanism." [82] J. William Thurmond was the father of the U. S. senator from South Carolina, J. Strom Thurmond. The young Strom Thurmond was often taken to Tillman's home by his father, and the impressionable lad observed close at hand the personality and character of Edgefield's fiery extremist.[83]

Senator Thurmond himself might not reject the label, "extremist," for it has been rightly noted that his "political fundamentalism . . . tolerates no compromises, no ambiguities, no equivocations, and no criticism." [84] As the presidential candidate of the States' Rights Democratic (Dixiecrat) party in 1948 and as a U. S. senator since 1954, J. Strom Thurmond gained national fame for his passionate Southern opposition to the movement for black civil rights in the 1940's to 1960's. In contrast to Tillman, however, there has been no tincture of violence in Thurmond's leadership. Thurmond's extremism has been confined strictly to politics and, in the style of a vigorous old-school Southern gentleman, to the ideological and philosophical spheres.[85] In this regard, the scholar, James G. Banks, has described Senator Thurmond as an extreme white Southern traditionalist.[86] "Strom's Edgefield environment," Banks wrote, "was the most influential factor in his development. Growing up in the area, coupled with the close association of his father, he absorbed the region's traditions and prejudices, while at the same time becoming aware of Edgefield's legacy to the South." "So important was his Edgefield beginning," concluded Banks, "that it is doubtful that Strom Thurmond would be what and where he is today had it not been for the legacy of Old Edgefield." [87]

Times change—but not completely. Edgefield's public high school (named after J. Strom Thurmond) now has an enrollment that is half black, but a private academy for whites flourishes, and the white people of Edgefield "still cultivate their roots to the past." [88] In spite of the staunch opposition of Edgefield's Senator Thurmond to desegregation and civil rights, race relations in South Carolina during the 1950's and 1960's—although undeniably marked by tension—were notably progressive and nonviolent[89] in contrast to its sister states of the deep South. South Carolina's record of improved race relations has owed much to the state's dominant Democratic party faction, the so-called Barnwell Ring (a bloc strongly opposed by Thurmond),[90] which has been oriented to the national Democratic party and to moderation in white-black relations.[91] The Edgefield tradition is now in eclipse, and South Carolina is at long last outliving its two-century heritage of extremism that grew out of the Back Country generation of violence.

Part III

VIGILANTISM: THE CONSERVATIVE MOB

THE MOB ASPECT OF AMERICAN vigilantism appears in its popular dimension: the participation of members of the local community of average or lesser status in vigilante activity justified by an ideology with such democratic elements as the concepts of popular sovereignty and the right of revolution. Yet, there is a deeply conservative basis of vigilantism, both in its aims and its adherents. The goal of vigilantism has characteristically been a conservative one: the perpetuation of established patterns of local community life, especially in newly peopled frontier areas where crime and disorder loom as a threat to honest, upright persons and their idealistic concepts of life and property. Moreover, vigilante movements have usually been led by the element of the local community with the greatest stake in the social status quo upheld by vigilantism: the elite group of leading businessmen, planters, and professionals.

With the coalition of elite leadership and middle- and lower-class deeds embodied in vigilantism, the typical vigilante movement was a paradigm of the broader local community with its upper, middle, and lower social strata. The American community at the local level has ordinarily exemplified the three-tiered structure thus noted—a structure generally characterized by harmonious relationships among its elements. There was nothing inherently wrong with the community leadership provided by the local elite. The distortion came, rather, with the extension of elite leadership into the extralegal sphere of vigilante violence. The local elite might better have been expected to set an example of scrupulous obedience to the law, but that it did not is one of the salient social facts of American vigilantism. Even so, the task here is to understand the distortion not merely to condemn it.

A case in point is the great San Francisco vigilante movement of 1856. It illustrates the pattern noted and vividly exemplifies the vigilante movement as a conservative mob of the American frontier.[1] The San Francisco organization was dually significant, for it also represented an aspect of vigilantism that became more prominent as the nineteenth century waned and the twentieth century waxed: the extension of vigilantism from its preoccupation with the problem of frontier disorder to an ill-starred attempt to deal with the problems of emergent, modern, urban America. As a transitional movement between the old and the new, the San Franciscans were thus pivotal in the history of American vigilantism.

In our own time Americans have been shocked by the involvement of leading lawyers and members (or former members) of the federal government in the 1972 break-in at the headquarters of the national Democratic Party in the Watergate building in Washington, D. C. and in related activities, such as the illegal tactics in the 1972 presidential primary campaigns, the burglary of the office of Daniel Ellsberg's psychiatrist, and the cover-up of the original Watergate break-in. Indicted, convicted, sentenced, or pardoned for participation in these matters have been thirteen prominent Americans, headed by former president Richard M. Nixon, former attorney general John N. Mitchell, and former chief presidential assistants H. R. Haldeman and John D. Ehrlichman.[2] Yet, there is nothing new in this pattern of involvement of public officials or former public officials (most of whom, as members of the bar, were—aside from official oaths—sworn to uphold the law) in illegal activity, for the history of vigilantism reveals that, long before Watergate, leading American lawyers, judges, and public officers from presidents on down have been ardent supporters of, or participants in, illegal vigilante action. Senators, congressmen, governors, judges, founders of state bar associations, legal philosophers, and even presidents have all endorsed, by word or deed, the taking of the law into one's own hands.

Chapter 4

THE AMERICAN VIGILANTE
TRADITION

*Every fibre of our frame vibrates with anger and disgust when we meet
a ruffian, a murderer or a marauder. Mawkish sentimentalism we
abhor. The thought of murdered victims, dishonored females, plundered wayfarers, burning houses, and the rest of the sad evidences of
villainy, completely excludes mercy from our view. Honor, truth, and
the sacrifice of self to considerations of justice and the good of
mankind–these claim, we had almost said our adoration; but for the
low, brutal, cruel, lazy, ignorant, insolent, sensual and blasphemous
miscreants that infest the frontiers, we entertain but one sentiment–
aversion–deep, strong, and unchangeable. For such cases, the rope is
the only prescription that avails as a remedy.*

Thomas J. Dimsdale, *The Vigilantes of Montana*

*We are believers in the doctrine of popular sovereignty; that the people
of this country are the real sovereigns, and that whenever the laws,
made by those to whom they have delegated their authority, are found
inadequate to their protection, it is the right of the people to take the
protection of their property into their own hands, and deal with these
villains according to their just desserts. . . .*

resolution of northern Indiana vigilantes (1858)

The vigilante tradition, in the classic sense, refers to
organized, extralegal movements, the members of which take the

law into their own hands. The first vigilante movement in American history was in 1767. From then until about 1900, vigilante activity was an almost constant factor in American life. Far from being a phenomenon only of the western frontier there was much vigilantism in the eastern half of the United States. Although the first vigilante movement occurred in Piedmont South Carolina, in 1767–1769, most of the Atlantic Seaboard States were without significant vigilante activity. But, beyond the Appalachians, there were few states that did not have vigilante movements. There may have been as many as 500 movements, but, at the present, only 326 are known.[1]

American vigilantism is indigenous. There were "regulators" in early-eighteenth-century London, who formed a short-lived official supplement to London's regular system of law enforcement,[2] but there was no connection between London's legal regulators and the South Carolina's Back Country Regulators of 1767 who constituted America's first vigilante movement. From time to time in Europe there appeared movements or institutions (such as the *Vehmgericht* of Germany and *Halifax law* of the British Isles),[3] which resembled American vigilantism, but these phenomena did not give rise to a vigilante tradition either on the Continent or in the British Isles. European expansion in other areas of the world has, similarly, failed to produce anything like the American vigilante tradition. Perhaps the closest thing to it was the *commando* system (against marauding *kaffirs*) of the Boer settlers in South Africa; the *commandos,* however, were more like the Indian-fighting rangers of the American frontier than the vigilantes.[4]

Vigilantism arose as a response to a typical American problem: the absence of effective law and order in a frontier region. It was a problem that occurred again and again beyond the Appalachians. It stimulated the formation of hundreds of frontier vigilante movements.[5] On the frontier, the normal foundations of a stable, orderly society—churches, schools, cohesive community life—were either absent or present only in rough, makeshift forms. The regular, legal system of law enforcement often proved to be woefully inadequate for the needs of the settlers.

Fundamentally, the pioneers took the law into their own hands for the purpose of establishing order and stability in newly settled areas. In the older settled areas, the prime values of person and property were dominant and secure, but the move to the frontier meant that it was necessary to start all over again. Upright and ambitious frontiersmen wished to re-establish the values of a property holder's society. The hurtful presence of outlaws and marginal types, in an area of weak and ineffectual law enforcement, created the specter and, often, the fact of social chaos. The solution was vigilantism. A vigilante roundup of ne'er-do-wells and outlaws followed by their flogging, expulsion, or killing not only solved the problem of disorder but had an important symbolic value as well. Vigilante action was a clear warning to disorderly inhabitants that the newness of the settlement would provide no opportunity for the erosion of the established values of civilization. Vigilantism was a violent sanctification of the deeply cherished values of life and property.

Because the main thrust of vigilantism was to re-establish, in each newly settled area, the civilized values of life, property, and law and order, vigilante movements were usually led by the frontier elite. This was true of the greatest American vigilante band—the San Francisco vigilance committee of 1856—which was directed by the leading businessmen of the city. Again and again, it was the most eminent local community leaders who headed vigilante movements.

"Vigilance Committee," or "Committee of Vigilance," was the common name of the organization, but, originally—and far into the nineteenth century—vigilantes were known by the now obsolete term of regulators. Variant names for vigilante groups were "slickers," "stranglers," "committees of safety," and, in central Texas, simply, "mobs." (In this study, "vigilante" will be used as a generic term to cover all phases of the general phenomenon of vigilantism.) The duration of vigilante movements varied greatly, but movements that lasted as long as a year were long lived. More commonly, they finished their business in a period of months or weeks. Vigilante movements (as distinguished from ephemeral lynch mobs) are thus identifiable by the two main characteristics of (1) regular (although illegal) organization and (2) existence for a definite (often short) period of time.

I

The first American vigilante movement—the South Carolina Regulators, 1767–1769—did not occur until 160 years after the first permanent English settlement at Jamestown. The reason for the late appearance of the phenomenon was the slow pace of frontier expansion. It was well into the eighteenth century before the settlement of the Piedmont began on a large scale, and, at the time of the Revolution, the settlement of the Piedmont was just coming to a close. Thus, frontier expansion proceeded at a snail's pace in the colonial period, and it was possible to provide adequate systems of law enforcement for the slowly proliferating pioneer communities. The one exception to this pattern of orderly frontier expansion occurred in the South Carolina Piedmont in the 1760's.

Newly settled and recently devastated by the Cherokee Indian War, the South Carolina Back Country of the 1760's was typical of later American frontier areas. As sketched in the previous chapter, this war so disrupted social organization that, by the mid-1760's, the whole of the Back Country was being terrorized by gangs of outlaws. A two-year campaign by the Regulators restored law and order, albeit violently. Regulator violence had become so brutal, however, that a counter-movement of "Moderators" was organized. The latter, along with the Provincial government's provision for district courts and sheriffs, caused the Regulators to disband voluntarily in 1769.[6]

An American tradition had begun, for, as the pioneers moved across the Appalachians, the regulator-vigilante impulse followed the sweep of settlement toward the Pacific. The model for dealing with frontier disorder established by the South Carolina Regulators was utilized over and over again by American settlers.

Geographically, American vigilantism divides into Eastern and Western halves. Eastern and Western vigilantism are similarly distinct, chronologically. Eastern vigilantism mainly came to an end in the 1860's whereas Western vigilantism began in the 1850's. Eastern vigilantism was largely a feature of the first half of the nineteenth century and Western vigilantism of the second. Eastern vigilantism fell between the Appalachian Mountains[7] and the 96th meridian, whereas Western vigilantism stretched from the 96th meridian to the Pacific.[8] The humid Mississippi Valley, Great

Lakes, and Gulf Coast regions furnished the main scenes of Eastern vigilantism; Western vigilantism took in the arid and semiarid Great Plains and the Rocky Mountains and the Pacific coast. Eastern vigilantism was a response, chiefly, to frontier horse thieves, counterfeiters, and ne'er-do-well whites. West of the 96th meridian the vigilantes were concerned largely with disorder in mining camps, cattle towns, and open ranges.

In early-nineteenth-century America, horse thieves and counterfeiters seemed to go together, and when they did a vigilante movement was not far behind. The vulnerability of the settler to horse theft needs no comment, but counterfeiting as a frontier evil is a bit less familiar. The money problem made itself felt at the national level in the age of Jackson in a number of famous issues, such as the Bank War, but it was no less a problem in the backwoods and border country. Not only did the frontier suffer from a money shortage, which counterfeiters as well as wildcat bankers tried to fill, but the frontier felt the lack of money especially in regard to the purchase of federal public land. Added to the lively demand for cash at the land office was the chaotic condition of the paper money system. The lack of an effective system of federal paper money and the plethora of private bank notes meant that never before or since in our history was counterfeiting easier.[9] *173809*

Horse thieves commonly organized into gangs, stealing horses in one area and disposing of them hundreds of miles away—preferably across state lines.[10] For obvious reasons, counterfeiting operations were best carried on in the same way, and it was simple to combine the two. The link between counterfeiting and horse theft affected the geographical distribution of regulator and vigilante movements. The latter tended to be found in wilderness areas, close to state lines, or near Indian borders—all were places favored by horse thieves and counterfeiters.

From the 1790's, and well into the nineteenth century, vigilante activity was generally local in Kentucky, Tennessee, Indiana, and Illinois.[11] Thereafter, there were four major peaks or waves of vigilantism. They occurred in the early 1830's, the early 1840's, the late 1850's, and the late 1860's. The first wave, from 1830 to 1835, took place mainly in the lower Southern states of Alabama and Mississippi, where Captain Slick's bands operated against horse thieves and counterfeiters[12] and vigilantes attacked gamblers and the alleged Murrell conspiracy.[13] The second wave, in the early 1840's, included the Bellevue vigilante war in Iowa,[14] the east Texas Regulator-Moderator conflict,[15] the northern and southern Illinois Regulators,[16] and the Slicker War of the Missouri Ozarks.[17] The vigilante wave of the early 1840's may have been a response to a shift in outlaw elements (caused by the 1830–1835 vigilante campaign) from the Lower Mississippi River region of Alabama, Mississippi, Arkansas, and Louisiana to the Upper Mississippi area (northern Illinois, eastern Iowa, and the Missouri Ozarks) and to the trans-Mississippi Southwest (east Texas).

The third peak of vigilantism, from 1857 to 1859, included the Iron Hills and other vigilante movements of Iowa,[18] the northern Indiana Regulators,[19] the San Antonio[20] and New Orleans[21] vigilantes, and the *Comités de Vigilance* of southwest Louisiana.[22] The movements of the late 1850's may have been inspired by the San Francisco Vigilance Committee of 1856,[23] which was well publicized throughout the nation. The fourth and final wave of vigilantism occurred in the immediate post-Civil War period (1866–1871) with major movements erupting in Missouri,[24] Kentucky,[25] Indiana,[26] and Florida[27] in a reaction to postwar lawlessness.

The nature of the natural resources of the West determined the types of frontier disorder that gave rise to vigilantism. Repeated strikes of precious and valuable metals in the Sierras and Rockies set off mining rushes that brought miners and others into raw new camps and towns by the thousands. In such places the law was often absent or ineffectual, with vigilantism the result. The other great natural resource of the West was the grassy rangeland of the Great Plains, the mountain plateaus, and the river valleys. The open-range system afforded an irresistible attraction to cattle and horse thieves, who, in turn, invited vigilante retaliation.

Beginning with the first significant vigilantism in the gold-rush metropolis of San Francisco in 1849, and continuing for 53 years down to 1902, there were at least 210 vigilante movements in the West. No vigilante movements in American history were better organized or more powerful than the San Francisco vigilance committees of 1851 and 1856. The San Francisco movements had an immense impact on American vigilantism, in general, and

Californian vigilantism, in particular. During the 1850's the San Francisco committees were copied all over the state in the new mining towns (Sacramento, Jackson, etc.) and in the old Spanish cities (Los Angeles, Monterey, etc.). Of California's 43 vigilante movements, 27 movements occurred in the 1850's.[28]

Montana was a most significant vigilante state. It had two of the most important movements in the history of vigilantism: the influential Bannack and Virginia City movement of 1863–1865 (which popularized the term "vigilante" in American English)[29] and the 1884 movement in northern and eastern Montana, which Granville Stuart led against horse and cattle thieves in a human roundup that claimed 35 victims and was the deadliest of all American vigilante movements.[30] In addition, Montana, from the 1860's to the 1880's, was in the grips of a territory-wide vigilante movement with headquarters, apparently, in the territorial capital, Helena.[31]

Texas had 52 vigilante movements—more than any other state. There were two important ante-bellum movements (Shelby County in east Texas, 1840–1844; San Antonio, 1857 and later), but the majority (at least 27 movements) occurred in violence-torn central Texas in the post-Civil War period from 1865 to 1890.[32] There were dozens and dozens of vigilante movements in most of the other Western states; only Oregon and Utah did not have significant vigilante activity. The 16 movements in Colorado were headed by the Denver vigilantes of 1859–1861.[33] New Mexico had three strong vigilante movements in Albuquerque (1871–1882),[34] Las Vegas (1880–1882),[35] and Socorro (1880–1884).[36] The Butler County vigilantes, who enlisted almost 800 members and claimed 8 victims, formed the most notable of Kansas's 19 movements.[37] To the north, Nebraska had 16 vigilante movements that were topped by the Sidney vigilantes (1875–1881) and the Niobrara region vigilantes (1883–1884), who accounted for 2 and 6 fatalities, respectively.[38] Wyoming vigilantism, swift, brutal, and deadly, began with two movements in the wild railroad boomtowns of Cheyenne and Laramie (1868–1869) and came to a climax with vigilantism's most famous failure, the cattlemen's Regulator movement, which precipitated the Johnson County War of 1892.[39]

All of the 326 American vigilante movements are listed alphabetically by state in Appendix 3. If the Eastern and Western vigilante movements are compared, it can be seen that there were about twice as many vigilante movements in the West (210) as in the East (116). (Here the figures probably understate the ubiquity of Eastern vigilantism. Regulator activity was general in the early years of settlement in Kentucky, Tennessee, Indiana, and Illinois, but records of only a few of these movements have survived.) The ratio of large, medium, and small movements in the West was about 1:2:2; in the East it was approximately 1:1:1. Of the 729 known victims killed by vigilantes, about five-sevenths were dispatched by western vigilantes.

There were 81 large movements; they extended, chronologically, from 1767 to 1897, and all are indicated in Appendix 3. Fifty-nine of the eighty-one large movements were clustered in the period from 1850 to 1889; forty-nine movements occurred in the mid-century decades from 1850 to 1879 when the nation was wracked by Civil War violence in the East and the tensions of rapid frontier settlement in the West. About three-fifths (190) of all vigilante movements took place after 1860, but, here again, it must be noted that the lack of specific information on many Kentucky, Tennessee, Indiana, and Illinois movements leads to an understatement of pre-1860 vigilante movements; 180 of the 190 movements were concentrated in the three decades from 1861 to 1890. By the same token, about five-sevenths (511) of all the killed victims of vigilantism perished after 1860.[40]

Behind the statistics lies the impact of vigilantism on the American consciousness. The original South Carolina Regulator movement of 1767–1769, with its success in restoring order in the Back Country, recommended itself to the pioneers who crossed the Appalachians and populated the Mississippi Valley. The regulator method was, hence, applauded as a tool for establishing frontier social stability until, in the 1840's, three anarchic movements in southern Illinois, the Missouri Ozarks, and east Texas gave regulators an increasingly bad name. Soon thereafter, in 1851 and 1856, the restrained San Francisco vigilance committees restored to vigilantism an enormous prestige, which it retained through the remainder of the century. Countless vigilante movements from coast to coast modeled themselves upon the San Francisco vigilance committees. One of these was the vigilante movement of the gold camps of Bannack and Virginia City, Montana (1863–

1865), which, in turn, had something of the same effect on American attitudes as the earlier South Carolina and San Francisco movements. Thomas Dimsdale's classic book, *The Vigilantes of Montana* (1866), not only spread the fame of the Montana movement but was a veritable textbook on the vigilante method.

Significant vigilante activity did not always involve a formally organized movement with officers, trials, etc. By the latter half of the nineteenth century the ritual-like action of organizing a vigilante movement had been carried out so many times on so many frontiers that to many settlers it often seemed an unnecessary delay to swift lynch-law justice. A local consensus in favor of immediate vigilante action without any of the traditional formalities produced *instant vigilantism*. Instant vigilantism was more prevalent in the West than the East. Many of the "one-shot" vigilante actions in Western states were the result of instant vigilantism. Thus, instant vigilantism existed side by side with more formally organized vigilantism. Instant vigilantism meant that the public mind had long since been made receptive to vigilante action when general conditions or a particular crime seemed to warrant it. The ritual process of organization had been gone through so many times, the rationale of vigilantism was so well understood, and the course of action so obvious on the basis of past precedents that the settlers readily proceeded to the lynching.

Instant vigilantism seems to have occurred in all the Western states but Oregon and Utah. Instant vigilantism was particularly effective in California. In the Golden State, regular vigilante action took 101 lives, but the toll of instant vigilantism from 1851 to 1878 was almost as high, amounting to 79 lives.[41] On a lesser scale, instant vigilantism occurred in other Western states, where, time and again, precipitate lynchings were justified by vigilante tradition.

II

Settlers ordinarily desire new opportunities but not social innovation. Their main desire is to recreate the life they left behind them, reconstructing the communities from which they came. This is no great problem for entire communities that migrate en masse. The

Pilgrim settlers of Plymouth, Massachusetts, and the Mormon migrants to Great Salt Lake, Utah, are notable cases of "colonized" new communities.

More common have been the "cumulative" communities of inhabitants thrown together helter-skelter by the migration process.[42] The migrants to San Francisco, California, in 1849 and after furnish an example of the cumulative new community. San Franciscans came from all over the world and were an immensely diverse lot. The only thing that united them, initially, was their desire to profit from the California Gold Rush.

Basic to the reconstruction of the community is the re-establishment of the old community structure and its values. To the extent that both are achieved, an orderly and stable new community life will be achieved. Although American frontiersmen of the nineteenth century came to their new localities from all points of the compass and were usually unknown and unrelated to each other, most came from essentially similar communities. The typical American community of the eighteenth and nineteenth centuries possessed a social structure of three levels:[43]

1. The upper level consisted of leaders and their families. Included were well-to-do businessmen, the most eminent professional men, affluent farmers and planters, and prominent men of whatever occupation. This was the local elite, and in it were concentrated the community leading men.

2. The middle level included the men of average means: farmers, craftsmen, tradesmen, and less eminent lawyers, teachers, and other professionals. The industrious, honest middle level formed the core of the community. In this sector resided the legendary but real American yeoman.

3. The lower level included the honest poor and also those who were either marginal to or alienated from the remainder of the community. In but not really *of* the community (and spurned by it) were the ne'er-do-well, shiftless poor whites. They constituted a true *lower people;* they were viewed with contempt and loathing by the members of the upper and middle levels who could not abide their slatternly way of life, their spiritless lack of ambition, their often immoral conduct, and their disorganized family life.[44]

The lower people were not outlaws but often tended to lawlessness and identified more with the outlaw element than with the law-abiding members of the community. The outlaw element lived on the fringes of the community. In some cases they sprang from the lower people, but they were also men of good background who chose the outlaw life or drifted into it. They were alienated from the values of the community, although some occasionally joined respectable community life as reformed men.

A community has behavioral boundaries just as it has geographic boundaries. When a new community establishes its geographic boundaries, it must also establish its behavioral boundaries. The latter represent the positive, mutual values of the community.[45] The values that supported the three-level community and the basis upon which it rested were the related ideals of life and property. The American community of the eighteenth and nineteenth centuries was primarily a property-holder's community, and property was viewed as the very basis of life itself.

The vigilante leaders were drawn from the upper level of the community. The middle level supplied the rank-and-file. Outlaws and alienated lower people represented the main threat to the reconstruction of the community and were the principal targets of the vigilantes.

In the cumulative new communities of frontier America, the alienated lower people and the outlaws met the representatives of the middle and upper levels in social conflict. The former wished to burst their subordinate bounds and take over the new communities. In sociological terms the outlaws and the hostile lower people (but not the honest poor) constituted a "contraculture."[46] They rejected the respectable values of life and property and wished to upset the social structure in which the upper and middle level men were dominant. The relative weakness of social bonds in the new settlements was their opportunity. On the other hand, men of upper level background or aspirations were determined to establish and strengthen the community structure in which they were dominant. In this they had the support of the middle level inhabitants, and, with them, they mounted vigilante campaigns to quell the insurgent outlaws and lower people.[47]

The danger of a takeover of newly settled areas by the alienated, outcast elements of society was a real threat. Whether or not the alleged Murrell conspiracy of the lower Mississippi Valley in the 1830's actually represented a concerted plot of white outlaws to raise a gigantic slave rebellion in the interest of an "underworld" dominion of the region, the phenomenon revealed the sensitivity of lawful society to the large numbers, aggressiveness, and alienation of the outlaws of the region. In southern Illinois, in the 1840's, the "Flathead" element of horse thieves, counterfeiters, brigands, slave stealers, and Ohio River-bottom dwellers triggered a violent Regulator reaction.[48] In east Texas, in the late 1830's, a similar combine of horse thieves, counterfeiters, slave stealers, and "land pirates" incited a countermovement by the Regulators.[49] By 1841, a group of outlaw gangs had virtually taken over the Rock River counties of northern Illinois until challenged by the Regulators in that year.[50] Much earlier, in South Carolina in the middle 1760's, a disorderly mixture of demoralized Indian war veterans, "straggling" refugee whites, "crackers," mulattoes, and outlaw horse thieves and counterfeiters well-nigh ruled the Back Country until honest men reacted in the Regulator movement.[51] West of the Mississippi and Missouri in the raw, new mining camps, cattle towns, railheads, and open ranges, the same threat emanated from the professional "bad men" and outlaw gangs, the "black-leg" element, and the always troublesome rustlers and horse thieves. These and other challenges were thus met head on by the vigilantes.

The masonic lodge was often found in frontier communities, and the relationship between Freemasonry and vigilantism was frequently an intimate one. Typical was the situation in Bannack, Nevada City, and Virginia City, Montana, rough, new mining camps in 1863–1864. There the leading members of the active vigilante movement of the winter of 1863–1864 seem initially to have formed a bond as a result of their common membership in the Masonic lodge.[52] The like happened elsewhere. The same impulse —desire to participate in the upper level dominance of the community—often caused the same person to join the masonic lodge (usually an elite local organization) and enlist in a vigilante movement. In Montana, Texas, and elsewhere, Freemasonry was often the shadowy background for the organization of a local vigilante movement.[53]

Sometimes the members of the upper level did not wait for an overt crime outbreak but formed a vigilante organization to prevent an outbreak and cement the three-level community structure. Thus, Thomas G. Wildman of Denver, Colorado, wrote back East on September 8, 1859:

> There is to be a Vigilance Committee organized in the town this evening. All of the leading men of the town has signed the Constitution, and its object is a good one. . . . It is thought that stabbing and drunkenness will be rampant here this winter, and we think that the rowdies and gamblers will be more careful when they find out that we are organized and that all the first men of the town are determined to punish crime.[54]

To the men of Butler County, Kansas, in 1870–1871, vigilante action was the cornerstone of community construction. After killing eight men they justified their action by declaring, "it has become a question whether honest men of the country shall leave, or this gang." Invoking "self-preservation" as "the first law of nature," they asserted that "however much we deplore the further use of violence in order to secure life and property . . . we shall not hesitate to do justice to the guilty if it is necessary."[55]

James Hall described the challenge which outlaws and lower people presented in the early years of the settlement of the Midwest:

> We had whole settlements of counterfeiters, or horse thieves, with their sympathizers—where rogues could change names, or pass from house to house, so skillfully as to elude detection—and where if detected, the whole population were ready to rise to the rescue. There were other settlements of sturdy honest fellows, the regular backwoodsmen in which rogues were not tolerated. There was therefore a continual struggle between these parties—the honest people trying to expel the others by the terrors of the law, and when that mode failed, forming *regulating* companies, and driving them out by force.[56]

An example of the problem was the bandit and "blackleg" community of the tamarack thickets and swamps of Noble County in northern Indiana. William Latta, William D. Hill, and George T. Ulmer were the pioneer founders and leaders of this illicit community, which thrived for 25 years. The banditti and their blackleg allies were sworn to uphold each other. They robbed, murdered, stole, gambled, burned buildings, and made and sold counterfeit money. They exerted a pernicious influence on the sons and daughters of their respectable neighbors, leading many young men and women into lives of crime, debauchery, and prostitution.[57] Finally, in 1858, 2,000 Regulators rose and scattered the blacklegs and outlaws once and for all.

The loathing of upper level men for the lower element—the contraculture—of the frontier was stated with feeling by Thomas Dimsdale, who cried that "for the low, brutal, cruel, lazy, ignorant, insolent, sensual and blasphemous miscreants that infest the frontier we entertain but one sentiment—aversion—deep, strong, and unchangeable." [58] At times the deep aversion expressed itself in grisly ways. Such an incident occurred in Rawlins, Wyoming, in 1881, where Dr. John E. Osborne (a future governor of Wyoming) attended the hanging of the brutal western outlaw, Big Nose George Parrott (or Parrotti). After the hanging, Dr. Osborne skinned the corpse and tanned the skin. The skin thus preserved was made into various mementos (including a pair of shoes that were put on years-long exhibit in a Rawlins bank), and, in effect, constituted an upper level trophy in tribute to the community values of life and property held by such men as Dr. Osborne.[59]

Vigilante movements varied in size from the 12 to 15 members in Pierre, South Dakota to the 6,000 to 8,000, who belonged to the San Francisco vigilance committee of 1856. Of the 326 documented vigilante movements, information has survived on the number of members in 50 movements. There were 13 movements of small size, varying from 12 to 99 members. At the other extreme were 9 movements ranging in order of size downward from 6,000–8,000 members to 700 members: San Francisco (1856), South Carolina (1767–1769), Attakapas region of Louisiana (1859), northern Indiana (1858), northern Illinois (1841), Idaho City, Idaho (1865), Bald Knobbers of Missouri (1885–1887), Butler County, Kansas (1870–1871), and Denver, Colorado (1859–1861). Predominant were the 28 movements, spread from 100 to 599 members—these were the movements of medium size. Thus, the typical vigilante movement was one of from one hundred to several hundred members. When we consider that the majority of American vigilante movements took place in new frontier localities of small population, the typical participation of from one hundred to a few hundred members underscores the extent to which the community as a whole participated in these movements.[60]

The characteristic vigilante movement was organized in command or military fashion and usually had a constitution, articles, or a manifesto to which the members would subscribe. Outlaws or other malefactors taken up by vigilantes were given formal (albeit illegal) trials in which the accused had counsel or an opportunity to defend himself. An example of a vigilante trial is found in the northern Illinois Regulator movement of 1841. Two accused horse thieves and murderers were tried by 120 Regulators in the presence of a crowd of 500 or more. A leading Regulator served as judge. The defendants were given a chance to challenge objectionable men among the Regulators, and, as a result, the number of Regulators taking part in the trial was cut by nine men. Two lawyers were provided—one to represent the accused and one to represent the "people." Witnesses were sworn, an arraignment was made, and the trial proceeded. In summation, the prosecuting attorney urged immediate execution of the prisoners. The crowd voted unanimously for the fatal sentence, and, after an hour allotted to the two men for prayer, they were put to death. The accused were almost never acquitted, but the vigilantes' attention to the spirit of law and order caused them to provide, by their lights, a fair but speedy trial.

Sentences of whipping and expulsion were common in the early decades of vigilantism, but, as time passed, killing—usually by hanging—became the customary sentence. Through 1849 there are only 88 documented fatalities resulting from vigilante action. In the next decade, 105 persons were killed by vigilantes, and it was at about this time—the 1850's—that the transition in the meaning of the term "lynching" from whipping to killing was occurring. The change, from whipping and expulsion to killing, in vigilantism, made firm in the 1850's, was accentuated during the remainder of the century; from 1860 to 1909 vigilantes took at least 511 lives.

The number of victims of the 326 organized vigilante movements upon which this chapter focuses is only a part of the total number of lynch-law fatalities in American history. Included in the larger context are the victims, also, of the unorganized, ephemeral lynch mobs. Attempts to arrive at a grand total are doomed to only partial success, since, in the centuries-long history of American lynch law, some evidence has been suppressed, lost, or scattered. Still, the available figures (although understating the total number of those actually killed) do afford a reasonable approximation of the number of those who thus lost their lives: 729 persons executed by organized vigilantes, 1767–1909; 4,730 persons executed by unorganized lynch mobs, 1882–1951; with 5,459 the grand total.

Since the grand total of 5,459 does not include the victims of the first and third Ku Klux Klans, nor the vigilante, lynch mob, White Cap, and Night Rider fatalities not compiled, a round total of 6,000 is probably closer to reality. Legal executions no doubt surpassed extralegal executions in the pre-Civil War period (as they have in the twentieth century), but with the wave of black lynchings in the South after Reconstruction, plus the continued widespread application of vigilantism in the West, the pattern was reversed in the late nineteenth century: during the period from 1883 to 1898, the number of persons lynched annually easily surpassed the yearly total of legal executions.[61]

Of the 326 known vigilante movements, 141 (43 per cent) were responsible for the death of 729 victims. Of the movements by category (i.e., large, medium, small), the large movements were, as might be expected, the most deadly, the medium movements less so, and the small movements hardly at all. Thus, the overwhelming number of deaths attributed to organized vigilantism, 704 (or 97 per cent of the total of 729), were exacted by 122 large and medium movements, which, however, amounted to only 37 per cent of all 326 vigilante movements.

The tendency among the 141 vigilante movements taking lives was to stop after claiming four or fewer victims. The most lethal of all vigilante movements was that in Montana in 1884 led by Granville Stuart; it accounted for 35 lives. The 10 other vigilante movements that killed 16 or more victims were, in descending order of deadliness, those of Lewiston, Idaho (1862–1864, 1871); Bannack and Virginia City, Montana (1863–1865); the entire Montana Territory (1862–1884); San Saba County, Texas (1880–1896); Madison and Hinds counties, Mississippi (1835); southern Illinois (1846–1849); Shackelford County, Texas (1876–1878); San Antonio, Texas (1857–1865); South Carolina (1767–1769); and the combined city of Cheyenne and Laramie County, Wyoming (1868–1869).

Although the trend was for the large movements to kill the most victims, it was not always necessary for a powerful movement to take a large number of lives. Often a vigilante movement could achieve its aims by taking only one or a few lives. The greatest of all vigilante movements (San Francisco, 1856) killed only four men. Two other significant movements—the northern Illinois Regulators of 1841 and the northern Indiana Regulators of 1858—executed only two men and one man, respectively. The fearful example of one or two hangings (frequently in conjunction with the expulsion of lesser culprits) was on many occasions enough to bring about the vigilante goals of community reconstruction and stability.[62]

Vigilante leaders wished to establish and strengthen the three-level community structure (in which they would be dominant) and the values of life and property that supported it. Specifically, they wished to check disorder and crime, but in some situations the threat of the latter was slight. In such cases, their desire to use vigilantism underscored their basic, implicit goals of implanting community structure and values.

All this they wished to achieve as cheaply as possible. They were the typical frontier entrepreneurs. Their enterprise in commerce or land was often speculative, and they frequently skated on economic thin ice. The delicate balance of their own personal finances could be easily upset; hence, they had a lively awareness of the cost of public services and a yen to keep them down, lest, as substantial taxpayers, their own circumstances should suffer. No better resolution of the conflicting goals of public order and personal wealth could be found than vigilantism, which provided a maximum of the former at minimum cost to the ambitious and well-to-do.

The typical vigilante leaders were ambitious young men from the old settled areas of the East. They wished to establish themselves in the upper level of the new community, at the status they held or aspired to in the place of their origin. Two notable but representative examples of aggressive young vigilante leaders were William Tell Coleman and Wilbur Fisk Sanders.

Coleman was head of the San Francisco vigilance committee of 1856 and was 32 years old at the time. His father had been a Kentucky lawyer and legislator but died a bankrupt when the son was only 9 years old. The future vigilante, deprived of the opportunity for an education, spent his early years moving restlessly about the Midwest (Illinois, Missouri, and Wisconsin) in a fruitless quest to regain the upper level status of his father.

Arriving overland in California in 1849, at the age of 25, Coleman embarked on a career, which, by 1856, found him to be one of San Francisco's most successful importers. His participation as a vigilante leader was, in effect, an action to cement his position in the upper level of the new city and to consolidate the three-level social system there.

Wilbur Fisk Sanders was the courageous and incisive prosecuting attorney of the vigilantes at Virginia City, Montana, in 1864. Like Coleman, Sanders came from an upper level background but had not yet made firm his own position. He was 29 years old when he served as a vigilante and had not long before accompanied his uncle, Sidney Edgerton (who had been appointed territorial chief justice by Lincoln), from Ohio to Montana. Sanders' vigilante service did much to establish the three-level system in chaotic early Montana, and it was the beginning of one of the most spectacular careers in the territory. Sanders went on to become one of the leading lawyers and top Republican politicians in Montana. He founded the Montana Bar Association and, in 1889, was elected one of Montana's first two U.S. senators.[63]

III

In frontier areas, law and order was often a tenuous thing. Outlaws—singly or in gangs—headed for the new areas and took every advantage they could of the social disorganization stemming from the newness of the settlement and the weakness of the traditional institutions of state, society, and church.

Law enforcement was frequently inadequate. Throughout most of the nineteenth century (and not just on the frontier) it was restricted to the immediate vicinity of county seat, town, or township.[64] Localities lacked the economic resources to support constables, policemen, and sheriffs in long pursuits of lawbreakers. A really large expenditure of funds for the pursuit, capture, jailing, trial, and conviction of culprits could easily bankrupt the typical frontier county or town.

There was also the handicap of poor transportation. The mobility of sheriffs and others was only as rapid and flexible as their horses could afford. A fugitive, having gained any sort of lead, was difficult to catch. The development of the railroad was a help but was not without its disadvantages. The officer was bound to the fixed route of the railroad. There were large gaps, also, between the railroad lines—gaps into which the fugitives unerringly headed. In the hinterland stretches not served by the railroads, the authorities were forced to make their way over poor roads and disappearing trails.

Linked with inadequate law enforcement was an uneven judicial system. Through fear, friendliness, or corruption, juries often failed to convict criminals.[65] The lack of jails (in the early days) or their flimsy condition made it nearly impossible to prevent those in custody from escaping.[66] The system presented numerous opportunities for manipulation by outlaws, who could often command some measure of local support. Whenever possible, outlaws would obtain false witnesses in their behalf, pack juries, bribe officials, and, in extreme cases, intimidate the entire system: judges, juries, and law enforcement officials.[67] Such deficiencies in the judicial system were the source of repeated complaints by frontiersmen. They made the familiar point that the American system of administering justice favored the accused rather than society. The guilty, they charged, utilized every loophole for the evasion of punishment. Compounding the problem was the genuinely heavy financial burden involved in maintaining an adequate "police establishment" and judicial system in a sparsely settled and economically underdeveloped frontier area.[68]

For many a frontiersman, vigilantism was the solution to these problems. W. N. Byers, an old Denver, Colorado, vigilante of 1860 reminisced:

> We never hanged on circumstantial evidence. I have known a great many such executions, but I don't believe one of them was ever unjust. But when they were proved guilty, they were always hanged. There was no getting out of it. *No, there were no appeals in those days; no writs of errors; no attorneys' fees; no pardon in six months. Punishment was swift, sure and certain.*[69]

Vigilantism could never have become such a powerful force in nineteenth-century America without having gripped the minds and emotions of Americans. This it did through a system of ideas and beliefs that emerged as the ideology of vigilantism. There were several elements in it.

In the nineteenth century the doctrine of "vigilance" suffused America in a way that had not been the case before or since. To be vigilant in regard to all manner of things was an idea that increasingly commanded Americans as the decades passed. The doctrine of vigilance provided a powerful intellectual foundation for the burgeoning vigilante movements, and, in turn, vigilante movements reinforced the doctrine of vigilance.

Vigilance committees were formed early for a host of things having nothing to do with the problem of frontier disorder. In 1813–1814, the leading men of Richmond, Virginia (headed by Chief Justice John Marshall), organized a committee of vigilance whose purpose was home-guard defense against a possible British attack during the War of 1812.[70] The attack never came, but the idea of vigilance did not die. In 1817, when Pensacola, Florida (at that time still under Spanish rule but soon to become American) was threatened by a ship of Mexican filibusters, the citizens established a committee of vigilance for home defense which, however, like that of Richmond was never put to the test.[71] American settlers in Texas on the eve of the Texan Revolution founded committees of vigilance in Nacogdoches, and other localities, in 1835–1836 by way of preparing for the looming hostilities with the Mexican mother country.[72]

The doctrine of vigilance had thus been utilized in regard to the early-nineteenth-century crises of war and expansion; so, too, was it put to the service of sectional interests as the North and South moved toward confrontation in civil war. Possibly the first "vigilance committee" involved in the sectional issue was that of the Ohio county of Meigs, which lay across the Ohio River from western Virginia. In 1824, Meigs County men organized a vigilance committee to prevent Virginians from pursuing fugitive slaves into their locality.[73] As early as 1838, Philadelphia and New York had vigilance committees to aid fugitive slaves. In the 1850's, Northern vigilance committees of this sort became increasingly common as they proliferated in response to the Fugitive Slave Act in Boston, Syracuse, Springfield, and smaller cities.[74] The South, conversely, fostered the founding of antiabolition vigilance committees as early as 1835 in Fairfax County, Virginia. Such committees spread throughout the South in the 1840's and 1850's.[75] By that time in Dixie abolitionists constituted an illusory threat at best. But the antiabolitionist vigilance committees probably helped increase the sectional solidarity of the South.

The doctrine of vigilance was not restricted to the great issues of war and sectional controversy but impinged upon the prosaic world of commerce. Thus, in a presage of the modern Better Business Bureau, the Merchant's Vigilance Association of New York City was organized in 1845 "to investigate and expose abuses in trade" and "to prevent frauds." [76] In time, the doctrine of vigilance merged with the earlier Regulator tradition (that went back to the South Carolina Back Country) and the result, by the 1840's and 1850's, was the vigilance committee dedicated to the eradication of frontier crime and turbulence.

Although the doctrine of vigilance was the context for the organizing of many vigilante movements, the vigilantes, knowing full well that their actions were illegal, felt obliged to legitimize their violence by expounding a philosophy of vigilantism. The philosophy of vigilantism had three major components: self-preservation, the right of revolution, and popular sovereignty. Reinforcing the threefold philosophy of vigilantism was an economic rationale for vigilante action. All these elements—the doctrine of vigilance, the vigilante philosophy, and the economic rationale—composed the ideology of vigilantism.

By the middle of the nineteenth century, self-righteous vigilantes in as widely separated locales as Washington Territory, Montana, Missouri, and Louisiana were routinely invoking "self-preservation" or "self-protection" as the first principle of vigilantism. Thus the June 1, 1856, Vigilance Committee of Pierce County, Washington Territory, justified its existence by citing "self-preservation [as] the first law of society, & the basis upon which its structure is built." [77] The French Acadians of the Louisiana *Comités de Vigilance* were no less sure of their ground when, on March 16, 1859, they declared, as a basis for taking the law into their own hands, that "self-protection is supreme." [78] The same note was struck by Thomas J. Dimsdale in his classic contemporary account when he stated that for the honest Montana miners of Bannack and Alder Gulch (1863–1864) the depredations of the "road agents" had narrowed the question down to "kill or be killed." Under the principle that "self-preservation is the first law of nature" the vigilantes "took the right side." [79] The very same language—"self-preservation is the first law of nature"—headed the resolutions of the Johnson County vigilance committee as it organized against post-Civil War horse thieves, murderers, and robbers in Warrensburg, Missouri, on February 28, 1867.[80]

The right of revolution was crucial, since vigilantes were well aware that their illegal action was, in effect, a blow at established authority. In order to deal with horse thieves and counterfeiters in Illinois in 1816–1817 "the people," Governor Thomas Ford later wrote, "formed themselves into *revolutionary tribunals* . . . under the name of regulators." [81] Vigilante penmen cut right to the heart of the matter by unequivocally invoking the right of revolution. A Louisiana *Comité de Vigilance* proclamation of March 16, 1859, explicitly avowed its character as a "revolutionary movement." [82] The authorized historian of the *Comité*, Alexander Barde, cited the American Revolution as a justified popular insurrection and precedent for the movement he described. To condemn the vigilance committee in the context of intolerable conditions of lawlessness (analogous to the lack of justice that brought on the Revolution of 1776), said Barde, would be "to condemn our history" and to say "that if Nero governed us, we should submit to Nero." [83]

Most vital to the philosophy of vigilantism was the democratic ideal of popular sovereignty whose origins, as noted in Chapter 2, went back to the era of the American Revolution. Aside from factors stated at the beginning of this chapter, an additional reason for the failure of vigilantism to appear before 1767 was the lack, up to that time, of a mature belief in democracy. The emergence of the popular-sovereignty doctrine in the revolutionary period was linked to the transition from deferential to democratic social values in America, a process that took from the time of the Revolution to the age of Jackson. By the latter age (which coincided with the firm establishment of the vigilante tradition), the rule of the people was acknowledged by all but the most skeptical and reactionary.

"Popular sovereignty" was much more than a slogan used by the ambitious Democratic party politician, Stephen A. Douglas, as an answer to the thorny problem of slavery in the territories; it represented a belief shared deeply by Americans of whatever political persuasion. The Regulators of the predominantly Republican party counties of La Grange and Noble in northern Indiana saw no inconsistency (as they prepared for a lynch-law drive) in stating as the first of their Resolutions on January 9, 1858:

> Whereas, We are believers in the *doctrine of popular sovereignty;* that the people of this country are the real sovereigns, and that whenever the laws, made by those to whom they have delegated their authority, are found inadequate to their protection, it is the right of the people to take the protection of their property into their own hands, and deal with these villains according to their just desserts. . . .[84]

The same idea was put a bit more pithily in 1902 when the following jingle was found pinned to the body of a man hanged by the vigilantes of Casper, Wyoming:

> Process of law is a little slow
> So this is the road you'll have to go.
> Murderers and thieves, Beware!
> PEOPLE'S VERDICT.[85]

"The *right of the people* to take care of themselves, if the law does not," said Professor Bigger of the local normal school to the Johnson County, Missouri, vigilantes in 1867, "is an indisputable right." [86] Hence, to nineteenth-century Americans the rule of the people was superior to all else—even the law. Vigilantism was but a case of the people exercising their sovereign power in the interest of self-preservation.

The economic rationale of vigilantism was tied to elite dominance of local vigilante movements. Thus, although vigilantism rested on a bedrock democratic premise, the vigilante operation in practice was often not democratic. Ordinary men formed the rank and file of the vigilante organization, but, usually, its direction was firmly in the hands of the local elite. The local vigilante leaders often paid the highest taxes. They had the customary desire to whittle down the tax rate and keep local expenses in check. From this point of view there was a persuasive economic rationale, for vigilante justice was cheaper, as well as quicker and more certain, than regular justice. This was a theme that the vigilantes sounded time and again.

In 1858, northern Indiana Regulators paraded under a banner that said, simply, *"No expense to the County."* [87] A *Denver Tribune* reporter probed opinion in Golden, Colorado, in 1879 after a recent vigilante lynching and found that "on every side the popular verdict seemed to be that the hanging was not only well merited, but a positive gain to the county, saving it at least five or six thousand dollars." [88] The redoubtable vigilance committee of Las Vegas, New Mexico, was (like many others) dominated by the leading local merchants. One night in the early 1880's the vigilantes entered the local jail, took out all the inmates, and chased them out of town. The reason for the expulsion was economy in government, as the inmates—"petty thieves, bunko men, and would-be bad men—were eating their heads off at the city's expense." [89] On September 3, 1887, the Meeker (Colorado) *Herald* praised a local vigilance committee and said, "We approve of this method of dealing with 'rustlers' as it is expeditious and saves the county the expense of prosecuting such cases." [90]

IV

Two "models" of vigilante movements developed. One was the "good" or socially constructive model, in which the vigilante movement dealt with a problem of disorder straightforwardly and then disbanded. The result was an increase in the social stability of the locality; the movement was, thus, socially constructive. The other model was the "bad" or socially destructive one, in which a vigilante movement encountered such strong opposition that the result was an anarchic and socially destructive vigilante war. Some movements were run according to the ideal theory of vigilantism whereas others were not. Some were socially constructive; others were not.

The socially constructive movement occurred when the vigilantes represented a genuine community consensus. Here a majority of the people either participated in the movement or approved of it. Vigilantism of this sort simply mobilized the community and overwhelmed the unruly outlaws and lower people. The community was left in a more orderly and stable condition, and the social functions of vigilantism were served: the problem of community order was solved by the consolidation of the three-level social structure and the supporting community values.

Although the methods used were often harsh and arbitrary, most vigilante movements—large and small—conformed to the socially constructive model. One of the best examples was the northern Illinois Regulator movement of 1841. The northern Illinois movement confronted a classic threat to community order: an agglomeration of outlaw gangs was nearing control of the area. With the regular government virtually powerless, the respectable leaders of the community upper level took the law into their own hands with the help of the middle level farmers.

Since 1835, the situation in the Rock Valley of northern Illinois had gone from bad to worse. Several gangs of horse thieves and counterfeiters found the Rock River country a convenient corridor for illicit operations in Wisconsin, Illinois, Iowa, and Missouri. The Driscoll and Brodie gangs had made Ogle and De Kalb counties a virtual fief. The Oliver gang dominated Winnebago County. The Bliss-Dewey-West ring waxed strong in Lee County, while the Birch gang of horse thieves ranged in all quarters. By 1840 the desperadoes were numerous enough to control elections in Ogle County and to similarly threaten other counties. One summer the outlaws even went so far as to burn down the newly constructed courthouse at Oregon, Illinois.

Finally, in April, 1841, 15 "representative men" of Ogle County formed the first Regulator company. In no time at all the counties were dotted with Regulator squads, but the most vigorous were those of Ogle. The Regulators embodied the social, economic, and political prestige of Ogle County: John Phelps was the county's oldest and wealthiest settler and the founder of the county seat, Oregon. Peter Smith combined a bank presidency with the ownership of 1,600 acres of land. The farmers who made up the bulk of the movement were substantial property holders; they had taken up Government land claims ranging from 240 to 600 acres. These solid citizens brooked no opposition. They burned the Rockford *Star* to the ground soon after it published an anti-Regulator editorial. But, on the whole, the local elite kept the movement well under control. Having accomplished their purpose in a campaign of whipping, hanging, and firing squads, the Regulator companies disbanded. Socially they left the Rock Valley in a better state than before they organized.[91]

The northern Illinois Regulator movement exhibited the major characteristics of the successful frontier vigilante movement. It was organized in a rational way. Mass participation of respectable men was the mode, but the movement was dominated, clearly, by the social and economic elite of the area. The Regulators were implacable in their war on the outlaws and unrelenting in the face of opposition. Although the Rockford *Star* opposed the Regulators, no anti-Regulator coalition, as a whole, developed. The outlaw gangs were isolated and broken up. The vigilante leaders desired the assurance of their position at the upper level of their communities but were not power mad. With the outlaw threat put down, peace and order reigned.

In the socially destructive model, the vigilante movement resulted in anarchy. Because there was no community consensus behind the vigilante movement, strong opposition appeared, and civil conflict flared. In the socially constructive model, opposition to the vigilantes was narrowly restricted to outlaws and lower people who could gain no support from the remainder of the community. For the vigilantes to be stymied, a large antivigilante coalition was necessary. The formation of an antivigilante coalition almost inevitably condemned the community to a chaotic internecine struggle between the vigilantes and their opponents.

Respectable men did not join the antivigilante coalition because of any great sympathy for the outlaws and lower people. They were impelled into opposition by things the vigilantes did or stood for. Sometimes two or three powerful local families would join the antivigilante movement. In some cases, a family had been carrying on a feud of sorts with a leading vigilante family.[92] Sometimes a local political party or faction went into the antivigilante movement, because the vigilantes were dominated by the rival party or faction.[93] In the 1830's–1850's if the leading Democrats of a community, for example, were found among the vigilantes, the antivigilante coalition would probably attract the local Whigs. Political rivalries were often linked to vigilante strife, for, in many instances, vigilante leaders harbored political ambitions and were not above using the movement to further their personal ambitions.[94] Economic rivalries among community leaders also were a factor in antivigilante and vigilante alignments; mercantile competition sometimes caused a leading storekeeper to go into the opposition if his rival were a vigilante.[95] Thus, personal, family, political, and economic antagonisms accounted for a ready-made vigilante opposition in some communities.

At other times, vigilante extremism drew into opposition decent men who otherwise probably would not have opposed vigilantism. The best of vigilante movements usually attracted a fringe of sadists and naturally violent types. Often these men had criminal tendencies and were glad to use the vigilante movement as an occasion to give free reign to their unsavory passions. It was always a problem for vigilante leaders to keep these elements under control, and sometimes a movement was taken over or seriously skewed by these social misfits. Sadistic punishment and torture, arbitrary and unnecessary killings, and mob tyranny marked vigilante movements that had truly gone bad.[96] When this happened, many sound and conservative men felt they must oppose the vigilantes with whose original objectives they had probably felt no quarrel.

Examples of the socially destructive model of vigilantism did not occur as often as the constructive model, but when they did extremely violent conflicts tended to appear. Among the leading instances were the east Texas Regulators (versus the Moderators), 1840–1844; the southwest Missouri Slickers (versus the Anti-Slickers), 1842–1844; and the southern Illinois Regulators (versus the Flatheads), 1846–1850.[97] Sometimes an antivigilante coalition arose, which, although unable to match vigilante strength, was able to call in outside help and, hence, could define the limits of vigilante power. The antivigilante Law and Order faction in San Francisco, in 1856, played this role. The vigilantes there would have liked to have hanged Judge David S. Terry but did not dare do so, for the Law and Order faction would have almost certainly obtained federal action against the vigilantes.[98] Similarly, the Moderators in the South Carolina Back Country, 1769, were not strong enough to overturn Regulator domination, but they did check the movement and bring its excesses to an end.[99]

If a socially destructive model of vigilantism gained power, the moral standing of the vigilantes and the opposing coalition tended increasingly to be compromised. As the struggle became more violent, the respectable men of the antivigilante coalition put a higher premium on the violent talents of the outlaw element with which they otherwise had nothing in common. So, too, did the original vigilantes themselves recruit and acquire a criminal fringe, which they put to mercenary use. With the community descending into bloody chaos, wise and prudent men left if they could. The opposing movements tended to fall more and more into the control of the worst and most extreme of their adherents. When this occurred, the desperate neutral residents would beseech state authorities for the intervention of the militia, and the "war" would subside fitfully in the presence of state troops.[100]

The Regulator-Moderator war of east Texas (1840–1844) was representative of this degenerate, socially destructive vigilante situation. The scene was the redland and piney wood country of east Texas in the days of the Lone Star Republic. The center of the conflict was Shelby County. Fronting on the Sabine River, where it formed the boundary between Louisiana and Texas, Shelby County lay in an old border area that had never been known for peace and calm. In 1840, the Regulator movement arose as a quite honest and straightforward attack on a ring of corrupt county officials who specialized in fraudulent land transactions. The rise of the Regulators was probably inevitable in any case, for the county had long wilted under a plague of counterfeiting, horse thievery, Negro stealing, and common murder and mayhem. The Regulators, however, overplayed their hand, especially after their original leader, Charles W. Jackson, was killed and replaced by the nefarious adventurer, Watt Moorman. Bad elements infiltrated both the Regulators and their opponents, the Moderators, but, by comparison, the latter seemed less obnoxious. Some honorable and level-headed citizens like John W. Middleton stayed with the Regulators to the end, but an attitude of wild vengefulness came to be more characteristic of the band. The early group of ne'er-do-wells among the Moderators dwindled. As more and more citizens were forced to take sides, many joined the Moderators, reacting to the sadism and vindictiveness of the swashbuckling Watt Moorman, who affected a military uniform and blew great blasts on a hunting horn to summon his henchmen.

The original reasons for the founding of the Regulator movement were all but forgotten. The war became a thing in itself, a complexity of personal and family feuds that was consuming the area in blood lust. Several attempts to restore peace failed. Complete anarchy was the situation in 1844 when an all-out battle between two armies of several hundred men each was forestalled only by the dramatic intervention of Sam Houston and the militia. After 4 years, 18 men had been killed and many more wounded. A stream in the vicinity was called "Widow's Creek." The killing of so many leaders and the exhaustion of the survivors probably explain why the war was not revived after Sam Houston and the militia withdrew. Ex-Regulators and ex-Moderators warily fought side by side in separate companies in the Mexican War, but for 50 years east Texans were reluctant to discuss the episode lest old enmities be rekindled.[101]

Vigilantism characteristically appeared in two types of situations: (1) where the regular system of law and order was absent or ineffective, and (2) where the regular system was functioning satisfactorily. The first case found vigilantism filling a void. The second case revealed vigilantism functioning as an extralegal structure of justice that paralleled the regular system.

Why did vigilantes desire to erect a parallel structure when the regular one was adequate? There were a number of reasons. By usurping the functions of regular law enforcement and justice or, at times, duplicating them, vigilante action greatly reduced the cost of local government. As taxpayers, the vigilante leaders and the rank and file benefited from the reduction in public costs. Second, the process of community reconstruction through the recreation of social structure and values could be carried on more dramatically by a vigilante movement than was possible through the regular functioning of the law. A vigilante hanging was a graphic warning to all potentially disruptive elements that community values and structure were to be upheld.

The sort of impression that vigilantes wanted to make was that received by young Malcolm Campbell, who arrived in Cheyenne, Wyoming, in 1868 at the age of 28. No sooner had he arrived than there were four vigilante hangings. "So in rapid succession," he recalled, "came before my eyes instances which demonstrated the strength of law [as carried out by vigilantes], and the impotence of the criminal. Undoubtedly, these incidents went far in shaping my future life and in guiding my feet properly in those trails of danger where I was later to apprehend some of the most dangerous outlaws of the plains." [102] (Campbell later became a leading Wyoming sheriff.)

Finally, the vigilante movement sometimes existed for reasons that were essentially unrelated to the traditional problems of crime and disorder. The San Francisco vigilance committee of 1856 is one of the best examples of the vigilante movement as a parallel structure. The San Francisco vigilantes spoke of a crime problem, but examination of the evidence does not reveal a significant upsurge of crime in 1855–1856. The regular authorities had San Francisco crime well under control. Fundamentally, the San Francisco vigilantes were concerned with local political and fiscal reform. They wished to wrest control of the government from the dominant faction of Irish-Catholic Democrats. The vigilantes actually left the routine enforcement of law to the regular police and intervened only in a few major cases. The parallel structure of the vigilante movement was utilized to organize a reform political party (the People's party) and to shatter the Irish-Catholic Democratic faction by exiling some of its leading operatives. [103]

Sometimes the regular and parallel structures were intertwined. Law enforcement officials often connived with vigilantes. Here a sheriff or police chief was not taken by surprise when a vigilante force bent on a lynching converged upon his jail, for he had helped plan the whole affair. Appearances were preserved, usually, by a token resistance on the part of the law officer, but it was well known in the community that he had shared in the vigilante plot. [104]

Why would men violate their oaths and subvert their own functions as officers of the law? For some men the reason was that they were little more than hirelings of the local vigilante elite to whom they were beholden for office. Other officers were large landholders or businessmen themselves; they shared the vigilantes' desire to keep down governmental costs. Little interested in legal niceties, vigilante-minded law officers were happy to have a bad man disposed of quickly, cheaply, and permanently by a lynching.

American vigilantism has been paralleled by a number of related movements. Such movements as the three Ku Klux Klans, the White Caps, and the Night Riders were illegal and usually violent. One legal, nonviolent movement existed side by side with vigilantism from the late eighteenth to the early twentieth century. This was the anti-horse thief movement. It is now almost forgotten, but hundreds of thousands of Americans from New England to the Rio Grande belonged to it.

The anti-horse thief movement consisted of local societies, clubs, and associations of men—mainly farmers—who banded together to detect and pursue thieves, especially horse thieves. The anti-horse thief societies were much like vigilante movements in respect to organization, objectives, and types of members. There was one crucial difference: they did not take the law into their own hands. Instead, they restricted themselves to the detection and pursuit of culprits whom, after capture, they dutifully turned over to local law enforcement officers. They eventually came to incorporate themselves under state law, and some states granted them constabulary powers.

The first anti-horse thief societies arose spontaneously just after the revolutionary fighting had ended.[105] The first such society was probably the Northampton Society for the Detection of Thieves and Robbers organized in Massachusetts in 1782. By 1800, similar groups had been founded along the Atlantic coast from Rhode Island to Delaware. The movement thrived in the northeastern United States as a legal supplement to regular law enforcement. It was vital and long lived in New Jersey—a typical state—where over 100 local societies were founded from 1788 to 1915. Official approval of the New Jersey societies was unstated until 1851, at which time the legislature explicitly approved organization of the societies; later it granted them the power of arrest. The societies flourished until the establishment of township police departments in the 1890's lessened the need for them. Inauguration of the state police in 1921 rendered them wholly unnecessary. Here and there they still exist but only as nostalgic social organizations.

The experience of New Jersey and the Northeast with the anti-horse thief movement was duplicated in the Mid- and Southwest. The movement got underway in Indiana in 1852 with the legalization of regulator bands as anti-horse thief societies. After the Civil War, the movement grew rapidly, and an interstate combine, the National Horse Thief Detective Association (with headquarters in Indiana) spread into Ohio and Illinois.[106] A similar development was seen across the Mississippi, where a movement that began in northeast Missouri in the 1860's had, by the 1890's and later, become the farflung Anti-Horse Thief Association with thousands of local chapters and over a hundred thousand members in Kansas, Oklahoma, Missouri, and Arkansas.[107]

Eventually the anti-horse thief movement succumbed to the automobile. The latter supplanted the horse as the means of transportation the members had joined together to protect. And the automobile immensely increased the range, mobility, and effectiveness of local law enforcement, thereby rendering obsolete the anti-horse thief society as a supplemental crime-fighting agency.

V

In the short run, the vigilante movement was a positive facet of the American experience. Many a new frontier community gained order and stability as the result of vigilantism that reconstructed the community pattern and values of the old settled areas, while dealing effectively with crime and disorder. A host of distinguished Americans—statesmen, politicians, capitalists, lawyers, judges, writers, and others—supported vigilantism by word or deed. Some of them were personally involved in vigilante movements; usually this was when they were younger men, but, in later life, they never repudiated their actions.

Men who were actually vigilantes or had expressed strong approval of specific vigilante movements included two presidents of the United States (Andrew Jackson, Theodore Roosevelt), five U. S. senators (Alexander Mouton, Louisiana; Francis M. Cockrell, Missouri; Leland Stanford, California; William J. McConnell, Idaho; Wilbur Fisk Sanders, Montana); eight governors of states or territories (Mouton, Louisiana; Stanford, California; McConnell, Idaho; Augustus C. French, Illinois; Fennimore Chatterton and John E. Osborne, Wyoming; Miguel A. Otero and George Curry, New Mexico); one congressman (Curry, New Mexico); and one minister to a foreign country (Granville Stuart, Montana, minister to Uruguay and Paraguay). Prominent writers who were outspoken in their support of vigilantism included historian Hubert Howe Bancroft, novelist Owen Wister, and university president and diplomat Andrew D. White.[108]

The nineteenth-century American elite walked a tightrope in

regard to vigilantism. Most of the elite held conservative social and economic views and were not attracted by the revolutionary and democratic rationales of vigilantism,[109] but, as late as World War I, members of the American elite looked with favor upon the vigilante tradition. In 1918, a group of distinguished writers formed an organization to promote the war effort. Significantly, they chose to call themselves "the Vigilantes." Invoking the vigilante heritage, their pamphlet announced:

> There has been a disposition to associate the Vigilantes with those beloved rough-necks of the early California days, who established order in frontier towns and camps by methods distasteful to tender souls. We find no fault with this. In fact, we are rather proud of being linked up with the stern and vigorous pioneers who effectually squelched the anarchists and I. W. W. of their day.

The membership list of the Vigilantes was a "Who's Who" of the writers of the day. Among those who belonged were Hamlin Garland, Booth Tarkington, Ray Stannard Baker, Irvin S. Cobb, Edgar Lee Masters, Theodore Roosevelt, and many others.[110]

The classic era of vigilantism had attracted the participation and support of elite Americans as well as rank and file frontiersmen. It came to an end around the turn of the century, but the vigilante tradition lived on into the twentieth century. In fact, it was extended into new areas of American life. Thus arose the later phenomenon of the new vigilantism, or neovigilantism.

Neovigilantism grew mainly after the Civil War and was largely a response to the problems of an emerging urban, industrial, racially and ethnically diverse America. The transition from the old to the new vigilantism was heralded by the San Francisco vigilance committee of 1856, which used the methods of the old vigilantism on the victims of the new. Virtually all the features of neovigilantism were present in the San Francisco movement of 1856. Neovigilantism was to be frequently urban rather than rural, as was the case in San Francisco. The old vigilantism had been directed mainly at horse thieves, counterfeiters, outlaws, bad men, and lower people. Neovigilantism found its chief victims among Catholics, Jews, immigrants, Negroes, laboring men and labor leaders, political radicals, and proponents of civil liberties. The actions and overtones of the San Francisco movement were strongly imbued with the passions and prejudices that came to be features of the neovigilantism.

The San Franciscan vigilantes were ethnically biased; their ire focused on one group: the Irish.[111] The vigilantes were anti-Catholic; their hero and martyr was the anti-Romanist editor, James King of William, and most of their victims in 1856 were Catholics. Although their ranks included laborers and mechanics, there was a distinct social class tinge to the 1856 movement: middle- and upper-class merchants were aligned against the lower-class supporters of the San Francisco Democratic machine. Last but not least was a disregard for civil liberties. Angered by the arguments of John Nugent of the San Francisco *Herald*, who came out in favor of regular justice, the merchant vigilantes of '56 quickly organized an advertising boycott that transformed the *Herald* overnight from the strongest to the weakest of the city's major dailies.

Allegedly concerned with a crime problem, the San Francisco vigilantes of 1856 were, in actuality, motivated by a desire to seize control of the municipal government from the Democratic political machine that found the nucleus of its support among the lower-class, Irish-Catholic workers of the city. Basic to the vigilante movement was the desire to establish a business-oriented local government, which would reduce expenditures, deprive the Irish-Catholic Democrats of access to municipal revenues, and lower taxes. To a considerable extent, the San Francisco vigilante episode of 1856 represented a struggle for power between two religious, class, and ethnic blocs. Thus, the vigilante leadership of upper- and middle-class, old American, Protestant merchants was aligned against a political faction supported by Irish-Catholic lower-class laborers. Such were the social and economic tensions that typically enlisted the violence of neovigilantism.

The protean character of neovigilantism precludes an extensive discussion of it. Only significant tendencies are noted here. Negroes have been the targets of three distinct Ku Klux Klan movements over a more than 100-year period, going back to 1867.[112] Catholics and Jews were singled out for verbal attack by the second Ku Klux Klan (of the 1920's), but the bulk of Klan violence in the 1920's seems to have been leveled against ne'er-do-well white Anglo-

Saxon Protestants, who did not measure up to the puritanical Klan moral standards,[113] and was similar to the White Cap movement, which violently regulated the immoral and shiftless from 1887 on into the twentieth century.[114] Immigrants were repeatedly the victims of neovigilantism. One of the most spectacular instances was the lynching of 11 Sicilians in New Orleans in 1891.[115] Laboring men and labor union organizers (many of whom were immigrants) were frequently the subjects of vigilante violence when they were striking or attempting to organize.[116]

Political radicals have often undergone vigilante harassment; one of the most striking examples was the arrest of thousands of Communists and radicals in the "Red raids" of January 1, 1920.[117] The raids were carried out under the color of law, but the whole action resembled nothing so much as a giant vigilante roundup. Proponents of civil liberties have at times fallen afoul of a quasi-vigilante spirit manifested in such waves of intolerance as the "McCarthyism" of the early 1950's.

During the turbulent, riot-torn, crime-ridden 1960's and early 1970's, three sectors of the American public have become vigilante-prone: (1) Members of black enclaves, North and South, who have felt the need for self-protective organizations against white harassment and violence. The Deacons for Defense and Justice of the middle and late 1960's illustrate the neovigilante spirit among black people. (2) White residents of urban and suburban neighborhoods, who have felt threatened by a possible incursion of black rioters and looters. The predominantly Italian-American membership of a North Ward Citizens' Committee (founded in 1967) of Newark, New Jersey, emerged as a leading example of this neovigilante impulse. (3) Residents of urban neighborhoods beset by crime. The Maccabees (1964–1966 and later) of Crown Heights, Brooklyn, arose as the prototype for this species of modern vigilantism. Although the Maccabees were mainly white (their core was composed of Hasidic Jews reacting against black street crime), black organizations similar to the Maccabees have appeared in high-crime black neighborhoods where they have been especially active in recent years against drug dealers.

These vigilante movements of the 1960's and early 1970's have differed from classic vigilantes in the sense that the current movements have not ordinarily taken the law into their own hands. (Since 1970, however, there have been reports that black and Puerto Rican vigilantes have executed drug dealers in New York City.) Instead, the main activity has been patrol action around neighborhoods in radio-equipped automobiles (linked to a central headquarters) for the purpose of spotting, reporting, and discouraging criminal acts against the residents of their communities. Characteristically, these up-to-date vigilantes cooperate with the police, but not always: the Negro organization of Deacons for Defense and Justice was formed, in part, to deal with white police harassment in black sectors in small cities of the deep South, whereas, as indicated, recent black and Puerto Rican urban vigilantes have supposedly levied summary justice on ghetto drug pushers. Despite frequent cooperation with police, the contemporary movements are in the authentic vigilante tradition, for they are associations in which citizens have joined together for self-protection under conditions of disorder. While usually not usurping the law, these movements have been commonly viewed as vigilantes by the public, the authorities, and themselves.[118]

VI

Despite the existence of some anarchic, socially destructive vigilante movements, the effect of vigilantism—as noted above—was to enhance social stability and order in frontier areas. Moreover, American opinion generally supported vigilantism; extralegal activity by a provoked populace was deemed to be the rightful action of good citizens. Thus, from the short-run perspective of frontier development the paradoxical aim of vigilantism—to uphold the law by breaking the law—was not only achieved but applauded. Yet, a long-range view of vigilantism casts doubt on its positive impact. We are and always have been a law-abiding people, but pervasive respect for the law has been counterpointed by a widespread spirit of lawlessness. Americans have long felt that intolerable conditions justify defiance of law and ultimately, if required, revolution.

The vigilante tradition has powerfully fostered American lawlessness. A part of the heritage of hundreds of American communities from the Piedmont to the Pacific, vigilantism—like the American Revolution—has taught the lesson that in certain cases defiance of law pays. The typical vigilante took the law into his own hands sincerely (but paradoxically) in the interest of law and order. He desired social stability and got it. But was it purchased at too high a cost?

Yes, said the principled opponents of vigilantism, who hammered home a philosophy of anti-vigilantism that went as far back as the opposition to the original South Carolina movement of 1767–1769. From the very beginning, anti-vigilante theorists cogently argued that due process of law was a precious Anglo-American legacy, that true law and order meant observing the law's letter as well as its spirit, and, finally, that the only way to obtain real and lasting law and order was to pour all one's power and substance into making the regular system work.

One trenchant opponent of the San Francisco Vigilance Committee of 1856 noted that "if the same energy which prompted the formation of the Committee and organized the armed force that assaulted the jail had been directed to strengthen the regular course of justice as public opinion can do it, there would have been no need for the [vigilante] outbreak. . . . The precedent is bad, the law of passion cannot be trusted, and the slow process of reform in the administration of justice is more safe to rely on than the action of any revolutionary committee, no matter how great may be the apparent necessity," he continued. "Better to endure the evil of escape of criminals than to inaugurate a reign of terror which to-day may punish one guilty head, and tomorrow wreak its mistaken vengeance on many innocent lives," he concluded.

Aside from the danger of vigilante action extending to extremism, the critics of vigilantism were upset by its fundamentally subversive character. A southern Illinois opponent of the Regulator movement in Pope, Johnson, and Massac counties, Richard S. Nelson, charged in 1847 that by attacking citizens and taking their property the Regulators had violated "those great principles of civil liberty" upon which the Illinois State constitution was based. Nelson also turned the vigilante justification of popular sovereignty against them by noting that, in forcing elected county officials to leave the county or surrender their offices, the Regulators had

"made a direct attack upon the sovereignty of the people." [119]
There is no doubt, however, that, for all the plausibility of Nelson's
invocation of popular sovereignty against vigilantism, the appeal to
popular sovereignty was made much more often by vigilantes than
by their opponents.

Occasionally, vigilante opponents discussed what they thought
were the sociological causes of the crime and turbulence that led to
vigilantism. The Reverend William Anderson Scott was a courageous opponent of the powerful San Francisco vigilantes of 1856.
In a sermon entitled "Education, and not Punishment, the True
Remedy for the Wrong-Doings and Disorders of Society," Scott
called for industrial education for the lower classes and for urban
eleemosynary institutions as means of eradicating the root sources
of crime. "You may depend upon it," he insisted, "the stream of
blood will never be staid [sic] while men take the law into their own
hands." [120]

Americans have for generations been ambiguous in their attitude
to law. In one sense, Americans are a law-abiding people of
exemplary character. But the many organized movements in our
history that have openly flouted and ignored the law (revolutionary
Whigs, Northern abolitionists, Southern filibusters, regulators,
vigilantes, Ku Klux Klansmen, White Caps, lynch mobs, etc.) show
that lawlessness has been rife. In 1837, the young Abraham Lincoln
delivered an address on "The Perpetuation of Our Political
Institutions" and found that the chief threat came from "the
increasing disregard for law which pervades the country—the
growing disposition to substitute the wild and furious passions in
lieu of the sober judgment of courts, and the worse than savage
mobs for the executive ministers of justice." [121]

The key to the apparent contradiction between our genuine
lawfulness and the disregard for law emphasized by Lincoln lies in
the selectivity with which Americans have approached the law.
Going back to the colonial period and the patriotic resistance to
the British mother country, "the Americans," observed James
Truslow Adams, "had developed a marked tendency to obey only
such laws as they chose to obey. . . . Laws which did not suit the
people, or even certain classes, were disobeyed constantly with
impunity." [122] Perhaps in the long run the most important result of

vigilantism has been the subtle way in which it has persistently undermined our respect for law by its repeated theme that the law may be arbitrarily disregarded—that there are times when we may choose to obey the law or not.

Chapter 5

PIVOT OF AMERICAN VIGILANTISM: THE SAN FRANCISCO VIGILANCE COMMITTEE OF 1856

All my interests were here [San Francisco], and I had expected to bring my family. I found a state of affairs not at all encouraging for the prospect of a comfortable residence, or the prosperity of the country, or security, social, political, or otherwise.

William T. Coleman, President of the Vigilance Committee of 1856

The old vigilantism, which arose mainly before the Civil War, was directed primarily against pioneer lawlessness and focused chiefly upon horse thieves, counterfeiters, and outlaws in the far-flung reaches of the Mississippi Valley and the West. It was a frontier phenomenon of the agrarian era of American history.[1] The new vigilantism, or neovigilantism, came to be a much broader and more complex thing. Not confined to frontier or countryside, it was a part of the transition from a rural to an urban America.[2] The new vigilantism found its victims among Catholics, Jews, immigrants, blacks, laboring men and labor leaders, radicals, free thinkers, and defenders of civil liberties.[3]

The San Francisco committee of 1856 is pivotal in the history of American vigilantism, because it signals the beginning of the transition from the old to the new vigilantism. The San Francisco vigilantes linked the methods (hanging, expulsion) of the old with victims typical of the new: immigrant Irish-Catholics in an intricate San Francisco context including allegations of a crime wave, electoral irregularities, and municipal corruption as well as ethnic and religious prejudice. Not only was the committee of 1856 the largest and best-organized vigilante movement in American history, but it was by far the best known. It received publicity on a world-wide scale and attracted the editorial approval of the eastern press.[4] The San Francisco vigilance committee was copied widely and even more widely admired [5] and had much to do with creating the favorable image of American vigilantism in the nineteenth century. It marked a turning point in American vigilantism, from a concern with rural frontier disorder to a groping—and unsuccessful—quest for solutions to the problems of a new urban America.[6]

Ethnically, there was perhaps no more cosmopolitan city anywhere in the Western world of the 1850's than San Francisco. Virtually all nationalities were represented in the population. Old-stock Americans; English, Scotch, and Irish; French, Germans, Italians, and Scandinavians; Mexicans, South Americans, Polynesians, and Australians; Jews, Negroes, Chinese, and many more were present. Many ethnic and religious groups had their own special societies and newspapers.[7] The French had not merely one newspaper but four, and, shortly after the height of the vigilante movement, a Negro newspaper hit the streets.[8]

In official pronouncements and editorials there was much ethnic tolerance and good will,[9] but under the surface ethnic hostility was rife. To a great extent, the political alignments of San Francisco represented the ethnic tensions of the fast-growing city. The Democratic party was split into two wings. One faction was Southern-oriented, but the dominant wing was the machine of David C. Broderick. Broderick, an aggressive political operator from New York City, introduced the system of New York ward politics into San Francisco.[10] The Broderick machine dominated the city by ballot-box stuffing, manipulation, and the strong-arm election efforts of Irish-Catholic "shoulder strikers" from the East.[11] It ran roughshod over the opposition of the Know Nothings who had inherited much of the old-stock appeal of the fading Whig party. There is no doubt that the Broderick machine considered the Irish and the Catholics and the black-leg and laboring elements of the population its backbone.

San Francisco was a seething cauldron of social, ethnic, religious, and political tensions in an era of booming growth. In the short space of seven years—from 1849 to 1856—the city had ballooned to a population of 50,000.[12] Streets were built, municipal services were established, the shoreline was improved, and wharves were constructed. But all this was done at the cost of enormous payments to the Broderick machine. Huge salaries, rampant graft, a soaring municipal debt, depreciating city scrip, and rising taxes were the signs of a fast-approaching municipal bankruptcy.[13] By 1855, the municipal budget had skyrocketed to $2,500,000.

It was against this background that the vigilance committee of 1856 was formed. The story begins in October, 1855, with the launching of the San Francisco *Daily Evening Bulletin* under the excited editorship of James King of William.[14] King wrote one sensational editorial after another, blasting the crime and corruption in the city.[15] Then, on November 17, 1855, an Italian-Catholic gambler named Charles Cora fatally shot the U.S. marshal, William Richardson.[16] When Cora's trial ended in a hung jury in January, 1856, King's flaming editorials in the *Bulletin* roused San Franciscans to a white heat. King had been a San Francisco vigilante in 1851, and the threat of vigilante justice frequently appeared in his columns.[17]

By the spring of 1856, King had created a near-panic psychology in San Francisco with his fulminations against the Broderick machine. Laying claim to a martyr's halo in advance, King predicted time and again that his enemies would get him. Finally, on May 14, 1856, his prediction came true when he was shot and fatally wounded by James P. Casey, an Irish-Catholic political manipulator and erstwhile inmate of Sing Sing prison.[18] The shooting of King hit San Francisco with sledge-hammer impact. The very next day the vigilance committee was organized by William T. Coleman and other leading merchants of the city, who were determined that Casey would not escape retribution as Cora had thus far.[19]

Within a matter of days the vigilantes tried and hanged both Casey and Cora. Two months later they hanged two more men;[20] and altogether, they expelled twenty-eight men. Meanwhile, thousands of San Franciscans flocked to join the vigilance committee. Soon its membership was approaching its peak figure of 6,000 to 8,000.[21] It was well understood at the time, and cannot be emphasized too strongly, that the vigilance committee was in the iron grip of the leading merchants of San Francisco, who controlled it through an executive committee.[22] In this body, William T. Coleman, one of the leading importers of the city, had near-dictatorial powers as president of the organization.[23] The papers of the vigilance committee have survived today in the manuscript collection of the Huntington Library, and numerous documents testify to its strong mercantile ethos. It was a rational movement with everything highly organized. Nothing was overlooked by the directing businessmen, who had the same passion for order and system in the running of a vigilante movement as they had in their own commercial affairs.

Possibly because of this background in commerce, the vigilantes used printed forms for membership applications. Out of a total membership of 6,000 to 8,000 some 2,500 applications have survived in the Huntington Library collection.[24] These constitute a unique file in the history of American vigilantism and provide a rather complete picture of the make-up of the 1856 committee. In addition to his name, each applicant was required to state his age, occupation, where he was from, and where he lived in San Francisco. On the basis of the data in these applications, it can be said, in general, that the vigilance committee was composed of young men in their twenties and thirties. Virtually every ethnic group, American state, and country of Europe was represented, but the American membership was predominantly from the Northeastern United States, from Maine to Maryland. There were also strong contingents from Germany and France. Significantly, few Irishmen were members. The fact that the bulk of the membership was drawn from the North Atlantic basin—that is, from the coastal states of the northeastern United States and from such Western European countries as France, Germany, England, and Scotland—seems to reflect the maritime orientation and origin of so much of San Francisco's population. As to occupation, the vigilantes came largely from the ranks of the city's merchants, tradesmen, craftsmen, or their young employees. Laborers were in a scant minority, and gamblers were forbidden to join.[25]

The mercantile complexion of the vigilance committee is the key to its behavior. The merchants of San Francisco depended on eastern connections for their credit.[26] Like most businessmen, the San Francisco merchants had an understandable interest in their

own credit ratings and the local tax rate. In the eyes of Eastern
businessmen, San Francisco economic stability was being jeopardized by the soaring municipal debt, rising taxes, and approaching
bankruptcy under the Broderick machine. The specter of municipal
bankruptcy made Eastern creditors fear that the city was on the
verge of economic chaos. The restoration of confidence in San
Francisco's municipal and financial stability was a *sine qua non.* It
had to be accomplished—and in such a way that would let
Easterners know that conservative, right-thinking men had definitely gained control.[27] Fiscal reform at the municipal level was
thus basic to the vigilante movement. But in order to bring about
fiscal reform it was first necessary to smash David C. Broderick's
machine.

Vigilante violence was the means used to destroy the Broderick
organization. Consider the hanging of James P. Casey: Casey had
recently broken with Broderick, but he had formerly served him as
a hard-hitting election bully and manipulator. The execution of
Casey not only had done away with the assassin of James King of
William, but it put Broderick's Irish-Catholic political henchmen
on notice of the sort of fate that might await them. Even more
important was the banishment of the 28 men, for it was their
expulsion that really broke Broderick's power. After the hangings
of Casey and Cora, the vigilance committee organized sub-commit-
tees and methodically went about collecting evidence of ballot-box
stuffing, election fraud, and municipal corruption.[28] The Irish-
Catholic "shoulder strikers" and bully boys who had bossed
elections were rounded up, jailed, tried, and sentenced to expulsion
from California. Broderick himself was called before the committee. There were rumors that he would be hanged or banished, but
this the committee did not quite dare do. Broderick was released,
but he had the wisdom to leave quickly for sanctuary in the
mountains.[29]

Broderick would come back to San Francisco another day, but
when he returned his chief lieutenants would be gone—put aboard
ships for foreign or Eastern ports with the warning never to
re-appear. To understand what happened, it is only necessary to
consider the names of those expelled. A Celtic tinge is unmistaka-
ble. Among the twenty-eight banished were Michael Brannegan,
Billy Carr, John Cooney, John Crowe, T. B. Cunningham, Martin

Gallagher, James Hennessey, Terrence Kelly, James R. Maloney, Billy Mulligan, and Thomas Mulloy.[30] The most famous of all—Broderick's trusted aide, Ned McGowan—ran for his life.[31] Thought to be involved in the shooting of James King of William, McGowan was sought for hanging by the vigilantes. He escaped to Santa Barbara, with neck unstretched, but he would no more turn out the vote for Broderick.[32]

With the Broderick machine in ruins, it was time to put something in its place. On August 11, the leaders of the vigilance committee initiated a political reform movement, which they called the People's party.[33] The People's party represented the consummation of the movement that began with hangings and banishments. The violent, illegal phase of the vigilance committee lasted only three months, from its organization on May 15 to its disbanding with a grand review and parade on August 18.[34] The legal, political phase of the movement, on the other hand, lasted for 10 years—until 1866—during which time the People's party was in power in San Francisco.

The call for the mass meeting at which the People's party was founded and the resolutions adopted, although mentioning crime, put the emphasis on municipal financial reform. Great complaint was made of "heavy taxes filched from honest industry," of the near prostration of city and county credit, and of the vast sums that went into the pockets of office-holding drones. The plea was made that the best men of the city give their attention to levying taxes and making public appropriations. An "economical administration of the public funds" was demanded. Close control of salaries and fees was stipulated.[35]

The call for the meeting had been signed by virtually all the San Francisco merchants. The "Committee of 21," which was chosen to make People's party nominations, was dominated by merchants. On September 16 the committee published its slate of candidates. It was a large list, but the candidates were chosen very carefully so as to give full representation to the business enterprises, trades, and professions of San Francisco. The appeal of the slate was to the commercial groups of the city rather than to the religious or ethnic groups.[36]

It was unmistakably a vigilante-dominated ticket. In the first place, support of the vigilance committee was demanded of the

entire list of People's party candidates. Beyond that, some of the
leading vigilantes were put at the head of the ticket. Charles Doane,
the commander of the vigilance committee's 5,000-man military
force, was nominated sheriff. Other prominent vigilantes ran for
chief of police and the state legislature.[37] The People's party
forbore making a choice in the presidential race between Bu-
chanan, Fremont, and Fillmore, but its sympathies were clearly
Republican. In fact, the opportunistic young Republican party of
San Francisco made its support of the vigilance committee a
principal appeal in the election. The Republicans endorsed all
People's party municipal and county candidates, and in return
gained endorsement of their state candidates who greatly benefited
from vigilante votes.[38] In time, most of the leading vigilantes
became Republicans in state and national politics.

The result of all of this was a smashing victory for the People's
party in the November general election. It buried the weakened
Democratic opposition by margins that often ran as high as two to
one. Not a single People's party candidate was defeated. The
reformers carried the entire city with the exception of the water-
front first ward. Even the sixth ward—formerly a Broderick
machine stronghold—went heavily into their column.[39]

In terms of a lower tax rate and lower municipal expenditures,
the People's party delivered on its promises. It drastically slashed
municipal expenditures from a height of $2,500,000 in 1855 to
$353,000 in 1857.[40] For 10 years the People's party held the
government, mainly on the basis of its platform of keeping the tax
rate down.[41] In proudly reviewing the history of the vigilance
committee from the vantage point of 1891, William T. Coleman
was in no doubt as to the significance of its offspring. The People's
party, he said, introduced a "new era" into San Francisco life by
lowering taxation and introducing "economies," which "radically
reduced" the municipal debt. "The credit of the city, State, and
people, which before all was uncertain," wrote Coleman, "soon
after took a foremost rank, which has since been finally held and
maintained." [42] Coleman's statement emphasizes that vigilante
action and the People's party fiscal reform raised the credit rating
not only of the city but of the "people." By "people" Coleman
meant San Francisco's businessmen—such as himself—who were
crucially dependent on Eastern lenders and suppliers.

To what extent did conditions of crime lead the businessmen of San Francisco to employ the traditional penalties of hanging and banishment that were often used by frontier vigilantes? In their rhetoric, both James King of William and the vigilantes in the early stages of their movement made much of a supposed crime problem. Did the reality support the rhetoric? The crime news in the San Francisco newspapers of 1855–1856 indicates that the regular organs of law and order had crime fully under control.[43] In keeping with the broader scope of the nascent new vigilantism, the main thrust of the San Francisco committee of vigilance was not against the regular criminal activity that characteristically energized the old vigilantism but was against what *the vigilantes saw* as a greater threat to the public good: the ruthless, corrupt political machine of Broderick and the Irish-Catholic Democrats. Thus, the vigilantes focused on the interwoven factors of society, politics, and government in San Francisco. In the largest sense they were concerned with the issue of municipal development in the booming city between the ocean and the bay. Ultimately, reform of the politics and government of San Francisco was the goal of William Tell Coleman and his vigilante colleagues. They wished to supplant the Broderick machine with a reform-minded political organization of their own creation.

This raises another question. If political reform was fundamentally the main concern of the vigilantes, why did they not try that in the first place? The answer of the vigilantes to contemporaries who asked that very question was that there was no possibility of political reform at the polls, since the corrupt element simply stuffed the ballot boxes and counted out the opposition. Hence, the vigilantes claimed, they were forced to take the law into their own hands.[44] That was their answer, but it is too simple. Implicitly, the reason why the reform-minded businessmen of San Francisco first resorted to vigilante violence rather than political action stemmed from the perennial problem of reformers: the difficulty of organizing apathetic and indifferent voters against an organized and entrenched political machine. Yet in the fall of 1856 the vigilantes did triumph at the polls by a two-to-one count. No amount of skulduggery by Broderick's henchmen could have overcome such an overwhelming majority.

The final question, then, is why did not the vigilantes invoke that overwhelming sentiment for reform in the first place and save themselves the trouble of the hangings and banishments? The answer, of course, is that it took the vigilance committee itself to break through the crust of apathy and bring about a mass movement for reform.

Before the founding of the vigilance committee there simply was no reform organization in San Francisco. To carry out the banishments and the fair hangings, the vigilance committee enrolled thousands of members. Since they had to control a large city, and, since they feared that the governor might raise a militia force against them,[45] the vigilante leaders felt it necessary to fashion a tightly organized movement with military discipline. Thus vigilantes were enrolled in companies of 50 to 100 members, which, in turn, were organized into battalions and regiments. The companies, battalions, and regiments all had officers.[46] The rank and file of the vigilantes elected representatives to an Assembly of Delegates of about 150 members, and the president of the vigilance committee in turn named an executive committee of about 40 members.[47] The military apparatus of the vigilante movement was headed by a grand marshal[48]; the president and the executive committee exercised autocratic control over the movement, and the Assembly of Delegates functioned merely as an organ for voicing rank and file opinion.[49]

Thus, the vigilance committee—organized in pyramidal, chain-of-command fashion and based on primary units of 50 to 100 members—was ideally constituted to assure success in an election. To win a smashing victory at the polls, all the People's party leadership had to do was to draw upon the vigilante apparatus—and that is exactly what it did.

Seen superficially, the San Francisco vigilantes were faced with the problem of a corrupt Irish-Catholic Democratic political machine. Their solution was to crush it. But in Broderick's approach to government, and in his appeal to the voters and his concept of municipal life, there was something more basic than boodle. At issue in the San Francisco of the 1850's were the same unresolved questions that came to typify American cities. Could extensive urban improvements be made only at the cost of wholesale corruption?[50] In ethnically mixed cities, would newcomers of minority-group status—Irish, Italians, Catholics, Jews, and others—be fully absorbed into American life, or would they be permanently condemned to economic degradation and social inferiority? [51]

To complex problems such as these the vigilance committee's starkly simple response of hanging and banishment was tragically inappropriate—tragic for the victims, of course, but tragic also for the vigilantes who thought they were solving something when they really were not. From his viewpoint of 1891, William T. Coleman complacently believed that the vigilance committee of 1856 had left San Francisco a permanent legacy of civic virtue and fiscal integrity. But he spoke too soon, for San Francisco was at that very time on the eve of the most turbulent period in its history: the era of the monumentally corrupt regime of Boss Ruef and Mayor Schmitz and the reform crusade of Fremont Older, Francis J. Heney, and Hiram Johnson.

The vigilantes of 1856 were on the right track when they abandoned the rope for the ballot box, but their People's party reform movement was much too narrowly concerned with fiscal matters to achieve any lasting solutions to San Francisco's problems. The vigilantes never had a real understanding of the fundamental issues involved.

The new vigilantism, of which the vigilance committee of 1856 was a harbinger, was one of the birth pains of urban America. But for the problems of the new America it was a symptom rather than a solution.

Chapter 6

LAWLESS LAWFULNESS: LEGAL AND BEHAVIORAL PERSPECTIVES ON AMERICAN VIGILANTISM

Lynch law is not unknown in more civilized regions, such as Indiana and Ohio. Now lynch law, however shocking it may seem to Europeans and New Englanders, is far removed from arbitrary violence. According to the testimony of careful observers, it is very seldom abused, and its proceedings are generally conducted with some regularity of form as well as fairness of spirit. What are the circumstances? Those highly technical rules of judicial procedure and still more technical rules of evidence which America owes to the English common law, and which have in some States retained antiquated minutiae now expunged from English practice, or been rendered by new legislation too favourable to prisoners, have to be applied in districts where population is thin, where there are very few officers, either for the apprehension of offenders, or for the hunting up of evidence against them, and where, according to common belief, both judges and juries are occasionally "squared" or "got at." Many crimes would go unpunished if some more speedy and efficient method of dealing with them were not adopted. This method is found in a volunteer jury, summoned by the leading local citizens, or in very clear cases, by a simple seizure and execution of the criminal. Why not create an efficient police? Because crime is uncommon in many districts—in such a district, for instance, as the rural parts of Illinois,—and the people have deliberately concluded that it is cheaper and simpler to take the law into their own hands on those rare occasions when a police is needed than to be at the trouble of organizing and paying a force for which there is usually no employment.

James Bryce, *The American Commonwealth*

Of all classes and professions, the lawyer is most sacredly bound to uphold the laws. He is their sworn servant; and for him, of all men in the world, to repudiate and override the laws, to trample them under foot, and to ignore the very bands of society, argues recreancy to his position and office, and sets a pernicious example to the insubordinate and dangerous elements of the body politic. It manifests a want of fidelity to the system of lawful government which he has sworn to uphold and preserve.

Joseph P. Bradley, *Ex Parte* Wall

This chapter deals with the attitudes of lawyers, judges, and legal critics—the legal illuminati—in late nineteenth- and early twentieth-century America in regard to vigilantism and lynch law. These attitudes were in response not merely to more than a century of American vigiliantism but more particularly to an outburst of extralegal violence that occurred in the last two or three decades of the nineteenth century. The late nineteenth-century rampages of Western vigilantes, Southern lynch mobs, and Northern and Eastern White Caps seemed to challenge the stability of American life. Was America threatened by this upsurge of violence, or was the violence itself an understandable—and not really harmful, indeed perhaps helpful—response to problems that were not being met effectively by the regular system of law and order? Many leading members of the legal profession, and other prominent Americans, answered the question by their actions; they participated in vigilante movements and lynch law action. The legal illuminati answered the question in their writings. Their conclusion, on the whole, was that vigilantes and lynch mobs acted in response to an unsatisfactory American legal system. To a qualified approval of vigilantism and lynch law, the legal illuminati added suggestions for the improvement of the legal system that would have moved it in the direction of lynch law.

On first reading this might seem a surprising state of affairs—that leading Americans and members of the legal profession should join the common people in the act of lynch law and that the legal illuminati, supposedly the element most vocal in support of due process of law, should speak out in approval of vigilantism. The explanation is to be found in behavioral terms. By definition, the legal profession and its more elite illuminati were the most vigorous exponents of law and order. But their conception of law and order in regard to the problem of criminal and disorderly behavior did not stress the method of due *process* of law but the *aim* of crime repression. In the vast majority of their actions, these attorneys, jurists, and legal writers were law abiding in deed and thought. But when they were confronted by the disorder of late nineteenth-century America, their devotion to the strict letter of the law gave way to their primary desire for order.

Whether behaving legally as lawyers or judges or extralegally as participants in lynch law these leaders of late nineteenth-century America were motivated by their desire to repress crime. To them the law, rigorously applied, seemed to hamper justice, whereas lynch law enhanced it. It is this that explains why some founders of state bar associations could also be unashamed participants in lynch law. They saw no contradiction. The legal illuminati who put their thoughts into print tended to reflect the views of their more action-minded colleagues. The illuminati rationalized the practice of vigilantism and sought reform not through aggressive law enforcement to suppress lynch law but through modification of the regular system of law and order in ways that would have accentuated the simplicity, certainty, and severity of vigilantism.

I

The traditional view has emphasized a sharp distinction between legal and extralegal justice, but the clear distinction between the regular system of courts and law enforcement on the one hand and vigilantes and lynch mobs on the other dissolves when the behavior of all elements is observed. Most striking is the wide extent of collusive practices and shared values that have united vigilantes and legal authorities. There are many instances of sheriffs and officials who have collaborated with vigilantes and lynch mobs.[1] Distinguished lawyers and judges and notable Americans and the public have seen vigilantism as fulfilling a necessary role in the over-all fabric of American justice. The legal-extralegal distinction, based as it is on a formalistic legal classification of activity, is less basic than an interpretation based on behavior. From the behavioral viewpoint the most important thing is not whether the actions of officials or vigilantes were legal or illegal but, rather, what the goal was in each case.

The legal scholar, Herbert L. Packer, advanced a behavioral concept of the contemporary process of criminal law[2] that will be applied here to replace the unsatisfactory legal versus extralegal perspective. In viewing the operation of the criminal law, behaviorally, Packer abstracted "from reality" two models of the criminal process: the "Due Process Model" and the "Crime Control Model." Neither is presented by Packer as "corresponding to reality or representing the ideal to the exclusion of the other," but both represent "an attempt to abstract two separate value systems that compete for priority in the operation of the criminal process." The due process model emphasizes procedural due process and the traditional presumption of the innocence of the accused. It is much less efficient in punishing criminals than the crime control model, for the due process model in operation resembles an obstacle course.

The contrasting assumption of the crime control model is that the accused is guilty, and this assumption allows it to deal effectively with large numbers of accused. Social control and efficiency are the main objectives of the crime control model. Packer's exposition of the "value system" of the crime control model refers to the legal administration of justice, but, in fact, it is a very accurate description of the value system that has supported vigilantism:

> The value system that underlies the Crime Control Model is based on the proposition that the repression of criminal conduct is by far the most important function to be performed by the criminal [*sic*] process. The failure of law enforcement to bring criminal conduct under tight control is viewed as leading to the breakdown of public order and

thence to the disappearance of an important condition of human freedom. If the laws go unenforced—which is to say, if it is perceived that there is a high percentage of failure to apprehend and convict in the criminal process—a general disregard for legal controls tends to develop. The law abiding citizen then becomes the victim of all sorts of unjustifiable invasions of his interests. His security of person and property is sharply diminished and, therefore, so is his liberty to function as a member of society. The claim ultimately is that the criminal process is a positive guarantor of social freedom. In order to achieve this high purpose, the Crime Control Model requires that primary attention be paid to the efficiency with which the criminal process operates to screen suspects, determine guilt, and secure appropriate dispositions of persons convicted of crime.[3]

Building on Packer's models, a more realistic, behavioral way of viewing American vigilantism is to see it in the context of a continuum of American justice that ranges between the poles of *due process of law* and the *control of crime*. (See chart "on facing page.)" Viewed in this way, vigilantism is not the opposite of legal justice, but, rather, possesses an affinity to the order of legal justice that emphasizes crime control rather than due process. The legal approach stressing crime control occupies a middle position between legal due process and extralegal vigilantism. The key point is that both extralegal vigilantism and legal crime control share the same overriding value emphasis: the repression of criminal conduct. The crucial distinction, then, is not legal versus extralegal action but extralegal and legal crime control versus due process of law.

It has been common for well-meaning opponents of vigilantism and lynch law to make the case that if vigilantes had "expended in the discharge of their duties as citizens the same energy and public spirit they displayed as vigilantes, officers could have been elected who would fearlessly and faithfully have performed their duty." [4] The sentiment is a laudable one, but it misses the point. The reality is that during the nineteenth century and on into the twentieth Americans supported a dual system of legal and extralegal justice by adherence to the primary value of repression of crime with little regard for procedural safeguards. Thus, Americans did not feel themselves any less public spirited when they participated in lynch law. Instead they saw vigilante participation as an act of public spirit as important in its own way as the election of upright

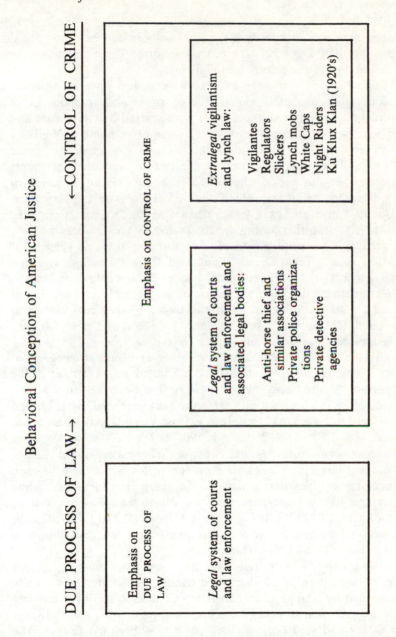

Behavioral Conception of American Justice

DUE PROCESS OF LAW→   ←CONTROL OF CRIME

Emphasis on
DUE PROCESS OF
LAW

Legal system of courts
and law enforcement

Emphasis on CONTROL OF CRIME

Legal system of courts
and law enforcement and
associated legal bodies:

Anti-horse thief and
similar associations
Private police organiza-
tions
Private detective
agencies

Extralegal vigilantism
and lynch law:

Vigilantes
Regulators
Slickers
Lynch mobs
White Caps
Night Riders
Ku Klux Klan (1920's)

officials. Americans felt that there were certain functions in preserving public order that the legal authorities would not, could not, or should not be expected to perform. These functions the people themselves assumed as vigilantes.

The decades from 1880 to 1910 were violent ones in America. Aside from industrial violence, race riots, and forebodings of proletarian revolution, these years were scarred by vigilantism and lynch law, and victims continued to mount in number. Vigilante activity was unflagging in the 1880's and 1890's—especially in the West and South. Two of the deadliest of all vigilante movements occurred in this period: the 1884 vigilante movement of northern and eastern Montana, which took 35 lives,[5] and the San Saba County "mob" in Texas, which accounted for 25 deaths from 1880 to 1896.[6] Altogether during the 1880's and 1890's, 157 persons were executed in vigilante movements.[7] In addition to the movements of Montana and Texas already mentioned, there were major vigilante movements in Las Vegas[8] and Socorro,[9] New Mexico; Seattle, Washington;[10] the Niobrara region of northern Nebraska;[11] Taney and Christian counties in southern Missouri;[12] the Creek Nation in present Oklahoma;[13] New Orleans, Louisiana;[14] Sevier County, Tennessee;[15] and Johnson County, Wyoming.[16]

To the long list of regulators, vigilantes, and other such agents of lynch law, the 1880's and 1890's contributed a new variant of the species: "White Caps." White capping first broke out in southern Indiana in 1887, spread into Ohio the next year, and, by 1889, had surfaced in New York, New Jersey, West Virginia, Arkansas, Iowa, and Texas. From 1887 through 1900 at least 239 cases of white capping occurred throughout America. Whereas organized vigilantism was largely a Western occurrence in this period and the mob lynching of Negroes mainly a Southern phenomenon, white capping had a great impact in the North and East as well as elsewhere. Of 239 White Cap incidents from 1887 to 1900, 102 took place in Northeastern states extending from Iowa and Illinois to Massachusetts and New Hampshire.[17]

White capping in its origin and thrust was a movement of violent moral regulation by local masked bands. The White Caps usually punished by whipping, and their most common victims were wife beaters, drunkards, poor providers, immoral couples and individuals, lazy and shiftless men, and petty neighborhood thieves. The

White Caps thus operated in the realm of human behavior where the authority of the law was either not clear or non-existent. In this sense, white capping fell into the vigilante tradition, but, in its use of masks, it was probably influenced by the Ku Klux Klan of the Reconstruction era. As the years passed, White Cap activity broadened into the economic sphere (sometimes with racial animosities added), and, by 1900, white capping had come to be a generic term for almost any sort of local violent group activity. The White Caps had also become such a large problem that a number of states—Ohio, Tennessee, Mississippi, and Texas among them—passed laws to suppress them.[18]

To many Americans the most appalling feature of late nineteenth-century violence was the wholesale lynching of southern blacks from the 1880's on. The practice was relatively new, for Southern Negroes had been lynched infrequently before the Civil War. During the Reconstruction period they were often the targets of Ku Klux Klan violence, but, after Reconstruction, the nation was increasingly shocked at the toll of Negroes taken by Southern lynch mobs. Due largely to the surge of Southern lynching, the number of persons illegally executed, annually, in the 1883–1898 period far exceeded those put to death legally. The *Chicago Tribune*'s annual publication of state and national lynching statistics beginning with 1882 did much to focus public attention on the immensity of the carnage. The *Tribune*'s figures clearly indicated that lynching was nationwide and not restricted to the South, but of the total of 3,337 persons of all races lynched from 1882 to 1903, nearly 60 per cent (that is, 1,985) were Southern blacks.[19] The nature as well as the quantity of the lynching of Southern blacks was horrifying, for they came to be regularly subjected to fiendish tortures that had seldom been inflicted on the white victims of lynch law. The lynching of Southern blacks routinely came to be accompanied by the emasculation of males and the burning of both sexes.[20]

The prevalence of vigilantism, white capping, and Southern lynching during the late nineteenth and on into the twentieth century led to much soul searching on the part of the American legal illuminati. The pervasiveness of lynch law was noted, the causes of the violent activity were analyzed, and, finally, reforms were suggested. This critical process revealed a surprisingly large amount of sympathy for lynch law. Insofar as the illuminati advocated legal reforms designed to diminish lynch law there was a tendency—in the interest of the overriding value of crime control— to bring the regular system of law and order closer to the spirit and practice of vigilantism.

II

When the legal illuminati considered why vigilantism and lynch law continued to flourish in America they found a basic cause in popular sovereignty. Roscoe Pound, who grew to manhood in late nineteenth-century Nebraska where vigilantism was common, placed the emphasis on "naive political theories of popular sovereignty," which "had much to do with fostering the practice of lynching." "Respect for law," wrote Pound, "seems to suffer when it is widely felt that law proceeds from the governed and is something which they may make and unmake at their pleasure." [21] O. F. Hershey, a prominent Baltimore lawyer writing in 1900, similarly saw approval of lynching by American public opinion originating in the "primitive democracy" of America. "The power to lynch," he asserted, "inspires in the American "a belief in the right to lynch." Lynching was a response to the American's "sense of self defense and self preservation." As a lyncher he "no longer looks to the appointed officers of the law for protection, but becomes in his own estimation an officer of the law himself, until consciously or unconsciously he comes to regard lynching as one of his more sacred and inalienable rights." Hershey noted a contradiction between the American lip service to the "Rule of Law" as conceived by Dicey and the fact that since colonial times because "we make our own laws . . . in certain cases, we feel unconsciously that we can be a law unto ourselves." Thus, concluded Hershey, "we actually have . . . a recognized public sentiment which it is not entirely absurd to call 'lynch law.' " [22] Commenting in 1902 on the long and violent history of California lynch law, a writer in the popular legal journal, the *Green Bag*, supported the popular sovereignty theme in his announcement that "the doctrine of vigilance, as of lynch law in general, is based upon the theory that the people have the right to hold perpetual vigil over all their institutions and to correct, where necessary, abuses and corruption which threaten the security of their lives and property." [23]

The role of popular sovereignty in vigilantism and lynch law was upheld during the nineteenth century by the vigilantes themselves. In drawing up formal resolutions on January 9, 1858, in order to justify what was to be an entirely successful drive on northern Indiana outlaws and blacklegs, the Regulators of La Grange and Noble counties invoked "the doctrine of popular sovereignty" to validate "the right of the people to take the protection of their property into their own hands" through the application of vigilante justice.[24] Late in the century, in a spectacular vigilante movement of 1891 headed by leading New Orleans citizens, the same motif appeared. The victims were 11 Italians who had allegedly participated as Mafia members in the assassination of the New Orleans police chief. W. S. Parkerson, a prominent New Orleans lawyer and politician who headed the vigilante organization, whipped up the emotions of a mass meeting before the lynching by declaring that "when the law is powerless the rights delegated by the people are relegated back to the people, and they are justified in doing that which the courts have failed to do." At the same mass meeting another vigilante leader, the New Orleans corporation lawyer, political reformer, and socialite, Walter D. Denègre, echoed this declaration: "The law" having "proven a farce and a mockery[,] it now reverts to us to take upon ourselves the right of self-preservation." [25]

As the insistence on popular sovereignty suggests, vigilantism was related directly to the behavioral patterns of American life in the nineteenth century. A cluster of attitudes involving "localism," the community, and an "instrumental" view of the law have been noted by James Willard Hurst. During the nineteenth century, Hurst has written, "localism" became deeply ingrained in American life, in part as "a natural accommodation to a frontier country of great distances and poor communications." In a "sparsely settled country with poor communications and people of small means, men naturally sought to bring the administration of justice closer to home." The legal trend emphasized by Hurst resulted in the prominence of the justice of the peace court as practically a "neighborhood" court and in the proliferation of state-created courts on a geographical district basis.[26] The extralegal components of this trend were the vigilante and lynch law movements; they, too, were organized on a neighborhood or community basis.[27] The pervasive localism of American life, which fed both the legal and extralegal streams of American justice, was related to another deep-seated American attitude, instrumentalism. The challenge of settling the continent, Hurst has said, caused us to want "to get on with the job most immediately at hand." "Our popular assemblies, our free religious congregations, the simplicity of our surroundings, and our need to use . . . government for . . . very tangible operations . . . taught us a matter-of-fact attitude toward government; government belonged to us, and it was an instrument of utility, not an object of awe." [28] The same "instrumental attitude" that caused Americans to approach law with a "readiness" to achieve "immediate practical results" ran as strongly in the extralegal domain with its stress on repression of crime as it did in due process of law.[29] In a similar vein, Roscoe Pound decades earlier had cited the popular assumption that the administration of justice is an easy task "to which anyone is competent." [30]

Vigilantism as an endeavor of the local community was the most extreme and final expression of a concept accented by G. K. Gardner and Henry M. Hart, Jr.—"the moral condemnation of the community." [31] "The essence of punishment for moral delinquency," writes Gardner, "lies in the criminal conviction itself. One may lose more money on the stock market than in a court-room; a prisoner of war camp may well provide a harsher environment than a state prison; death on the field of battle has the same physical characteristics as death by sentence of law. It is the expression of the community's hatred, fear, or contempt for the convict which alone characterizes physical hardship as punishment." [32] Underscoring Gardner's thesis, Hart emphasized that what separates "a criminal from a civil sanction and all that distinguishes it . . . is the judgement of community condemnation which accomplishes and justifies its imposition." [33] The Gardner-Hart analysis of legal criminal conviction applies doubly to its extralegal analogue of vigilantism, for "community condemnation"—shorn of the intermediary of the law between people and criminal—was expressed most starkly and brutally by vigilante lynching.

The "aversion—deep, strong, and unchangeable" of upright men for "the low, brutal, cruel, lazy, ignorant, insolent, sensual and blasphemous miscreants" [34] of the frontier was vented in grisly form by the practice of taking trophies from the bodies of vigilante victims. The habit appeared early in the history of American vigilantism with the display in Kentucky in 1799 of the head of Micajah Harpe,[35] one of a brother duo of fearsome outlaws who had plagued the Tennessee-Kentucky settlers until checked by regulators. Trophies were still being taken as late as 1891 when in the frontier community of Rawlins, Wyoming, a leading citizen, Dr. John E. Osborne—a future governor of Wyoming—participated in the vigilante hanging of the ferocious bandit, George (Big Nose) Parrott. The next day Dr. Osborne "skinned 'Big Nose' George and cut away the top of the skull, in order to remove the brain. The skin was tanned and made into a medical instrument bag, razor strops, a pair of lady's shoes, and a tobacco pouch. The shoes were displayed in the Rawlins National Bank for years." [36] Lynching was thus the extreme in "physical hardship as punishment," and the retention for display of a part of the body of the lynched victim was the ultimate expression of "community condemnation."

The late nineteenth-century commentators on vigilantism pointed to the wishes of economy-minded Americans as another factor in the popularity of lynch law. One legal journal concluded "that lynching is now done by tax-payers out of the mere design of ridding the State and county of the enormous cost, often as high as twenty thousand dollars, of convicting a known murderer and bringing him to the gallows." [37] J. S. Tunison, an Ohio and New York journalist, commenting several years earlier on the extralegal execution of Southern Negroes, found "the most potent reason for the practice of lynching, the reason which only the most outspoken will acknowledge and the one which will sustain it longest in the region where it flourishes" to be "the view taken of it as a measure of economy. To have strung up the alleged murderer, whether he be guilty or innocent, obviates the expense which his trial would have laid on the body of tax-payers." [38] Vigilantes were open in their avowal of the economy factor: the northern Indiana Regulators of 1858 stressed the lack of expense to the county in regard to their executions[39]; Golden, Colorado, vigilantes gained approbation in 1879 for the way in which their extralegal justice saved the public thousands of dollars[40]; and the same sentiments were expressed in support of vigilante movements in Las Vegas, New Mexico, in the early 1880's[41] and Meeker, Colorado, in 1887.[42] Emphasis upon the economic factor is not surprising, for the maintenance of an adequate police system and judicial establishment in the sparsely settled and economically underdeveloped areas of the South and West during the nineteenth century was a genuinely heavy financial burden for communities that were often impoverished and usually dependent on the narrow tax base of a thin population.[43]

Although great weight must be attached to the roles of popular sovereignty and economic pressure, the factor that aroused the greatest interest of the legal illuminati in their analyses of vigilantism and lynch law was the archaic American judicial system. The latter contained so many procedural defects that respectable men, it was observed, were often forced to the conclusion that lynch law was the only solution. The most significant exposition was Roscoe Pound's incisive treatment of "The Causes of Popular Dissatisfaction with the Administration of Justice" in 1906.[44] Pound's critique is important not only for the wide attention it received, but because it amounted to a persuasive summation of defects in legal procedure that had been noted by other commentators. Pound, of course, was not in any way sympathetic to vigilantism (as were some of the other critics), but his shrewd dissection of the antiquated American legal order laid bare one of the major causes of nineteenth-century American lawlessness and vigilantism.

Pound found the greatest cause of the popular dissatisfaction with the administration of justice to be America's obsolete and inappropriate system of courts and procedure: The result of this anachronism was "uncertainty, delay and expense, and above all the injustice of deciding cases upon points of practice, which" were "the mere etiquette of justice." [45] Also emphasizing the problem of delay in the legal system was Justice Henry Bischoff of the New York state supreme court. While strongly opposing delay as a justification for lynch law, Bischoff none the less conceded that "the demands" upon the judicial system were "too great for a system planned to accommodate scarcely half the business now presented, and making no elastic provision for enlarged requirements." [46] Among the other analysts of the shortcomings of the

American legal system who concentrated on procedural defects were Henry A. Forster, who underscored the inadequacies of the American system in comparison to other "Anglo-Saxon countries," [47] and Charles J. Bonaparte (1899) and David J. Brewer (1903), who called for drastic revisions in American legal procedure as a means of eliminating lynch law.[48]

Of the many weaknesses in the American judicial system "the common law doctrine of contentious procedure" was, in Pound's view, one of the greatest flaws. The effect of contentious procedure (that is, the adversary system), Pound argued, was to turn litigation into a "game." It caused, among other things, an undue reliance on procedure, which, in turn, led to an excessive number of new trials. In contrast to England, where this game-like contentiousness had been severely curbed, the long-run result in America had been to give the "whole community" a false notion of the purpose and end of law. A consequence was "the modern American race to beat the law" in which the entire legal system was involved. Hence, Pound concluded, "the courts, instituted to administer justice according to law" had become "agents or abettors of lawlessness." [49]

Related to the emphasis on contentious procedure was a host of technicalities that skewed the administration of justice.[50] Pound felt that the "worst feature of American procedure" was "the lavish granting of new trials." [51] Charles J. Bonaparte cited as an evil the double jeopardy prohibition when it was based upon a technicality such as the law error of a trial court.[52] The general inadequacy of the jury system was widely seen as a defect.[53] Specific evils were abuse of the jury challenge privilege, the lack of real necessity for grand juries, and the low quality of the petit jury. Cited as an abuse beyond the scope of the judicial system, but closely related to it, was the excessive use of the power of pardon by the executive branch of government.[54]

The defects in the procedural system scored by the legal illuminati had long since been acted upon by vigilantes through resort to lynch law. Thus, the role of packed juries, perjured evidence, and changes of venue in early Illinois history had caused frequent recourse to vigilantism by the pioneers.[55] The way in which pre-Civil War outlaws exploited the jury system through packing juries and inspiring false witnesses was seen by the *American Whig Review* in 1850 as a major inducement to vigilantism.[56] An old Colorado vigilante of 1860, W. N. Byers, told how vigilante lynchings cut through the complexities of procedural problems: ". . . when [culprits] were proved guilty, they were always hanged. No, there were no appeals in those days; no writs of errors; no attorneys' fees; no pardon in six months. Punishment was swift, sure and certain." [57]

Early in the twentieth century a flagrant case of vigilantism occurred that illustrates vividly the deep popular dissatisfaction with procedural delays and safeguards that underlay these outbreaks. It is a glaring example, too, of the way in which the authorities and vigilantes often cooperated to subvert due process of law; it was a flagrant case because it involved defiance of the U. S. Supreme Court. The incident was a lynching in Chattanooga, Tennessee, on March 19, 1906—the day before a Negro prisoner, Edward Johnson, was scheduled to be executed legally for the crime of rape. Although there was reason to believe that he was not guilty of the charge of raping a white school girl, Johnson was convicted on February 11, 1906, in the Hamilton County criminal court in Chattanooga. Johnson's trial was perfunctory, and he was not very diligently defended by his attorneys, who feared mob violence. An appeal was made in behalf of Johnson, and on March 19, 1906, U. S. Supreme Court Justice John M. Harlan announced that the court would hear Johnson's appeal on the ground that he had been denied his constitutional rights by an extremely speedy conviction. On the afternoon of the 19th a telegram was sent to U. S. circuit court Judge Charles D. Clark in Chattanooga informing him that the appeal would be heard and that Johnson was thereafter to be considered a federal prisoner. This information was communicated to the sheriff of Hamilton County, Joseph F. Shipp.

News of Justice Harlan's allowance of the appeal, which thus stayed the execution of the death sentence against Johnson, was published in the Chattanooga *News* late in the afternoon of the 19th. The result was that several hours later—between nine and midnight—12 men broke into Johnson's jail cell, took him out, and, joined by about 60 persons or more, lynched him by hanging and shooting. Although Sheriff Shipp and Deputy Sheriff Jeremiah Gibson had not taken part in the lynching, the Supreme Court later found that they had connived at it and hence were guilty of contempt of court. As Chief Justice Melville W. Fuller III wrote in the court's majority opinion, "Shipp and Gibson were in sympathy with the mob while pretending to perform their official duty of protecting Johnson, and . . . they aided and abetted the mob in prosecution and performance of the lynching." Fuller noted that the militia had been drilling in the armory that night only three blocks from the jail, but the sheriff had made no effort to summon them for the protection of the prisoner. The distinction made by Chattanooga public opinion and implicitly supported by Sheriff Shipp in an interview he gave the Birmingham *Age-Herald* was that there was not only a proper time for legal procedure but a rightful time for extralegal justice: "The people of Hamilton county were willing to let the law take its course," explained Shipp, "until it became known that the case would not probably be disposed of for four or five years by the Supreme Court of the United States. The people would not submit to this, and I do not wonder at it." [58]

III

Although the principals in the Shipp case were outrageous in their defiance of the U. S. Supreme Court, other offenses almost as gross were committed. There is a wide range of evidence illustrating the collusion between law officers and vigilantes, the participation of lawyers and leading men in vigilante movements, and the sympathy with which members of the legal illuminati viewed vigilantism and lynch law.

Cooperation between public officials and vigilantes was both overt and covert. Among the examples of overt collusion were cases in Nebraska, Missouri, and Texas. In 1867 near Columbus, Platte County, Nebraska one Ransel B. Grant was murdered by an acquaintance, Robert Wilson. Grant's brother organized a vigilante movement to dispose of Wilson, and when the justice of the peace, Hudson, tried to prevent the lynching, the sheriff, John Browner, and his deputy, Wash Fulton, pinioned him so that the hanging could proceed. [59] The turbulent Missouri-Kansas border area, which two years after the Civil War was still in the grip of violence and banditry, produced a similar case. To deal with horse thieves in Vernon County, Missouri, citizens organized a vigilance committee, and one of its leaders was the county attorney, one Birdseye.[60] In the decades after the Civil War, Texas was swept by waves of vigilantism. Especially violent was the tricounty area of Comanche, Brown, and Erath. The lair of one of the most dangerous desperadoes in American history, John Wesley Hardin, this central Texas region was seared by continuous strife. The outcome in 1872 was that the officials in all three counties participated in fatal vigilante actions as the aroused citizenry tried to end the plague of violence.[61] A decade later and further to the north in Texas, along the main routes of the cattle drives to the northern plains states, Wilbarger County men organized a vigilance committee against cattle rustlers. Among the vigilantes who took the lives of several rustlers was the acting sheriff, A. T. Boger.[62]

Collusion between vigilantes and officials was exemplified not only by the Shipp case in Chattanooga but a century earlier by the situation in territorial Illinois where, in 1816–1817, horse thieves and counterfeiters were rampant. Governor Thomas Ford later described how Illinoisans had organized themselves as regulators to deal with the problem and how "the governor and judges of the territory, seeing the impossibility of executing the laws in the ordinary way against an ordinary banditti who set all law at defiance, winked at and encouraged the proceedings of the regulators." [63] In early frontier days there were always strong pressures for officials to tolerate vigilantism and lynch law, but as the regular law became more strongly established the expectations of more orderly behavior increased. Yet these expectations were not always met, as in the early twentieth-century case in Chattanooga and the collusion between officials and vigilantes in the lynching of 11 Italians in New Orleans in 1891. The mass lynching of the New Orleans Italians was a striking example of the failure of officials to act when faced with a clear and present danger of lynching.

The background of the New Orleans lynching lay in the assassination in 1890 of the city police chief, David Hennessy. It was widely believed that the chief had been murdered by a Mafia faction of immigrant Italian dock workers whose anger Hennessy had aroused. In retrospect, it appears that Chief Hennessy's behavior was ambiguous. There was a second faction of Italian dock workers, and Hennessy seems to have sided with them against the so-called Mafia faction. In any case, 11 supposed members of the Mafia in New Orleans were brought to trial in 1891 but not convicted. Amid high public indignation arising from the belief that the jury had been tampered with, a dormant vigilante movement—whose core was composed of leading citizens—was quickly re-activated with a mass lynching in mind. Neither Governor Francis T. Nicholls,[64] Mayor Shakspeare, nor Sheriff Villere (all of whom were in the city at the time) took any steps to prevent the lynching. This lack of action was in spite of ample warning that a lynching was about to occur, for, on the day of the lynching, the morning newspapers had appeared with a notice for a mass meeting calling on all citizens to come "prepared for action." The lynching followed the mass meeting and was one of the most brutal in a brutal century. The vigilantes burst into the jail and pursued the terrified victims through the building. Once cornered, they were shot down or taken outside for hanging before a throng of thousands. The case was one more example of the convergence of crime-repressive attitudes among people, public officials, and lynchers, since the lynching—led by some of the city notables[65]—went uncondemned by a single New Orleans newspaper. The city, reported the *New York Times*, was "unanimous in upholding the action of the mob." [66]

The open cooperation or collusion of officials with lynchers had become such a scandal that after 1892 a number of states adopted legislative or constitutional provisions designed to end the evil. Alabama by constitutional provision in 1901 and Indiana by a 1905 law levied penalties of fine and removal from office against sheriffs who through fault or neglect lost prisoners to mob violence.[67] A similar Illinois law of 1905 struck hard at covert cooperation by providing that a prisoner taken from a sheriff or deputy and lynched was *prima facie* evidence that the officer had not done his duty and was thus removable by the governor. This law was applied in 1909 when the governor deprived of his office the sheriff of Alexander County, Illinois, from whose custody two prisoners had been taken and lynched.[68] An Ohio law of 1896 enacted the liability of counties for damages to mob victims or their legal representatives up to $5,000 depending on the serious-ness of the offense.[69] South Carolina in its 1895 constitution provided for removal of officers who participated in or connived at lynchings and for the liability of counties for damages. Other state provisions before 1930 aimed at curbing lynching and relevant to the problem of official collusion were those that punished individuals who took part in mob violence or lynching, who broke into jails or seized persons in the custody of officers, or who interfered with sheriffs or others in the execution of court orders. Another anti-lynching approach was to give special powers to law officers to summon posses for the protection of prisoners.[70] Although these measures were largely ineffective, they were an index of a growing public opinion that, in the 1920's, began to turn decisively—in contrast to New Orleans in 1891 and Chattanooga in 1906—against lynching.

Collusion between officials and vigilantes is not particularly surprising when one considers that some of the leading Americans of the nineteenth and the early twentieth century participated in vigilante action or strongly encouraged it and that among these prominent Americans were a number of lawyers and politicians. Most of them took part in vigilante movements as young men, but in later life they never repudiated their roles in extralegal justice. They were proud of their vigilante service.

The "Who's Who" of American vigilantism[71] begins with presidents of the United States. As president, Andrew Jackson once advised Iowa settlers to punish a murderer by lynch law action,[72] and, in his youthful ranching days, Theodore Roosevelt sought—unsuccessfully—to join a vigilante movement. The young Roosevelt was most anxious to lead a vigilante drive against Montana and Dakota horse and cattle thieves, but veteran cattlemen discouraged him. Actually, the cattlemen *were* planning a vigilante movement, but they did not want the impetuous young Roosevelt associated with them for fear that indiscretions on his part might lead to damaging publicity. With Roosevelt safely out of the way and back on his North Dakota ranch, the vigilantes ranged over northern and eastern Montana in 1884. They disposed of at least 35 rustlers and thieves in a wave of vigilantism that accounted for more victims than any other such movement in American history.

It is fair to say that Theodore Roosevelt had a lifelong affection for vigilantism. As late as 1915—only a few years before his death—he wrote with approval, "Before there was law in California and Montana, and indeed as a requisite for bringing the law there, the Vigilantes had to . . . hang people. Technically this was murder; practically, it was the removal of murderers." Significantly, this salute to vigilantism was delivered in connection with another Roosevelt enthusiasm, imperialism. In the course of a letter to William Roscoe Thayer on July 10, 1915, Roosevelt made an analogy between vigilantism and the imperialist actions of the British against Egypt and Sudan, the French against Algeria, the Germans against East Africa, the Russians against Turkistan, and his own presidential actions against Panama. These feats, like vigilantism, he saw as being "very useful to mankind." Roosevelt praised the Montana vigilantes of 1884 by writing in 1885 that, despite several unjust executions among some "sixty odd," "the outcome of their efforts" was "in the main wholesome." It should be noted that the Montana vigilante campaign of 1884 took place not "before there was law" in Montana but while the law was functioning regularly and had been for years. Roosevelt simply ignored this. As president, he was stern in his denunciation of anti-Negro Southern lynch mobs, an attitude, however, that was undercut by his own favorable view of vigilantism in the West. A recent biographer has cited Roosevelt's good fortune in being rebuffed by Granville Stuart and the other Montana "stranglers" of 1884, for the unfavorable publicity in the East that might have arisen from Rooseveltian vigilantism could have stunted his political career.[73] But attitudes toward vigilantism were so indulgent at this time that he might have suffered only a temporary setback, if that.

Two members of the San Francisco committee of vigilance of 1856 who went on to gain fame in business and politics were William Tell Coleman and Leland Stanford. Coleman, a prominent capitalist and importer, was the main leader of the 1856 San Francisco vigilante movement. In addition to being a leading California businessman (until his business failed in 1886), Coleman was active in politics. In 1865 he received 26 votes in the California state senate for the office of U. S. senator, and in 1884 Charles A. Dana of the New York *Sun* boomed him for the presidency.[74] Leland Stanford, one of the "Big Four" builders of the Southern and Central Pacific Railroads, had been a San Francisco vigilante at the age of thirty-two. A Republican, after serving as governor from 1861 to 1863 Stanford served in the U. S. Senate from 1885 to his death in 1893. In 1885 he founded Stanford University as a memorial to his deceased son.[75]

Other leading politicians had been vigilantes. Among them was Senator Francis M. Cockrell of Missouri. On February 28, 1867, at a public meeting in Warrensburg, Missouri, Cockrell spoke strongly in favor of forming the Johnson County vigilantes, who ultimately killed ten men. A lawyer and a former Confederate general, Cockrell served Missouri in the U. S. Senate from 1875 to 1905, and he was on the Interstate Commerce Commission from 1905 to 1910. In 1904 his name was placed in nomination for president at the Democratic national convention.[76] A prominent Louisiana politician who had a vigilante career was Alexander Mouton, an example of a man at the peak of his state and national standing who chose to become a vigilante. One of the wealthiest sugar planters in Louisiana, Mouton had been trained in law at Georgetown College. After serving as a U. S. senator (1837–1842) and as governor of Louisiana (1843–1846), Mouton became president in 1859 of the vigilance committee of Cote Gelée in Lafayette Parish, Louisiana.[77] Although not a vigilante himself, the Louisiana governor, William Pitt Kellogg, in 1872 encouraged a powerful vigilante movement that was to claim 12 lives. Kellogg was a lawyer by profession and had been chief justice of Nebraska Territory in 1861. Coming to Louisiana during the Civil War, he served the state in the U. S. Senate (1868–1872, 1877–1883) and House (1883–1885) as well as the governor's chair.[78] Much earlier, and as a young man, Governor Augustus C. French of Illinois had taken part in a regulator movement in the early days of Edgar County. A lawyer and a Democrat, French became a two-term governor of Illinois from 1846 to 1853. He ended his career as a law professor at McKendree College in Illinois.[79]

A host of Western "first citizens" participated in vigilante movements. Montana's leading pioneer and one of its most distinguished inhabitants, Granville Stuart, was a prime leader of the Montana vigilante movement of 1884 Theodore Roosevelt had sought unsuccessfully to join. At that time Stuart was one of the largest cattle ranchers in Montana as a member of the company of Davis, Hauser & Stuart. Later he became state land agent; American minister to Uruguay and Paraguay, 1894–1898; president of the Montana Historical Society, 1890–1895; and, in 1904, city librarian of Butte, Montana.[80] Another Montana vigilante of distinction was Wilbur Fisk Sanders, who had been a notable vigilante at the age of twenty-nine in 1864 when he served as prosecuting attorney for the Virginia City, Montana, vigilantes. The nephew of Montana's territorial chief justice, Sidney Edgerton, Sanders went on to become one of the leading attorneys and Republican politicians in the state. He was the founder of the Montana Bar Association and in 1889 was elected to the U. S. Senate in Montana's first delegation to that body.[81]

William J. McConnell was one of Idaho's first two U. S. senators (1890–1891) and was governor of the state from 1893 to 1896. He was the author of a book for juveniles in which the Idaho vigilantism of the 1860's (as well as his own role as a leading Payette Valley vigilante) was glorified. Believing the book to be essentially a treatise on good citizenship for youth, McConnell had wished to dedicate it to the Boy Scouts of America! Senator William E. Borah of Idaho, one of the leading progressive statesmen of his generation, and a lawyer himself, was conscious of no indiscretion in writing a favorable introduction to McConnell's book on vigilantism.[82] Two of the early governors of the state of Wyoming were participants in one of the most famous episodes of Wyoming vigilantism: the lynching of the brutal George (Big Nose) Parrott, in Rawlins in 1881. Dr. John E. Osborne, a leading Rawlins physician who later, from 1893 to 1895, was governor of the state, was an enthusiastic participant.[83] The other distinguished Wyoming vigilante was Fennimore Chatterton, an eminent lawyer, a businessman, and a promoter of irrigation projects. Chatterton was governor of Wyoming from 1903 to 1905.[84] Vigilantism in Wyoming, as in all states, was bipartisan; Osborne was a Democrat and Chatterton was a Republican. Undoubtedly the weight of their presence at the lynching of Parrott enhanced public acceptance of the act.

New Mexico, too, had two governors with vigilante backgrounds. Miguel A. Otero, son of a well-to-do merchant (who himself had also been an active vigilante in Kansas and New Mexico), took part in the Las Vegas, New Mexico, vigilante movement of 1881–1882 when he was twenty-two. Becoming one of the most prominent New Mexicans of his time, Otero was governor from 1897 to 1906. In politics he was a Republican and, later, a

Bull Moose Progressive.[85] New Mexico's other vigilante governor was George Curry who had been a member of the Colfax County vigilance committee of 1885. Curry was later a Rough Rider protégé of Theodore Roosevelt and, partly on the basis of that connection, became a provincial governor in the Philippine Islands and the governor of New Mexico from 1907 to 1911. From 1912 to 1913 Curry served as one of New Mexico's first congressmen.[86] The ranks of American vigilantism thus included men who were to gain the highest political positions in territory, state, and nation.

Literary men often wrote in support of vigilantism. Hubert Howe Bancroft, who produced many volumes on Western history and who built his San Francisco publishing house into one of the leading businesses on the Pacific Coast, contributed a vigorous and highly favorable account of the 1851 and 1856 San Francisco vigilance committees in his massive two-volume work, *Popular Tribunals* (1887)—a history that drew upon the recollections of many of Bancroft's elite San Francisco friends who had been vigilantes in younger days.[87] Thomas J. Dimsdale, the English-educated Montana superintendent of public instruction, published a popular and highly laudatory account, *The Vigilantes of Montana*, in 1866 as did Nathaniel Pitt Langford (the father of Yellowstone National Park) later in *Vigilante Days and Ways* (1890), another classic defense of vigilantism.[88] Owen Wister, the socially prominent Harvard graduate and scion of an aristocratic Philadelphia family, strongly praised vigilantism in his immensely popular novel, *The Virginian* (1902),[89] and in so doing summed up the opinion of many elite Americans. Among them was Andrew D. White, university president, historian, and diplomat, who maintained that "there are communities in which lynch law is better than any other." [90]

A leading lawyer who participated in lynch law in Tampa, Florida, on March 6, 1882, was Joseph B. Wall. One of Florida's most prominent attorneys, he played an influential role in a lynching that took place at the doorstep of a sitting federal court. Thirty-five years old at the time, the son of one of the pioneer settlers of Hernando County, Florida, Wall had served in the Confederate army and was a graduate in law from the University of Virginia. In 1872 he had moved to Tampa where he formed a law partnership with H. L. Mitchell, who ultimately became a state supreme court justice and governor of Florida. Wall himself served as state's attorney in Tampa from 1874 to 1878 and in 1880 became a brigadier general of the Florida national guard. By 1882, the year of the lynching, Wall was thus a figure of note in his city and state. Although it caused his disbarment from the federal district court, participation in the lynching did not check his career. In 1886 he was elected to the state senate, and in 1889 he became its president. At home in Tampa he was a large real estate developer and a leader in community affairs.[91] On the morning of the lynching, the United States circuit and district courts of the southern district of Florida were meeting in the courthouse in Tampa with Judge James W. Locke presiding.[92] Locke adjourned the court for the noon meal, and, as he left the building he noticed a prisoner, one "John" (who apparently was a Negro), being brought into the jail. During the noon hour adjournment a mob of 100 persons, including Wall, took the prisoner out of the jail and, over the protests of the sheriff, hanged him from an oak tree in front of the courthouse steps, the victim "hollowing" the while. The judge returned from his meal to find the corpse dangling at the entrance to his court. The next day, acting on the basis of dependable information that Wall had been a member of the crowd, Locke removed him from the bar of his court. Although Wall had been only a passive member of the mob, such was "his influence in this community," Locke charged, "that his presence" was "ample encouragement to others" at the lynching. Locke's disbarment of Wall was upheld by the U. S. Supreme Court when the Tampa attorney appealed it.[93] That the legal profession of Florida saw nothing unseemly in Wall's participation in the lynching was revealed five years later in 1887 when it elected him the first president of the newly founded Florida State Bar Association.[94] Like Wall himself, the majority of Florida's lawyers—like so many other American lawyers of the time—undoubtedly felt that lynch law had a legitimate role at the far, extralegal end of the spectrum of American justice.

IV

Apart from the eminent American lawyers who participated directly in lynch law, there were attorneys and jurists who stated their approval and understanding of the process. At the annual meeting of the Georgia Bar Association, July 1–2, 1897, five leading Georgia lawyers and jurists formed a symposium on the question, "Is lynch law due to defects in the criminal law, or its administration?" Four of the five members of the symposium supported the legitimacy of lynching. They conceded that there were problems in regard to the criminal law and its administration in Georgia but did not see them as crucial factors in regard to lynching. The chief cause, they felt, was simply the rape of white women by Negroes, especially in the rural areas of the state.[95] In effect, the four men (Henry T. Lewis, Burton Smith, Lewis Thomas, and G. P. Munro)[96] excused lynching on the ground that it was the traditional way by which Anglo-Saxons in America and Georgia defended their women against sexual crime. The Negro rapist was lynched, Georgia supreme court justice Henry T. Lewis held, not because "the lynchers have less regard for law and order, but because they have more concern for the sanctity of home and the protection of its inmates." [97]

A more general defense of lynch law was made by one of the most distinguished citizens and jurists of the South, Judge Walter Clark of North Carolina.[98] While serving as an associate justice on the supreme bench of North Carolina in 1894, Clark contributed a strong endorsement of lynch law to the *American Law Review*. Exemplifying Herbert L. Packer's contention that repression of crime rather than maintaining due process is often the chief goal of American lawyers and judges, Clark attacked the defects in American legal procedure and justified lynching: "The cause of lynching is not a spirit of lawlessness. As a rule the men who participate in it wish ardently to enforce justice. The truth is society feels that it must be protected against crime. Whenever society has lost confidence in the promptness and certainty of punishment by the courts, then whenever an offense sufficiently flagrant is committed society will protect itself by a lynching." "The purpose in hanging a man is not to reform him but to deter others," Clark announced. "To have that effect the punishment must be prompt and certain whenever guilt is clear beyond all reasonable doubt. This principle which is so often ignored by the courts," the judge found, "is the one which instinctively actuates lynching mobs." [99]

While generous in his attitude toward lynch law, Clark, at least, had not announced it from the high court upon which he sat. Occasionally, however, judges endorsed or seemed to endorse vigilantism while wearing judicial robes. In doing so their tendency was to grant legitimacy to lynch law in the pioneer period of settlement. Thus Chief Justice H. L. Hosmer of Montana Territory, in an 1864 charge to the grand jury of Montana's first judicial district, began by vigorously saluting the Montana vigilantes of 1863–1864 who had taken nearly 30 lives as "voluntary tribunals of the people partaking more of the nature of self-defence than the comprehensive principles of the Common Law." He lauded the vigilantes as members of an "organization, which, in the absence of law, assumed the delicate and responsible office of purging society of all offenders against its peace, happiness and safety." Vigilante movements, Hosmer said, originated in "necessity" and "have been common of late years in communities without law." Giving the vigilantes a clear stamp of judicial approval, he continued: "Their adaptation to the necessities of new settlements, has obtained for them an approbation so universal, that they are the first measures resorted to, by well intentioned men, to free themselves of that vile class of adventurers which infest all unorganized communities for purposes of fraud, robbery and murder." [100] Hosmer's extravagant praise was a preface to his plea that with the job now "so well done" the methods of vigilantism should be "forever abandoned" so that the law, under Hosmer's own authority, might take its regular course. Far from discouraging vigilante activity, however, Hosmer's praise probably had the opposite effect. Despite Judge Hosmer's plea for its end, vigilante action continued with vigor during the 1860's, and, as late as 1884, a massive vigilante drive in northern and eastern Montana took 35 lives.[101]

A similar tolerant perspective on vigilantism in the early pioneer period informed the opinion by which the U. S. Supreme Court upheld the disbarment of Joseph B. Wall as a result of the Tampa lynching. Justice Joseph P. Bradley, writing the opinion for the court, forthrightly denounced lynching as a "prostration of all law and government; a defiance of the laws; a resort to the methods . . . of those who recognize no law, no society, no government." But later in the opinion Bradley made a Hosmer-like distinction between lynching in a frontier locale and in an old, well-settled area (such as Florida) that, in effect, suggested the propriety of frontier vigilantism. "Whatever excuse," wrote Bradley, "may ever exist for the execution of lynch law in savage or sparsely settled districts, in order to oppose the ruffian elements which the ordinary administration of the law is powerless to control, it certainly has no excuse in a community where the laws are duly and regularly administered." [102] This was at best a guarded and ambiguous endorsement of frontier vigilantism, but that the highest court in the land should even by implication suggest the legitimacy of vigilantism in any time or place is at first glance remarkable. On closer examination, however, it fits easily and significantly into the concept of American justice as a continuum ranging from due process legality to crime repression extralegality.

Moreover, whereas Justice Bradley was from the Eastern non-vigilante state of New Jersey, the court in 1882 did have two Westerners whose background was such as to make them personally familiar with frontier vigilantism: Justice Samuel Miller from Iowa and Justice Stephen J. Field from California. Miller was born in Kentucky in 1816; when he left Kentucky at the age of thirty-four the state continued to harbor regulator movements that must have been known to Miller. Moving to Iowa in 1850, Miller entered that state at the beginning of a turbulent decade in which it had ten active regulator or vigilante movements.[103] Even more disorderly was Justice Field's state of California. During Field's period of California residency from 1849 to 1863 (when he was appointed to the Supreme Court) there were 31 vigilante movements, including the largest and most famous such episode in American history, the San Francisco committee of vigilance of 1856. In California Field went about armed, and, in the words of Robert McCloskey, "it is likely that he enjoyed a fight." [104] As a local judicial official in the violent mining town of Marysville, Field opposed lynch law, but in so doing (see below) he felt obliged to adopt an aspect of vigilantism. Bradley's statement suggesting the propriety of frontier vigilantism probably seemed unexceptionable to both Miller and Field.

Vigilantism had a "feedback" effect upon the legal system of justice. "A frontier society," Roscoe Pound commented, "in which men were prone to set right their own wrongs, conduct feuds, organize vigilance committees, hold lynchings, and exert offhand extra-legal pressure on those whose conduct varied from the locally recognized ethical norm, are in the background of more than one unhappy feature of our criminal justice." [105] Much earlier, in 1837, the English observer, Francis J. Grund, had noted the close relationship between vigilantism and legality: "Lynch law, is not, properly speaking, an opposition to the established laws of the country, or, is at least, not contemplated as such by its adherents; but rather as a supplement to them,—a species of *common* law, which is as old as the country, and which . . . has . . . been productive of some of the happiest results." [106] The feedback effect of vigilantism into the legal administration of the law is illustrated especially well by the early experience of the Supreme Court justice, Stephen J. Field, as a local judge in the gold rush days of California. Field had dissolved his New York law partnership and gone to California in late 1849 where, in the tough mining camp of Marysville, he had been elected to the position of *alcalde*. In the pioneer state of things the *alcalde,* a judicial official with powers similar to those of justice of the peace, assumed virtually unlimited powers to preserve local order,[107] and as *alcalde* Field dealt out quick, effective justice which on occasion turned into illegal, vigilante-type corporal punishment. Thus, after he had conducted a trial that resulted in the conviction of a gold dust thief, there had been "a great crowd and much excitement," Field recalled, "and some talk of lynching. . . . What was to be done with the prisoner? How was he to be punished? Imposing a fine would not answer; and, if he had been discharged, the crowd would have immediately hung him." The prosecution did not have sufficient funds to send him to San Francisco where he could have been securely imprisoned. Nor was it "at all likely that the people would have consented to his removal. Under these circumstances," Field decided, "there was but one course to pursue, and, however repugnant it was to my feelings to adopt it, I believe it was the only thing that saved the man's life. I ordered him to be publicly whipped with fifty lashes, and added that if he were found, within the next two years, in the vicinity of Marysville, he should be again whipped." After the flogging the scamp "went off and never came back." "The sense of justice of the community was satisfied," Field concluded. "There had been no hanging; yet a severe public example had been given." Field's use of illegal whipping had thus worked well, and occasionally in the future he used it again.[108]

By 1906, extralegal punishments had become so routine a part of the "unwritten law" of American justice that a prominent Louisiana attorney, Thomas J. Kernan,[109] was moved to sketch a "jurisprudence of lawlessness" as it really functioned in America. After a Louisiana husband had killed to avenge a verbal insult to his wife, a newspaper had queried Kernan for his views on the extent to which Americans felt justified in taking the law into their own hands. By way of answering, Kernan outlined the following descriptive decalogue of familiar American extralegality:

1. A rapist may be lynched.
2. An adulterous man may be killed by the wronged husband.
3. A seducer of a virgin may be slain.
4. A traducer of a woman may be shot unless he apologizes.
5. The survivor of a fair duel may be acquitted.
6. The killer in a fair fight may be acquitted.
7. The lie direct or an opprobrious epithet justifies assault.
8. In a legal trial an accused horse or stock thief is presumed guilty. (This, Kernan felt, was a legalization, as it were, of the vigilante tradition.)
9. Defendant corporations are presumed guilty in the civil suits of individuals.
10. The presumption is with an employee in a damage suit against an employer.[110]

The last two points of Kernan's table of lawlessness revealed his own bias in favor of the legal position of corporations, an area in which—in contrast to the other eight points—the feedback effect of lynch law was slight.

The impact of vigilantism extended not only to the realm of judicial practice (the young Stephen J. Field) and citizen action (Kernan's "jurisprudence of lawlessness") but also to the conduct of the police. The current controversy over "police brutality" is not a new one. Wide public discussion of the issue was precipitated in 1931 by the National Commission on Law Observance and Law Enforcement, headed by the distinguished attorney and public servant, George W. Wickersham. In its *Report on Lawlessness in Law Enforcement*, the commission found use of the "third degree—that is, the use of physical brutality, or other forms of cruelty, to obtain involuntary confessions or admissions"—to be "widespread." Illegal detention, refusal to allow access of counsel to the prisoner, and violence and brutality in arrests were also found to be common police practices.[111] Drawing in part on the Wickersham Commission investigation, Ernest J. Hopkins published in 1931 a study of what amounted to police vigilantism. Hopkins condemned "direct-action police work" as a response to the "war theory of crime control." Direct-action police work involved the use of overt illegal methods by police. It was not the result, Hopkins believed, of the modern crime problem but had been "well ingrained" in American police work for a long time. Both the judiciary and the police acted all too frequently on the vigilante-like theory that the public was in a war against crime, and, hence, any action taken against it was justified. "Judicial acceptance of direct-action police work means, simply," Hopkins wrote, "that we tend to abandon the basic right of individuals under pressure of crime as we did under pressure of war—but more subtly, and permanently." Both the police and the public united against the criminal in a spirit that was reminiscent of vigilantism and lynch law: "My oath of office requires me to protect this community," a Buffalo, New York, police official declared and then added, "If I have to violate that oath of office or violate the Constitution, I'll violate the Constitution." In effect, the police behaved almost as vigilante agents of the citizens, for, as Hopkins said, "Police brutality, in short, is less a matter of the individual policeman than of the [community] sanctions behind him." [112]

The influence of vigilantism and lynch law on the legal illuminati was exemplified at the close of the nineteenth century by the reform pleas of three ornaments of the Northeastern legal establishment, Charles J. Bonaparte, David J. Brewer, and Simeon E. Baldwin. Using the *Yale Law Journal* as his forum, Bonaparte called in early 1899 for drastic changes in the criminal law, which would, in short, have legalized a quasi-lynch law. Born in 1851, Charles J. Bonaparte graduated from Harvard College (1872) and Harvard Law School (1874). By the time he turned his attention to "Lynch Law and Its Remedy" in 1899, Bonaparte had long since established himself as a prominent Baltimore lawyer and civil service reformer. He had become a friend of Theodore Roosevelt, and the high regard Roosevelt had for him would eventuate in his appointment as secretary of the navy in 1905 and attorney general in 1906. Always of a progressive bent, Bonaparte was founder of a leading reform organization, the National Municipal League, and in 1912 he supported his old political chief, Theodore Roosevelt, in his Progressive party candidacy for president.[113]

Hence, it was with impeccable social, educational, legal, political, and progressive credentials that the "patrician reformer" Bonaparte addressed the subject of legal and extralegal justice in the *Yale Law Journal*. For some years Bonaparte had been well disposed toward lynching. In 1890 he had addressed the graduating class of the Yale Law School on "The Strength and Weakness of Popular Government in the United States." In the course of his remarks Bonaparte commented on the "much misjudged custom of lynching." "Judge Lynch," he said, "may make mistakes, and his mistakes can be corrected by no writ of error, but if the number of failures of justice in his Court could be compared with those in our more regular tribunals, I am not sure that he need fear the result. I believe that very few innocent men are lynched, and, of those who have not committed the past offense for which they suffer, a still smaller proportion are decent members of society. It is, of course, an evil that the law should be occasionally enforced by lawless means, but it is, in my opinion, a greater evil that it should be habitually duped and evaded by means formally lawful." [114]

In the *Yale Law Journal* Bonaparte noted the close connection between lynching, vigilance committees, Regulators, and White Caps, and sounded a familiar theme: "The underlying purpose in all these cases is not to violate, but to vindicate, the law; or to speak more accurately, the law is violated in form that it may be vindicated in substance, its 'adjective' part (*i.e.*, matter of procedure) is disregarded that its 'substantive' part may be preserved." [115] Delving into the ancient lore of the law, Bonaparte cited Bracton, Fleta, Britton, and Glanville as evidence that in olden times "in some cases of violent presumption" summary execution was legitimate. One of the functions of justice, Bonaparte claimed, had been to determine whether a trial, or, in effect, a lynching should occur. Two or three hundred years before, the legal system had made executions painful as a result of man's vengeful feelings, Bonaparte asserted. The sentiment of vengefulness he saw surviving in lynching. By reference to ancient legal practice and tradition Bonaparte had sought to clothe lynching with a dignity not always given it, but in regard to the contemporary problem of crime prevention Bonaparte was unabashed in his praise of lynching. He found lynchers to be sound in their instinct to do away with incorrigibly recidivistic persons whom, he felt, no amount of penal discipline would ever restore to legal behavior.[116]

To get at the twin problem of crime prevention and lynching, Bonaparte proposed a "remedy" for lynching that would, by making the criminal law more effective and realistic, forestall lynch law. Bonaparte's suggested "reforms" adopted the spirit and some of the simplicities of lynch law. Bonaparte wanted to do away with uncertainties stemming from procedure by abolishing grand juries, instituting elite petit juries, excising the peremptory challenge for jurymen, and doing away with the double jeopardy prohibition when based on the law error of a trial court. He favored also the abandonment of technical impediments (such as the term of a court) to the trial of the accused. Bonaparte's bias as a progressive civil service reformer became evident when he cuttingly asked that public prosecutors be competent and upright lawyers, not venal politicians oriented toward the criminal. He advocated, as well, the removal of the pardoning power from the executive branch to the judicial in order to prevent its abuse. The most drastic of Bonaparte's proposed reforms was one that would have introduced a measure of judicial lynch law into the system. This was a provision whose aim was the utter "extirpation" of habitual criminals. Here Bonaparte asked for an increase in the number of capital offenses, and he recommended that the death sentence be imposed upon the third conviction for a "serious" offense. In Bonaparte's view, serious offenses were felonies or "such misdemeanours as argue exceptionally great depravity or involve grave injury or danger to society."[117] That a man with such views became attorney general of the United States only seven years after expressing them is believable when one notes that he was appointed by a president who had sought as a young man to become a part of the vigilante movement—a desire he never repudiated.[118] But in later years both Roosevelt and Bonaparte were interested in other things, and Bonaparte's chief impact as attorney general was not in criminal law but in trust-busting.[119]

Another prominent member of the turn-of-the-century legal establishment who proposed drastic procedural reform was Justice David J. Brewer of the Supreme Court. Brewer was a nephew of

Stephen J. Field, and, like Field, his service on the Supreme Court was prefaced by a judicial stint in a Western state in which vigilantism thrived. While Brewer resided in Kansas from 1858 to 1889 there were 19 vigilante movements. On the U. S. Supreme Court from 1890 to 1910 Brewer was a highly conservative jurist of staunch social darwinist views.[120] In 1903, Brewer aroused controversy by his call for the abolition of the *right* of appeal in criminal cases as a means of "checking the fearful habit of lynching." "Is it strange," asked Brewer, "that a community incensed by some atrocious offense, aware of the common experience of [delay in] criminal proceedings, takes the law into its own hands and summarily punishes the offender?" [121] Like Bonaparte, Brewer tended to seek the cure in the malady, for, in abolishing the right of appeal, Brewer would have brought into legal justice one of the salient characteristics of lynch law: its irrevocability. Brewer, however, did make a careful distinction that modified to some extent the severity of his suggested reform. He emphasized that he did not wish to do away entirely with appellate court reviews of trial court decisions. Instead of appeal being a matter of *right* he desired that "whether there be a review with the consequent delay should be determined by the Appellate Court in the exercise of a sound discretion, upon fixed rules, and not upon the will of the beaten party." [122]

Even more vivid than Bonaparte's plea for the execution of serious offenders, or Brewer's call for erasure of the right of appeal, was Judge Simeon E. Baldwin's appeal in 1899 for the legalization of whipping and castration. Aside from the savagery of the punishments advocated, Baldwin's program was a sensational one because of his high standing in American life. Possessed of the weightiest achievements and honors in academic, legal, judicial, and political life, Simeon E. Baldwin, "Connecticut's first citizen," was one of the most distinguished Americans of his time. Born in 1840, Baldwin studied law at Yale and Harvard and in 1869 joined the Yale law faculty, a position he held until 1919. A most successful lawyer, he also served as a Connecticut superior court judge before joining the Connecticut Supreme Court in 1894. He remained on the state supreme court until 1910, eventually becoming its chief justice. During the 1870's and 1880's he was prominent in the movement to simplify Connecticut legal procedure. Baldwin was an active member of many legal and learned societies and was honored with the presidency of several of them including the International Law Association (1889), American Social Science Association (1897), Association of American Law Schools (1902), American Historical Association (1905), and the American Political Science Association (1910). He had been a founder of the American Bar Association and gained its presidency in 1890. The climactic honor of a life filled with distinctions came with his election to two terms as governor of Connecticut, 1910–1914.[123]

Simeon E. Baldwin was a participant in the movement that got under way in the 1880's to legalize whipping. Delaware had never forsaken the punishment, but, by the middle of the nineteenth century, all other states and the federal government had outlawed it. Maryland reinstated whipping in 1882 as a penalty for wife beaters, and from 1885 to 1887 the American Bar Association considered the suitability of whipping as a punishment. In 1885, the New York lawyer and former Reconstruction governor of South Carolina, Daniel H. Chamberlain,[124] presented to the American Bar Association a resolution calling for a study of whipping and its desirability. The resolution was referred to a committee consisting of Baldwin, Henry Hitchcock of St. Louis,[125] and Skipwith Wilmer of Baltimore. The committee, no doubt influenced by Baldwin's views, reported favorably on whipping in 1886. The Association debated extensively a resolution in favor of whipping in 1887 but, in effect, killed it by voting 63–28 to table it.[126] It is noteworthy that the movement to legalize whipping became spirited at the time— the 1880's and 1890's—the White Caps were using whipping all over the country as an extralegal punishment for wife beating, immorality, shiftlessness, and petty thievery—precisely the sort of small offense against which the movement to legalize whipping was mainly directed.[127]

The campaign to legalize whipping had been reinvigorated in 1898 by Virginia's passage of a law to provide whipping for juvenile offenders, and to Simeon Baldwin the time doubtless seemed right to argue once again for the legalization of whipping on a broader scale. To promote his views, he turned to the pages of the *Yale Law Journal* in 1899 shortly after Bonaparte had used the same magazine to praise lynch law and promote the execution of serious offenders. Baldwin's agenda for reform of the criminal law was more restricted than Bonaparte's and of a wholly different nature from Brewer's, but in calling for castration as well as whipping Baldwin—then an associate justice of the Connecticut Supreme Court—went beyond either of them.

Judge Baldwin advocated whipping in place of fine or imprisonment for "young offenders," for molestation of female children, and "for some minor offenses by full grown men." [128] He based his position on the principle that "retributive justice" was sanctioned by St. Paul in the Bible (*Romans*, xiii, 4) and that the "human sanction" should be added to the divine—"the sentence of the courts to the sentence of the conscience and the community." "The nature of things," he continued in a darwinian tone, "would seem to require that he who strikes shall be struck back." This, Baldwin claimed, "is the rule of reason for the administration of justice." To support his advocacy of whipping in place of fine or imprisonment Baldwin cited, as vigilantes had so often, the economic factor. Imprisonment for minor offenses had "added enormously," he said, to the cost of government. And in a slap at the correctional system Baldwin charged that jailing had "taken thousands . . . of people from their natural surroundings and opportunities for profitable industry" and had shut them up in an artificial, unnatural, and usually immoral atmosphere. To this Baldwin added the common—and apparently fallacious—argument that whipping reduced recidivism.[129]

Baldwin's call for castration of convicted rapists was motivated partly by his desire to salvage the dignity of the law that, by 1899, had been buffeted by the lynching of hundreds of Negroes for rape—lynchings that had come increasingly to include castration and unspeakable tortures. After citing precedents for castration for rape in European and early American law, Baldwin fell back on the need to invest the illegal but popular penalty of emasculation with the dignity of the law. "Is it too much to say," he asked, "that if the courts are not ready to apply these, the people will?" It would be more appropriate, he contended, for the courts to inflict the penalty of castration, since the people—and not "the best people"—would lynch the offender anyway and "probably rush into acts of savage cruelty." Baldwin sought to depict castration as a humanitarian reform on the ground that it did not take life whereas lynching did.

Influenced, perhaps, by the eugenic theories of the day,[130] Baldwin also argued that castration would not only be an absolute prevention of the future crime of rape by the convicted but would "end the line of a family which is misusing the earth." Baldwin was not alone in favoring castration. He noted that "some years ago" a delegation of District of Columbia ladies headed by the wife of then Chief Justice Morrison R. Waite petitioned Congress to adopt castration as a District punishment for rape. He cited, too, the approving view of John Hooker, former reporter of the Connecticut Supreme Court (a man of "humane temperament and philanthropy"), as well as a recent contribution to the Women's Christian Temperance Union magazine by a Dr. Thomas D. Crothers of Hartford.[131]

That a man of Simeon E. Baldwin's undoubted learning and benevolence should unashamedly advocate the cruelty of whipping and the atrocity of castration is an indication, in part, of the way in which the prevalence of lynch law and vigilantism in the nineteenth century had brutalized attitudes and shaped the area of debate. Although more extreme than most, the views of Baldwin, Brewer, and Bonaparte were symptomatic of the impact vigilantism and lynch law had made by the end of the nineteenth century on American legal thought.

Part IV

VIOLENT PATHS TO THE PRESENT

THE TWO MOST NOTABLE EPISODES of violence in our generation have been the massive black ghetto riots of the 1960's and the direct American participation in the Vietnam war, 1965–1973. To place both episodes in perspective, the historical background of each must be considered: the centuries of violence marking relations between blacks and whites in America and the central Texas origins of Lyndon B. Johnson, the major protagonist of the American role in the Vietnam war.

The historical context of the burst of black ghetto rioting in the 1960's is to be found in the courageous but, with the striking exception of the Florida Maroons, usually unsuccessful black insurgencies in the slavery period, in the pre-1960 Northern and Southern riots and the post-Civil War Southern lynchings by which whites forcefully kept free blacks in a subordinate position, and in the demographic revolution of the twentieth century (the aggregation of blacks in huge urban enclaves) with the accompanying surge of black consciousness so basic to the black violence of the 1960's.

Attention to the local roots of Lyndon B. Johnson indicates much about the nature of American violence as well as the genesis of U. S. military intervention in Vietnam, for the history of central Texas provides a microcosm of rampant American disorder. The historical conditions making the people of central Texas especially prone to violence fostered a regional ethic of violent self-defense (and self-redress) serving to reinforce the general tendency to violent behavior initiated by such factors as the Civil War and Reconstruction, Indian warfare, frontier turbulence, community feuding, cattle industry conflict, and racial hostility. The production of violence in central Texas through the interaction of historical conditions and behavioral patterns affords a regional example, as did the old Back Country of South Carolina (Chapter 3), of the way in which violence has often become endemic in America.

LIVING TOGETHER VIOLENTLY: BLACKS AND WHITES IN AMERICA FROM THE COLONIAL PERIOD TO 1970

The history of the American Negro is the history of . . . [the] longing to attain self-conscious manhood . . . .

William E. B. DuBois

The decisive and pivotal centers of Negro life in America are to be found in our northern industrial cities . . . .

Richard Wright, introduction to
Drake and Cayton, *Black Metropolis*

What produces riots is the shared agreement by most Negro Americans that their lot in life is unacceptable, coupled with the view by a significant minority that riots are a legitimate and productive mode of protest.

T. M. Tomlinson, "The Development of
a Riot Ideology among Urban Negroes"

A̲s this chapter is being completed, racial violence has flared up in Boston,[1] the cradle of American abolitionism. Despite its notable history as a stronghold for the promotion of black freedom and opportunity, this is not, however, the first time that Boston has experienced violence between whites and blacks.[2] The ambiguous history of race relations in Boston illustrates the paradox of the title above, "Living Together Violently: Blacks and Whites in America from the Colonial Period to 1970." Indeed, the title suggests a question: Can a violent life really be a meaningful life? Yes, it can, under particular conditions, for, the strain of violence aside, the central truth of black-white relations in America is that whites and blacks have endured together for more than three and one-half centuries.[3] But it has been a stormy endurance—for most of this long period an existence of unhappy duress for blacks, a duress habitually enforced by acts of white violence and the even more constant threat of violence—a duress periodically shattered by desperate, usually fruitless insurgent black violence.

The violent travail of white-black relations is the subject of this chapter, not the far more numerous—and ultimately more significant—contacts of constructive relationship. Yet, the violence in our race relations stands, historically, as an index of the difficulty of achieving in this country a mutually satisfactory life for blacks and whites together in the face of all that has served to divide them. The following study of black-white violence concludes with a treatment of the widespread black ghetto riots of the 1960's, the greatest wave of racial violence yet experienced by America. Crucial to the surge of black violence in the riots of the 1960's was a concurrent rise of ghetto-based black consciousness and pride the like of which the country had not seen. Ironically, the revolution in black consciousness and pride that underlay the riots of the 1960's may have, in the long run, more important nonviolent consequences for positive relations between the white and the black races. The heightened racial self-identity gained by blacks during this period may yield—and probably already has yielded—an increased respect for blacks by whites (as well as a greater black pride) necessary for constructive race relations unmarred by hatred, bitterness, and the extreme emotions of superiority and subordination.

Since the establishment of slavery in the colonial period, three major phases of black-white violence stand out: (1) an initial phase of sporadic black revolts (and plots for revolt) during the long period of slavery; (2) a middle, long-term era of mainly white initiated violence (riots and lynching, especially) carried out to maintain post-slavery white supremacy in America; and (3) the recent 1960's cycle of massive ghetto riots in reaction to the deprivations suffered by blacks in the United States. All three phases have been closely connected to the demographic character of black life in America. Despite heavy concentrations of blacks in certain rural areas during the slavery period, blacks were greatly outnumbered by whites in the over-all population of America. Realization of their cumulative numerical inferiority made blacks wary of the highly risky strategy of slave revolt in noteworthy contrast to the actions of slaves in the Caribbean region and South America where a much more favorable black-white population ratio brought success to many slave uprisings.[4] With the end of slavery the demographic situation did not alter significantly: in totality, blacks were still overwhelmingly the minority in this country. The dismantling of the slavery system with its militaristic, authoritarian apparatus for the control of blacks did leave an instrumental void in the maintenance of white supremacy, which an aroused white population successfully sought to fill with a century-long campaign of riots, lynching, and Ku Klux Klan violence. By the middle of the twentytieth century, a major demographic change had occurred. The minority status of the black population did not significantly change, but its distribution did. In contrast to slavery and post-slavery times, black people were now heavily concentrated in enormous urban enclaves, which were formidable enough to preclude the customary untrammeled punitive violence with which whites had kept blacks in subordination. Instead, for the first time in American history, blacks became violent aggressors on a large scale with the shattering black ghetto riots of the middle and late 1960's.

I

During slavery, despite deep black resentment of bondage, there were only seven major black uprisings or planned slave revolts: two New York City affairs, 1712 and 1741; the Stono slave revolt of 1739 in South Carolina; the Gabriel Prosser plot for a slave rebellion in Virginia in 1800; the Louisiana slave uprising of 1811; the plot for a slave revolt in South Carolina headed by Denmark

Vesey in 1822; and Nat Turner's rebellion in Virginia, 1831. None of the four actual uprisings (New York City, 1712; Stono, 1739; Louisiana, 1811; and Nat Turner's, 1831) gained anything more than the most temporary success before succumbing to the forces of massive white suppression, whereas the Gabriel Prosser and Denmark Vesey plots for mass urban uprisings were nipped in the bud after whites were warned by black informers.

The failure of black uprisings in America is in contrast to the success of many such efforts in the West Indies and South America. Among the most notable of the black rebellions in the latter areas were the black runaways' "Republic of Palmares" in Brazil, 1630–1697, as well as other uprisings in Brazil on into the nineteenth century;[5] the Bush Negroes of eighteenth-century Surinam who fled in rebellion into the jungle back country and replicated their pre-slavery African existence in belligerent seclusion,[6] as well as the ferociously insurgent slaves of British Guiana and Venezuela;[7] the Maroons and other rebels of Jamaica;[8] and, most dramatically of all for their impact on the white (and perhaps the black) consciousness of America, the triumphant slave revolutionaries in St. Domingo, 1791–1804.[9] The black rebels elsewhere in the Western Hemisphere do not seem to have been any more avid for their freedom than were the enslaved blacks of the United States, but the former rose in the context of more favorable black-white population ratios than were to be found in America. For example, in St. Domingo, the huge slave population outnumbered whites and free mulattoes and free blacks ten to one.[10] In the much smaller colony of Dutch Guiana (Surinam), the white population was too small for successful action against the escaped slaves in their interior refuge.[11] The thirteen to one black-white ratio of Jamaica in the era of British colonial control was such that, although some slave rebellions were repulsed, others—headed by the fierce Maroon rebels—were successful.[12] In contrast to the frequent large slave majorities in the Caribbean and South America, the reverse was true in the ante-bellum American South: only two states—South Carolina and Mississippi—had a majority of slaves, and the majorities were slight in both cases, while the two states that had the largest minorities (44 to 47 per cent) were counterpointed by the nine others whose slave minorities ranged from only 1.5 to 33 per cent.[13]

Focusing on the United States alone, it is evident that the slaves' demographic handicap limited their resistance to the white masters. There is much to indicate that in the eighteenth-century formative period of American slavery the African agrarian background, village existence, and premodern world view prepared blacks for a successful adjustment to comparable agricultural livelihoods on the plantations and to life in the slave quarters.[14] But accommodation to slavery did not mean acceptance of it. "In fact," announces Eugene D. Genovese in his monumental new study of American slavery, *Roll, Jordan, Roll*, "accommodation itself breathed a critical spirit" and "might best be understood as a way of accepting what could not be helped without falling prey to the pressures for dehumanization, emasculation, and self-hatred."[15]

Thus, blacks resisted slavery constantly throughout the existence of the institution but in ways that were often subtle and not understood even by their white masters. Because of the over-all black demographic disadvantage, the success of black resistance varied inversely with the amount of the violence. The most pervasive resistance to slavery was actually nonviolent in the form of a cumulative, spontaneous, unorganized slowdown of slave labor; slaves loafed at their tasks, worked carelessly and inefficiently, committed acts of sabotage, and malingered.[16] Such resistance was indirect, implicit; there was no direct challenge to the slavery system. Resistance did, however, become overt in countless acts of low level violence against slavery. As the black historian, John W. Blassingame, has written, "hundreds of slaves . . . ran away from their masters, assaulted, robbed, poisoned and murdered whites, burned their master's dwellings," and "hundreds more fought whites in self-defense and were guilty of insubordination." Slaves also "were often unruly, refused to learn trades, and burned plantation buildings in retaliation for mistreatment." [17] Based upon an analysis of a published compendium of court records, Blassingame's statement undoubtedly understates the amount of low level violent resistance to slavery, since thousands upon thousands of low level individual actions (assault, murder, arson, and running away) surely remain unrecorded or hidden in records unquantified by historians.

Still, the amount and degree of organized violent resistance to slavery should by no means be minimized. The revolts and authenticated plots for revolts (that did not take place) were the tip of the iceberg of black rejection of slavery. Although relatively few and far between, the uprisings that did occur were understood by both whites and blacks to be an index of unremitting Negro hostility to slavery. White fear of black rebellion, in fact, greatly exceeded the actual rebellions. In the heavily black plantation districts from the colonial period on, whites lived in fear of black insurgence. The point that blacks were in the over-all minority in America was scant comfort to those whites who lived on plantations in sectors where the black population was weightily in ascendance. All knew that a sudden slave uprising would over-whelm the luckless whites immediately in the path of the rebels; this happened in the Stono revolt of 1739, the 1811 Louisiana outburst, and the Nat Turner rebellion of 1831. The psychology of the situation was that at all times whites, surrounded by their restive black chattels, lived in a profound unease that, on no few occasions, rose to the level of hysteria—notably in Mississippi in 1835[18] and all through the deep South in the summer of 1860[19] as well as in the aftermaths of the Gabriel Prosser and Denmark Vesey plots and the Stono, Louisiana, and Nat Turner uprisings.

There were at least forty-three significant actual slave revolts or aborted slave revolts from the seventeenth century to the time of the Civil War. Of these events, twenty-nine were conspiracies that were prevented by white vigilance or black betrayal from reaching the point of actual rebellion, whereas fourteen were real uprisings.[20] All forty-three affairs are listed in Appendix 4. Among the forty-three planned or actual insurgencies there were, as noted above, four major rebellions (New York City, 1712; Stono, 1739; Louisiana, 1811; Nat Turner, 1831) and three major conspiracies (New York City, 1741; Richmond, 1800; Charleston, 1822).

The first of these major events was the New York City insurrection on the night of April 6, 1712. About twenty slaves set a fire and then killed nine whites and wounded others. The whites of New York believed that only the presence of a British military contingent saved the inhabitants from massacre and the city from being burned to the ground. In the aftermath the process of investigation, trial, and conviction suggests that at least a score more slaves took part in the enterprise. The legal retaliation was the most brutal ever levied upon American slave rebels and slave conspirators, not in the number executed (eighteen—a figure exceeded later) but in the horrid character of the executions: in addition to the thirteen victims who received the normal fate of hanging, one was starved to death in manacles, three were burned at the stake, and one was broken on the wheel. In the face of such medieval retribution it is not surprising that six rebels forestalled execution by committing suicide.[21]

A generation later, New York City succumbed to an even greater hysteria—the worst ever to occur in America as the result of a slave rebellion, actual or planned. An outbreak of fires in New York City in 1741 (in a climate of white anxiety fed not only by memories of the insurrection of 1712 but by slave unrest in neighboring New Jersey) led to a probe that ultimately gained sixty-seven slave confessions and renewed the specter of 1712: a slave conspiracy (this time allegedly assisted by ne'er-do-well whites) for the burning of the city and the slaughter of its residents. The confessions were undoubtedly tainted by the duress under which they were obtained and the terror of the times for the accused, but a reasonable conclusion is that white fears (although surely exaggerated) of a slave insurgency were well founded. In any case, the convicted slaves paid a terrible price, whether guilty or not: eighteen were hanged (as were four whites) and thirteen, in the manner of 1712, died in flames at the stake. An additional seventy slaves were exiled to the West Indies, and in all, one hundred and fifty slaves (and twenty-five whites) fell afoul of the remorseless New York justice.

With the waning of slavery in the North, the major slave rebellions and conspiracies were all to be found in the South. The earliest there was South Carolina's Stono Rebellion of 1739, which appears to have followed a large importation of new Negro slaves from Africa (historians have viewed newly arrived Africans as having been particularly prone to insurrection in America and elsewhere). The rebel core seems to have been made up of Angolans led by one Jemmy. The outbreak came on the Stono River in St. Paul's Parish about 20 miles from Charleston on the morning of Sunday, September 9, 1739. The rising was well planned. Despite the proximity to Charleston, the capital of the province, the slaves had no designs on the city. Instead, their objective was to escape to Florida where the Spanish authorities had promised freedom to fugitive Carolina slaves. The rebels realized that they would have to fight their way out of South Carolina, and this they attempted. Once under way they marched in order with two drums beating, a flag flying, and repeated shouts of "Liberty." They burned and plundered plantations and stores and killed more than 20 whites as they moved toward the crossing of the Edisto River at Jacksonborough Ferry. Here the approximately 60 to 100 insurrectionaries were met by a force of about the same number of whites rallied by Lieutenant Governor William Bull (who happened to be in the vicinity when the rebellion broke out) and a local leader, the Reverend Archibald Stobo. The white attack shattered the slave force; at least 14 slaves were killed, and it was said that as an example to the plantation slaves the whites "cutt off their heads and set them up at every Mile Post they came to." But this was not the end. About 30 rebels escaped the slaughter at Jacksonborough Ferry, and a remnant had gotten 30 miles closer to Florida a week later when whites caught and overwhelmed it. Still, there were fugitive rebels and sporadic guerrilla-type attacks on whites for about another six months thereafter. The coda to the Stono uprising came a year later with a black plan for a large-scale rebellion north of Charleston in the parish of St. John's Berkeley. The whites got wind of it and executed at least 50 plotters. The Stono Rebellion with its features of "total surprise, ruthless killing, considerable property damage, armed engagements, [and] protracted aftermath" was a traumatic experience for white South Carolinians. They reacted by legislating the Negro Act of 1740, a harsh, systematic curtailment of slave liberties and privileges, which remained the core of South Carolina's rigid system of slave control right down to the time of the Civl War.[22]

Little is known of the Louisiana slave rebellion of 1811, but the scanty evidence indicates that it was our largest slave revolt.[23] This insurrection was similar to the Stono Rebellion and the later Nat Turner uprising. The scenario of a sudden outbreak put down within forty-eight hours held in all three cases. In Louisiana the revolt started on the night of January 8, 1811, in the plantation country of St. Charles and St. John the Baptist parishes about 35 miles from New Orleans. Some 400 to 500 slaves took part, the largest force of rebellious slaves in American history. They first overwhelmed the plantation of one Major Andry and then, with guns, drums, and flags, and supposedly under the leadership of, among others, Charles Deslondes, a free mulatto refugee from St. Domingo, commenced ravaging plantation after plantation as white refugees streamed toward the safety of New Orleans. Meanwhile, Governor William C. C. Claiborne and others swiftly mounted a counterattack. Hundreds of militia men in two forces from New Orleans and Baton Rouge converged on the rebels and struck them on the morning of January 10, smashing the insurgent band and killing or executing sixty-six of the revolutionaries on the spot. Mopping up—at times out of control—of the shattered rebels continued for at least a week thereafter, and disturbances further up the Mississippi River were put down by military force. Sixteen of the captured rebels headed by a slave, Gilbert, were tried and executed in New Orleans. As in the earlier days of Stono, "their heads were strung aloft at intervals from New Orleans to Andry's plantation." It appears that white casualties were light (at least two whites were killed but apparently no more), yet property damage was high. The "ferocious sanguinary" white reaction testified to the trauma felt by the Louisiana slaveholding class, and for the year following the district of the revolt was troubled with apprehensions of more insurrectionary activity.[24]

The still somewhat mysterious rural Louisiana uprising of 1811 was bracketed in time—a decade hence and a decade after—by two great conspiracies for urban slave revolts: that of Gabriel Prosser in Richmond, Virginia, 1800, and that of Denmark Vesey in Charleston, South Carolina, 1822. The similarities between the Richmond and Charleston plots are striking, and, as will be seen, the complex, urbanized society in which each conspiracy grew afforded, for the black rebel planners, a frustrating contradiction in terms: on the one hand *sophisticated, skilled slaves and free blacks of the urban community* capitalized on their intellectual and ideological resources in the plotting of their ventures, but, on the other hand, *the complexity of the urban black community* with all its anxieties, confusions, and dissonances was such that, in each case, Negro turncoats betrayed the black rebellions to their white masters.

Gabriel Prosser's conspiracy for a slave insurrection in Richmond and environs was a product of the citified, riverine, relatively open society of Richmond and tidewater Virginia. The leaders of the conspiracy comprised an urbanized black elite assimilated to

American culture. Well treated and quite independent, even though slaves, these conspirators yet coveted freedom. They were acculturated enough to American society to have absorbed the libertarian ideology of the American revolutionary era. Utopian in retrospect, their goal was a political one: to capture Richmond and then negotiate for and gain their freedom whereupon they would take their place in Virginian and American society as free citizens.

The conspiracy was centered in Richmond and its outskirts, but it stretched from Gloucester County on Chesapeake Bay to the Piedmont uplands of Albemarle and Cumberland counties. The plan was that 200 blacks would, on August 30, 1800, assault Richmond at midnight, but the leaders hoped for an uprising of from 3,000 to 10,000 Negroes all the way from tidewater to the Piedmont. Not until the day before the projected rebellion did the whites at last (after the slaves and some free blacks had kept their plans a secret all summer) gain knowledge of the plot through Negro informers. A heavy rain forced the plotters to postpone the rebellion one day, and this, too, helped save the whites from the onslaught.

Gerald W. Mullin, the leading authority, feels that the plot of Gabriel Prosser and his followers failed because it did not sufficiently enlist the plantation field slaves who were less assimilated to the dominant white culture. These slaves might have been reached, so Mullin contends, through a religious appeal that would have drawn on the fairly primitive slave religion that was, broadly, a syncretism of African and Christian elements. One of the leaders of the conspiracy was George Smith who did make a religious appeal but who failed to really integrate it into the call for insurrection by the elite black rebel leaders headed by Gabriel Prosser. The latter was both the chief and typical of the instigators of the projected uprising. Gabriel Prosser was a skilled worker, a blacksmith on the plantation of his well-to-do master, Thomas H. Prosser, located not far outside of Richmond. Other skilled occupations found among the leading black conspirators were those of coal miner, iron founder, ropemaker, boatman, warehouseman, and postman, and there were such domestic workers as waiter, janitor, custodian, and houseman. As soon as Governor James Monroe got wind of the planned uprising he quickly took steps to suppress it, with the upshot being that, of about forty slaves arrested, about twenty (including Gabriel Prosser, "the Main Spring and Chief Mover") were executed.[25]

Twenty-two years after the abortive revolt in Richmond there was a second vast conspiracy for an urban slave uprising in the great South Atlantic metropolis of Charleston, South Carolina. The leader of the Charleston plot was a literate, prosperous free Negro, Denmark Vesey who in 1822 was a respected 55-year-old carpenter. Born in either Africa or the West Indies, Denmark Vesey had been a Charleston resident for 40 years and a free man since 1800. Despite his prosperity Vesey had a grievance: his wife (and also his children) were the slaves of a white man. Moreover, Vesey had been much affected by the example of the successful St. Domingo uprising two decades earlier and also by the much more recent antislavery statements made in Congress during the Missouri Compromise (1820) debate, which he had followed closely in the newspapers.

Hence, in 1822 Vesey began planning an enormous slave rebellion. Among his chief lieutenants were Peter Poyas and Gullah Jack, with the latter, Gullah Jack, making a mystical appeal to the superstitious plantation slaves of the Charleston area. The religious aspect, although not dominant, was significant for the conspiracy. In addition to the sway of Gullah Jack, there was much quoting of scripture and preaching by Vesey in the meetings held to plan the insurgency. At the core of the plot, however, were elite slaves and free Negroes of Charleston and environs who, like Vesey (and like earlier plotters in the Prosser conspiracy in Richmond), were often skilled and literate persons. The plot may have included as many as 9,000 blacks (mostly slaves but with a significant contingent of Charleston's free Negroes) and was said to have extended as far east in South Carolina as Georgetown, as far north as the parish of St. John's Berkeley, and as far west as the Combahee River.

The rebellion was set for July 14, 1822, a Sunday, with seven separate forces from inside and outside Charleston slated to capture the city. There was to be a general massacre of whites. After Charleston was secured, it was to serve as the center of a wide uprising in South Carolina or, alternatively, the rebels would gain freedom by commandeering shipping for transportation to the black republic of Haiti that had been created by the victorious St. Domingo slave insurgents. Indeed, the model for the revolution planned by Vesey was the St. Domingo uprising and its capture and destruction of the capital, Cap Francais, in 1793. But in May, 1822, a slave informer revealed the plot to the white hierarchy of Charleston. When the plotters learned that their secret was known, Vesey decided to shift the revolt back to Sunday, June 16, but this, too, had to be canceled when white officials brought massive reinforcements into the city on the weekend of June 15–16. The arrests began on June 18, and Vesey—detained on June 22—was speedily tried, convicted, and hanged. During the ensuing summer the courts were busy in Charleston, with the result, ultimately, that a total of 35 accused blacks were executed, with 42 more blacks banished from South Carolina.

As in the case of Gabriel Prosser's conspiracy in Richmond, a generation earlier, the Denmark Vesey plot drew upon the sophisticated, urbanized black slaves and freemen of the complex secular and religious black community of Charleston and its suburbs. Thus, the skilled or semi-skilled occupations of carter, drayman, sawyer, porter, stevedore, mechanic, lumber worker, and carpenter were represented among the plot's leadership. Yet, unlike Prosser and Richmond in 1800, the Vesey plot seems to have had a considerably broader rank-and-file base among the plantation slaves of the outlying area. This was probably due in large part to Gullah Jack whose chief value was "his great sway over the superstitious [plantation] slaves who regarded him as a conjuror with the power to both charm and curse." Gullah Jack operated within a "Gullah Society which met regularly and whose members were bound to Jack by a shrewd combination of magic and discipline." But all came to naught. The careful planning, organization, and preaching of Vesey and the religious appeal of Gullah Jack were wiped out by a slave informer.[26]

The otherworldly element, whether in terms of orthodox Christianity or surviving African religious traditions or syncretisms of the two, was a key factor in the planning of black rebellions. In this connection, Gerald W. Mullin has noted a spectrum of religious motivation in the three great planned slave uprisings in the nineteenth century: from (1) the almost wholly secular plot of Gabriel Prosser to (2) the Denmark Vesey design with its dominantly urbanized, worldly base that was, however, significantly tinctured by the conjures of Gullah Jack and the preaching of

Vesey himself to (3) the only one of the three that was carried through from planning to action: Nat Turner's messianic, religiously focused revolt in Southampton County, Virginia. Ultimately Denmark Vesey failed declares Mullin, because "like Gabriel . . . his rebellion was" at its core "urban-based and restricted to artisans, shopkeepers, and free Negroes. Only Nat Turner, who charged his plan with supernatural signs, and sacred, poetic language that inspired action, was able to transcend the worlds of the plantation and the city. Only Turner"—a "seer and a holy man" who headed "plantation slaves in an economically backward area"—"led a 'sustained' insurrection." [27]

There was slave unrest in Virginia in the years around 1829–1831. Southampton County below the James River was one of the leading agricultural and slaveholding counties in tidewater Virginia, but it was not a county of large slaveholders nor of particularly prosperous ones. The county's plantation economy was in serious decline, and its plantation proprietors, owning only small- or medium-sized contingents of slaves, were unable to arrest the downturn.

America's most noted slave rebel, Nat Turner, had been born in the county in 1800. He was noticed in his childhood as a remarkable youngster, and he came early to believe that he was destined to be a prophet. He was literate and sharply intelligent, and in time he gained high standing among neighborhood blacks as a Baptist "exhorter." Beginning in 1825 he began to have visions marked by blood and by intimations of violent liberation for slaves. The idea of a slave rebellion—the "great work"—grew in Turner's mind, and he awaited a definite sign from heaven to proceed. It came in early 1828 with an eclipse of the sun. Thereupon Turner began to tell others of his plan for an uprising, which he first scheduled for July 4, 1831—a significant anniversary! —but then put off for a time. Final intentions were confirmed at a feast around a campfire in the woods on the afternoon of Sunday, August 21, 1831, when Turner met with his core of six slave adherents: Henry, Hark, Sam, Nelson, Will, and Jack. Several hours later they broke out in revolt before daylight on Monday, August 22, hitting first the dwelling of Turner's master, Joseph Travis, and killing the entire family. In the next 2 days, the insurrectionaries attacked about 20 plantations over a twisting

30-mile route along which the force of 60 to 80 blacks killed about 65 whites.

"Liberty" was the goal, and, under Turner's leadership, the rebels were convinced that the only way to gain it was a general execution of whites along the path toward their immediate objective: the capture of the county seat Jerusalem (later renamed Courtland). Beyond this their plans, if any, were not revealed by Turner in his subsequent confession. The revolt was crushed in less than 48 hours with Turner's dwindling band overrun by a militia attack on the morning of August 23. For several days following the denouement of that Tuesday morning white vigilantes in Southampton County conducted a largely indiscriminate roundup of slaves and free Negroes that resulted, apparently, in at least sixty black fatalities and perhaps hundreds more. Meanwhile, the survivors among the rebels were quickly brought to the bar of justice. About twenty were tried and executed, and one was banished. Turner himself escaped into the woods and remained a fugitive until captured on October 30 whereupon he was speedily tried and sentenced and, finally, executed on November 11, 1831. Nat Turner died composedly and without remorse after having given a remarkable confession to one of his white captors.[28]

Of the seven great slave rebellions or plots for rebellion in American history, then, none were successful. Yet, the long history of slavery in the United States did produce one triumphant campaign of violent black resistance, and this was an instance of the Maroon mode of insurgency, which, all through the Western Hemisphere, afforded the most successful cases of slave dissidence.

In terms of sharp, decisive defiance of the slave system, running away was undoubtedly the act most commonly resorted to by discontented slaves. Most runaways acted alone (and there was a major sanction against running away—not simply the forcible control of the master, but the reluctance of the slave to sever his, or her, personal connections with family and the slave community, a break that was the personal, emotional penalty that even successful runaways often paid for their flight),[29] but some of them gathered together in forest refuges, supported themselves in small illicit communities, and made frequent forays (for food and necessities) against plantations and white settlements. The organized runaways were the Maroon bands, which, in their sporadic acts of violence, conducted, virtually, a guerrilla war against their erstwhile white masters. ("Maroon," a word of Spanish origin, was the generic term in the New World for organized groups of rebellious fugitive slaves.) Most Maroon violence was localized and ordinarily involved only a handful to about a score of blacks (and often including whole families) in the bands that harried the flanks of the American slavery system.

In his study of Maroon activity in the United States, Herbert Aptheker, the most thorough historian of black slave rebellious activity, describes at least fifty Maroon communities that existed in the period from 1672 to 1864 from the region of Chesapeake Bay to the bayou country of Louisiana with the following eight states (in order of magnitude) harboring the most troublesome activity: South Carolina, North Carolina, Virginia, Louisiana, Florida, Georgia, Mississippi, and Alabama.[30] (Although Florida ranked low in the number of its Maroon movements, it had by far the largest one—described below.) Thirty-seven of these Maroon movements are listed in Appendix 4.

With its wild haunts well suited to refuge from pursuing whites, the Dismal Swamp region of the Virginia-North Carolina border country was a favorite precinct of Maroons as were other swampy, heavily wooded wilderness areas elsewhere in the South. North Carolina was the home of many intrepid Maroon groups. Among the known Maroon leaders in the Tarheel State were Tom Copper (of the Elizabeth City vicinity) in 1802; Billy James (alias Abaellino) of Wake County in 1818; one Harry of Gates County in 1820; and one Isam (known as "General Jackson") in the tricounty Carteret-Onslow-Bladen area in 1821. In North Carolina and other states the existence of Maroons in a district was often blamed by whites for causing unrest and unruliness among the plantation slaves. This was the case in the environs of Elizabeth City, North Carolina, where the Maroon leader, Tom Copper, flourished in 1802, and it was the same a generation later in a wide section of North Carolina (Sampson, Bladen, Onslow, Jones, New Hanover, and Dublin counties) in 1830 when whites complained that slaves, spoiled by the example of Maroons, had become "almost uncontrollable. They go and come and when and where they please, and if an attempt is made to correct them they immediately fly to the woods and there continue for months and years Committing grievous depredations on our Cattle, hogs, and Sheep." [31]

For years Maroon communities and their denizens eluded vengeance-minded whites but not always. In North Carolina, in 1830, "the inhabitants of Newbern [*sic*] being advised of the assemblage of sixty armed slaves in a swamp in their vicinity, the military were called out, and surrounding the swamp, killed the whole party." [32] This episode was still in the minds of whites when the Nat Turner rebellion erupted a year later in 1831 with Virginians wondering, at first, whether the Turner uprising was connected with the New Bern Maroon activity. [33] Another example of the way in which angry whites went after Maroons occurred in Mobile County, Alabama, where for years a clutch of Maroons had been plundering plantations until, in 1827, a three-day attack by whites shattered the community of black fugitives who had almost completed a defensive stockade before the whites overran them.

By far the most significant locale of Maroon activity was the vast hammock and swamp land of Florida. Here, as Maroons, American blacks (most of whom were ex-slaves of whites) made their only successful organized, violent resistance to the system of slavery. This they did in the conflict of 1835–1842, known as the Second Seminole War. As far back as 1687, slaves of American colonists in the Carolina region began escaping southward to the sanctuary of Spanish-held Florida, but it was during the British regime in Florida (1763–1783) that black slave escapees from the north became an important element among the Seminole Indians of northern Florida. In addition to the Negroes who came among the Seminoles as refugees, blacks were also purchased as slaves by the Seminoles. Seminole slavery, however, was far milder than the American system of bondage. The Seminoles let their slaves lead an autonomous life in their own black villages and on their own farms, with the Indians contented to take from their nominal slaves only a ten-bushel share per farm of their annual corn crop. In reality they were more like tenants than slaves.

By 1812, there were, among the Seminoles, a number of Negro towns containing several hundred fugitives from Georgia and the Carolinas. In effect, these "Seminole Negroes" were Maroons, and the lot of an inhabitant of one of these black Maroon enclaves was colorful and pleasant: "He lived in a Negro village, separate from that of the Indians with whom he was associated, in a house built after the Indian style of palmetto plants lashed to upright posts and thatched with palmetto leaves, but usually of better construction, in the midst of well-cultivated fields of corn, rice, sweet potatoes, melons, beans, peppers, and cotton. Horses, cattle, and swine belonging to him grazed in the woods and on the savannas. He dressed after the Indian fashion, on occasions of particular festivity wearing moccasins, leggings, a long full smock, or hunting shirt of gaudy hue. . . ."[34] The Negroes had their own captains who served under particular Seminole chiefs, but whites felt—apparently with justification—that these black subordinates actually exercised a dominant influence over the Seminole chiefs in many cases. The blacks, some of whom were literate, from the white perspective lived on a higher cultural level than the Indians and apparently imparted some of the agricultural and other facets of white civilization to the Seminoles. On the whole, the Negroes among the Seminoles were slaves in name only. In fact, they constituted, in peace and war, an elite in the Seminole confederation.

The almost idyllic existence that these elite Florida Maroons enjoyed in the Seminole land was increasingly threatened by the hostility of the American slaveholders above the Florida boundary. The latter launched a series of military campaigns to take Florida, recapture the Maroons, and defeat the Seminoles who were the nominal masters of the Maroons.[35] There were four phases of the slaveholders' anti-Maroon, anti-Seminole operations: the "Patriot movement" of 1812–1814; the drive against "Negro Fort" of 1815–1816; the First Seminole War of 1817–1818; and the climactic Second Seminole War of 1835–1842.

The Patriot movement, composed mostly of Georgians, was a by-product of the War of 1812 in the South. Anti-Florida in character, the Patriot campaign against Florida was repulsed mainly by the Maroons who, fearing re-enslavement at the hands of the Americans, rose in arms and defeated Major Daniel Newnan of the Georgians and, later, killed the Patriot leader, General Buckner Harris. Despite these early successes the Maroons and Seminoles, although not defeated, were forced to give ground, in the face of a massive 1813 invasion by Tennessee militia and U. S.

troops, when they moved from their homes in the Alachua district of north Florida to a more southerly location toward the Suwanee River.

Meanwhile, as a result of the 1813–1814 Alabama phase of the War of 1812, a thousand Negro refugees crossed into the Florida panhandle and settled for a distance of fifty miles along the Appalachicola River. At the mouth of this river these Negro Maroons built a strong point that became known as "Negro Fort." This bastion had a population of 300 blacks, and under its fearless Maroon commander, one Garcon, it anchored the thriving Negro community along the Appalachicola until, in 1816, American gunboats destroyed Negro Fort with a lucky shot into its magazine that blew up most of the black garrison.

With the fall of Negro Fort the Maroons of the Appalachicola retreated east to the Suwanee (just as in 1813 the Maroons of the Alachua district had been forced to flee toward the Suwanee), where, under their head man, one Nero, they settled with a faction of the Seminoles led by Chief Bowlegs. Continuing the pattern of separate but related village settlements, the Indians dwelled along the east bank of the Suwanee, while the blacks began life along the west bank where the main Negro village extended about three miles along the river. Border warfare between Georgians and Seminoles resulted in the invasion of Florida by Andrew Jackson in 1818. Jackson made straight for the Indian and Negro villages along the Suwanee, and, with a force greatly outnumbering the Maroons and Seminoles, forced them to flee, while Jackson, after fending off a sharp rear-guard action by the blacks, was left free to destroy the Suwanee settlement. Following this campaign Jackson committed his notorious executions of the Scottish trader of St. Mark, Florida, Alexander Arbuthnot (whose main offense was that he had traded with and befriended the Negroes and Indians), and Robert C. Armbrister, the soldier of fortune and ex-British lieutenant who had been functioning informally as the military commander of the Seminole-Maroon force along the Suwanee. Before his death Arbuthnot warned the Indians and Negroes that Jackson's principal objective was "to destroy the black population of the Suwany [*sic*]," and Jackson himself spoke of his successful campaign as "this savage and negro war."

The three anti-Maroon/anti-Seminole campaigns of 1812–1818

were effective. They pushed the Indians and their black colleagues out of the north Florida districts of Alachua, Appalachicola, and Suwanee and down into the Lake Harris-Tampa Bay region of central Florida far away from the Alabama and Georgia boundaries. Yet, the black Maroons continued to thrive among the Seminoles, and this never ceased to rankle the American slaveholders of Alabama, Georgia, and north Florida who could not abide the thought of a growing, prospering, free community of slave refugees flourishing beyond their reach. Not only was the constant trickle of slave escapees to the Maroons worrisome, but many whites dreamed of large economic gains to be made by the wholesale re-enslavement of the Florida Maroons. All of this, and the perennial land hunger of American settlers for the Seminole domain in Florida, was the prelude to the Second Seminole War, which finally came in 1835.

The status of the Maroons among the Seminoles was a key issue in the white-Indian strife. The black Maroons played a crucial role in the disagreements that led to and prolonged the war. One reason that the Seminoles rejected the white offer of resettlement in the West (the present eastern Oklahoma—a refuge that had been accepted by the five other Civilized Tribes) was the lack of a guarantee that their black co-tribals, the Maroons, would be allowed to go with them and not be sent back into slavery.

The Second Seminole War, 1835–1842, has generally been considered the greatest Indian war in American history, and the statistics bear this out: among the American military forces, nearly 1,600 men died or were killed during the war, and many, many more were wounded or became sick; the money cost of the long conflict was an enormous $30–40,000,000. In spite of its traditional designation as an Indian war, the leading U. S. commander during the war, General Thomas S. Jesup, termed it "a negro, not an Indian war," and with the benefit of tireless research and historical perspective, Professor Kenneth W. Porter, has delivered the careful judgment "that Negroes were more important than Indians in bringing it about and keeping it up and bringing it to a conclusion." In a similar vein the great historian of the removal of the Six Civilized Tribes from the Southeast to what is now Oklahoma, Grant Foreman, felt that the war was "conducted largely as a slave catching enterprise for the benefit of the citizens of Georgia and

Florida." [36] Indeed, the war was a bivalent black-Indian struggle against their common white antagonists. In emphasizing the crucial nature of the Maroon participation in the war, it is not necessary to denigrate the Indian role in the conflict, but it would be wrong to adopt the traditional view that it was solely an Indian belligerency.

From the outset, the Maroons were a spearhead of the Seminole resistance to the whites. "When it came to fighting," writes John K. Mahon, the leading historian of the war, "the Negroes . . . were armed, capable, and willing, and they proved to be fiercer warriors against the white men than the Indians themselves." [37] At the war's outbreak there were anywhere from 500 to 1,000 Seminole Negroes (of whom about four-fifths were technically Maroons—that is, escaped slaves of the whites—with the remaining one-fifth composed of lawful slaves of the Indians and lawful free Negroes), who were thus a formidable force even when compared to the approximately 2,000 Seminoles in the war. As noted earlier, the leading blacks served as deputies to (but, in actuality, often exercised influence over) the Indian chiefs. During the war, the top black leaders were one Abraham (head counselor of the main chief, Micanopy), John Cavallo (close associate of Chief Coacoochee or Wild Cat), and John Caesar (second in command to the chief, King Phillip). Moreover, the warriors of the most famous Seminole chief of the war, Osceola, were largely Negro.[38]

Always outspoken and bellicose in the Seminole councils of war, the black Maroons were equally active in the field. At the war's beginning, when the Seminoles scored a shocking victory by massacring the 100-man force of Major Thomas Dade, there were 30 to 50 avid Maroon participants in the slaughter committed by Micanopy's band of 200 to 250 men. And on another occasion the Maroon, John Caesar, led a guerrilla force to within two miles of St. Augustine in one of the most daring exploits of the war.

The turning point of the war came in 1838 after three years of bitter fighting in which the Maroons were in the forefront. The key event, in early 1838, was General Jesup's concession that the Maroons would not be re-enslaved, should the Indians come to terms, but would be allowed to accompany the Seminoles in freedom to their new home in present Oklahoma. The leading Maroon, John Cavallo, accepted this guarantee, and, with their black comrades satisfied, the Seminoles (now urged on by the blacks) and the Maroons began their voluntary exodus to the West. Some torrid fighting remained as a holdout faction of Seminoles fought on for four more years until they were granted sanctuary in the Everglades, but for the black Maroons and the great majority of the Seminoles the war was over.[39]

The achievement of the Maroons was an imposing one. In alliance with their Seminole co-tribals, they fought off the vigorously, copiously applied might of the U. S. government and gained their objective: protection from re-enslavement and the grant of a life of freedom in the Seminole's new Oklahoma domicile. It was a triumph of black resistance to American slavery, and, although smaller in size, it is worthy of citation along with the great implacable Maroon communities of South America and the Caribbean: the Republic of Palmares in Brazil, the Bush Negroes of Surinam, and the Maroons of Jamaica.

II

As slavery ended gradually in the North and abruptly in the South, the pattern of black-white violence changed drastically. Before the abolition of slavery, blacks usually initiated violence in a brave but futile resistance to slavery, but, with the end of slavery, the pattern switched from black-initiated rebelliousness to white-originated violence to maintain Caucasian supremacy. Urban riots in the North and South and lynchings, especially in the rural South, were the major aggressive violent means by which whites kept blacks in their inferior status once slavery was outlawed. In a slaveless society, riots and lynchings were used by whites to maintain the boundary of white supremacy over which blacks dared not step (or even signal a willingness to step) without suffering the all-out violent retaliation of whites. As sociologist Allen D. Grimshaw has noted, "the most savage oppression" of whites over blacks "whether expressed in rural lynchings or in urban race riots, has taken place when the Negro has refused to accept a subordinate status. The most intense conflict has resulted when the subordinate group [blacks] has attempted to disrupt the *status quo* or when the superordinate group [whites] *has defined the situation as one in which such an attempt is being made* . . . ."[40]

Thus, from about 1825 to 1960, white *perception* of black aggressiveness, not merely the act of black aggressiveness, triggered violent white reprisal. With the decline and, finally, end of slavery and its associated legal system of authoritarian control of blacks, whites came to feel the need for an informal, extralegal system of violent suppression to replace legal slavery in keeping blacks at the bottom of American society. The informal, extralegal pattern first emerged in the North during the second quarter of the nineteenth century, a period in which slavery had all but vanished above the Mason-Dixon line. In the pre-Civil War period, the urban race riot of the North (copied in the postwar South) became the characteristic means of keeping the black in his place. In the period from 1824 to 1849 John M. Werner has found that 39 race riots took place in Northern cities "as a result of real or imagined assaults by blacks on the established structure" of white dominance. (All 39 riots are listed in Appendix 4.) At least fourteen of these riots were of major significance, with three occurring in Providence, four in Cincinnati, one in New York City, five in Philadelphia, and one in Columbia, Pennsylvania. Other cities with riots were Boston, Hartford, New Haven, Detroit, Newark, Trenton, Buffalo, Pittsburgh, and the smaller communities of Palmyra, New York; Camden and Burlington, New Jersey; Zanesville and Troy, Ohio; Evansville and New Albany, Indiana; and New London, Connecticut.[41]

The underlying causes of these riots were white fears of social amalgamation with blacks, distrust of black education, dislike of black efforts at self-improvement, and hatred of abolitionism. Basic to these widely prevalent emotions of hostility to blacks was the deep-seated racial prejudice (whose roots Winthrop D. Jordan, in a stunning scholarly achievement, has traced not only far back into the colonial period but into the pre-colonial era in England),[42] in which whites saw blacks as "something less than human." As a Boston publication sympathetic to blacks noted in 1842, "all the mobs by which the people of color have been hunted and persecuted, have been directed against their efforts and means for improvement. A negro brothel, or a dance house, might have stood in Moyamensing [a Philadelphia suburb noted for anti-black violence] for a century, without being mobbed by the populace, or torn down as a nuisance . . . . But a negro church or school house, or temperance hall, is not to be tolerated at all." Hence, the most frequently attacked targets by whites in the 1824–1849 period were black churches, benevolent institutions, schools, and businesses—"in short," states Werner, "places that served as tangible signs of black attempts at improvement." [43]

The powerful instinct of whites to maintain the boundary of dominance over blacks was demonstrated most brutally in such fast-growing, turbulent large cities as Philadelphia and Cincinnati, but the anti-black animus was every bit as strong in smaller towns in which a resident, prospering black population made whites uneasy. Such was the case in Columbia, Pennsylvania, a bustling community of about 2,000 (of whom one-quarter were blacks) on the banks of the Susquehanna River. Columbia was the scene of prolonged rioting against blacks from August 16 to October 2, 1834. The main cause of the violence was white resentment at the success and aggressiveness of black artisans and workingmen in a town economy that was dominated by transportation, lumbering, and business. A significant part of the animosity of Columbia whites was directed against an affluent, self-made, successful black, Stephen Smith, whose prosperity as a lumber and coal dealer and as the largest stockholder in the local bank did not seem to many whites to be a fitting status for a black man. After a time the riots subsided but not before Columbia whites, stricken by the success of Smith and the laboring blacks and sensitive to the social boundary between the races, met in public meeting to declare their fear of black-white intermarriage and their detestation of black labor competition.[44]

By the 1820's and 1830's the first black ghettos were rising in the cities of the North: "Little Africa," "Bucktown," and "the Swamp" in Cincinnati, "Five Points" (with both black and white inhabitants) and the district of Orange, Mulberry, Anthony, and Leonard streets in New York City; "Negro Hill" in Boston; "Snow Town" in Providence; and Philadelphia's south side and its contiguous suburb of Moyamensing.[45] These nascent black ghettos were populated by upstanding workers and businessmen as well as by poverty-stricken blacks. The experience of Philadelphia, with five major and four lesser race riots in the 1824–1849 period, was representative of the large cities. In 1830 Philadelphia and its closely associated suburbs had a population of 161,271 of whom close to 10 per cent were free Negroes. At this time the "City of

Brotherly Love" was, in fact, an enclave of rampant racism with a caste system featuring pervasive racial segregation. The riot of August 11–14, 1834, although not the city's first anti-black disturbance, inaugurated Philadelphia's pre-Civil War epoch of race rioting. Angered by black job competition, irate whites invaded the black shantytown on the south side, beating their hapless victims and destroying property. Riots against blacks in Philadelphia occurred in 1835 and 1837 and reached a peak in the riot of May 17–18, 1838. The latter outburst was touched off by the dedication of a new abolitionist meeting place, Pennsylvania Hall. Racist Philadelphia whites felt that the builders of the hall were promoting not merely abolitionism but, even more disquietingly, social equality for blacks. That whites and blacks were to gather in unsegregated abolitionist meetings in Pennsylvania Hall—with perceived implications of miscegenation and intermarriage—was intolerable to Philadelphians, who reacted in a furious riot during which the new building, on which deep anxieties about white dominance had come to focus, was razed by a rampaging mob.[46]

Following the end of slavery in Dixie, the prototype of the anti-black urban race riot that had been pioneered in such Northern cities as Philadelphia, Cincinnati, and Columbia was seen in the South almost at once with the outbreak of vicious pogroms in New Orleans (34 blacks killed) and Memphis (46 blacks killed) designed to suppress the former slaves whose well-being as freed persons was being promoted by the federal policy of Reconstruction. Other riots of this sort occurred in the South during the postwar period to 1876 (see Appendix 4), but the restraint on Southern whites imposed by the threat of federal interference kept the South relatively free of urban race riots until the turn of the nineteenth century. At this time the South experienced two significant race riots—in Wilmington, North Carolina, and Atlanta, Georgia—when white residents perceived a dangerous black aggressiveness. In each case, the result was a pogrom that harked back to the New Orleans and Memphis riots of 1866 and the much earlier riots in the North.

The Wilmington riot of November 10, 1898, was, in effect, an armed *coup d'état* by whites, which terminated the participation of blacks in the local government and brought the expulsion of black activist leaders from the vibrant leading port city of the Tarheel

State.[47] As such, the Wilmington riot was a meaningful episode in the climatic period, 1890–1910, during which whites re-established an iron-clad system of white supremacy after the black surge toward equality in the post-Civil War period. Throughout the South, in the 1890's, blacks were systematically disfranchised and deprived of civil rights and social and economic privileges, usually through the nonviolent means of state constitutional conventions and legal enactments but also, on certain significant occasions, as in the case of Wilmington, by violence.

By 1898 not only had blacks become leading and substantial (though not the dominant) officeholders in Wilmington and surrounding New Hanover County, but there was a thriving black community (comprising more than one-half of Wilmington's population) that had its own impressive cadre of enterprising business-men and professionals notable, especially, for its able and aggressive lawyers, doctors, and editors. Black attorneys and physicians had, indeed, cut into the business of their white counterparts, and there was also vigorous competition in the lower-class labor market as the city became a mecca for ambitious black workers and craftsmen. These were the general reasons for the riot in which hundreds of whites swept through Wilmington, but the direct reason was an article a few months earlier in the forthright black newspaper of Wilmington, the *Record*, edited by Alex Manly, which daringly advanced the view that often alleged sexual assaults by black men on white women were actually not attacks at all but the result of spurious white accusations in regard to instances in which white women surreptitiously but willingly granted their favors to black men.

Manly's article enraged Wilmington whites, but they bided their time until November 9, 1898, the day after white-supremacist Democrats won a decisive election in city and county. On the ninth, Wilmington's white power elite, acting through the "Secret Nine," issued a Declaration of White Independence in which they bugled their intention to overturn black officeholding, oust Negroes from jobs, and close down Manly's offending *Record*. In less than 24 hours, without even giving the black community a chance to comply with this program (couched in the form of demands), the riot erupted. More a massacre than a riot, the white mobs, suffering no casualties, by their own admission killed at least 30 blacks. The toll of black lives was undoubtedly much higher, although probably falling short of the hundreds of black bodies a Wilmington Negro leader claimed were dumped into Cape Fear River. The white protagonist of the riots was a noteworthy Wilmington citizen of aristocratic bearing, Alfred M. Waddell, who had a statewide reputation as a vitriolic, white supremacist orator. Vividly exemplifying Grimshaw's thesis that savage white oppression followed black refusal to accept cravenly subordinate status, Waddell stirred up Wilmington whites with his charges that "nigger lawyers are sassing white men in our courts; nigger root doctors are crowding white physicians out of business." On black officeholding Waddell vociferated: "We will not live under these intolerable conditions. No society can stand it. We intend to change it, if we have to choke the current of Cape Fear River with negro carcasses." Waddell's threat became history immediately after the carnage of November 9th: Wilmington's leading black officeholders (the police chief, county treasurer and coroner, deputy sheriff, city jailer, federal collector of customs, and four city aldermen) were, along with their white fusionist colleagues, forced out of office. When Waddell took over as mayor, the principal blacks of Wilmington were fortunate to escape with their lives to refugee careers in the North.

The Atlanta riot of 1906 was an outgrowth of a Southern white attitude that, in Atlanta, Wilmington, and other cities, favored black genocide and rationalized it as protection for Southern white women supposedly threatened by the "New Negro Crime," rape, which blacks had adopted, so it was felt, in frustration over their failure to gain the social equality that had emerged as a goal during Reconstruction. Under the delusion that blacks were avid rapists of white women a leading Southern editor, John Temple Graves, called for the castration of black men involved in incidents with white women, and one Georgian wanted all black women "unsexed" to forestall the rise, so he alleged, of another generation of rapists.[48] This was the background of the riot of September 22–26, in Atlanta, a city where white prejudice had been inflamed by an 18-month long gubernatorial election campaign featured by the Negro-baiting of top candidate Hoke Smith and brought to the point of violence by a newspaper campaign, September 17–22, against a less than genuine epidemic of black rape.

Early in the evening of September 22nd, black-white scuffles led to a riot that broke out in the Decatur Street black area of central Atlanta. White mobs, meeting ineffective resistance by city police, raged out of control during the night—a night when the young Atlanta black, Walter White (destined to be the great NAACP leader of the mid-twentieth century), "learned who I was": a member of an oppressed race. The pogrom proceeded as blacks were murdered and their businesses pillaged and destroyed. Blacks did resist. One young woman on Cain Street "denounced white oppression and called on black men to rise up and take a life for a life," but, with the white militia actually abetting the rioters and in a city where blacks were outnumbered eight to five, the human targets of the white violence usually had to retreat but not before they did indeed rise up and fight pitched battles with a white mob (supported by police and militia) that invaded the Negro college district of "Brownsville" in south Atlanta. When the six days of rioting ended twenty-five blacks (and only one white) were dead, hundreds were injured, and over a thousand fled the city.

The pogrom type of riot, first seen in pre-Civil War Northern riots, as a "one-sided attack, generally by the majority community upon members of the opposite community" [49] did not disappear after the Wilmington and Atlanta riots but, not restricted to the South, lasted until the middle of the twentieth century. Pogrom-style riots, in which whites freely assaulted blacks, included those of Springfield, Illinois (1908);[50] Omaha, Nebraska (1919);[51] Columbia, Tennessee (1946);[52] and Cicero, Illinois (1951).[53] In the riot-torn World War I era and its aftermath there were three massive riots of this type: East St. Louis, Illinois (1917);[54] the village of Elaine, Arkansas, and its rural environs (1919);[55] and Tulsa, Oklahoma (1921),[56] with black fatalities estimated, respectively, at 100, 60 to 75, and 60 to 125.

Yet, during the period of the first World War and after, in which there were 13 major race riots (and at least 15 minor ones in 1919 alone) a new type of riot emerged: the "communal" (or "contested area") riot in which, although whites were still generally dominant, the riot activity was more equal, featuring "mass, uncoordinated battle" in which "large, relatively evenly-matched sections of each [black and white] community attacked members of the other communities." Characteristically, "the mobs rarely attacked each other, but moved en masse against the less protected elements of the opposite community," and, in a particular city, "the most frequent locales for attack were the mixed areas where one community was in a distinct minority, and the borderline areas between strongholds of opposing communities." [57] Among the notable communal riots of the time of World War I were those of Houston, Texas (1917)[58] and Knoxville, Tennessee (1919),[59] but the greatest communal riots shook Washington, D. C., and Chicago in 1919 and, a generation later, Detroit in 1943.[60]

The basic cause of the communal type of riot remained in most cases the white perception of black aggressiveness and desire to alter the *status quo* of white dominance in race relations. Thus, "whites responded to Negro 'insubordination' and 'pushiness' by direct assault upon the minority." [61] The massive Washington, Chicago, and Detroit communal riots were all set off by such white perceptions. The Washington violence of July 19–22, 1919, produced an estimated fifteen deaths of which five were blacks. This riot stemmed from white dislike of wartime gains by blacks, the feeling that blacks were unduly ambitious for an improvement in their situation, and the precipitating factor: the *Washington Post*'s sensational coverage of an alleged crime wave in which black rapes were emphasized.[62] Following quickly in the wake of the Washington turmoil was the much larger Chicago riot of July 27–August 2, 1919.

In the background of the Chicago outbreak were worsening race relations that had been festering for several years when a massive influx of Southern blacks altered Chicago's population, especially during the war years. At the crux of Chicago's racial crisis was the competition for housing and living space. With the burgeoning black element trapped in the developing Southside ghetto of Chicago, border districts between white and black dominated localities became "contested areas" into which desperate blacks, attempting to escape the intolerable overcrowding of the ghetto, sought to move, while whites struggled just as frantically to keep them out. A few years of sporadic violence came to a head with the tragic, but revealing incident that sparked the explosion of the summer of 1919. A fracas in which whites stoned to death a young black on the city's Lake Michigan shore after the latter had wandered into a bathing beach area claimed by whites escalated within a few hours to a week-long cataclysm in Chicago. It was a prototypical communal riot as independent white and black mobs, rather than fighting pitched battles, pounced on isolated victims of the opposite race. The white mobs tended to dominate the rioting as the casualties indicate: When the violence was over, there were 23 black and 15 white dead, with well over 500 of both races injured.[63]

Two and one-half decades after the giant Chicago race riot another huge communal conflict occurred in the Northern industrial metropolis of Detroit in 1943. There were important similarities between the two riots. In both cases, wartime conditions of crowded housing exacerbated tensions between the races. Also, in both cases, the majority white populations of each city, in the face of swiftly growing enclaves of blacks, were disturbed by black advances that seemed to threaten the *status quo* in which the whites were the clearly dominant race. In Detroit itself, a climate of visceral white racism was fueled by the anti-black agitation of the fascistic Black Legion and two leading clerics, the Catholic Father Coughlin and the Protestant Reverend J. Frank Norris. The smoldering racial animosities of Detroit during the 1930's were further enflamed in the early 1940's when thousands of Southern whites and blacks were drawn to the Motor City to man its mighty World War II industry. By the summer of 1943, Detroit was extremely riot prone: whites were restive over gains made by blacks in regard to jobs and income, and blacks, too, were irritable over typically negative conditions in housing, police practices, etc. As in the case of Chicago, the triggering event of the riot occurred at a location where blacks and whites were apt to encounter each other in social contact and conflict. This place was the Belle Isle amusement park, where the first violence broke out toward the end of a hot early-summer Sunday afternoon. The riot in Detroit was shorter than the one in Chicago (two days against seven), but it was even more violent. The pattern of the communal race riot with rival black and white mobs avoiding mass confrontations in favor of attacking defenseless victims obtained, but the blacks were more decidedly less aggressive than the Chicago blacks. After only two days of rioting, fatalities in Detroit were almost as high as in Chicago in 1919, but the proportion of black to white dead was much higher in Detroit: twenty-five blacks killed, and only nine whites.[64]

The pogrom-style race riots of the nineteenth and twentieth centuries often approached the character of racial massacres of blacks by whites. The great communal riots of World War I and World War II in which blacks, although almost invariably the losers, inflicted serious casualties on their white urban tormentors were a transition to the numerous riots of the 1960's that found blacks initiating and dominating the violence. The historical significance of both the pogrom and communal type race riots during the long period from 1825 to 1960 was that urban whites employed them to enforce their dominance, extralegally, over blacks who had gained the legal status of free persons in both the North and the South.

In the post-Civil War South, a differing kind of violent intimidation of blacks by whites was used in the extensive rural areas where population was dispersed and blacks were often a numerical majority. The tactic, adopted as early as Reconstruction, was the lynching of blacks—often for trivial or nonexistent offenses—by white supremacists. The occasional black who violated the prescribed system of racial etiquette in the small towns and country districts of the South came to grief at the hands of a lynch mob. Like the urban riot, rural Southern lynching was a violent instrument to keep inviolate the invisible but real social boundaries between whites and blacks.

Although frequently employed against black murderers and rapists, many lynchings were for lesser offenses, and, indeed, the basic lynchable offense was not any particular act but rather any mood or inclination among blacks deemed by whites to be anything less than the complete subservience demanded by the "master" race. Lynchings of Negroes in the South before emancipation were rare, because the slavery system was sufficient to maintain the unquestioned ascendancy of the whites. Sometimes slaves were legally executed, but, in such cases, the slaveholder received state reimbursement for the loss of his property.

After the Civil War, the lynching of blacks by whites became a crucial extralegal prop for the reality of white superiority. The Ku Klux Klan during Reconstruction initiated the wholesale lynching of blacks, and, from 1868 to 1871, there were over 400 Klan lynchings (see Appendix 4). Beginning in the 1880's, as whites began to construct the rigid apparatus of white supremacy, which was completed by the early part of the twentieth century, the number of blacks lynched annually in the former slave states rose steadily. In the 70-year period, 1882–1951, for which complete lynching statistics in the United States are available, a total of 3,437 blacks were lynched (against only 1,293 whites), and, therefore, over 70 per cent of the persons lynched in this country from 1882 to 1951 were blacks. In that time span, a staggering total of 3,328 blacks were lynched in the former slave states, while elsewhere only 109 blacks met such deaths.[65] The most intense period of lynching in the South was the latter part of the nineteenth century and the early part of the twentieth. These were precisely the years when the most telling legal blows were struck at Southern blacks with political disfranchisement, greatly increased segregation, and drastic erosion of civil rights becoming the rule below the Mason-Dixon line. The decade of the 1890's was particularly bad, with the number of Southern blacks lynched usually over a hundred annually. In the entire 1889–1918 turn-of-the-century period, 2,460 blacks were lynched in the former slave states. In the states of the lower South the carnage was appalling, as the following figures for all of the former slave states, 1889–1918, demonstrate:[66]

360, Georgia	117, South Carolina
350, Mississippi	67, Virginia
264, Louisiana	51, Missouri
263, Texas	41, North Carolina
244, Alabama	36, Oklahoma
182, Arkansas	22, West Virginia
162, Tennessee	15, Maryland
161, Florida	1, Delaware
124, Kentucky	2,460, Total

Although nearly two-thirds of the black victims in this period were killed for alleged murders, rapes, or attacks upon white women—the crimes for which white Southerners chiefly rationalized the institution of lynching—the remainder were lynched for less serious allegations, some so vague that the records list only white racial prejudice as the offense.[67]

In contradiction, then, to the folk tradition that lynching was used only to punish black murderers and rapists, the practice was much broader and more significant: fundamentally, it was a violent bulwark for strict white supremacy. Lynching was well understood by both blacks and whites to be a warning to any uncowed blacks who were inclined to step out of line not to do so. This is not to say that blacks were supine in the face of such unrelenting white dominance. At times blacks did resist the emergent system of white supremacy as in the case of Jack Turner, the activist black leader of Choctaw County, Alabama, but Turner himself was lynched on August 19, 1882, and the black movement of his Black Belt county was snuffed out.[68] Indeed, lynchings may well have constituted an index of black opposition to oppressive white regimes in certain small towns and rural areas. This was quite possibly the case with some of the mass lynchings that occurred—among them the thirteen blacks lynched at St. Charles, Arkansas, March 26, 1904, and the eight lynched, respectively, at Juliette, Florida (March 5–15, 1897); Watkinsville, Georgia (June 29, 1905); Barnwell, South Carolina (December 28, 1889); and Hemphill, Texas (June 22, 1908).[69] The crushing retaliation these mass lynchings represented—and the lynching of several blacks at a time was common—was no doubt more deeply aimed at obliterating the spirit of black resistance rather than punishing the serious crimes usually alleged to have been committed.

The most effective black opposition to lynching was the nonviolent tactic by which blacks sought to mobilize public opinion against lynching. The anti-lynching movement was a broad one in which many whites, North and South, ultimately joined, but the first person to gain an important hearing for anti-lynching views was apparently the black activist, Ida B. Wells. The latter was a pretty young woman who, born in Mississippi, went to Memphis where she became the co-editor (with J. L. Fleming) of a militant black newspaper, the *Free Speech and Headlight*. Wells and Fleming promoted the idea of black self-defense in the columns of their newspaper. In a July, 1889, editorial they applauded some Georgetown, Kentucky, blacks who, by setting fire to the town in revenge for a lynching, had shown "some of the true spark of manhood by their resentment" and, after excoriating blacks in Tennessee, Arkansas, and Mississippi for not resisting lynchings, went on to assert that "so long as we permit ourselves to be trampled upon, so long will we have to endure it. Not until the Negro rises in his might and takes a hand in resenting such cold-blooded murders, if he has to burn up whole towns, will a halt be called in wholesale lynching."

Three years later, in 1892, Wells and Fleming turned their attention to their own city of Memphis when they strongly protested the lynching of three blacks, an act that climaxed a hot commerical rivalry between an established white business and its aggressive new black competitor, the People's Grocery Store. But, following the publication of an editorial in which she accused white women of being attracted to black men sexually and attempting to seduce them, Wells and her co-editor were forced to flee north to Chicago where she resumed the anti-lynching campaign on a broader front. With trips to England, lectures in the North, and publication of pamphlets, Ida B. Wells effectively whipped up anti-lynching sentiment. Her vigorous attacks on the lynching record of the supposedly more orderly urban metropolis of Memphis (ten blacks killed, 1892–1894) before a disapproving international audience stung the power elite of the city, and its white newspapers, at last, came out against lynching.[70] As time passed, the anti-lynching crusade gained increased support by whites in both the North and the South, and the measure of success for the blacks who had so long opposed lynching began to appear in the 1920's and 1930's when lynching sharply declined in the South as it was increasingly condemned by leading citizens and public officials.[71]

Although the quantitative impact of Southern lynching was enormous, the qualitative aspect of lynching as a community ritual dedicated to the perpetuation of white supremacy was no less significant. By the 1890's, the typical lynching embodied stylized features calculated, by a combination of racism and sadism, to have a maximum intimidative effect on the entire black population of a locality and its surrounding region. Usually applied to the accused black rapist or murderer, the macabre ritual included the following aspects: (1) Ample notice of a day or two so that whites from neighboring areas (or from areas even further away) could stream into the site of the lynching by train, buggy, or car to join local whites in witnessing the lynching. Railroads sometimes ran special trains and frequently assigned extra cars to regular trains to accommodate the demands of lynch-minded crowds. (2) The lynching itself thus became a mass spectacle with thousands of whites, in gatherings up to as high as fifteen thousand persons, participating as spectators. (3) The doomed victim was burned at the stake—a process that was prolonged for several hours, often, as the black male was subjected to the excruciating pain of torture and mutilation (frequently initiated by the masculine relatives of the wronged white in the case) climaxed, ordinarily, by the hideous act euphemistically described as "surgery below the belt." (4) Nor did the obscenely sadistic ritual end with the death of the victim. Souvenirs from the body, taken in the course of the mutilation process, were collected, and picture postcards of the proceedings were sold (sometimes for years thereafter) by enterprising photographers. (5) Although the leading participants in the lynching were well known, having been observed by thousands and with their identities often highlighted in newspaper accounts, the whole affair was concluded by the automatic verdict of the coroner (or his jury) that the lynching was committed by parties unknown. Resistance to the lynching by local law enforcement officers was usually either perfunctory or altogether absent.[72]

The entire lynching ritual was structured to give dramatic warning to all black inhabitants that the iron-clad system of white supremacy was not to be challenged by deed, word, or even thought. Editorials in Northern newspapers were scathing in their denunciations of these horrendous lynchings, for the spectacles were well reported in the nation's press, but Southerners continued, undaunted, to relish the ferocious extralegal executions, which, although diminished in number, extended well into the 1930's.

III

From 1963 to 1970 America was rocked by well over 500 race riots with at least 263 persons killed and property damage of $160–200,000,000. Virtually all of these riots were initiated by Negroes as hundreds of thousands of urban blacks rose in violent protest over the squalid conditions of their ghetto existence in a white-dominated nation. After almost 20 years with no extraordinarily large race riots (i.e., none since the 1943 outbursts in Detroit and

Harlem), the trend reversed in 1963 with riots in Birmingham and Philadelphia. Four more riots (Harlem and Bedford-Stuyvesant in New York City, Rochester, and Philadelphia) in 1964 were but the prelude to the first of the super-riots of the 1960's: the August 11–16, 1965, Watts riot in the Los Angeles area, with thirty-four killed and $35,000,000–40,000,000 in property damage. Other notable riots of the traumatic 1965 to 1968 period were the Chicago and Cleveland uprisings of 1966; the gigantic 1967 riots in Newark with twenty-three killed and $10,250,000 in property damage and in Detroit with forty-three killed and $40,000,000–45,000,000 in property damage. Following the assassination of Martin Luther King on April 4, 1968, there was a massive wave of 125 riots (led by those in Washington, Baltimore, Chicago, and Kansas City, Missouri), with 46 deaths and $70,000,000 in property damage.

In the background of the aggressive black rioting of the 1960's was a highly significant demographic change in the lives of black people, which, during the twentieth century, found them largely transformed from rural dwellers in the South to urban ghetto inhabitants of the North and West. At the beginning of the twentieth century, 90 per cent of U. S. blacks lived in the South and less than one out of four were urbanites, but, by 1960, three-quarters of all blacks were urbanites and about one-half lived outside the South. In 1960, the urban black population was most heavily concentrated in the North and West where 95 per cent lived in cities, but even in the South almost two-thirds had forsaken the country for city life.[73] The rise of huge urban ghettos in the twentieth century was paced by the growth of massive black populations in New York City and Chicago. New York's 1910 black population of 91,709 was substantial but only 1.9% of the total inhabitants of the city, but, after 1910, the Harlem enclave grew rapidly, and, by 1920, more blacks lived in New York than in any city in the United States—Gotham had gained a primacy that for three decades had been held by a border city, Washington, D. C. In 1930, New York's 327,706 blacks were heavily concentrated in Harlem, but by 1960, the city's 1,087,931 Negroes had burst the bounds of Harlem to go to another huge ghetto, Bedford-Stuyvesant in Brooklyn, and other sections of the city. And, in 1970, one of every five New Yorkers was a black, with the Negroes totaling 1,666,636.[74] A comparably massive growth of Chicago's black population occurred during the same period: from being only 2.0 per cent of the population in 1910, the Negro masses of the lakeshore colossus soared to 35.7 per cent in 1970. In 1920, Chicago's 109,458 blacks were crammed into a narrow Southside slum, in contrast to the vast ghetto expanses of the South and West Sides that held most of Chicago's 1,102,620 blacks in 1970.[75]

The spectacular gains in the size of the black populations of New York and Chicago were mirrored in dozens of other American cities. Although only five cities (Washington, Baltimore, New Orleans, Philadelphia, New York) had more than 50,000 blacks in 1900, there were forty-eight such cities in 1970. In 1970, only New York and Chicago had over a million blacks, each; but four more cities (Detroit, Philadelphia, Washington, Los Angeles) had over one-half million, each; nineteen had between 100,000 and 500,000, each; and twenty-three had between 50,000–100,000. The striking increase, in absolute terms, of the black populations of large cities was punctuated by the concentration of Negroes in ghetto areas as the percentages reveal: In 1910, 22 large cities had black populations exceeding 10 per cent of their total populations, but only 3 cities (Baltimore, Washington, Louisville) were outside the former Confederate states. By 1970, the situation was dramatically different. Then, of the 48 cities with over 50,000 blacks, each, all but 2 cities had black populations in excess of 10 per cent of their total residents, but, of these 46 cities, more than one-half (28) were outside the former Confederate states, divided as follows in terms of the black percentages of total population:

10–19%, 8 cities	50–59%, 2 cities
20–29%, 7 cities	60–69%, 0 cities
30–39%, 6 cities	70–79%, 2 cities
40–49%, 3 cities	10–79%, 28 cities

Of these 28 Northern and Western cities, the 10 cities with the largest black populations are shown on facing page. Hence, in these great Northern and Western cities, the black population ranged from 17.9 per cent in Los Angeles to 71.1 per cent in Washington.[76]

By the eve of World War I, nascent black ghettos thus existed in New York (Harlem), Chicago (State Street on the Southside),

City	Black Population (1970)	Total Population (%)
1. New York	1,666,636	21.2
2. Chicago	1,102,620	32.7
3. Detroit	660,428	43.7
4. Philadelphia	653,791	33.6
5. Washington	537,712	71.1
6. Los Angeles	503,606	17.9
7. Baltimore	420,210	46.4
8. Cleveland	287,841	38.3
9. St. Louis	254,191	40.9
10. Newark	207,458	54.2

Philadelphia (the 7th Ward), Washington (Northwest Neighborhood), Baltimore (Druid Hill Avenue), and Louisville (Chestnut Street and Smoketown), among other cities.[77] Such districts (and others in cities like St. Louis, Pittsburgh, Cleveland, and Detroit) absorbed the tremendous influx—"the Great Migration"—from the South during World War I. The population surge of the Great Migration was the first stage in the ghettoization of blacks in the North. The Great Migration, in turn, was the result of a number of complex factors that pushed Negroes out of the South and pulled them into the North. Apart from the constant tyranny of white supremacy, blacks were pushed out of the South by the depression in the cotton economy heightened by the inroads of the boll weevil. An economic pull-factor was the lusty demand of Northern industry for black workers to make up for the cutoff of white European immigrant labor by the war. Moreover, the lure of manifold opportunities for blacks in the relatively free, open cities of the North was tirelessly promoted by the likes of Negro publisher Robert S. Abbott in the pages of his *Chicago Defender*, which circulated widely among Southern blacks.[78]

The pace of migration out of the South lagged during the post-World War I depression, resumed smartly during the boom of the 1920's, languished again during the economically slack 1930's, and became a torrent during World War II and its aftermath in the 1940's to the 1960's.[79] There were two great northward migratory paths: Negroes of the South Atlantic states went north to Harlem (and such other East Coast cities as Washington, Baltimore, Philadelphia, Newark, Jersey City, and Boston) over the routes of the Southern Railroad, the Seaboard Air Line Railroad, and the Atlantic Coast Line Railroad.[80] Blacks of the vast south central region from Alabama to Texas utilized, especially, the popular direct route of the Illinois Central Railroad, paralleling the Mississippi River, to converge on Chicago, while growing contingents of blacks from the Gulf South states followed other trunk lines to such Midwestern industrial centers as Detroit, Cleveland, Gary, Indianapolis, St. Louis, Kansas City, and Akron.[81] Mainly as a result of the attractions of the defense plant industry of World War II in Los Angeles, Oakland, and other Pacific Coast cities, a trend, which for the first time produced a mass migration of Southern and Southwestern blacks to the Far West and its most notable ghetto, the Watts district of Los Angeles, was established.

The demographic revolution in the black population was the setting for an equally significant revolution in black consciousness. Before 1900 blacks were, in the main, a people widely dispersed over the rural South, defensive and demoralized under the oppressive pall of white supremacy. The increasing concentration of Negroes in Northern cities brought in its train a new, upright pride in being black. This revolution in consciousness occurred among both the Negro elite and the black masses. The impulse for the new black consciousness came out of the burgeoning black ghettos of the North, especially those of New York and Chicago. Central to the new black consciousness was, in the words of William E. B. DuBois, the "longing to attain self-conscious manhood." [82] Thus, many of the great protagonists of heightened black consciousness in the first half of the twentieth century were nurtured by the new black ghettos. Harlem was the stronghold of the charismatic leader of the black masses, Marcus Garvey, and, in elite, intellectual terms, the Harlem Renaissance of the 1920's brought forth the prototype of the "New Negro." To the west, Chicago's teeming Southside Black Belt was the inspiration of the powerful black writer, Richard Wright; the subject of the remarkable tome of black scholarship, *Black Metropolis* by St. Clair Drake and Horace R. Cayton; the bailiwick of the first successful twentieth-century black ghetto politician, Oscar DePriest; and the base of the

significant religious leader of the ghetto lower class, Elijah Muhammad, supreme minister of the Black Muslims. A galaxy of other
notable twentieth-century blacks emerged from ghetto life—among
them journalist Robert S. Abbott (Chicago), novelists Ralph
Ellison and James Baldwin (Harlem), politicians Adam Clayton
Powell, Jr. (Harlem), and Shirley Chisholm (Bedford-Stuyvesant),
athletes Joe Louis (Detroit) and Bill Russell (Oakland), singer
Mahalia Jackson (Chicago), religious leaders W. D. Fard (Detroit)
and Father Divine (Harlem), and militant leaders Malcolm X and
Stokely Carmichael (Harlem) and Huey Newton and Bobby Seale
(Oakland).[83]

By 1920, New York City's 150,000 blacks were heavily concentrated in the fast-growing ghetto of Harlem, which formed the
human backdrop for the emergence of the "New Negro," mentioned earlier.[84] The Harlem Renaissance was a movement of elite
intellectuals and artists who were inspired by race pride and driven
to express in passionate, critically acclaimed works of prose and
poetry the plight of the American Negro—the atrocity of lynching,
the onus of segregation, the denial of social equality, the blight of
discrimination, and the squalor of black life. One of the most
remarkable literary flowerings in American history, it found its
keynote in the significantly entitled book of 1925, *The New Negro*,
edited by Alain Locke.[85] Despite artistic problems, ambiguous
relationships with white patrons and critics, and the perplexities of
the quest for an independent black identity,[86] the Harlem Renaissance produced an exhilarating sense of the possibilities of black
life in America as well as a blazing rejection of the disabilities of
such a life.

The Harlem Renaissance left untouched the black multitudes of
the ghetto. The literary exponents of the New Negro were sensitive
to the hard lot of the ghetto lower class, but the latter had no
inkling of the writings of the black intellectual elite. Instead, the
masses of Harlem and other districts responded to the spectacular
leadership of Marcus Garvey, the Jamaican immigrant founder of
the Universal Negro Improvement Association (UNIA). Garvey
was everything the members of the Harlem Renaissance were not.
Whereas the Renaissance protagonists were often light skinned,
generally integrationist, intellectual, and profoundly committed to
black improvement in America, Garvey was blatantly the opposite.

A full-blooded black himself, Garvey was hostile to the mulattoes found in disproportionate numbers among the Negro elite.[87] He attacked intellectuals, was proudly anti-white, and carried his bellicose separationist views to the point of advocating mass migration to Africa. The meteoric career of the UNIA, initiated in Harlem in 1917, was plagued with impracticality and bad management, and, by the mid-twenties, Garvey's dream of the return to Africa was in ruins, but the dual achievement of the Garvey enterprise was one of the most significant in black American history: it was the first movement to win a mass following in the black ghettos, and it was Garvey who "brought to the Negro people for the first time a sense of pride in being black." [88]

Although the post-1920 period did not bring forth any unified movement of black letters comparable to the Harlem Renaissance, the post-Renaissance *oeuvre* of black writers, responding to the impact and inspiration of ghetto life, has far surpassed that of the earlier Harlem community both artistically and in its insight into black life. Ralph Ellison's novel, *Invisible Man* (1947), transcends the black experience, but in the course of it he offers, through the eyes of a young black refugee from the South, a vivid canvas of the Harlem ghetto in what has been authoritatively judged to be the finest American fiction published since World War II. Notable, too, among many outstanding works by recent black writers, is James Baldwin's semi-autobiographical, Harlem-centered novel, *Go Tell It on the Mountain* (1953).[89] Yet no piece of black fiction has been more pointedly the product of the traumatic ghetto experience than Richard Wright's searing novel, *Native Son* (1940). Bigger Thomas, the fictional "native son" of Wright's book, is a sort of Everyman for all black youths lost amid the poverty and degradation of the ghetto. Here Wright dealt with the lower class social stratum of the ghetto to which the Garvey movement most powerfully appealed. In Wright's story, Bigger, trapped by his hapless Southern background and the blighted Chicago ghetto environment, commits a brutal murder for which he eventually pays with his life. The luckless Bigger Thomas was no mere literary construct. He was based in part upon Wright's own transition from the deep South to the peril of street life in the ghetto of Chicago and in part upon a convicted black murderer Wright interviewed in a Chicago jail.[90] The tale of Bigger Thomas was grounded, too, as

Wright acknowledged, on a rich tradition of scholarly study of Chicago's black ghetto.[91] The learned treatment of Chicago's Black Belt reached its epitome in the classic sociological study, *Black Metropolis* (1945), by the black scholars St. Clair Drake and Horace R. Cayton.[92] Thirty years after its publication *Black Metropolis* remains the most complete, authoritative, and representative study of Northern ghetto life.

In their research, Drake and Cayton found that, although most ghetto dwellers did not participate in organizations for "racial advancement" like the NAACP or Urban League, "when some inciting incident stirs them deeply, they close ranks and put up a scrap—for a community housing project, to remove a prejudiced policeman, to force a recalcitrant merchant to employ Negroes." The people, Drake and Cayton observed, were responsive to the "most persistent theme of speeches and editorials" in the Black Belt: "Negroes must learn to stick together." [93] As World War II drew to a close, Drake and Cayton saw that Chicago's ghettoized black people were "rather definite about what they want"—the abolition of job discrimination, adequate housing, equal access to all public accommodations, unrestricted social contact among blacks and whites who wanted it, and they wanted these things "extended to all of America—including the South." [94]

The burgeoning pride discovered by Drake and Cayton in Chicago's Negro ghetto during the 1930's and 1940's has been tapped since the 1950's on an increasingly large scale in Chicago and other major black urban enclaves by the Lost-Found Nation of Islam, known to outsiders as the Black Muslim movement. The sect originated in the Detroit ghetto of the early 1930's under the guidance of the shadowy, soon-to-disappear W. D. Fard. The latter's successor, Elijah Muhammad, operating from headquarters moved to Chicago, provided astute leadership for the steadily growing movement that emerged from obscurity after 1955 with an inspired response to the conditions of urban ghetto life. The strident anti-white ideology of the Black Muslims enlisted the emotions of the downtrodden, demoralized lower- and lower middle-class elements of the ghetto. Yet, the life style the Black Muslim faith requires of its adherents represents a forthright rejection of the ghetto culture of poverty as revealed in *Black Metropolis* and other leading accounts of ghetto life.[95]

The Black Muslims' aggressive anti-white ideology is coupled, paradoxically, with a code of morals and behavior that is the essence of the puritanical, white, middle-class way of life. Thus, the Black Muslim movement prohibits tobacco, pork, alcohol, drugs, gambling, dancing, card playing, cosmetics, and sexual laxity. On the other hand, bourgeois traits of work and thrift, along with an emphasis (in Black Muslim schools) upon traditional three-R's education, are prescribed with the result that "many members who were once degraded or criminal," writes black historian Edgar A. Toppin, have become "honest, clean-living, hardworking people as Muslims." [96] All of this has been achieved with a notable increase in black consciousness and pride among practitioners of the rite of the Lost-Found Nation of Islam. Moreover, the Black Muslim movement has raised the level of black consciousness and pride in the ghetto as a whole—not merely among its own members but also among those non-Muslim ghetto dwellers who, although unwilling to subscribe to the rigorous Muslim personal code, have nonetheless felt a deep pride in the achievements of the following of Elijah Muhammad. Yet, for all its impact on the ghetto, the Black Muslim movement never gained the huge membership that seemed to be its destiny in the early 1960's. The reason, probably, is that the worldly behavior required of Black Muslim religionists was too sharp a rejection of the ghetto life style idealized during the 1960's and 1970's in the mystique of Soul. [97]

For the millions of Southern blacks who streamed into the Northern and Western cities from World War I on, the ghetto was, at first, a promised land. Spared the oppression of Southern white supremacy, blacks reveled in the freedom and opportunities for advancement that they found outside Dixie. But, as the years passed, the mood of ebullience waned as blacks realized they had exchanged the hell of Southern life for the purgatory of the Northern ghetto. The grinding poverty, social dislocations, and emergent patterns of discrimination that so many urban Negroes experienced tended to fix in them considerable emotions of shame and disgust in regard to ghetto life. It was difficult for blacks to feel any positive identification with the ghetto, and, in this sense, their ghetto residence was scarcely less demoralizing than their previous habitation in the South. During the 1960's, however, blacks came increasingly to feel that their ghetto culture was a precious heritage worthy of a full measure race pride.

What are the positive aspects of ghetto culture? Black scholar Charles Keil and many other scholars, black and white,[98] see them to include black music, humor, speech, nonverbal expressiveness, religious preaching, and food—in short, all the cultural components that are subsumed under the concept of Soul. The inclusive mystique of Soul was crucial to the unprecedented surge of black consciousness and pride that both supported and transcended the ghetto riots of the 1960's. A direct expression of the link between Soul-based black consciousness and pride and black militancy emerged in the middle and late 1960's with the metamorphosis of the formerly socially centered rhythm and blues music of the 1940's and 1950's (the racially primal mode of urban bluesmen Bobby Bland, B. B. King, Ray Charles et al.)[99] into the politicized "soul music" of the riot-torn decade. In this development, declares Marien Tally Brown, "phrases were taken out of black culture and were loaded with personal, religious, [and] political suggestions" in the lyrics of the new soul music that reflected the "mood of growing confidence" of blacks and the "aggressive well-defined image" of black assertiveness. A high point in this trend was the recording in 1967 by Aretha Franklin (daughter of the important black preacher of Detroit, the Reverend C. L. Franklin) of the song, *Respect*, whose title (and words), says Brown, summed up the object of black desire in that era of violence and protest.[100]

Current scholarly books on the black ghetto by Kenneth B. Clark, Elliott Liebow, and Ulf Hannerz[101] show that, in comparison to Drake and Cayton's study of the 1930's and early forties, the ghetto way of life, especially its lower-class component, has changed relatively little in recent decades. Yet, as Marien Tally Brown's critique of soul music shows, there has been a remarkable alteration in the self-perception of ghetto blacks. Thus, during the 1960's, ghetto life, more and more epitomized by blacks as a lower-class life, came to be viewed as a cultural unity under the label of Soul. A mystique of the ghetto—something that had been largely lacking before—became central to ghetto self-appraisal. Blacks were heard to speak knowingly and proudly of the "soul brother" and of "soul food" as well as soul music. By "soul" was meant, Ulf Hannerz wrote, "the essence of Negroness" in regard "to the kind of Negro with which the urban slum-dweller" was "most familiar—people like himself." "In fact," continued Hannerz, "soul seems to be a folk conception of the lower-class urban Negro's own 'national character.' " [102]

Soul, too, was a prideful concept, for those deemed lacking in soul—whites, of course, but also upper- and middle-class blacks stained by the accretion of particular white cultural traits—were considered inferior. The very term "soul," in drawing upon the strong religiosity of the black masses itself, arrogated to its possessors alone, as it were, the fully human quality. By implication those without Soul were "somewhat less human." In effect, suggests Hannerz, as lower-class ghetto blacks were increasingly blocked from social flow into the mainstream of American life (a stoppage that became all the more galling in the vaunted "affluent society" of the post-World War II United States), they reacted by ideologizing their lower-class life style as Soul.[103] The result, then, was a significant transformation of values from a negative estimate of black slum life to a positive valuation of such life as the basis of Soul.

The contemporary goal of "black power," closely related to Soul, like Soul draws upon the ghetto for its demographic base. Studies of the ghetto view of black power reveal that "the rhetoric of black power is essentially a call for the black man to rediscover himself as a substantial human being. Its primary themes center around black pride, black cohesiveness, and the need for political and economic power." In the ghetto, real black power was seen to be dependent on and subordinate to self-discovery and identification. A black youth thus expressed it in the ghetto vernacular: "For a man to be a man, he must make an effort hisself to find hisself and be hisself and not keep on being a nigger with his hand out, dependent on somebody else all the time." [104]

IV

The massive demographic build up in the black ghettos of America and the rising, ghetto-connected black consciousness produced the riots of the middle and late 1960's. The black ghetto riot prototype of the 1960's embodied the following stages of background grievances, precipitating incident, large scale rioting, and declining violence:[105]

1. Long-term background grievances in regard to discrimination, employment, housing, and the like, common to ghetto blacks everywhere in America.

2. Short-term grievances, particular to a specific city, in a period of months or weeks before the precipitating incident.

3. A precipitating event that sets off a riot—often a trivial occurrence as in the cases of the 1965 Watts riot (a traffic-violation arrest) and the 1967 Detroit riot (a police raid on an after-hours drinking place) but sometimes a major happening as in the 1968 Washington, Baltimore, and Chicago riots (the assassination of Martin Luther King).

4. Initial phase (immediately following the precipitating incident on the first day of the riot) of crowd-police confrontation with growing excitement among ghetto blacks but only minor violence.

5. Major phase (on the first or second day of the riot) of "extensive looting, selective attacks on stores, and attacks on control agents"—police, etc.—"who attempt to intervene." [106] The major phase lasts one, two, or several days, depending on the size of the riot. The principal form of riot activity, attack on property through looting and burning, is the distinctive feature of ghetto violence in the 1960's.

6. "State of siege" with increasing arson, fire bombing, property damage, and reports (usually exaggerated) of sniping accompanied by a cessation in negotiations between white officials and representatives of aggrieved ghetto dwellers. The escalation in violence by ghetto people results in the hallmark of the state of siege, a "massive law enforcement response" [107] in which the strategy, typically, is for military forces (the National Guard usually but sometimes federal troops as in Detroit) to seal off the riot area.

7. Subsiding stage in which the riot gradually winds down to conclusion because of "the wounds and exhaustion of the rioters" and the "massive crushing force" being employed by the authorities.[108]

Fully exemplifying this seven-stage riot prototype was the Newark, New Jersey, violence of July 12–16, 1967. The Newark riot was not the first of the super-riots of the 1960's, however. That distinction belongs to the Los Angeles area's Watts riot of August 11–16, 1965, which burst like a bombshell on the American scene in the middle 1960's.[109] Nor was the Newark riot the largest riot of the 1960's; primacy in size apparently goes to the Detroit riot of July 23–30, 1967.[110] Although exceeded in magnitude by the Detroit riot and in fame by the Watts riot, the Newark riot was representative of the super-riots of the period. During the 1950's and 1960's Newark, a city of 400,000, had been losing large numbers of its white inhabitants (e.g., 70,000 from 1960 to 1967) to the suburbs as Negroes, Cubans, and Puerto Ricans flowed into ghetto areas.[111] In a six-year period, Newark's demography reversed from 65 per cent white to 52 per cent black. The demographic transition was accompanied by the typical panoply of afflictions of ghettoized blacks: poor housing, unsatisfactory employment, bad schools, etc., as well as police practices the Newark blacks believed to be brutal and discriminatory. These grievances festered for years before the 1967 riot, but a complex of pre-precipitating–event disputes in the months and weeks immediately prior to the riot put the Newark black community at the flash point. The political alliance in Newark between Negroes and Italians within the Democratic party foundered upon the shoals of increasing black resentment over the white near monopoly of positions in the political establishment: whites outnumbered blacks by identical seven to two counts on both the City Council and the Board of Education, and they also dominated the important Planning Board as well, with a white holding the office of mayor. As the riot neared, blacks were more and more incensed over two issues: (1) a plan to locate a new medical and dental school on a 150-acre plot in the midst of the Central Ward black ghetto, which, if it had been carried out, would uproot poor blacks and significantly dilute black voting power in the ward, and (2) the rejection by Mayor Hugh Addonizio of the black nominee to succeed the retiring white Secretary of the Board of Education—a key position in regard to a school system with an enrollment that was 70 per cent black.

With black discontent thus running high by the mid-summer evening of Wednesday, July 12, 1967, it took only a minor incident to precipitate the riot that was to last 5 days, take 23 lives (21 blacks), and result in over $10,000,000 in property damage. The typically trivial triggering event was the arrest of an erratic black cabdriver for a tailgating offense. The rumored beating of the cabdriver inside the 4th precinct police station that night touched off the initial phase of violence, which, the next day, rose to engulf eventually a 2-mile district. With the Newark police well nigh powerless to curb the riotous looting, fire bombing, burning, and occasional sniping, the third day of violence, Friday, July 14th, saw the entry of state troopers and National Guardsmen upon the order of Governor Richard J. Hughes. As the massively reinforced riot-control forces sealed off the wounded ghetto area with 137 roadblocks the violence tapered off Sunday and came to an end on Monday, July 17th, whereupon the state forces were withdrawn and the city returned to normal.

As the Newark riot indicates, the main type of violence by rioters was destruction of ghetto property (usually owned by whites) rather than killing of whites. Although whites who happened to pass through the ghetto during the early stages of the riot were subject to physical assault (ordinarily not fatal), the mass confrontations between black and white civilians that characterized the communal race riots of the nineteenth and twentieth centuries (best illustrated in Chicago in 1919 and in Detroit in 1943) were missing in the 1960's. The rigid enclave character of the middle twentieth-century black ghettos served to separate the two races. Anti-Negro white urban residents dared not invade the huge, densely populated black ghettos, while the ghetto blacks never made good their rumored intentions of storming white districts in the city or the suburbs. So notable a feature of the 1960's riots was the property-destruction factor that sociologist Morris Janowitz, in reference to the focus on material property, termed them "commodity riots." [112] A paradoxical result of the 1960's riots is that, despite massive black aggression, white casualties were consistently fewer than black injuries and deaths. The explanation is that the punitive actions of the predominantly white, crowd-control forces (police, state troopers, and state and federal military contingents) inflicted heavier losses on the rioters than the rioters did on them. Highly publicized media accounts of rioters sniping at police, troops, and firemen seem, in retrospect, to have been wildly exaggerated. Such sniping did occur but not at all on the scale that riot-control forces believed to be the case during the riot, and the mistaken impression (understandable in the confusion of the riot) of the riot-control forces led to an overreaction on their part in regard to the supposed snipers. In fact, ghetto rioters concentrated on destruction and looting of property rather than on assaults on riot-control personnel. The casualty figures for the riots in both Newark (twenty-three killed of whom only two were white) and Detroit (thirty-three killed of whom only ten were white) are typical, and they illustrate the pattern of predominantly black fatalities. Even so, the number of blacks killed in each super riot was only the scantiest handful of the thousands of rioters who participated in each event.

Ghetto-resident participation in the riots was very high, ranging, for example, from about 15 per cent of the black inhabitants (i.e., teen-agers and older) in the instances of Watts, Newark, and Grand Rapids (1967) to about 30 per cent in the Detroit, New Haven (1967), and Dayton (1967) riots.[113] In the Watts riot, approximately 30,000 blacks took part of whom nearly 4,000 were arrested and about 1,000 were injured, with only about 30 blacks killed. The character as well as the number of riot participants has been carefully studied. In its profile of "the typical rioter in the summer of 1967"—a profile that stands up, generally, for the entire 1960's—the National Advisory Commission on Civil Disorders (Riot Commission) described "a Negro, unmarried male between the ages of 15 and 24." (Females and older blacks, on into the age bracket of 60–70, were active riot participants everywhere, but here the Riot Commission is emphasizing the typical.) He was not a migrant from the South but a lifelong resident of his city. His economic status was comparable to that of non-rioting ghetto men, but he was a bit better educated (with some high school attendance) than the average ghetto black. If employed he was usually in a menial or low-status position and subject to frequent periods of joblessness. Eager for better work, he attributed his underemployment to white prejudice rather than to lack of ability or training. With strong race pride, he was "extremely hostile to whites" but with his hostility "more apt to be a product of social and economic class" for he was "almost equally hostile toward middle class Negroes." [114]

Confirming the Riot Commission's profile of the typical ghetto protagonist of violence, T. M. Tomlinson saw such rioters as the "cream of urban Negro youth in particular and urban Negro citizens in general," [115] and Nathan Caplan and Joe R. Feagin and

Harlan Hahn have carried this analysis to an even higher level of social generalization in referring to the 1960's rioters as examples of the "New Ghetto Man." [116] The New Ghetto Man, say Feagin and Hahn, is "politically more active, more likely to vote, more critical of responsiveness of local authorities, more distrustful of politicians, more knowledgeable about political affairs . . ." than non-riotous ghetto blacks.[117] The New Ghetto Man "believes that he can and must control his own present and future. He is a black man resolutely dedicated to the eradication of exploitation and oppression by open confrontation with white America even to the point of collective violence if that is necessary. Here then is a man who contradicts traditional white stereotypes of the black man: allegedly lazy, shiftless, docile and unwilling to protect his own or his family's interests." [118] This New Ghetto Man is in significant contrast to the "New Negro" of the 1920's. The more recent term concisely typifies the revolutionary changes in black demography, consciousness, pride, and militance of the 1960's. The New Negro of the 1920's drew his spiritual strength from the nascent black ghetto represented by Harlem, but the New Negro himself was no typical ghetto resident; instead he was an elite, intellectual writer or artist of middle- or upper-class social status among Negroes. While expressing a new militancy in intellectual and artistic terms, the New Negro of the 1920's was more *in* the ghetto than *of* it. Unlike the New Ghetto Man of the 1960's, the earlier New Negro dared not participate in or even encourage a violent ghetto movement for black self-determination. In kind with the changing times and the emergent ghetto mystiques of Soul and black power, the New Ghetto Man (lower class or lower middle class, socially) represented the enormous demographic shift to ghetto concentration, which enabled the riotous ghetto black masses of the 1960's to strike out in violent protest against white domination in America.

Interwoven with the new concepts of Soul and black power was the unique "riot ideology" of the New Ghetto Man. Studies of ghetto attitudes during the riot period of the 1960's reveal clearly an ideology of violent insurgency that rested on a long pent-up resentment over a history of "economic exploitation, racial discrimination, and police malpractice." [119] These grievances were seen as plaguing all ghetto blacks in America and not just those of a particular city.[120] In even more general terms, "the continued exclusion of Negroes from American economic and social life" was "the fundamental cause of the riots." [121] To the ghetto people these grievances amounted to "legitimate reasons" for rioting.[122] The many important scholarly studies of the riots have uncovered no evidence that, as some persons have charged, the riots were planned in advance or directed by outside agitators. But the rioters felt themselves to have acted in an organized way, and it was their riot ideology that caused them to act in a concerted way as they looted and burned. Thus, with riots neither preplanned nor directed from above or outside, their organized nature stemmed from an implicitly purposeful character owing to the generally structuring impact of the commonly, enthusiastically held riot ideology.[123] It was a key part of the ideology of the rioters that their "dominant" purpose was "to call attention to Negro problems" by violence as well as to express the "hostility, resentment, or revenge" of a "fed up" people. Ghetto blacks were strong in their belief that their main needs in regard to jobs, housing, education, police practices, etc., were ameliorable by society acting through government.[124] Thus, ghetto rioting was not "meaningless or pathologically destructive behavior" [125] but, rather, in rational terms a message—a violent message—sent to "merchants, police, and white people in general" [126] voicing their determination to suffer no more and to reverse the pattern of white domination. In short, the ghetto riot ideology was "the shared agreement by most Negro Americans that their lot in life" was "unacceptable, coupled with the view by a significant minority that riots are a legitimate and productive mode of protest." [127]

To Feagin and Hahn, the scholars who have made the most complete study of the 1960's black ghetto riots, riots were acts of political violence. These riots, along with the black power movement, are, in their view, "in contrast to earlier demands emphasizing integration" as involving, rather, a "black struggle for self-determination and equality." [128] But, contend Feagin and Hahn, blacks did not mean to abandon traditional nonviolent means of political protest. Implicitly, though, blacks came to feel in the 1960's that decades of conventional, peaceful actions in behalf of black self-improvement had failed to move, significantly, the white local and national power structures and had not accomplished enough,[129] a perception that was made more acute as increasingly restless blacks watched the dramatic rise in the living standard of affluent white Americans during the 1950's and 1960's.[130] Hence, for a time during the 1960's ghetto blacks made a decision, in effect, to resort to political violence—to add "various types of collective violence," headed by rioting, to their array of established tactics that included "electoral politics, nonviolent demonstrations, boycotts, [and] civil disobedience." [131] In thus turning to "collective political violence," ghetto blacks, as Feagin and Hahn correctly note, have drawn upon "a tradition that dates back in this country to the revolutionary period, and even before in the lengthy English tradition of popular violence." [132] Ghetto blacks, at last, became one with earlier violent Americans in employing "one of the violent weapons of any people whose political aspirations remain significantly unfulfilled after other alternatives have been tried." [133]

Chapter 8

THE VIOLENT REGION OF CENTRAL TEXAS: LAND OF LYNDON B. JOHNSON

. . . long after Texas entered the Union . . . violence was still common; indeed, the state's reputation for lawlessness seemed to increase rather than to diminish with economic and political maturity. The question therefore arises as to why Texas maintained a frontier mentality that condoned acts of violence by her citizens until well after the physical frontier had moved on. Perhaps the answer lies in her unique history.

W. Eugene Hollon, *Frontier Violence*

In Texas the folk law of the frontier was reinforced by the unwritten laws of the South and produced a habit of self-redress more deeply ingrained, perhaps, than anywhere else in the country. The grievances and abuses of the bad days after the Civil War gave extraordinary scope for the application of the old ways of dealing justice, and even today there are many vestiges of frontier days and the Old South in the Texan's attitude toward crime and punishment.

C. L. Sonnichsen, *I'll Die before I'll Run*

Sitting in . . . the Oval Office and surveying the troublesome world, he [Lyndon B. Johnson] was the President from Texas. His was the land of the Alamo, where outnumbered men chose to die to show their bravery. He saw himself as a tall Texas Ranger riding into town to take charge and brooking no interference. Unable to grow beyond his limited heritage and outlook, Sam Johnson's boy could not become more than the President from Texas.

Alfred Steinberg, *Sam Johnson's Boy*

An earlier chapter explored the generation of Back Country violence in South Carolina and its crucial role in the genesis of a strain of extremism that characterized South Carolina political behavior from Nullification and Secession down to the implacable conservative of our own time, Senator J. Strom Thurmond.[1] One of our most violent regions has been the compact area of southern Illinois and western Kentucky. From the murdering Harpe brothers in the 1790's[2] through nineteenth-century vigilantism,[3] Civil War turbulence, and the mass uprising of the tobacco-belt Night Riders of the early twentieth century[4] to the bloody labor violence of the 1920's[5] and the recent racial strife of Cairo, Illinois,[6] this southern Illinois–western Kentucky enclave has suffered through nearly 200 years of violence.

No region, however, has surpassed the acute, long-term violence of central Texas, the extensive region stretching from Texas's northern boundary on the Red River down to the Gulf of Mexico. Its heart is the triangular area whose points are the cities of Houston, San Antonio, and Dallas–Ft. Worth. When the line running from Dallas–Ft. Worth to San Antonio is pushed westward about 100 miles, the central Texas area of about 90,000 square miles is circumscribed. The image of Texas as one vast monotonous plain is belied by the diversity and beauty of the "varied physical arena of woods and prairies, hills and plains, rich river bottoms and thin-soiled cuestas" that is central Texas.[7] The rich blackland prairies in its eastern sector are indeed flat and treeless, but as one moves west into the Cross Timbers and the limestone mountains and sparkling streams of the Hill Country, post-oak groves, cedar brakes, and brushy mesquite thickets are encountered.[8] Central Texas approximates the "core area" of Texas described by the cultural geographer, Donald W. Meinig.[9] Dominated by westward-moving native Southerners, central Texas was also an area of cultural convergence for German immigrants, blacks, and Hispanos.[10] One consequence of this ethnic and cultural variety (exacerbated by long-term Indian warfare) was tension resulting in violence, our subject here.

From 1860 to about 1890, historical events made central Texas the focal area for a wide variety of violence stemming from Civil War and Reconstruction troubles, Indian warfare, vigilantism, cattle industry conflict, outlaw activity, community feuds, ethnic tension, agrarian discontent, and political tumult.[11] It was a land without surcease from killing, and, as one type of disorder fed another, a distinct regional style of violent behavior emerged. In these turbulent conditions, an ethic of individual violent self-defense and self-redress arose, which, in turn, made central Texans more prone to settle difficulties by resorting to violence. With the most dramatic events of the region's history suffused with violence, and its social landscape awash with it, central Texans embraced a mystique of violence. By the close of the formative period (roughly, 1890) the pattern of central Texas violence was set. Not even the waning of some of the most important causes of the violence— Indian warfare, vigilantism, cattle industry conflict, and banditry— was sufficient to change the pattern. Repeated acts of violence on a large scale had created a habit and tradition in which violence became self-perpetuating. Central Texans were irrepressibly prone to violence. Thus, a cultural disagreement in the modern, urban setting of the central Texas educational center of Waco should have been restricted to controversy in public print; instead, the central Texas ethic of violent self-redress produced the violent Baylor-Brann killings of 1898. To understand the significance of the Baylor-Brann feud, one must imagine that, by analogy, Clarence Darrow and William Jennings Bryan had settled their differences with guns rather than peaceably at the bar of public opinion. The tradition of central Texas violence has survived in a real although an attenuated form in the Ku Klux Klan activities of the 1920's, the currently high homicide rate, and, so it will be argued, in the foreign affairs leadership of the late President Lyndon B. Johnson, whose ancestors settled in the heart of central Texas during the period of greatest violence, whose Christian name, Lyndon, was his father's tribute to the hero of a classic episode of central Texas violence, and whose Vietnam policy was a throwback to the central Texas ethic of violent self-defense.

I

In the summer of 1860 a hysterical mania, the Great Fear, swept over the Deep South. In a broad belt from the Atlantic to Texas, Southerners thought they had uncovered plots by secret abolitionists and Unionists to sponsor slave rebellions. The distraught slaveholders were probably incited more by apocalyptic visions of the consequences of the coming election of Abraham Lincoln to the presidency than by the reality of the image of a gigantic slave conspiracy, but, fanciful or not, Southerners, as they had in the past,[12] met the "threat" with a wave of vigilante lynchings and terrifying expulsions.[13]

Central Texas was one of the focal points of the farflung Great Fear. In the background of the 1860 trouble was the belief, in 1856, that a plan for a slave uprising in Colorado County (the future scene of a bloody central Texas community feud in the late nineteenth century) existed.[14] This belief precipitated vigilante action that resulted in the execution of four blacks and the expulsion of all Mexicans, who had been accused of connivance with the slaves (a month-long vigilante campaign in Austin in 1854 resulted in an expulsion of lower-class Mexicans, who were charged with abetting the flight of slaves to Mexico),[15] from Colorado County, as well as punitive action against certain whites said to be implicated in the plot.[16]

Contributing also to the outbreak of the Texas panic in 1860 was the widely known fact that northern Texas (including the northern portion of central Texas) was a center of Unionist and anti-slavery sentiment. Violence was acute in the northern part of central Texas during the summer of 1860, but it soon permeated the remainder of central Texas and eastern Texas as well. Excitement mounted with the great national events of 1860 and peaked in August when numerous fires—thought to have been connected with the slave uprisings presumably planned by abolitionists to occur on the day before the August election day—broke out around the state. Although no slave revolt ever occurred, public feeling in Texas rose, with vigilance committees being formed everywhere. Time and again the vigilantes obtained confessions—probably spurious —from Negroes who were in fear for their lives and under intense pressure to tell the vigilantes what they wanted to hear.[17]

The first notable fire ravaged the town square of Dallas on July 8, 1860, doing more than a quarter of a million dollars of damage. About the same time a big fire hit the neighboring town of Denton, and the idea grew that both fires were the result of arson. Reports of fires elsewhere, mingled with Negro confessions and rumors and disclosures of plots for slave rebellions, increased. Vigilance committees mushroomed, including one in Dallas, which, on July 24th, whipped 70 to 80 blacks and hanged 3 others accused of being the ringleaders of the arsonists. The blacks had supposedly imbibed abolitionist sentiments from two preachers, McKinney and Blount, whom the Dallas people had driven away in 1859.[18] On August 5th, the town square of Henderson was destroyed by fire, and two days later a vigilance committee was formed. The vigilantes obtained black confessions and followed them up with two executions.[19] The apparent epidemic of fires had quickly produced an even wider epidemic of vigilantism with movements springing up in the central Texas counties of Hunt, Kaufman, Navarro, Fayette, Austin, Grimes, and Lavaca.[20]

The violence of 1860 came to a climax with the Bailey (or Buley) incident. In late August and early September, a letter signed "W. A. Bailey" was published in newspapers all over Texas. It had been found near Ft. Worth, the seat of Tarrant County, and it was allegedly written by the Reverend W. A. Bailey (or Buley) who had been among a number of supposedly abolitionist preachers expelled earlier from nearby Fannin County. The letter sketched a secret plan for an abolitionist take over of Texas that would follow the destruction of Texas business places (hence, the fires), the ruination of their Texas proprietors, and their replacement by merchants of free-soil sentiments. Following the sensation of the Bailey letter, Bailey's two sons were apparently seized and hanged by vigilantes. Bailey himself escaped from Texas but was captured in Arkansas and brought back to Tarrant County where, in the fall of 1860, he was hanged at a spot west of Ft. Worth.[21]

Frank A. Smyrl, who has written the most detailed account of the Great Fear in Texas, does not dismiss the apprehensions of white Texan slaveholders in 1860 as groundless. "There had indeed been a large number of fires in the state in a very short period," he writes, "and separate confessions of Negroes and whites in different areas exposed very similar details of a supposed plot," yet the white reaction was more likely a "social hysteria" similar to that which had panicked Mississippians in 1835 in the face of a still unproven conspiracy for a slave rebellion that, as in Texas in 1860, never occurred.[22] Whether groundless or not, the central Texas vigilante lynchings of the summer of the Great Fear initiated the region's slide into a decades-long period of endemic violence. The lynching of Bailey did not, however, end the central Texans's campaign of extralegal violence against suspected abolitionists and Unionists. Indeed, the events of 1860 were only a prelude to what was probably the greatest mass spectacle of lynch law in American history, an event known in Texas annals as the "Great Gainesville Hanging." The latter occurred in the fall of 1862 after the Union Loyal League was discovered in north-central Texas. In the entire "great hanging area" of the four counties of Cooke, Wise, Denton, and Grayson, the number of illegally executed persons has been put as high as 171. The center of the killing was Gainesville, the Cooke County seat, where, of one hundred and fifty detained for alleged Unionist sympathies, forty-two were put to death in October (forty by hanging—of whom nineteen were dispatched on a single occasion—and two shot trying to escape) after sentencing by an extralegal jury established by a public meeting in Gainesville.[23]

The Great Gainesville Hanging capped a vendetta of several years' length against Unionist and anti-slavery elements in north-central Texas, but elsewhere in central Texas during the Civil War the strife was more along the lines of guerrilla warfare levied by the likes of the "Heel Flies" and the "Haenger Bande." In addition to the north-central region, another belt of pro-Union, anti-slavery feeling was found among the German settlers in the Hill Country west of Austin. The Haenger Bande was what the Germans of Fredericksburg and Gillespie County came to call the J. P. Waldrip gang. Waldrip had gotten along well with his German neighbors before the Civil War, but, during the war, he became a self-styled "frontier captain" in the Confederate army and led his murderous band against the Unionists—mostly Germans (Gillespie County, dominated by Germans, had voted 400 to 17 against secession)—whom he harried and hanged. The professed anti-Unionism of the Waldrip group of 60 members was largely a sham; they were "little more than a gang of ruffians and bandits, hanging, robbing, and burning out anyone they wanted to." Among their exploits—and a measure of how false were their Confederate loyalties—was an attempt to kill Charles Nimitz, the local Confederate conscription officer (of the same family that would later give us Admiral Chester B. Nimitz, the World War II naval commander), who had attempted to draft them into the regular army. More serious was the fate of at least seven men the Waldrip blackguards hanged. The Haenger Bande troubles lasted until 1868 in Gillespie County, but the climactic event came in 1867 when Waldrip was shot to death near the Nimitz Hotel in Fredericksburg by the revenge-minded Captain Philip Broubach whose father-in-law had been killed by the Haenger Bande.[24]

The activities of the Confederate Home Guard in Texas repeated on a wider scale the atrocities of the Haenger Bande. The Home Guard was designed to include all those too young, too old, or too infirm to serve in the regular Confederate military service, "but undesirable characters had little trouble getting in" and in many localities the Home Guard fell "into discredit and became more of a menace than a help" to the populace. The Home Guard often did catch deserters from the Confederate forces, but many Home Guard companies degenerated into little better than thieving bands more intent on harassing honest citizens than in protecting the home front.[25] In some cases, they resorted to rebranding the cattle of their absent neighbors who, as one old-timer recalled, "on returning began counterbranding these stolen cattle and horses; this caused many rows frequently resulting in shootings between former friends. Soon vendettas formed during the late sixties and seventies . . . and hundreds of murders was the consequence." [26] In time, the people began to call the members of the Home Guard " 'Heel Flies' after a mischievous insect which runs horses crazy in the summertime." [27]

The Heel Fly activity in Bell County, north of Austin, illustrates the marauding activities of the Home Guard and the post-Civil War violence thereby engendered in central Texas. "Very active and very obnoxious" were the Heel Flies of Bell County under the leadership of John Early, whose brutality was matched only by the shallowness of his Confederate allegiance—after the war he aligned himself with the military government of the victorious Union forces. Among the exploits of the Early company of Heel Flies was the 1865 lynching of three accused deserters from the Confederate army. This was followed by the abuse of an upstanding settler, Drew Hasley, whose son, Sam, was serving as a Confederate soldier at that very time. Sam Hasley swore to avenge the indignity against his father, and, after the war, this personal grievance was elevated to a factional fight in Bell County, a fight that saw the Hasley-McRae-Griffin group of Confederate loyalists in a violent confrontation with the Early-Christian-Clark group of Heel Flies and supporters of the Reconstruction government. Several years of forays peaked in 1869 with "a state of semi-war" in Bell County along the Leon and Little rivers. By the time the shooting was over, six lives had been lost in this aftermath of the old Heel Fly troubles. Related to this tumult was a vigilante movement in Bell County in 1866, which apparently originated in the Hasley–anti-Heel Fly faction. The vigilantes executed eight men charged with horse theft, including the leader of the tough Shackelford gang.[28]

II

The tensions of the Civil War era thus caused violent divisions among the white settlers of central Texas, but the wartime conflicts were bracketed, before and after, by an external threat that united them. Before the Civil War, and for some years after, the western and northwestern reaches of central Texas comprised the Comanche-Kiowa frontier where one of the most brutal and lengthy of all American wars between whites and Indians kept the land on the ragged edge of chaos. Of the two tribes, the Comanches posed the greatest danger. The more restricted raids of the Kiowas were confined to the far northwestern stretch of the central Texas frontier.

From 1855 until the end of the Comanche and Kiowa incursions, the frontier of Indian warfare remained in a broad belt of about 32 central Texas counties in a long northeast to southwest diagonal, angling downward from Montague and Cooke counties to the southwestern counties of Kimble, Kerr, Bandera, and Medina.[29] Conditions for the white settlers had worsened by 1870, and in 1870–1871 the state established ranging companies in the strategically located central Texas counties of Wise, Erath, Coleman,

Lampasas, Mason, Gillespie, Kimble, and Kerr to protect the pioneers. These ranging companies (not to be confused with the Texas Rangers, who were not revived until 1874) did kill 21 Indians, but they were not as effective as had been hoped.[30] Consequently, they were replaced from 1872 to 1874 with state-supported, but locally recruited and based Minute Men Companies in the 27 counties of central Texas most seriously harassed and threatened by the Indians.[31] The Minute Men were not much of an improvement on the previous ranging companies and were hampered by a provision that limited their paid service to no more than ten days per month. It remained for the thoroughly professional Frontier Battalion of the Texas Rangers (established in May, 1874, under the aggressive command of Major John B. Jones) to end the Comanche raids by a tireless campaign in 1874–1875.[32]

Indian tactics against the pioneers were those of guerrilla warfare. The Comanches raided in small bands, preferring to make sudden, swift attacks by moonlight or to surprise undefended, isolated settlers during the day. The Comanches characteristically killed the men, made prisoners of the women, and adopted captured children into the tribe.[33] White families broken up in this way were one of the tragic features of central Texas life. Wives and children taken by the Comanches were often regained by their kin, but there were many cases in which the captives had become irretrievably acculturated to Comanche life. The most notable example of this—one that became a legend for the people of central Texas—was Cynthia Ann Parker and her half-Comanche son, Quanah Parker, who became the last of the great Comanche chiefs.

During the early 1870's, when the counties of the Indian frontier were settling rapidly and the cattle industry was booming, the annual average number of Comanche raiding parties was about forty.[34] The ordeal faced by the white settlers is well illustrated by the 1870 experience of the Buckmeyer family who lived in the German community of Loyal Valley in southeastern Mason County. In the spring the Buckmeyers had a son stolen from them by the Comanches. Then on the afternoon of July 18th, while Mr. Buckmeyer and the oldest son were away, the mother and the remaining children were sent to the house in flight when eight Indians descended on the place. By the shooting of Spencer rifles and the hurling of large stones, the Comanches tried to force their way into the house through a window but were met with two blasts of buckshot from the double-barreled shotgun of the cool Mrs. Buckmeyer. With two of their number wounded, the Indians dashed off amidst parting whoops and yells. The pioneer wife had bravely defended her family, but the raid was, nonetheless, a costly one to the Buckmeyers: The Comanches had driven off all their horses and destroyed valuable bedding, clothing, harnesses, and household necessities kept in a storeroom.[35] The raid on the Buckmeyers was typical, and it reveals how—despite the efforts of ranging companies, Minute Men, federal troops, and Texas Rangers—the settlers were usually on their own against the Indians.[36]

To the northward, in 1870, the Kiowas were no less active than the Comanches. In July a large band of 50 to 100 Kiowas crossed over the Red River into Texas and assaulted settlers west of the town of Montague; they stole horses and killed cattle, killed three men, and captured the wife and five children of one of the men as well as another child.[37] On December 2, the Kiowas struck again with a night attack on a house 12 miles southeast of Montague where no men were present; it was a brutal event in which a mother was killed and scalped, her three children murdered, and another woman slain.[38]

The Comanches continued to rampage. "The counties of Llano, Mason, and Gillespie swarm with savages," reported the Austin *Daily State Journal.* "The farmers are shot down in their fields, and their stock stolen before their eyes and in open day. Not for twenty years back have the Indians been so bold, well armed and numerous as now. At Llano the frontier is breaking up in consequence of these incessant and ferocious raids." [39] The frontier held together, but with suffering such as that in San Saba County where, during a "light moon," 75 horses were run off, and one man was killed and two children were captured by the Comanches.[40] Lampasas County, too, found itself "infested by large bodies of hostile Indians" during "the last moon." A raid near the town of Lampasas relieved the inhabitants of some fine horses, but far more unfortunate was one P. H. Healy who was "brutally murdered and scalped by the red fiends of Hell. He was coming into town in a wagon" when "he was set upon by the Indians, and having only a single six-shooter, was evidently soon overpowered and murdered. His body was found a few days afterwards most horribly mutilated . . . ." [41] Even bolder were the Comanches who made a raid well behind the frontier in the vicinity of Belton, Bell County, capturing 59 horses.[42] Finally, in late 1870, a Comanche troop cut a wide swath through central Texas when they raided down through Brown County (doing much "mischief") and on into Blanco County where "a party of men ran upon them and scattered them." Thus repelled, the band turned northward through Burnet County, hitting the Cedar Mills section and "in their exit from [the] county . . . murdered a gentleman by the name of Whitlock and his entire family; at the same time burning his house and all furniture." [43]

The horrors of 1870 were a thing of the past by the end of 1875, for, in a relentless campaign from May, 1874, to November, 1875, the Frontier Battalion of Texas Rangers ended the Comanche raids into central Texas for all time. The concluding skirmishes in this long war were fought near Brownwood in Brown County, in Lost Valley of Young County, and in Menard and Mason counties.[44] The Indian war was over, but its impact had been to foster the central Texan's tendency to violence. As Walter Prescott Webb noted, these pioneers had "constantly faced danger from Indians," and "they carried arms at all times. Where all men are armed, conflicts among them are inevitable and the violent death of some is certain." [45] With the Civil War's legacy for central Texas "a social debris in the place of an organized and well-ordered society"; with "the war psychology" of the returning Confederate soldiers, whose war-time experiences had inured them "to bloodshed and to violent death"; with the onset of Reconstruction, which, in the wake of a deadly hatred between Democrats and Republicans, destroyed "whatever was left of self-respect, decorum, and fine morale"; and with the rapid post-war growth of the turbulent cattle industry erected on the combination of the "cow–horse–man–six-shooter complex" central Texas became "a lawless land." [46]

III

Walter Prescott Webb's vivid sketch of chaotic post-Civil War central Texas failed only to mention the horse and cattle stealing gangs who lurked in the blacklands, hid out in the Hill Country and Cross Timbers, and flayed the honest settlers. "There was a chain of outlaws from Red River to the lower Rio Grande," wrote George W. Tyler, "and all along the intervening country there were allies to harbor and protect them." Stolen horses were moved along the illicit chain to be sold "at some place far distant." Fugitive murderers and robbers were likewise passed along the route to safety. The "mountainous cedar brakes" and the "dense thickets" of certain areas of central Texas were "a secure retreat for the lawless." Upright men "were intensely aroused but were powerless, for their lives and their property were alike at the mercy of these outlaw gangs." [47]

With the local people intimidated, things were not much better when the hated state police of Governor E. J. Davis were sent in, for the latter met with "obstructionism" from the Southern-minded citizens who detested Davis's Reconstruction regime. Thus, with the regular means of law and order either ineffective or ignored, the people of central Texas resorted to vigilantism. Seldom was the county sheriff even informed of a crime. Punishment was immediate—usually by the many vigilante groups that sprang up through central Texas, their actions and memberships kept closely guarded secrets by the people.[48]

Vigilante violence continued long after the end of Reconstruction, for, by then, a pattern had emerged that only the passage of decades would erode. Hence, in 1878, a central Texas editorialist wrote that "by common practice in rural districts every [thief] caught is either shot on the spot or hung on the nearest tree" with the "law" paying not "the slightest attention to the lynchers of this kind." [49] With the demise of Davis's state police, the Texas Rangers, who enjoyed the confidence of law-abiding people, were revived. The Rangers were called upon time and time again—usually to pacify communities where vigilante-bred strife had gotten out of hand. But one time the Rangers were posted to clean out a locality, Kimble County, where there were not even enough honest men to launch a vigilante movement.

The Kimble County roundup of 1877 by the Texas Rangers is one of the most remarkable episodes in the annals of American law enforcement, for the Rangers applied to the capture and trial of men exactly the same techniques that Texas cowboys used for the roundup of cattle. Just as cowboys would surround a range and drive all the cattle before them to a corral where certain animals would be cut out for further disposition and others retained, so did squads of Texas Rangers sweep through Kimble County from one end to the other, driving men before them toward the county seat where a grand jury trial, in effect, cut out the blameless and indicted the criminal.

Kimble County, a broken land of brush far to the west of Austin, had gained a reputation as a "thieves stronghold." In all the lawless central Texas region, Kimble County was the most untrammeled—the one county where there was not even a pretense of law and order. As "the great head quarter for men loaded with crime from all parts of the state," Kimble County had a corps of 40 to 100 renegades, abetted by the sheriff and county judge, who nullified the regular working of the courts. Conditions were so bad in the spring of 1877 that the only solution seemed to be the Ranger roundup to separate the few honest men from the dishonest ones and to bring the latter to trial. Under Major John B. Jones, the intrepid commander of the Frontier Battalion of Texas Rangers, the roundup proceeded, with three companies of Rangers participating. Divided into four detachments poised on the southern and western borders of the county, the Rangers on April 19, 1877, rode down four watercourses (the South Llano and North Llano rivers, Johnson's Fork, and Menyard's Creek) to the county seat, Junction, herding all men before them. Securing their captives, the Rangers spent an additional three days scouring all other parts of the county. The result of the 4-day roundup was 37 arrests followed by a grand jury trial eventuating in 25 indictments. It was estimated that, aside from the members of the grand jury, there were fewer than a dozen honest men in the entire county.[50]

Seldom were upright men so lacking, as in Kimble County, that Texas Rangers had to carry out a campaign that, while strictly legal, resembled a vigilante drive. In practically all other central Texas counties, there was a core around which vigilante movements could form. Hence, from the end of the Civil War down to 1900 at least 27 vigilante movements flourished in central Texas.[51] The 27 vigilante movements are those for which evidence has survived, but there were probably as many as 50 or 60 movements, altogether, in this period of central Texas history, with 16 of the 27 vigilante movements occurring during the 1870's, the leading decade of vigilante activity. Many, however, continued on into the 1880's, during which 5 new vigilante movements arose. In all, 38 counties[52] had some sort of organized vigilante action, and the odds are that most of the remaining counties of central Texas had vigilante movements of which no trace can be found.

So endemic did vigilantism become in central Texas that the area developed its own special term for the phenomenon of the vigilante movement: "mob." Elsewhere in the United States the term "mob" ordinarily referred to any spontaneous, unorganized, ephemeral group of violent persons, but in central Texas during Reconstruction days and thereafter "mob" was an accepted label for an organized vigilante movement. The most tenacious of all these mobs was that of northern San Saba County. In existence as early as 1880, the San Saba Mob was still going strong in the middle 1890's.[53] It was probably the last of the central Texas mobs.

Typical of the vigilante-dominated counties was Erath, southwest of Ft. Worth, where it "was not uncommon to ride down a road and see several men hanging from trees," as in 1872 when vigilantes took four men out of the county jail and lynched them.[54] Adjoining Erath was the prototypically violent Comanche County, where active vigilantes often cooperated with vigilantes from Erath.[55] On the northern margin of the central Texas region, Montague County vigilantism, organized as an active Law and Order League, peaked in 1872.[56] Hill County, in the blackland region was plagued by endemic vigilantism, which reached a height in 1873. In the same vicinity was rugged Bell County, which had gone through one vigilante war in 1866–1867 as two factions resorted to "scouting and forting up and watchful waiting on both sides," only to be plagued later by an outbreak of horse stealing, which was brought to an end one night in 1874 when 300 to 500 vigilantes overwhelmed the county jailer and shot to death 9 culprits confined in an iron cage.[57] Mason County in the wild Hill Country to the west of Austin was the scene, in 1875, of a major conflict when the German settlers organized as "Hoodoos" against a faction of native-Southerner outlaws.[58] The neighboring Hill Country counties of Llano and Burnet were also troubled in the late 1870's with their "black period," which was terminated when

Miles Barler and Bob Rountree led a far-flung vigilante movement that broke up the infamous Roberts gang and other lawless combines.[59]

East of Austin, in the tri-county area of Bastrop, Lee, and Williamson, the Yegua Knobs region was a festering locale from 1876 to 1883. A faction of outlaws and small cattlemen, the Yegua Notch Cutters (who counted their victims by gun notches), incited the large cattlemen and their townsmen allies to periodic retaliation by vigilante action. The climax came in 1883 in the little town of McDade with a triple hanging by vigilantes on Christmas eve and a wild shootout the next morning that brought death to two Notch Cutters.[60] Far to the northwest, in sanguinary Shackelford County, a similar tangle of range-land hatreds bred a relentless vigilante movement that from 1876 to 1878 terrorized the county, in which Sheriff John M. Larn, accused of cattle theft, along with 18 other men, was executed.[61] The long-standing vigilantism of Coryell and Hamilton, two brawling counties west of Waco, reached its apex in the early 1880's. Pro-vigilante community sentiment in Hamilton County was well expressed by the sheriff when, upon being asked if he would resist a vigilante raid then in progress on the jail, he replied, "Hell, no, I have too many friends outside to shoot and kill any of them for a damned horse thief." [62] In even tougher Coryell County, vigilantes dominated an "era of mob violence" rent by the "lynching of white men who happened to know too much concerning a fellow criminal, or who, in one way or another had fallen into disfavor with the ruling lights of mobdom." [63] By 1885 vigilantism was declining in central Texas, with the notable exception of violence-spattered San Saba County in the Hill Country. In the northern part of the county, the San Saba Mob was a law unto itself; it accounted for about 25 fatalities from 1880 to 1896 before the intervention of Texas Rangers and the dauntless prosecution of the district attorney quelled the Mob.[64]

Although central Texas mob action as vigilantism sometimes got out of hand and was subverted by evil men who had no interest in the ultimate goal of law and order, the best people in central Texas were often enthusiastic members of these mobs. They saw participation in vigilante mobs as a necessary and legitimate, although illegal, exercise of their right of self-protection. This was the theme of James B. (Buck) Barry, one of the leading pioneers of central

Texas, who had a legendary reputation as an Indian fighter and a Texas Ranger and who served as county sheriff and legislator; he was also a Populist candidate for state treasurer.[65] Buck Barry had been a vigilante before the Civil War, and he enlisted in a similar movement in strife-ridden Bosque County after the war. In reply to an anti-mob editorial in the Austin *Weekly Statesman*, July 18, 1874, he passionately expressed the self-protection rationale of central Texans, defiantly upheld "mob law," and declared, "I would call you all miscreants and cowards were you to stand by and witness your neighbor robbed, his life taken, his women ravished, and not use your manly strength to avenge his wrongs in the most certain way to expedite justice." [66]

IV

Co-existing with the turmoil of vigilantism in central Texas was a 40-year-long era of community feuding during which, from the late 1860's to the early 1900's, central Texas was the scene of 8 major feuds that took at least 75 lives.[67] Although family loyalties were critical in these feuds, they were generally more complex than the simple family versus family prototype would indicate. Usually growing out of a particular troubling issue, hostility rose to a feud level involving an entire community. The encompassing term that applies to these feuds is not family feud but *community feud*. The origins of strife often had to do with cattle-range or land disputes, local political conflict, or racial tensions. With the outbreak of enmity, from whatever cause, two opposing core groups emerged. Each core group was ordinarily composed of a particular family along with its nearest kin and closest friends. The core group was not always family centered but was, at times, a political faction. The feuding alignment did not stop with the competing core groups, but, rather, extended into the larger community in a network of distant relatives, sympathetic acquaintances, and others linked by common interests or attitudes. In the classic feud of central Texas, the communal boundary was usually that of a county with the actual killing often occurring in the county seat. Some feuds did not extend over the entire county or engage most of its residents, but most did. The greatest feud of all, the Sutton-Taylor feud, spanned several counties. Centered in DeWitt County, it washed over the neighboring counties of Gonzales, Karnes, Wilson, and Lavaca.

The eight great feuds of central Texas were, in chronological order:

> 1867–1877, DeWitt County (and the surrounding counties of Gonzales, Karnes, Wilson, and Lavaca), Sutton vs. Taylor, 35 killed; 1873–1875, Hood County, Truitt vs. Mitchell, 5 killed; 1877, Lampasas County, Horrell vs. Higgins, 2 killed; 1888–1889, Young County, Marlow vs. big cattlemen, 7 killed; 1888–1890, Ft. Bend County, Jaybird vs. Woodpecker, 7 killed; 1890–1906, Colorado County, Townsend vs. Stafford and Townsend vs. Reese, 11 killed; 1895–1898, city of Waco, Baylor vs. Brann, 4 killed; and 1905, Waller County, Wet vs. Dry, 4 killed.

Examination of this list shows that the feuds tended to last three or four years or less, but two feuds were much longer: the DeWitt feud was an eleven-year-long conflict, and the Colorado County trouble flamed intermittently for seventeen years. The thirty-five men killed in the DeWitt vendetta was an exceptionally high total. The remaining seven feuds were bloody enough, however, with fatalities ranging from two to eleven.

There were certain geographical and chronological patterns. Three of the feuds (DeWitt, Hood, Lampasas) were bracketed by the years 1867 to 1877. Then there was a hiatus of 10 years (1878–1887) without major feuding, followed by a wave of new vendettas (Young, Ft. Bend, Colorado, Waco, Waller) lasting almost 20 years, from 1888 to 1906. Geographically, there were three clusters. In the northern part of the central Texas region were the Hood County and Young County feuds. The feuds in Lampasas County and the city of Waco were in the central area. In a southern belt were the DeWitt, Ft. Bend, Colorado, and Waller county feuds.

Like the contemporaneous feuds of the Kentucky and West Virginia mountaineers, political conflict was often the root cause of a feud or a major factor in continuing a feud. The most common pattern was for a strongly entrenched local political faction of "ins" to attract violent opposition. The Woodpecker, Townsend, and "Wet" (versus "Dry" in a prohibition controversy) political factions dominated the governments of Ft. Bend, Colorado, and Waller counties, respectively, and the Helm-Sutton ring was dominant in DeWitt County. The politically based feuds that erupted in the southern belt after 1890 hinged, in part, on a waning phase of Texas political history that went back to Reconstruction times: In the three counties of Ft. Bend, Colorado, and Waller, social and economic conditions had a Deep South character with large black populations present. The ascendant, white-controlled Woodpecker, Townsend, and Wet factions in these counties maintained political power with the support of black votes in the face of increasingly restive white residents. The feuds that broke out after 1890 were, in effect, a violent protest against black voting—against the black political participation that here and elsewhere in Texas was terminated during this period. In the middle and northern stretches of central Texas, where blacks were a less significant part of the population, economic disputes replaced political struggles. The Marlow affair in Young County and the Horrell-Higgins feud in Lampasas County both stemmed from range-land troubles involving charges of cattle stealing—against the Horrell brothers by the Higgins clique and against the Marlow brothers by the large cattlemen of the vicinity. The more restricted Truitt-Mitchell feud in Hood County grew out of a land dispute between the two families, who were neighbors.[68] A special case was the Baylor-Brann feud in Waco, a cultural conflict in which William C. Brann's free-thinker, anti-Baptist sentiments clashed with dominant community attitudes.[69]

Community involvement in a feud typically arose out of a specific *casum bellum* (e.g., a political or economic dispute), which led to fighting and shooting between two families or political factions. The next step upward in the violence was the rallying of near relatives and close friends and associates around the opposing core groups. The third and final stage was the polarizing of the community—a situation in which neutrals were squeezed out or forced to choose sides. In the final stage—which occurred in all but the Hood County and Lampasas County disputes—the feud was upon the point of escalating to local civil war. Elevation to an all-out civil war was narrowly averted in three of these feuds (DeWitt, Ft. Bend, Colorado) by the timely intervention of the Texas Rangers.

Although the Texas Rangers successfully intervened in many of the feuds, the ineffectiveness of the courts in ending the disputes is striking. Courtroom convictions did not end a single feud. In their practical effect, the courts were a nullity. It is true that an occasional strong judge, such as W. A. Blackburn in Lampasas County or H. Clay Pleasants in DeWitt County, helped bring peace (although even in their cases the Texas Rangers were much more effective), but, for the most part, the courts did not convict, and, among the few convictions that were obtained, only one man, Nelson Mitchell of Hood County in 1875, paid with his life. No long prison terms were ever served. Of the hundreds of participants in the 8 feuds that produced 75 fatalities, only one person was seriously punished by the law. The ineffectiveness of the law was not due to legal inaction. The authorities frequently launched prosecutions, but nothing much ever came of the case, whether the trial was held in the home county or changed, as often happened, to another venue. Plagued by postponements and rehearings, legal proceedings time and again withered away with the passage of the years. Just as frequently, a trial was never held or, if held, failed to bring conviction despite the most damning evidence. Jaybird feudist Volney Gibson, for example, was never even brought to trial for the killing of Kyle Terry, a Woodpecker enemy, even though the act took place before a crowd of witnesses in the rotunda of the Galveston courthouse. The failure to obtain convictions was sometimes due to the intimidation of judges and juries by feudists, but the reason, more often, was, it seems, that the people, long inured to central Texas violence, were simply indifferent to the notion that feud killings should be opposed with convictions and legal penalties. The self-defense syndrome that motivated the feudists in the first place was so generally accepted among central Texans that there was little appetite for punishment by the law. Central Texans preferred to let the feudists settle the issues themselves or to support the peace-keeping activities of the Texas Rangers when communities were about to disintegrate.

In default of law-enforcing activity by the courts, a common outcome was for a feud simply to fade away after most of the protagonists had been killed or forced to flee. This happened with the all-consuming DeWitt vendetta and in the Hood County, Young County, Colorado County, and Waco feuds. The Jaybird-

Woodpecker feud of Ft. Bend County was the single case resulting in a definitive victory for one side, the Jaybirds. Most unusual of all was the truce by which Major John B. Jones of the Texas Rangers ended the Horrell-Higgins fracas of Lampasas County. Major Jones's successful peacemaking effort was unusual, because truces among feudists were notoriously unstable.

In the high age of violence, from 1860 to 1910, central Texans naturally went feuding. The dramatic vow to kill the opposition in allegiance to the I'll-die-before-I'll-run mystique of self-defense was a staple feature in these terrible vendettas. Bill Mitchell in Hood County, Jim and Bill Taylor in DeWitt County, and Walter Reese in Colorado County took such pledges and thereby fought their feuds to a bitter end. The tenacity with which the feuds were fought in the lust for self-redress of affronted honor was equaled only by the depths of their tragedy. In conducting interviews during the 1930's and 1940's among the descendants and partisans of the feudists a half century, more or less, after the killings were over, C. L. Sonnichsen, author of classic accounts of the feuds, found bitterness rampant and sadness deep. Moments of joy were high and almost hysterical after a particularly satisfying feud killing, but the elation soon palled. Visitors to Richmond, county seat of Ft. Bend County, in the years just after the feud there found the town sunk in an oppressive gloom despite the notable victory of the Jaybirds.

A more pointed perspective on central Texas feuding is afforded by profiles of the two leading feuds of the region: the Sutton-Taylor feud of DeWitt County and environs and the Jaybird-Woodpecker feud of Ft. Bend County. Biggest of all, the DeWitt County feud fed on a complex of family and factional hatreds stemming from the Reconstruction era of Texas history. Twenty years later, the Ft. Bend County feud exploded as if at the end of a slow fuse of racial and political animosities that itself stretched back to Reconstruction. Dissimilar in their histories, these awesome feuds were alike in the carnage and tragedy that overwhelmed their respective communities.

The greatest feud of central Texas and perhaps the greatest feud in American history was the Sutton-Taylor feud centered in DeWitt County but with extensions into the adjacent counties of Gonzales, Karnes, Wilson, and Lavaca,[70] although 13 of its 35 killings took place in DeWitt County. Most of the remainder took place in the nearby counties, but killings did take place over an imperial area ranging from Mason County 160 miles to the northwest, to Bastrop 80 miles to the north, and to Indianola 70 miles to the southeast on the Gulf of Mexico. Beginning in 1867, the killings took place with regularity, except for an interlude in 1871–1872.

Although the Taylor faction lost 22 lives compared to only 13 fatalities among the Sutton faction, neither side was victorious. The killing went on until most of the leaders on both sides had fallen, and then the feud melted away as the Texas Rangers took an increasingly watchful stance in turbulent DeWitt County. The worst slaughter took place in DeWitt's old county seat, the town of Clinton, where nine perished, in the new town of Cuero across the Guadalupe River from Clinton, and in the Yorktown vicinity of the southwestern part of the county.

The Sutton-Taylor conflict was a community feud *par excellence,* and, to some extent, the Sutton and Taylor labels for the warring parties are misleading. Only one member of the Sutton family, William E. (Bill) Sutton, was among the leadership of the side that took its name. Up to his death, in 1874, Bill Sutton had indeed emerged as the dominant figure on his side, but the faction known as the Suttons was a very broad group, with widespread community support and with key leaders in the persons of Jack Helm, Jim Cox, Joe Tumlinson, and Rube Brown. The opposing leadership was much more tightly concentrated among the Taylors (Buck, Pitkin, Bill, and Jim), but the Taylor faction had ties ramifying widely through DeWitt, Karnes, Gonzales and other counties and was far from being just Taylors. John Wesley Hardin, the desperado living as a cattleman in Gonzales County, given his choice of joining either side, opted for the Taylors, and quickly rose to a position of leadership equal to that of Bill and Jim Taylor. The all-inclusive community involvement in the feud reached its most dangerous point in the summer of 1874, when Texas Rangers were sent into DeWitt County to forestall civil war as 2,000 men prepared for battle.

The evolution of the DeWitt County feud was typical of central Texas. Arising out of Reconstruction troubles when two young Confederate veterans, Hays and Doboy Taylor, killed five members of the Union army of occupation in 1867–1868, the feud quickly evolved into a morass of vengeful strokes and counter-strokes among the driven participants. With the murders of Hays and Doboy Taylor as background, the feud proper got underway in 1868 when forces led by Bill Sutton (who had allied himself with the Reconstruction regime) killed first Charley Taylor and then Buck Taylor in 1868. The feud mounted with seven killed in 1869–1870, ebbed slightly in 1871–1872, and then erupted anew in the vicious slaying of patriarchal Pitkin Taylor in March, 1873. The killing of old Pitkin Taylor brought his redoubtable sons, Bill and Jim, into the fray and with them a host of young daredevils (including John Wesley Hardin for the Taylors) on both sides.

In the history of the DeWitt feud, the funeral of the venerable Pitkin Taylor had disastrous consequences, for it led to a classic central Texas vow to annihilate the other side. The family historian of the Taylor side, Jack Hays Day, described the oath taken along the bank of the Guadalupe River several miles from Cuero. "It was," he wrote, "a grim and tragic scene" as the family of old Pitkin gathered around the grave on a shadowy rise above the river. In outrageous affront to the funeral proceedings, Bill Sutton and his followers celebrated the misfortune of the Taylors "with raw drink and coarse jest and wild firing of guns." Stung by the profane hilarity of the Sutton crowd and overcome by her grief, Pitkin's widow heard her son, Jim, pledge to "wash my hands in . . . Bill Sutton's blood!"—a deadly vow repeated by five other young relatives present.[71]

Jim Taylor was as good as his word and, along with his brother, Bill, and John Wesley Hardin, went to work quickly. An attempt against Bill Sutton on April 1, 1873 only wounded him, but human game almost as big as Sutton was bagged in May and June when Jim Taylor and another brother, Scrap, fatally ambushed Jim Cox in Karnes County and when John Wesley Hardin (accompanied by Jim Taylor) shot Jack Helm to death in front of a Wilson County blacksmith shop. Helm and Cox were nearly co-equal with Sutton, but still the Taylors and Hardin stalked Bill Sutton. Finally, on March 11, 1874, Jim Taylor gunned down Sutton and his friend, Gabe Slaughter, on a steamship deck in the Gulf port of Indianola.

A paroxysm of vengeance followed the slaying of Sutton. The enraged Suttonites struck back a month later when they overwhelmed the guard at the Clinton jail, took out three young Taylor cowboys (Scrap Taylor, Kute Tuggle, and Jim White), and lynched them under cover of a dark, stormy night. Soon the Sutton faction scored again with the killing of George Tenelle, a Gonzales County comrade of John Wesley Hardin. By now DeWitt County and its feud had gained a national reputation for bloodshed. With the violence about to spiral upward to a fight to the finish between the two feuding armies, calamity was averted by the intervention of the intrepid Texas Rangers, performing as a pacifying army of occupation. While the Rangers cooled things off, the courageous judge of DeWitt County, H. Clay Pleasants, presided over a determined but ultimately unsuccessful prosecution of the leading feudists. Outside the courtroom and beyond the sway of the Rangers, the feud moved through its last violent phase as the main leaders on each side departed the scene in 1874–1875. The Suttonites lost venerable Joe Tumlinson in an almost miraculous peaceful death in late 1874, whereas a Taylor crew finished off Rube Brown in a Cuero saloon on November 17, 1875. The Taylors similarly lost their leaders when Bill Taylor fled the country and Jim Taylor and two others were killed by a Sutton posse in Clinton on December 27, 1875. The violence terminated with three more murders in 1876–1877, but none involved major figures.

The Jaybird-Woodpecker feud, 1888–1890, was an outgrowth of political and racial tensions in Ft. Bend County and its seat, Richmond, 25 miles southwest of Houston.[72] The Woodpecker political faction had controlled the county since Reconstruction days. The Woodpecker leaders were white, but they dominated the county (in which Negroes outnumbered whites about five to one) by their control of black votes. In return, black people held county offices, often with Woodpecker white men actually carrying out the duties as deputies.[73] By 1888, Ft. Bend was one of the few remaining counties with large-scale Negro voting and officehold-ing, and the minority white population of the county, with a plantation society and economy based on rich cotton crops in the Brazos River bottoms, was restive. Affecting the style of a Deep South aristocracy were the young hotbloods of the Jaybird faction, who began organizing for an attempt to win the election of 1888, capture the county, and establish an iron-clad system of white supremacy. Tempers mounted as the political contest turned into a blood feud. Leading the Jaybirds was the popular proprietor of Richmond's Brahma Bull and Red Hot Bar, H. H. Frost, while at the head of the Woodpeckers were Judge C. W. Parker and Sheriff Jim Garvey.

The violence began on August 2, 1888, when a wealthy planter and Jaybird organizer, J. H. Shamblin, was shot to death in his home—apparently by Negro followers of the Woodpeckers. A month later, Frost narrowly escaped assassination by blacks, and the result was the expulsion of the black leadership from the county. The Woodpeckers nevertheless maintained their dominance by easily winning the fall election on the strength of rank and file black votes. A victory celebration by the Woodpeckers led to the killing of young Ned Gibson, a Jaybird, by the Woodpecker bully, Kyle Terry, and the Terry-Gibson rivalry smoldered as a sub-feud of the larger Jaybird-Woodpecker strife. Hatred was quiescent until August 16, 1889, when a wild gun battle exploded on the streets of Richmond. The shooting began as Judge Parker and W. T. Wade of the Woodpeckers encountered Volney and Guilf Gibson of the Jaybirds. With the first sounds of gunfire, Jaybirds and Woodpeckers rallied to the scene from all over town and blazed away at each other in front of the courthouse. When the fight was over, two Woodpeckers (Sheriff Garvey and old Jake Blakely) and one innocent bystander were killed, one Jaybird, H. H. Frost, was fatally wounded, and six persons were injured.

The climactic fight of August 16th was a defeat for the Woodpecker stalwarts who hastily left the county, never to return. The white-only Jaybird Democratic Association (with its 15-foot monument later erected to "Our Heroes") began 70 years of unchallenged rule in the county. The final fatal shooting of the feud came six months later on January 21, 1890, in the Galveston courthouse as Kyle Terry ascended the staircase to stand trial for the killing of Ned Gibson. Volney Gibson, standing in wait, shot Terry through the heart. Although casualties in the year-and-a-half feud were even (three Jaybirds and three Woodpeckers killed), the Jaybird shots had nullified the Woodpecker ballots. The Jaybird victory was hollow: Stunned by the tragic feud, the once ebullient town of Richmond sank into a stupor. Carry Nation, who lived in Richmond during the feuding days, reported the change when she returned for a visit in 1902. "I never saw such a difference," she said. "A pall of death seemed to be over the whole place, and one coming into the town would feel a desire to leave it as quickly as possible, if there was not some interest independent of the town. God said: 'They shall eat the fruit of their own doing.' " [74]

V

Fueled by the disorders of the Civil War and Reconstruction, Indian warfare, vigilantism, feuds, cattle industry conflict, and banditry, the spirit of central Texas violence gripped all alike: the upright and the ignoble, the law abiding and the lawless, the rough and the genteel. Although often calculated, violence in central Texas, in thousands of long-forgotten incidents, time and again erupted from a long-simmering hostility in a flare up of killings, such as the ones described in the regional dialect by the pseudonymous "Lunar Caustic" in 1867. The account of this typical and "very good fight" was told to "Lunar Caustic" by a schoolmaster of DeWitt County:

> Hit seems John Bell and Walt Edwards had words up on the Sandies, and Bell sent Edwards word not to come stock hunting on his range. Well, they met out on Lower Hog Eye, hits' a branch of the Cabasas over in the edge of Karnes [County], and who begun and shot first he couldn't ondertake to say, but hit was a very good fight and only four men in it, there was old man Edwards and Walt agin John Bell and Charley Thee *[sic]*, two and two a side and a very good fight. Walt Edwards and Charley Thee was shot down directly, but Charley kept a shootin' at old man Edwards long as he could raise his weepin—it was a very good fight and John Bell emptied his six-shooter and never missed only one shot, Walt Edwards and Charley Thee fell in their tracks and was killed on the ground, and old man Edwards is dead since, of a wound through his shoulder, and John Bell was the only one not hurted and hit was a very good fight.

Could not the fight have been stopped? "Well, the boys was all around; they was on a stock hunt and nigh the pen, but it come on a suddint, and was all over in half a minute; only four in it; two and two a side, but it was a very good fight"—"the best" the schoolmaster "had heerd on since the war." [75] All over in 30 seconds, this "very good fight," with three out of four men being killed and, as C. L. Sonnichsen has noted, women heartbroken and children orphaned.

The 1867 shoot-out on the Lower Hog Eye in DeWitt County had been between rough-hewn frontier stockmen, but even genteel professional men who taught Sunday school packed guns and lived nervously on the edge of the abyss of central Texas violence. Thus, the scholarly Dr. J. B. Cranfill, "a famous Baptist leader in Texas," a resident of Coryell County, seat of a mordant mob, commented on "the pall of mob murder" that placed good citizens in "hourly dread" of the band of county assassins to the extent that never, winter or summer, was a lamp lit without the curtains first being closed. Cranfill was a respected Sunday school teacher, but, for personal safety and against his peaceful instincts, he felt obliged always to carry a Colt .45 revolver in his hip pocket. "Indeed," he conceded, "I would have felt much more comfortable going up the street without trousers than I would have without a gun." [76]

Offered here are sketches of three prototypically violent central Texas individuals. The first is John Wesley Hardin, nonpareil killer, the most famous and dangerous outlaw of the region—notable both as a product and a producer of the regional style of violence. Next is an obscure but significant figure, Bill Mitchell, whose thirst for vengeance in troth to the central Texas code of violent self-redress made him a life-long fugitive. Finally, there is the upstanding man of large property, Print Olive—community pillar and killer, who violently defended estate and kin from the prairies of central Texas to the plains of Nebraska.

Billy the Kid, Jesse James, and Wild Bill Hickok were far more famous gunmen than was John Wesley Hardin of central Texas, but Hardin was the top killer of them all.[77] In a single decade, 1868–1878, Hardin killed well over 20 men. The claim of his biographer, Lewis Nordyke, that Hardin killed more men in personal combat than anyone else in the nation's history seems to be correct. Hardin had the intelligence and flair for learning that, in a quieter time or place, might have resulted in a distinguished career in law or politics, but, growing up among the hatreds and atrocities of the Civil War and Reconstruction period, Hardin emerged a killer instead. Born in 1853 and raised along the eastern border of the central Texas region, Hardin sprang from a highly respectable family—his father was a Methodist circuit rider and a great uncle was a signatory of the Texas Declaration of Independence. But his violent tendency appeared early; by the age of eight he was known to pack a .44 caliber pistol, and he stabbed a boy, non-fatally, in a schoolyard quarrel over a girl. According to family tradition the young Hardin, while in his teens, was embittered by a tragedy that was typical of this violent era in Texas history: Soon after the Civil War the family (wife, son, and daughter) of a maternal uncle was massacred by Unionist bad men with the women raped and the house set afire. From this time on, highly partisan Southern sympathies and rabid anti-Negro prejudice— both common in central Texas—inspired Hardin's career.

John Wesley Hardin's remarkable autobiography is one of the key documents in the history of central Texas violence, for he made his home in the region from 1869 to 1874, and he operated across its length and breadth. His baleful annals touched almost every aspect of the searing central Texas violence of the time. As an ardent white racist he took delight in killing Negroes—his first kill, at the age of fifteen, was an ex-slave bully.[78] As a partisan Democrat and violent Confederate sympathizer, he carried on a vendetta with the despised state police of Governor E. J. Davis's Reconstruction administration. As a cattleman, Hardin became involved in more than one killing scrape, both in Texas and on the trail north to Kansas. As a leading gunman on the Taylor side, Hardin had a key role in central Texas's most frightful feud, that in DeWitt County. Finally, Hardin's most notable killing took place in Comanche, a central Texas county known for its violence.

Beginning in 1869 with his first stand-up, face-to-face gun killing—of desperado Jim Bradley—on Christmas night in Hill County, Hardin's central Texas residency was punctuated repeatedly with sudden bursts of violence. He was just a boy of sixteen when he killed Bradley and a mere twenty-one, when, with a trail of spectacular killings behind him, he was forced to flee central Texas in 1874. An athletic, brown-haired, gray-eyed, 5-foot, 10-inch 155-pounder with a hair-trigger temper, Hardin had a gift for horsemanship and a penchant for gambling and drinking. In his liking for a fight and his carefree ways, Hardin was little different from thousands of wild young central Texans of his time but for one thing: his lightning fast draw that made him a winner in every test of his fame as a gun slinger.

After the Bradley shooting Hardin knocked about central Texas for a time, killed three state policemen near Belton in early 1871, and then settled down to cattle ranching in Gonzales County, where his widely connected Clements relatives lived. A bracing interlude came during the summer of 1871 when Hardin went up the Chisholm Trail to Kansas, made some kills along the way, and in Abilene (so Hardin claimed in his autobiography—Hickok partisans disagree) faced down Wild Bill Hickok, then serving as marshal. Back in Gonzales County, Hardin killed a black state policeman in September, 1871, married Jane Bowen of the locality, and, in April, 1873, shot down the belligerent and quarrelsome J. B. Morgan outside a bar in Cuero, the new county seat of neighboring DeWitt County. It was in 1873 that Hardin was drawn into the calamitous Sutton-Taylor feud of DeWitt and other counties on the side of the Taylor faction with whom he had many ties of kinship. In May, 1873, a shootout between the two factions found Hardin disposing of two members of the Sutton group, and later, on the 17th of May, Hardin struck a crippling blow against the Suttons and achieved one of his most famous killings by blasting the notable bravo, Jack Helm, in the town of Albuquerque, Wilson County.

As a master of the quick draw, John Wesley Hardin was unequaled in the history of the West. Many of his kills were due to the lithe grace and lightning speed with which he could draw and fire. Despite the endless movie episodes, television skits, and fictional accounts to the contrary, there were probably only a very few who could draw second and still get off the first shot. John Wesley Hardin could. On May 26, 1874, in the wild town of Comanche, he did so and achieved the epitome of his many kills when he gunned down an outclassed deputy sheriff, Charles Webb, who had come to town for the declared purpose of killing Hardin.

Fresh from his triumphs on the Taylor side in the DeWitt County feud, in late April, 1874, John Wesley Hardin stormed into Comanche County to join his wife who was staying with his father, brothers, sister, and other kin. Tension induced by Hardin's threatening presence built toward a showdown battle between John Wesley and the self-appointed local champion of gunplay, Charles Webb. The day of the clash, May 26, 1874, was a festive one of races in the town of Comanche. John Wesley Hardin's horses finished one-two-three in the main event. A big winner of $3,000, 50 head of cattle, and 15 saddle horses, Hardin set out toward the end of the day with his comrade Jim Taylor and cousin Bud Dixon for a last celebratory drink at Jack Wright's saloon. The stage was thus set for that legendary event of Western violence, the dusty-street, sundown, man-to-man gun duel: Charles Webb, an arrogant deputy sheriff of neighboring Brown County, had come to Comanche that day vowing to kill Hardin. With rumors of Webb's mission circulating around him, John Wesley was on edge despite the amiable introduction to Webb he had received on his way to the saloon. To Hardin's face Webb denied any hostile intent, and the two men, with others, headed for the saloon entrance. In that instant Webb took "the drop" on Hardin: "As I turned around to go in the north door," John Wesley recalled, "I heard some one say, 'Look out, Jack.' It was Bud Dixon, and as I turned around, I saw Charles Webb drawing his pistol. He was in the act of presenting it when I jumped to one side, drew my pistol, and fired. In the meantime," went on Hardin, "Webb had fired, hitting me in the left side, cutting the length of it, inflicting an ugly and painful wound. My aim was good and a bullet hole in the left cheek did the work. He fell against the wall"—dead.[79]

The killing of Webb made central Texas too hot for Hardin, who fled with his family to Florida later in 1874. Hardin's career as a central Texas bad man was over. After being captured in Florida and serving a term in the Texas state prison, Hardin, upon his release in 1892, resided in Gonzales County and Junction, Kimble County, for a time before drifting on to El Paso where, in 1895, only a shadow of his former self, he was fatally shot in the back, ironically, by another old central Texas gunman, John Selman, who in the 1870's had been chased out of Shackelford County by vigilantes.

In the annals of central Texas violence John Wesley Hardin was both effect and cause. Reaching young manhood in a volatile and violent time of racial, political, and feuding strife, Hardin was unable to transcend his background, and the result was his desperate, mordant career. The forces of central Texas violence converged to produce John Wesley Hardin, the outstanding individual example of the turbulence of the period. Molded by his time, Hardin, in turn, shaped it. He was a spearhead of the native white Texan's successful campaign against Governor Davis's state police of Reconstruction. By his killings he helped escalate the level of violence in the trouble-ridden cattle industry. Weighing in on the Taylor side at a crucial time, he tilted the advantage from the Suttons to the Taylors in their tragic, unremitting feud. And it was Hardin who figured in one of the most notable episodes of violence in troubled Comanche County. Unequaled as a gun slinger and killer in individual combat, Hardin's impact was yet more important in the general sense. He never killed for money and, while frequently spoiling for a fight, most of his kills—and certainly his best-known ones—were in defense of causes that central Texans deemed honorable: the ideals of white supremacy and unreconstructed Democracy, his associates in an endless community feud, and his own life when challenged by the likes of Charles Webb. John Wesley Hardin's incredible feats powerfully affected the imagination of his region. They nourished the self-defense syndrome—the "I'll die before I'll run" mystique of central Texas violence.

John Wesley Hardin was almost a mythic figure in central Texas, but the violent code by which both the famous and the forgotten central Texans lived is illustrated, too, by the little known outlaw, Bill Mitchell. Just an average central Texan, Mitchell was not a dazzling gun slinger or a noted killer, yet the tenacity with which he followed the central Texas code of individual honor and his single-minded willingness to kill in its behalf go to the heart of central Texas violence.

Bill Mitchell's life-long career as an unsung outlaw grew out of the 1874 Truitt-Mitchell feud of the central Texas county of Hood.[80] Compared to such colorful feudists as Bill Sutton, Jim Taylor, and others, Bill Mitchell was unglamorous, but nevertheless, he was the prototypical feuding Texan as his biographer, C. L. Sonnichsen, contends: Texas feuds were fought by hundreds of men resembling Bill Mitchell in their devotion to "folk justice"— the individual self-redress Mitchell and so many others relentlessly practiced.[81]

The scene of the Truitt-Mitchell feud, Hood County (with its county seat of Granbury) was about 30 miles southwest of Ft. Worth. A land of fields and woods, it was crossed by the Brazos River. In the early 1870's, the Truitts and Mitchells were neighbors in the Mitchell's Bend area of the Brazos section of the county.[82] They had been close and friendly at first, but, as a result of a land dispute, a feud was born about 1873. The killing began on March 28, 1874, after a court session in Granbury involving the two families. Wending their way home from the courthouse were two groups. One consisted of James, Sam, and Isaac Truitt. In the Mitchell party were the father and patriarch, Nelson Mitchell; his son, Bill Mitchell; and Mit Graves, William Owens, and D. A. Shaw. As they rode toward Mitchell's Bend, the two feuding parties crisscrossed along the road, traded insults, and, finally, in a timber thicket, commenced shooting. After the guns fell silent, Jim Truitt was unscathed, but Sam and Isaac Truitt were dead. Bill Mitchell raced off and out of the country immediately after the shooting.

Old Nelson Mitchell had not yet reached the thicket when the gunplay occurred, but he was tried for the murders on the grounds that he had "premeditated and instigated them." He was convicted and sentenced to hang. Shortly before the hanging, Nelson Mitchell's teen-age son, Jeff, climbed up the Brazos River bluff to the jail one dark night—probably to smuggle poison to the old pioneer so that he could commit suicide and escape the ignominy of hanging. In the gloom the guards heard someone coming up the bluff, fired away, and blasted the youngster's head off. The Mitchells thought that the guards had been tipped off to Jeff's mission and that his slaughter had been planned.

Two days later, on October 5, 1875, Nelson Mitchell was hanged in Granbury. Game but frail with a long white beard, the old man made a dramatic speech from the scaffold, levying a central Texas curse on the Truitts: "He called on his son Bill, wherever he was, whatever he might be doing, and however long it might take, to even the score with his father's murderers." [83] Though it took 11 years of waiting and plotting, Bill Mitchell honored his father's cry for vengeance.

Bill had been a fugitive since the 1874 killing of Sam and Isaac Truitt. He found his way to the wild country along the upper West Fork of the Nueces River in the brushy wilderness of Kinney County 100 miles southwest of San Antonio. Here Bill Mitchell "began his lifelong habit of camping out and wandering restlessly from place to place," [84] and here he lived under an assumed name, married, and gained a primitive livelihood for himself and his family as a hunter and herder. It was a life of privation and hard living, a sacrifice of himself and his wife and daughter to his revenge against the Truitt family. Bill bided his time until at last, in 1886, with the Truitt-Mitchell feud and himself long forgotten, he rode off in pursuit of Jim Truitt who, married, was by now a prospering professional man—a newspaper editor and part-time Methodist minister—in the east Texas piney-woods town of Timpson in Nacogdoches County. Bill Mitchell reached Timpson on July 20, 1886, a hot, lazy day. Just at dusk Bill walked without knocking right into the Truitt living room where, as Mrs. Truitt watched in horror, Bill killed the unsuspecting Jim Truitt with a pistol and fled.

Eluding pursuit, Bill Mitchell got back to his Kinney County hideout where he managed to escape capture by both the Texas Rangers and the sheriff of Nacogdoches County. With Kinney County now too hot for comfort, Mitchell and his family moved on to another wild, isolated locale: the White Sands areas of southern New Mexico where he lived under an alias, Baldy Russell, as a crusty old rancher. Finally, in 1907—33 years after the initial killings in 1874—old Bill was arrested at his ranch house in New Mexico, tried and convicted in 1910, and sent to prison in 1912. Bill Mitchell was never a criminal in the ordinary sense of the word. He had killed only for revenge.[85] Long after the events of 1874 and 1886, the law had merely gone through the motions when it imprisoned Bill Mitchell. After two years in prison he escaped and lived out his last fourteen years, until dying in 1928, still a fugitive but one no longer really wanted by the authorities. Thus, Bill Mitchell spent forty-seven years of his life as an outlaw, a fugitive from justice. Shaped by the violent culture of central Texas, Bill Mitchell—alias Baldy Russell—was as tough and typical as the land that produced him.

Central and south Texas was the great motherland of the American range cattle industry. Ranchers, cowboys, and herds flowed through central Texas outward to the ranges of the Great Plains, the Rocky Mountains, and the Southwest. The great Chisholm Trail that fed cattle into the towns of Abilene, Wichita, and Ellsworth, Kansas, in the late 1860's and the 1870's split central Texas with its main stem and branches. The main stem struck straight north from Karnes County through Gonzales

County, on to Austin and through Williamson, Bell, Coryell, Bosque, and Hill counties toward Ft. Worth, the Montague County crossing of the Red River, across what is now Oklahoma, and into Kansas.

Most of the other wild old counties of central Texas were bisected by feeder trails to the main Chisholm Trail. A southeastern feeder angled from Lavaca Bay through Victoria and DeWitt counties to the main-trail junction at Gonzales. There were two western feeders. The first ran through Bandera, Kerr, Gillespie, Llano, Lampasas, Hamilton, and Bosque counties and the second, to the big trail in Hill County, coursed from Mason County through San Saba, Mills, Comanche, and Erath counties northward to the Red River crossing.[86] By the 1880's, however, the Chisholm Trail to Dodge City, Kansas, had been largely supplanted by the Old Western Trail, which ran along the western margin of the central Texas region from Pleasanton, south of San Antonio in Atascosa County, northwestward through Medina, Bandera, Kerr, Gillespie, Mason, McCulloch, and Coleman counties to Abilene in Taylor County and thence northward through Knox County and into Oklahoma at Doan's Crossing of the Red River in Wilbarger County.[87]

These routes through central Texas are among the most significant lines of cultural diffusion in our frontier history. By them knowledge of the range-cattle industry was sent outward from Texas. Exported to the north and west along with the techniques of the ranching livelihood was the violent subculture of central Texas. A host of influential American cowmen had a central Texas origin as did many of the most famous protagonists of Western violence. In many of these old-time central Texans, who went north or west, a tendency to violence was combined with cattle-industry expertise. Such a person was I. P. (Print) Olive who gained a notoriety both for the size of his herds and the macabre deaths that befell his rustling enemies.

The dauntless Olive clan—the father, James, and his five sons, Print, Jay, Ira, Bob, and Marion—had its roots in the rich, rugged farm and range country about 30 miles northeast of Austin.[88] Among the first pioneers into the region before the Civil War, the Olives settled in southwest Williamson County. Things were quiet before the Civil War, but, after 1865, with young Print home from the Confederate army, the Olives ran into increasing opposition as they carved out a local ranching empire between the Yegua (pronounced "Yawah" by the inhabitants) and Brushy creeks. By 1869, the Olives, headed by Print, were engaged in what amounted to constant guerrilla warfare with cattle rustlers affiliated with the fearsome Yegua Notch-Cutters, who were quartered along Yegua Creek and among the Yegua Knobs bordering the three counties of Williamson, Lee, and Bastrop. In 1870, Print Olive killed a young connection of the Yegua gang, Dave Fream, in an exchange of gunfire, but it was not until 1876 that the strife between the Olives and those who harassed them rose to the level of a true central Texas conflict.

It was Bob Olive who made the first kill, dropping Lawson Kelley in early 1876. Later, about September 1, 1876, Bob won another shootout—this time with Lawson's even tougher brother, Dock Kelley, who had been running with the Ringo-Gladden gang of central Texas. Bob Olive's slaying of Lawson and Dock Kelley was topped by an all-out war that raged between the Olives and the Crow-Turner-Smith-Nutt faction. The Olives got in the first lick in March, 1876, with the execution of James H. Crow and Turk Turner who were caught disposing of some slain Olive cattle. Even more sensational than the murder of Crow and Turner was what the Olives did to their lifeless bodies in an affair probably supervised by Print. They sewed up the corpses in the green skins of the dead cows and left them on the open prairie with the Olive brands turned out as a warning to others.

The killing of Crow and Turner triggered a series of acts of revenge against the Olives that were led, apparently, by James H. Crow's son, Grip, and Cal Nutt and some of the numerous Smiths of the vicinity. In July, Bob Olive killed a black youth who, so he claimed, had been sent to assassinate him. Soon the Olives got word from an informer that the Yegua gang was planning a raid to exterminate the Olives. Determined to repel the blow, the Olives and their cowboys holed up at their stock pens where they hoped to lead their opponents into a trap. With a guard mounted nightly, the Olives were nonetheless surprised on the night of August 1, 1876, when about 15 or 20 men launched a blazing attack. The Olives fought off their assailants with many wounded on both sides. When Jay Olive died several days later, Print and Bob invoked in their brother's behalf "the feudal code of Brotherhood in the Texas of that day—'You kill my brother and I'll kill you.'" [89] Print and Bob focused their revenge on the Smiths and Cal Nutt, who they accused of planning the raid. Meanwhile, in early September, an Olive cowboy killed a Turner in the Williamson County town of Round Rock, later to be famous as the site of outlaw Sam Bass's demise. And, a day later, on September 7, Print Olive rose from a nap at his own house to shoot down a black, Banks, who had been sent on another mission of murder, and to wound Banks's accomplice, a second black named Donaldson.

In September, also, the neighborhood heard that one of the Smiths was missing. Olive family tradition holds that Print killed the missing Smith as the latter crossed Brushy Creek in an attempt to leave the country. Print then secretly buried the body, so the tradition runs. Cal Nutt, the other main target, met his end in Austin's Iron Front Saloon when he lost a flash-quick gun battle to Bob Olive in December, 1876.

With the killing of Smith and Nutt, the Olives had settled the score with the rustlers and were ready to leave Williamson County. The Olives were never people to run from a fight, but the constant feuding took too much time and energy. They were also eager to leave Williamson County where an increasing population blocked their ambitious plans to increase their herds. Their destination was the thinly settled open-range country of Custer County, Nebraska, with its lush grasses.

The Olive brothers' central-Texas scenario of a death-struggle with rangeland opponents was to be repeated in Nebraska. Print, who had already made many drives up the nearby Chisholm Trail, led the Olive exodus to Nebraska. Bob Olive, wanted by Texas Rangers for the slaying of Cal Nutt, came along under an alias. Establishing themselves in 1877 on a huge range along the Middle and South Loup rivers, the Olives were soon embroiled with their neighbors there.

The Olive group brought with them a mean reputation as a "gun outfit" gained in the central Texas war—an image accentuated by the bestowing of the Olive name on a new flapless revolver holster designed for quick-draw action. In a prelude of the trouble to come, Ira Olive killed one of his own vaqueros in a senseless quarrel. As they settled down in Nebraska, the Olives and their cowboys were decidedly on the shoot.

The Nebraska violence was set to brewing on the eastern border of the Olive range by two pugnacious homesteaders, Luther Mitchell and Ami Ketchum. Print Olive and his brothers charged that Mitchell and Ketchum were rustling their cattle and selling it on the sly. Conversely, Mitchell, Ketchum, and their settler allies claimed that the Olive "gun outfit" was trying to push all the homesteaders off the land. It was a classic confrontation between large cattlemen (for the Olives had supporters among the other big ranchers of Custer County) and sod-busting small farmers. It bore some resemblance to the earlier conflict in Williamson County, Texas, and it was a confrontation that would reappear again and again in the West. The Custer County situation was a more ambiguous one than that in central Texas where the Olives had been quite clearly beset by genuine cattle rustlers. But the Olives, with their patience already tried to the breaking point by the Texas battles, were in no mood to try to understand the homesteaders' point of view.

The climax came in December, 1878, just two years after the Olives came to Nebraska. Bob Olive got himself sworn in as deputy sheriff after he saw cattle bearing the Olive brand in a railroad stockyard with papers that traced them back to the Mitchell-Ketchum group. Bearing a warrant for Ketchum's arrest for cattle rustling, Bob led a party to the homestead where Mitchell and Ketchum waited. The guns on both sides spoke at once, leaving Bob Olive dead and Mitchell and Ketchum in flight. The central Texas pledge of "you kill my brother, and I'll kill you" was decisive once more for Print Olive.

The fate of Mitchell and Ketchum was sealed when pro-Olive officers caught them and turned them over to Print in return for a large reward. The result came quickly on the morning of December 11, 1878, when, at Devil's Gap a few miles from his ranch, Print Olive presided over the lynching of Mitchell and Ketchum. But what happened next was greeted by Nebraska and the nation as a greater atrocity than the hanging and shooting, for the two inert bodies were then burned almost beyond recognition and tossed into a loosely covered grave. Print Olive blamed his henchmen for the burning, but, as his biographer notes, it "was forever linked to the name of I. P. Olive . . . a harsh retribution for taking the law into his own hands, a distressing and unshakable cross which he would carry for the balance of his days." [90]

With a photograph of the two charred corpses circulating widely, indignation against Print Olive mounted, and the man-burning event continued to claim headlines while Print Olive's trial dragged along in 1879. Print regained his freedom in 1880 after serving only a year and a half of a lifetime prison sentence, when his lawyers won a reversal of his conviction. He remained in Nebraska for a few more years and then transferred his ranching operations to western Kansas. Not long after, Print Olive died by violence. On August 16, 1886, Print walked unarmed and unsuspecting into an eastern Colorado saloon and was shot down by Joe Sparrow, a ne'er-do-well old acquaintance out of Goliad County, central Texas, whom Print had taunted the day before as a deadbeat.

The violent record of the Olives is awesome. Of the five Olive brothers, only one, Marion, lived a peaceful life. Print, Bob, and Jay were all shot to death, and Ira killed a man.[91] Print Olive typified the two-fisted central Texas man of property who would kill without remorse in the defense of himself, his family, and his possessions. Print and his kin were typical in their commitment to the central Texas code of violent self-defense and self-redress. They were exceptional only in the number of their victims.

VI

Counterpointing the innumerable violent individuals exemplified by John Wesley Hardin, Bill Mitchell, and Print Olive were the many violent localities of far-flung central Texas. Among the wild, tough counties of that land, Comanche County bears examination as a microcosm of the region's violence. Not really more extreme in degree of violence than such counties as Shackelford, Brown, Erath, Lampasas, Llano, Coryell, Kimble, Gonzales, DeWitt, and others, Comanche County was, however, remarkable for the variety of its violence. Indian raids, cattle rustling and horse stealing, desperado activity (by John Wesley Hardin), endemic vigilantism, racial violence, and agrarian discontent beset the turbulent county.

The only major form of central Texas disorder absent was that of the community feud.

Within the broader tradition of central Texas violence, Comanche County gained its own distinct image. As late as the 1940's, Comanche County still had a reputation for lawlessness but a pale one compared to its fame in the 1870's and 1800's. Located at the southern end of the wooded Cross Timbers country astride "a high tableland broken by a jumble of hills and fertile valleys" about 80 miles southwest of Ft. Worth, Comanche County became a favorite place of the "hardy ranchers who dared to push their herds out into the Indian country" in the early days.[92] Comanche was one of those counties in the area subject to Indian attacks from 1870 to 1875 with local men obliged to join a Minute Men Company in 1872 to fend off the Indians for whom the county was named.[93] Productive cattle ranches in Comanche County, although served by a branch of the old Chisholm Trail,[94] were plagued by violence-engendering cattle rustling and, later, fence-cutting.

Defending the community by extralegal action was a tradition in Comanche County. As one old timer recalled of the county-seat town (also named Comanche), "the tree on the square was the gathering point for a meeting of any sort. There were lots of things settled there that could not be taken care of in the Court House." [95] But violence was general throughout the county and not restricted to the county seat. Sipe Springs in the northwest part of the county was visited several times by vigilantes intent on stamping out cattle rustling,[96] but an even more violence-prone locale was Hazel Dell in the northeast sector. Beset by horse stealing and other nefarious activity, Hazel Dell in the 1870's had "more gun play and rope stretching" than any other town in the area.[97]

It was at Hazel Dell that vigilantes from counties east of Comanche committed "one of the most unfortunate mob actions to occur in central Texas." The vigilantes raided the James Mackey place looking for Mackey's two sons who "had gone wrong" and were thought to have stolen some horses. The father—who had a good reputation—was away at Waco, and the two boys escaped. But later, after old man Mackey had returned, the vigilantes paid another visit. They dragged James Mackey out of his house and up a creek a few hundred yards and hanged him to an oak. Mrs. Mackey followed with a butcher knife intending to cut him down

before he expired, but one of the vigilantes saw her and shot
Mackey dead through the head.[98]

Another brutal lynching occurred at Hazel Dell, about 1882,
when thirteen members of a mob wrested the two Frailey brothers,
accused of stealing seed cotton, from the custody of an officer. The
two Fraileys had been chained together before being taken to the
county seat, Comanche. The older of the two told the mob that his
18-year-old brother had had nothing to do with the stealing and
pleaded that he be spared. In response a member of the mob
declared that "it was too blankety-blank much trouble to unchain
them" whereupon the brothers were taken a few miles away and
hanged from an old oak tree.[99] As late as 1886 Hazel Dell's
vigilante "Committee of 100" circulated an expulsion notice to
three residents, and, in the same year, one William Pruitt, wanted
by the vigilantes, was lynched near Sipe Springs.[100] Thus, the
mortality rate for the earliest settlers of Hazel Dell was a high one.
At least nine met violent deaths: the aforementioned James
Mackey and the Frailey brothers; Bill and Nute Jeffreys, hanged
by vigilantes in the Hamilton County town of Meridian; Joe
Hardin done in by Comanche County vigilantes; and M. M. Stone,
W. D. McFall, and Dan Mackey—all three shot to death but not
by the vigilantes.[101]

The remainder of Comanche County was not much quieter than
Hazel Dell. On the night of October 20, 1872, before the county
even had a jail three prisoners were being taken to Stephenville in
adjacent Erath County for safekeeping. The trio consisted of a
murderer, T. D. Reynolds, and two horse thieves, Mason and
Roberts. Although headed by a deputy sheriff, the escorting party
of several members was planning a lynching; one of its members
had purchased a 36-foot rope before leaving Comanche. The result
appeared the next day when the three prisoners were found
hanging from a tree limb six miles out of Comanche on the road to
Stephenville. The deputy claimed that the prisoners had been taken
from his party by a mob.[102]

Five days later, on October 25, 1872, Comanche County was the
scene of another multiple lynching, although in this case the
lynchers came from Erath County. On the night of the 25th, five
men—J. B. McDow, James M. Latham, Fayette Latham, Noble
Hardin,[103] and James Coates—were being held in the Erath County

jail for horse theft. A guard of sixteen men probably connived in the action of the mob, which broke into the jail that night and took the five men. Two men escaped the mob, but James Latham was killed in the act of capture, and two others, McDow and Hardin, were hanged. The Adjutant-General of Texas, investigating conditions in the vigilante-ridden area, consulted the district judge and others, and concluded that Comanche and Erath counties were experiencing a "reign of terror" under which it would be impossible to empanel a jury in either county that would convict "the members of these mobs, no matter how strong the evidence." [104]

The "reign of terror" continued on into 1873 and then reached a climax with the events of 1874 centering on John Wesley Hardin.

John Wesley Hardin's dispatch of deputy sheriff Charles Webb in the pre-dusk gunfight of May 26, 1874, set off a chain reaction of vigilantism that missed its main mark of John Wesley but bagged his brother and four of his associates. Comanche County feelings were aroused against John Wesley Hardin because he had killed the community favorite, Webb.[105] Mixed into the fatal maelstrom of hatreds, too, was the long-standing resentment of Comanche County people against John Wesley's brother, Joe, whose land fraud schemes in the Hazel Dell section had cost settlers many a dollar. No accusation of thievery against John Wesley Hardin has survived, but such was not the case with his brother Joe, a lawyer. As one old settler recalled, "Joe Hardin was hung on that land stealing business; by God there ought to have been lots more hung besides Joe. Old Steen was mixed up in that. Joe Hardin would come down here and he and old Steen would stay in the clerk's office all night fixing things . . . . Joe Hardin had a lot of seals he used in making fraudulent titles. I know of several parties that had to buy their places over . . . ." [106] An aged resident of Comanche, a contemporary of Joe Hardin, recalled, too, that "Joe was tricky . . . he was involved in some funny land deals, and his wife was hiding the deeds." [107]

With this backlog of hostility against John Wesley Hardin and his brother, the justice of lynch law was soon to come. After the killing of Charles Webb by John Wesley, a general roundup of the latter's friends and relatives took place. Three of the Hardinites—brother Joe and cousins Tom and Bud Dixon—were shut up in the county courthouse when, late on June 4, 1874, "in the dead hours of midnight," as John Wesley lamented, vigilantes had "come into the town of Comanche, had thrown ropes around the necks of Joe, Bud, and Tom, and had led them, bareheaded and barefooted, through the streets and out to some post oaks near by, where they hung them until they were dead." The next morning a posse fell upon Aleck Barrickman and Ham Anderson, two followers of John Wesley Hardin, at the Bill Stone ranch near Hazel Dell and shot them both to death.[108]

Night riding and mob action continued on into the 1880's in Comanche County and hit a new peak in the troubled year of 1886. The Committee of 100, a vigilante group, was active, and Comanche's newspaper, the *Town and Country*, asserted on June 20, 1886, that there had been more lawlessness in Comanche in the past ten months than in the previous ten years. People were getting tired of "a murder every month," said *Town and Country*. The newspaper, in an obvious allusion to the 1874 lynchings of the Hardin party, noted that "mob law" had once had an "effect for good." Added to the upsurge of disorder and vigilantism were the economic hard times, which caused the Democrats of the county to quarrel among themselves.[109] Such was the background for the explosion of violence that took the form of a vendetta against the county's blacks.

With the tumult of the 1870's focusing on horse stealing and cattle rustling and on desperado activity, epitomized by John Wesley Hardin, racial conflict in Comanche County had been kept in the background,[110] but in 1875 there had been a portent of trouble to come when a black, Mose Jones, had run amok and killed two young Negro girls and two white boys and was, in turn, killed by a search party. This episode ended without further violence, but a hatred of the county's blacks took hold among some whites. Violent racial prejudice surfaced soon after the July 24, 1886 murder of Mrs. Sally Stephens by her young black employee, Tom McNeel, after she had spoken sharply to him. A posse quickly captured McNeel and took him to the farm of one Green Saunders near DeLeon in the northern corner of the county. Then on July 26th he was taken to the scene of his crime where, over the protest of deputy sheriff W. D. Cox, he was hanged by a mob led by Saunders. DeLeon Negroes were forced to bury the corpse minus souvenirs of the body (and bits of the hanging rope), which were still being sold as late as 1898.

After the lynching of McNeel, and before the crowd dispersed, Green Saunders launched into a furious speech demanding the expulsion of all blacks from the county as retribution for the recent crime of McNeel and that of Mose Jones 11 years before. The crowd responded favorably, and the blacks of the DeLeon vicinity were given a warning to leave. Late that night "the mob, masked, rode into Comanche and visited every shack in the negro section with the warning to pack up and get out within ten days or be killed." The expulsion notice touched off a debate among the county's whites, with some of the latter coming to the defense of the blacks. At least one prominent family was divided on the issue of expulsion. Jim Nabers, a surviving brother of the two white boys whom Mose Jones had murdered, took part in the lynching of McNeel, but the father of the Nabers brothers, T. J. Nabers, was instrumental in convening a mass meeting on July 27th that drew 55 citizens, who, thereupon, passed resolutions in favor of law and order and against the expulsion. As the August 6, 1886, deadline approached political gibes were hurled (the pro-Negro mass meeting of July 27th was branded a Republican assembly composed of "nigger lovers"), one white pistol-whipped another, and threats were made. Two white men offered to defend their black employees against the mob, but the blacks decided to leave anyway lest the lives of their white sponsors be jeopardized. The Texas Rangers were sent for to restore order in the county, but they did not arrive in time to prevent (if, indeed, they would have moved to prevent) the forced exodus of the blacks. Although tragic in its impact, the departure was not huge, for the total black population of Comanche County numbered only forty or fifty. The expulsion was qualitative rather than quantitative in significance, for the event was a traumatic one for the county. Sixty years later the expulsion of the blacks was still remembered (with shame by some whites), and Comanche was still a whites-only county.

Symptomatic of a broader range of central Texas troubles was the political dissension that permeated Comanche County in its 1886 days of violence. The economic distress of the year weighed heavily on the less well-to-do farmers, a fact that resulted in a conflict among the county's Democrats, pitting the "Human party" of farmers and tenants against the Democratic regulars.[111] The pattern was not atypical. As the 1870's and 1880's wore on, the violence tended to be linked more and more with agrarian conflict, which stemmed from the more complex economic conditions in contrast to the pioneer economy of earlier times. The linkage of central Texas violence with the newer economic problems is revealed both by the rise of the Farmers' Alliance and the outbreak of the "Fence-Cutters' War."

The Farmers' Alliance that spread like wild fire in Texas and the South in the 1880's (with a booming Northern branch as well) is familiar to historians as a key progenitor of the great Populist movement of the 1890's—one of the most important movements of agrarian reform in American history.[112] It is not generally known, however, that the Farmers' Alliance was a direct outgrowth of central Texas violence. The Farmers' Alliance was initially organized in Lampasas County in 1874 or 1875 (and in Wise, or Parker, County in 1876) as a quasi-vigilante anti-horse thief organization.[113] The emergence of the Farmers' Alliance was a natural central Texas response to the chaotic conditions in wild Lampasas County. It was about this time, for example, that the Horrell-Higgins feud—in which there were accusations of cattle rustling—was lacerating the county, and, in this period, vigilantism was rife in central Texas.

Dr. C. W. Macune, the greatest leader of the Farmers' Alliance at the state, regional, and national levels in the 1880's and 1890's, had bounced around some of the most violent parts of central Texas (Burnet, 1874–1875; Georgetown, Williamson County, 1875; San Saba, about 1875–1876; and Junction, Kimble County and Fredericksburg, Gillespie County about 1879) as a cattle drover and editor before turning to the alleviation of farmer grievances in his ascendant role in the Farmers' Alliance.[114] Macune was well acquainted with the era of central Texas violence that produced the Alliance, and he later reminisced about the origins of the Alliance in the 1870's. With the operations of a gang of horse thieves "becoming more and more annoying," Macune recalled, a number of settlers agreed to organize to assist civil officers against the outlaws. "As all the members of this new organization were farmers, they decided to name it The Farmers [*sic*] Alliance." Using "passwords, signs, and grips," the original Farmers' Alliance was a secret society in the broad tradition of vigilantism.[115]

Conditions of economic hardship for the farmers of central Texas in the 1880's transformed the quasi-vigilante Farmers' Alliance into a nonviolent political and economic movement for broad agrarian reform. The reverse situation occurred when economic discontent among the small ranchers and farmers of central Texas led to a 20-year period of sporadic violence, in 1880–1900, capped by the Fence-Cutters' War of 1883–1884. The 1880's was a period of transition, during which much of the open range was fenced in. Fences were put up by the owners of large cattle ranches, who wished to secure their four-footed property, and by some farmers. Ranchers who owned from 15 to 200 head of cattle on 100 acres or less needed the open range to supplement the small amount of land they owned in fee simple. Although much of the fence-cutting violence was directed against regular farmers, farmers themselves occasionally joined in the cutting. Generally speaking, there was an alignment of the less affluent and the poor (the fence cutters) against the more prosperous (the fence owners). The result was a sharp, violent struggle in central Texas. During the fall of 1883, the contention "reached the proportions of open warfare," and thousands of miles of fence were cut by night. Fence cutting was generally widespread in central Texas in 1883–1884, but the worst outbreaks seem to have occurred in the counties of Clay, Brown, Coleman, Denton, Falls, Karnes, Medina, Tarrant, and Wise. Men were killed in Clay County and in Comanche County's bumptious neighbor, Brown County. In Brownwood, the county seat of Brown County, a gun battle was narrowly averted when the fence owners barricaded themselves in the courthouse against the farmer and the stockmen fence cutters, who had taken over the local opera house. The 1884 passage of a state law making fence cutting a felony brought the war of 1883–1884 to an end, but fence cutting on a smaller scale continued in central Texas until the turn of the century. Fence-cutting incidents were reported as late as 1897 in McCulloch County and 1898 in Brown and Waller counties.[116]

VII

While the rural precincts of central Texas—ranch, farm, and dusty town—were being buffeted by the exploits of the fence cutters and other protagonists of strife, the growing cities and educational centers scarcely escaped the regional plague of violence. Such is the significance of the tragic career of Will Brann, the victim of a cultural conflict.

William Cowper Brann ("Brann the Iconoclast") has gained standing in the history of American reform journalism for his promotion of free thought deep in the Bible Belt of Texas. Brann's monthly *Iconoclast*, in which he published slashing attacks on his fundamentalist Baptist neighbors of Waco, Texas in the vitriolic style of American personal journalism, is still remembered. All but forgotten, though, is Brann's fatal entanglement with the tradition of violence of central Texas. From the opening of his prose assault on Waco's Baptist establishment (centered on the local Baylor University), Brann's days were numbered, given the hair-trigger sensitivities of the central Texans of his era.[117]

Will Brann was born (*ca.* 1855) and reared in Illinois. He came to Texas as a reporter around 1883 or 1884 and in 1895 began publication of the *Iconoclast* in Waco. With a population of 25,000, Waco was one of the larger and certainly one of the more genteel cities of central Texas. It was an educational, a religious, and an intellectual center set in a rich, cotton-growing blackland. Waco's reputation as "the Athens of Texas" rested primarily upon the standing of Baylor University (enrollment 500), Texas's leading Baptist institution, along with the two other colleges and the one academy that thrived in the city. But, as Brann's biographer, Charles Carver, has noted, there was a darker side to Waco. Its other label was "Six-Shooter Depot." Back in the brawling 1860's and 1870's, McLennan County, of which Waco was the county seat, had had its fair share of the central Texas vigilantism and violence of the time. " 'Six-Shooter Depot' was a title," Carver states, "bought with the blood of hot-tempered citizens who adjusted their differences according to a relaxed interpretation of the dueling code of the Old South. In the days of the cattle drives following the Civil War, Waco lay close to the Chisholm Trail, and the town supplied the drivers with recreation, which often involved high-spirited killing of one another. This buoyant mood lasted through the century—as long as guns were a usual item of wearing apparel." [118]

Into this tinderbox of Baptist fervor and violent action, Brann brought his defiant *Iconoclast*.[119] In the very first issue, of February, 1895, he outraged Baptist readers with the bland claim that "the Sacred Books of all the centuries are essentially the same," and the Baylor-Brann feud was on. Not until five months later, however, in the July, 1895 *Iconoclast* did Brann publish an all-out attack on Baylor, with a scorching blast against Baylor and its aged, dignified president, Dr. Rufus C. Burleson. The cause was the Antonia Teixeira scandal. Antonia was a Brazilian teen-ager brought to study at Baylor to prepare for a missionary life in her native country. She lived at Dr. Burleson's home while attending Baylor and, in return for assisting Mrs. Burleson with the household chores, was given board, room, and tuition. Suddenly, in early 1895, Antonia's pregnancy was disclosed. When she publicly accused Steen Morris (the brother of Dr. Burleson's son-in-law, the Reverend Silas Morris) of raping her in the Burlesons's yard, the matter became a Waco sensation.

Brann rushed to the columns of the *Iconoclast* to heap scorn and contumely on Burleson, Baylor, and the Baptists for Antonia's luckless condition. The Baylor president replied with a pamphlet defending Steen Morris's innocence and assailing Antonia as a wanton who shamelessly pursued men and boys.[120] For more than a year the controversy over Antonia raged, and Brann delivered barrage after barrage against her Baptist detractors. Finally, in late 1896, Antonia returned to Brazil,[121] and the scandal faded. Yet, Brann did not lay down his cudgels against Baylor and the Baptists. The provocative character of Brann's anti-Baylorism appears in the typical words of odium he aimed at the Baptist center in deriding a report that Dallas had offered Baylor $50,000 to $75,000 to move to that city. "There isn't a town in this world that wants it except Waco," Brann fumed. "Its students are chiefly forks-of-the-creek yaps who curry horses or run errands for their board and wear the same undershirt the year round. They take but two baths during their lifetime—one when they are born, the other when they are baptized. The institution is worth less than nothing to any town. It is what Ingersoll would call a storm-center of misinformation. It is the Alma Mater of mob violence. It is a chronic breeder of bigotry and bile. As a small Waco property owner, I will give it $1,000 any time to move to Dallas, and double that amount if it will go to Honolulu or hell." [122]

Brann had good reason to refer to Baylor as "the Alma Mater of mob violence," for not long before, on October 2, 1897, Baylor men had abducted him, taken him to the campus, beaten him, and had been only narrowly restrained by their professors from lynching him. The violence escalated. On October 6, 1897, Judge John Scarborough, the father of a Baylor student, cane-whipped Brann on the street in front of the *Iconoclast* office. Baylor tempers waxed hot, for a booming circulation carried the *Iconoclast*'s taunts beyond Texas to a delighted nation-wide audience. Threatened repeatedly, Brann did have defenders in Waco. One of them was Judge George B. Gerald who had the hot, steely temper of the old-time central Texan. As a result of an incident growing out of the Baylor-Brann feud, Judge Gerald killed the *Waco Times-Herald* editor, J. W. Harris, and his brother, W. A. (Bill) Harris, in a burst of gunfire on the main street of Waco on November 19, 1897—a double slaying worthy of the skill of a John Wesley Hardin.[123]

The Gerald-Harris shootout illustrates the suddenness of central Texas violence and its tragic depth. "In his cold fury," writes Carver, "Gerald had approached so close to Bill Harris before firing that the dead man's collar had been set smouldering by the flame from the pistol. It was a sobering thought that a man could walk out of his house on a sunny afternoon, alert and sensible, perhaps kiss his wife good-by—but more likely just call out casually the hour he expected to return—and within the hour become a grotesque burning doll in a rubbish-strewn gutter." [124]

Brann's own time drew near. More denunciations of Baylor followed the Harris killings, and the city remained heavy with peril for Brann. The end came on the afternoon of April 1, 1898, just as Brann was preparing to depart on a lecture trip with his wife. As Brann strolled near the center of Waco, a "vocal anti-Brann citizen," Tom Davis, shot him in the back. Badly hurt but not felled, Brann wheeled to retaliate, and a staccato gun fight erupted. In seconds, though, both men sank down, each fatally wounded.

With the Baylor-Brann feud the central Texas tradition of violence expanded beyond the lost, sunswept counties and villages of the Cross Timbers and Hill Country to the urban bosom of genteel Texas religion and education. It destroyed a leading journalist at the peak of his national reputation. William C. Brann sought no battles except the polemical ones in the pages of his *Iconoclast*. He did not fire first, but, in Waco, in the late year of 1898, he packed a pistol and dropped the man who shot him. In his own way Will Brann was as much an exemplar of the central Texas self-defense syndrome as Bill Mitchell, John Wesley Hardin, or Print Olive. Brann was both protagonist and victim of the violence of the region.

VIII

The fatal climax of the Baylor-Brann conflict and the waning of the frontier period did not signal the end of significant central Texas violence. Community feuds flared up on into the twentieth century.[125] Oil-boom towns rocked with violence as the new century wore on,[126] and, from time to time, there were searing deeds of mob violence, such as the 1929 lynching of bank robber Marshall Ratliff in the town of Eastland.[127] Of larger proportion was the wave of Ku Klux Klan violence in the post-World War I period.

Ku Klux Klan activity in central Texas in the early 1920's, although part of a nation-wide movement, was a throwback to the acute violence of the post-Civil War era. In the Southwest, more than anywhere else in the United States, the revived Ku Klux Klan of the 1920's "became a device for the ruthless dictation of community morals and ethics." [128] A major cause of this was the explosive growth of such central Texas cities as Dallas, Ft. Worth, San Antonio, and Houston from 1910 to 1920. In that period, the population of Dallas jumped from 92,000 to 159,000; Ft. Worth from 73,000 to 106,000; San Antonio from 77,000 to 161,000; and Houston from 79,000 to 138,000. This rapid urban increase was accomplished largely by a flow of rural migrants into the cities. Texas's oil and cotton boom created commercial and industrial opportunities in the cities and induced ambitious men to leave the ranches, farms, and small towns of central Texas for the better economic prospects of the city. Urban prosperity appealed to the migrants, but the conditions of city life were often disquieting. The loose living, immorality, and crime of the booming cities were an affront to the rural standards of morality of the migrants, and they enlisted in the Ku Klux Klan by the thousands in an attempt to reimpose the strict morality of their origins on the chaotic cities.[129]

The principal leader of the Klan in Texas and the Southwest in the early 1920's was a dentist, Dr. Hiram W. Evans, of the central Texas metropolis of Dallas. Evans led the frequently successful Klan effort in Texas politics, but he did not scorn to foment and participate in violence. Evans was the leader of a Dallas foray in which a Negro bellhop, Alex Johnson, was dragged out of the Adolphus Hotel to have the initials K. K. K. branded in acid on his forehead.[130] Although Klan violence in Texas was, thus, at times directed against black people, it was more characteristically turned against white "moral transgressors and bootleggers" of the same ethnic stock (Anglo-Saxon, generally) as their Klan tormentors. In a "crusade for conformity," the Klan, in February, 1921, initiated in Houston a two-and-a-half year campaign that found Klan bands behaving as "masked regulators" in fifty-two violent actions in which the Klansmen "took the law into their own hands" against those whose behavior violated Bible Belt moral standards.[131] Tarring and feathering was common, and, although the violence spread throughout Texas, much of it was concentrated in the central region. In McLennan County, the strong Baptist city of Waco (the scene of Will Brann's ill-fated journalistic career) became a Ku Klux Klan hotbed, and, in October, 1921, a Klan parade in Lorena, south of Waco, led to a riot in which one person was killed and several others were wounded. The Lorena violence received national publicity, and community sentiment in favor of the Klan was revealed when the McLennan County sheriff, who had tried to stop the parade, was not only wounded on the occasion but publicly rebuked by the grand jury of the county.[132]

The Ku Klux Klan violence of the 1920's has faded, but the violent proclivities of individual central Texans has not. In a study of modern Texas, John Bainbridge found the Lone Star State still very much under the sway ·of the self-redress and self-defense syndrome that emerged in the central Texas post-Civil War era of acute violence. In June, 1960, the school-board secretary in the town of Brownsboro, Bainbridge noted, "punctuated years of bitter feuding over local affairs by shooting and killing a fellow-towns-man after a free-for-all at a school board meeting." [133] As an accurate statement of the contemporary Texas temper, Bainbridge quoted C. L. Sonnichsen's declaration that "today, if a man's life and his livelihood are endangered and he has no recourse to law, he will resort to folk justice, as did his ancestors." [134] Even the Reverend Billy Graham, a man deeply sympathetic to Texans, once found it appropriate to refer to Houston as the "murder capital" of America,[135] and Bainbridge, in his account of crime and violence in modern Texas, described repeated acts of homicide in Dallas, Houston, and smaller central Texas cities.[136]

Many of the murders cited by Bainbridge were committed under the old central Texas ethic of self-redress,[137] and the statistics of homicide collected by the Federal Bureau of Investigation in its annual *Uniform Crime Reports* reveal that Texas continues to be a national leader in the category of homicide. As late as 1970, the Texas per capita rate for "murder and nonnegligent manslaughter" was 11.6 per 100,000. This was far above the national rate of 7.2 and greatly exceeded the rates of the supposedly crime-prone states of New York, California, and Illinois where the rates were, respectively, 7.9, 6.9, and 9.6.[138] In absolute terms, the 1970 toll in Texas was very high, with a total of 1,294 murders and nonnegligent homicides—a figure that was surpassed only by the states of New York (1,439) and California (1,376) with their far larger populations. The only other state that had over a thousand such killings was Illinois, with 1,066, an amount well below that of Texas.[139] No separate figures for central Texas are available, but, by 1970, the two metropolises of the region were Houston and Dallas. With their huge populations of 1,213,064 and 836,121, respectively, these two urban giants nonetheless exemplified, among their residents, the cultural mores and tendency to violence of the old central Texas region. It is significant that, in 1970, among the 12 largest "standard metropolitan areas" in the United States, Dallas ranked second and Houston third for the per capita rate for murders and nonnegligent homicides. The Dallas and Houston rates per 100,000 were 18.4 and 16.9, respectively. They were far in excess of the New York City rate of 10.5, of Chicago's 12.9, Detroit's 14.7, and also of the rates for Los Angeles, Philadelphia, Baltimore, Washington, Cleveland, St. Louis, and San Francisco.

Only Atlanta's rate of 20.4 was greater.[140] Thus, the violence-prone character of nineteenth-century central Texas has survived down to the present. John Bainbridge attributed the continuing wave of murder in Texas to a historical factor stressed in this study: the tradition of the ethic of self-defense and self-redress,[141] accentuated by the easy availability of firearms and the long-time habit of carrying a gun.[142] C. L. Sonnichsen states that violent feuds (of which detailed descriptions are not yet advisable) continue to flourish in contemporary Texas.[143] In our own time, Texas juries frequently decline to indict or to convict in flagrant cases of murder committed in allegiance to the self-redress ethic.[144] In fact, the highest court in Texas, in contrast to other states, has given special recognition to individual self-protection: "In other states a man has to 'retreat' as far as he can before he kills an attacker," but "in Texas he can stand his ground. The lawyers say he doesn't have to retreat any farther than 'the air at his back.' " [145]

Three of the most notable individual criminal episodes in twentieth-century American history have taken place in recent years in central Texas: the assassination of President John F. Kennedy; the campus murders by the sniper, Charles Whitman; and the killings by Dean Allen Corll. In the first of these crimes—the slaying of Kennedy, Dallas was, in the early 1960's, in the grips of a right-wing mood that approached hysteria.[146] Of course, Lee Harvey Oswald, the 1963 assassin of President Kennedy was a self-styled Marxist and by no means a part of Dallas's frenzied rightist faction, but it is quite possible—perhaps even probable—that the extremist mood of Dallas in 1963 (which was reminiscent of the ambience of Waco during the Baylor-Brann feud of the 1890's) affected Oswald. The mounting extremism of Dallas may well have triggered Oswald's feelings against Kennedy, which seem to have been largely psychotic in character[147] despite the veneer of ideology. While a historical trajectory of violence may be drawn from the post-Civil War period time of central Texas to Oswald's crime of assassination (and Jack Ruby's counter-assassination of Oswald in the Dallas jail two days later—a classic example of the self-redress ethic: Ruby killed Oswald, he said, not only to avenge the fallen president but also to spare Mrs. Kennedy the painful ordeal of a public trial of her husband's killer),[148] the same is not true for the two other notable crimes of contemporary central Texas. Neither the seriously disturbed Charles Whitman who fatally shot 13 persons from his tower perch on the University of Texas campus in Austin in 1966[149] nor Dean Allen Corll of Houston, the allegedly homosexual murderer of at least 23 boys over a period of 3 years[150] in two of the largest homicidal sprees in American history seem to have been affected by the tradition of central Texas violence, but there is an apt, if macabre, historical symbolism in the location of these shocking episodes in central Texas.

IX

As noted in the introduction to this book, American life has been split between the lawless and the law abiding, between extremism and moderation, between the violent and the peaceable. The presidential leadership of the late Lyndon B. Johnson, with his central Texas heritage, exemplifies this dichotomy. In the realm of peaceful domestic accomplishments no president did more to advance the causes of civil rights, equal opportunity, and education for all Americans than Lyndon B. Johnson, and, with his appointment of four great study commissions on assassination,[151] law enforcement and the administration of justice,[152] race riots,[153] and violence,[154] no president has exceeded Lyndon B. Johnson's sensitivity to violence in America and the need for its eradication. Despite the tragic violence of the Vietnam war, one must acknowledge that Johnson kept his pledge of no nuclear war (though not his promise of no wider war in southeast Asia) and had inaugurated a de-escalation before leaving office.

Yet, when all this has been said, there remains the problem of understanding the relationship between this man of civility and reform and the *bête noire* of his administration, the Vietnam war.[155] The point to be developed here is that Lyndon B. Johnson's historical heritage—the violent tradition of central Texas—was crucial to the formation of the policy that led to the all-out American war in Vietnam. The effect of the central Texas tradition of violence was to mold an individual character structure in which violence was vested with a high degree of legitimacy when exercised in behalf of what was thought to be a good cause.

President Lyndon B. Johnson, as leader of the national war effort in Vietnam, is a striking example of the central Texas ethic of violent self-defense that crystallized after the Civil War.

Still, Lyndon B. Johnson was far from being the only prominent American who favored military intervention in Vietham. Lyndon B. Johnson's central Texas ethic of self-defense led him to approve arguments from *others* for the escalation of American military involvement in Vietnam. As for the "others"—chiefly the circle of elite Eastern bureaucrats and intellectuals President John F. Kennedy had brought to the fore, and to whom Lyndon B. Johnson turned for advice, their motivations were entirely different, combining an elitist, confident commitment "to a new American nationalism, bringing a new, strong, dynamic spirit to our historic role in world affairs, not necessarily to bring the American dream to reality here at home, but to bring it to reality elsewhere in the world." [156] Just as Lyndon B. Johnson was pushed ever deeper into the quagmire of Vietnam by his origins amid the tradition of violence of central Texas, so, too, were the Kennedy-circle proponents of the Vietnam war the product of a historical tradition—a totally different tradition: a tradition of paternalistic American intervention in the world that flourished among the Anglophile elite of the eastern United States, dating back to the late nineteenth-century imperialism (e.g., the Spanish-American War and the takeover of the Philippines) and the early twentieth-century diplomacy of President Theodore Roosevelt and a circle that included Secretary of State John Hay and Roosevelt's young protegé, Henry L. Stimson. Exclusive prep schools, Ivy League universities and law schools, aristocratic gentlemen's clubs, and the genteel drawing rooms of the cultured well-to-do were the formative context of the interventionist tradition of the Eastern elite,[157] a tradition that beneath its urbane patina was every bit as violent, ultimately, as that of central Texas. The late Howard K. Beale described the origins of the elite Eastern interventionist tradition in his massive *Theodore Roosevelt and the Rise of America to World Power*,[158] and David Halberstam has perceptively traced the connection between the elite tradition and the architects of our Vietnam policy in his book, *The Best and the Brightest*.[159] Among those architects is the Kennedy-Johnson national security chief, McGeorge Bundy[160]—brilliant, incisive Boston Brahmin, Groton and Yale graduate, Harvard professor and dean, literary collaborator of Henry L. Stimson, direct legatee of the Roosevelt-Hay-Stimson interventionist approach to foreign policy, and hawkish promoter of the American military adventure in Vietnam. It will never be known whether John F. Kennedy, had his presidential career not been cut short by assassination, would have led us into the sort of full-scale Vietnam war presided over by Lyndon B. Johnson, but Kennedy himself did sponsor a significant escalation of our role in Vietnam that was a prelude to the massive commitment of combat air power and soldiers in 1965. John F. Kennedy, too, was schooled in the elite Eastern tradition of paternalistic military intervention.[161]

By the time Lyndon B. Johnson took office as president in late 1963, McGeorge Bundy and other influential exemplars of the elite Eastern interventionist tradition were in the process of forging an option for enormous American military activity in Vietnam.[162] A complete stranger to the elite Eastern interventionist tradition by virtue of a decidedly different personal background, Lyndon B. Johnson might well have rejected that option. Instead he chose to exercise it, true to the tradition that nurtured him. He was a life-long superhawk in regard to American foreign policy—toward the Nazis and Japanese and, later, the Russians and the Red Chinese. Johnson's most thorough biographer, Alfred Steinberg, has noted that before he became president Johnson's most consistent theme in 24 years in Congress as a representative and senator was "his recurring call that the nation become an armed camp."[163] Thus, as early as 1940 in his first campaign for the Senate on the eve of World War II, Johnson made military preparedness his keynote.[164] Johnson, as president, personalized his leadership of military operations during the war. As the war progressed in 1965 Johnson "visualized himself on the battlefields and in field headquarters. 'I've got to go to Da Nang,' he said as he excused himself from partying White House guests with a heavy sigh, signifying that duty called him back to work. 'I could have bombed again last night, but I didn't,' he told a visitor."[165] The President's customary late-night vigils, while American planes were flying over North Vietnam became one of the legends of the war. For the origins of this mind-set one must revisit central Texas.

Lyndon B. Johnson's ancestral home in Johnson City, Blanco

County, was in the heart of the violent country of central Texas during the Civil War and after. Blanco County was the scene of desperate fighting with the Indians, and the Johnson home ranch was the target of a Comanche raid.[166] The county had its own vigilante movement, and it was in the frontier belt where Major John B. Jones's Frontier Battalion of Texas Rangers pursued Indians and outlaws in the 1870's. Moreover, Blanco County was surrounded by the scene of some outstanding events in central Texas violence. In Gillespie County, on Blanco's western boundary, the Haenger Bande killed German settlers during the Civil War. Blanco County was 30 miles southwest of Mason County, locale of the Hoodoo vigilante war of 1875 and of the slaying of federal soldiers by Hays and Doboy Taylor in the turbulent period of Reconstruction. It was immediately below the vigilante disturbances of Llano and Burnet counties in the late 1870's and 70 miles southeast of the operations of the San Saba Mob. The Texas Rangers conducted their roundup of bad men in Kimble County 60 miles to the west, and the same distance to the north was Lampasas County, site of the Horrell-Higgins feud and the quasi-vigilante origins of the Farmers' Alliance; 40 more miles to the north was the fearsome Comanche County. The Waco arena of the Baylor-Brann conflict was 100 miles to the northeast and only 50 miles to the east were the Williamson County precincts where Print Olive led his clan in a death struggle with the Yegua gang and where outlaw Sam Bass perished in an ambush.[167] To the east and southeast, at distances ranging from 90 to 160 miles, were DeWitt, Colorado, Ft. Bend, and Waller counties, known for their community feuds, and Blanco County was in the area from Comanche to DeWitt roamed over by John Wesley Hardin. During all these episodes, the grandparents, great-uncles, and parents of Lyndon B. Johnson were establishing themselves deep in the heart of the violence-prone region of central Texas.

Shortly after the establishment of Blanco County in 1858 three brothers—Andrew Jackson Johnson, Jesse Thomas (Tom) Johnson, and Sam Ealy Johnson, Sr.—pioneered in the settlement of the Pedernales River valley in the central part of the county.[168] Sam Ealy Johnson, Sr., the grandfather of Lyndon Baines Johnson, and his brother, Tom, settled on a Pedernales River ranch near the site of the present town of Johnson City. (Johnson City was not founded until 1879 in which year James P. Johnson, the cousin of Lyndon's father, Sam Ealy Johnson, Jr., laid out the town.) [169] Sam, Sr., and Tom "built a log cabin and a rock barn with portholes for use in case of Indian attack" and raised cattle.[170] Sam, Sr.'s growing prosperity as a cattle rancher was interrupted by a stint in the Confederate army during the Civil War, but by 1870 he and Tom were among the largest drovers of cattle northward to Kansas from the central Texas area of the counties of Blanco, Gillespie, Burnet, Llano, Hays, Comal, and Kendall.[171] At Sam's side was his young wife, Eliza (nee Bunton), whom he married in 1867 and whom the historian and University of Texas dean, T. U. Taylor, years later labeled as one of the "leading pioneer women of Blanco County." [172] Eliza Bunton Johnson earned Dean Taylor's accolade by her heroism during the Comanche onslaught against Blanco County in the late 1860's. On one occasion, while alone at the ranch, she saved herself and her children in an Indian raid.[173] At this time, August 15, 1869, Mr. and Mrs. Tom Felps, neighbors of the Johnsons, were brutally killed and scalped by the Indians. Ten days later, in retaliation, ten young men of Blanco County routed the Comanches at the battle of Deer Creek, which took place only three miles from the ranch of Sam and Eliza Johnson. Three of the wounded men from Blanco County were carried to the Johnson ranch for treatment after the battle.[174]

The Indian warfare ended, but in 1871 Sam Ealy Johnson, Sr., suffered grave economic reverses in his cattle business. The family moved away for a while but returned to the Pedernales by 1877 when the father of Lyndon B. Johnson, Sam Ealy Johnson, Jr., was born. Sam Ealy Johnson, Jr., became one of the leading men of his sector of central Texas. Although he developed his small farm in Blanco County into one of the best in the area, Sam Ealy Johnson, Jr., made his mark in the field of politics and public service. He served twice (1904–1908, 1918–1923) in the state legislature, representing the central Texas bloc of Blanco, Llano, Kendall, and Gillespie counties in his second term. In the legislature he was anti-big business, pro-small farmer, and strongly pro-education. In his 1918 to 1923 term, he was one of the prominent liberal members of the house of representatives, with some significant progressive legislation to his credit.[175]

In 1907 Sam Ealy Johnson, Jr., married Rebekah Baines, the

daughter of Joseph W. Baines, a leading Blanco County lawyer and state legislator and a descendant of pioneer Texans.[176] To this union the future president, Lyndon Baines Johnson, was born on August 27, 1908, on the family farm along the Pedernales. Sources on the life and family background of Lyndon B. Johnson reveal that he was raised among the living traditions of central Texas violence. In fact, his Christian name, Lyndon, was bestowed as a tribute to one of the heroic opponents of central Texas disorder who in a crisis was more than willing to resort to violence himself. In her book of family history, Lyndon's mother, Rebekah Baines Johnson, recalled that three months after his birth she and her husband still had not agreed on a name for the baby boy. One morning Rebekah said, "Sam, I'm not getting up to cook breakfast until this baby is named. He is nearly three months old and the most wonderful baby in the world and still called 'Baby.' I've submitted all the names I know and you always turn them down. Now you suggest and I'll pass judgment." "What do you think about Linden for him?", was Sam's question. The mother replied, "That's fine, if I may spell it as I like. Lin*den* isn't so euphonious as Lyn*don* Johnson would be." "Spell it as you please," Sam agreed, *"he will still be named for my friend Linden.* So now the boy is named Lyndon Baines Johnson." [177]

The man after whom the future commander-in-chief of the Vietnam war was named was W. C. Linden, a good friend of Sam Ealy Johnson, Jr., a frequent visitor to his home, and a prominent central Texas attorney.[178] Ten years before the birth of his namesake, Lyndon B. Johnson, young W. C. Linden had, as the elected district attorney of San Saba County, broken up the murderous San Saba Mob of vigilantes in one of the most courageous prosecutions in the legal annals of central Texas.[179]

The San Saba Mob was a long-term vigilante movement whose operations were centered in northern San Saba County but extended into the neighboring counties of Mills, Brown, Coleman, and McCulloch. It was headed by leading cattlemen who impressed their fanatically religious moral piety on the vicinity by lynch law, mostly in the form of killing from ambush. From shadowy origins in the early 1880's the San Saba Mob had, by 1888, established a reign of terror over a wide locality. With Texas Rangers in the county seat, San Saba, to preserve order, the newly elected W. C. Linden undertook the prosecution of the leaders who had terrorized their own and other counties for so many years. In April, 1898, eight members of the Mob were brought to trial in the town of San Saba. Among the eight being tried was Little Jim Ford, son of Mat Ford, a "bellerin' Methodist" and the chieftain of the Mob. The eight men were charged with only two murders, but over the years it is estimated that the San Saba Mob had done away with twenty-five lives. Their victims had been horse thieves, cattle rustlers, and even ordinary lawful citizens who merely dared to voice opposition to their high-handed ways. Until the young district attorney began his prosecution, the Mob had been "all but invincible" in tough San Saba County.

W. C. Linden's closing speech for the prosecution on the last afternoon of the trial was a fiery one. He knew that the Mob would not hesitate to ambush him, given the opportunity. Hence, he went armed at all times, and "once when Linden made a quick turn in front of the jury box, his Prince Albert coat swung open to reveal a pearl-handled six-shooter on his hip and somebody in the audience gasped audibly. 'Yes, I carry a gun,' he told them. 'I carry it for just such occasions as this, and you all know I can use it.' " [180] Linden then quickly concluded his speech, and the case went to the jury.

The high point in the whole affair came not in the courtroom but as W. C. Linden walked back to the hotel to wait for word of the jury's verdict. It was an episode that Linden proudly recounted to his friends and one that Lyndon B. Johnson, as a young boy, may well have heard on one of Linden's many visits: As Linden walked back from the courthouse to his hotel, he found Little Jim Ford, Mat Ford, and their henchmen in the San Saba Mob loitering along the street with the obvious intention of carrying out a plot to murder him. Little Jim held a knife and the others had their coats on to conceal guns. Linden met Little Jim's provocative words by quickly drawing his pistol and challenging the Fords and their accomplices to open fire if they dared: ". . . you don't know which one of you I'll kill while you're killing me. But I know." Announcing his intention to "get three of you before you get me," Linden ordered the sinister group to leave the scene and threatened to shoot the first man to stop or turn around. But in the face of Linden's implacability, these members of the San Saba Mob melted away, and a few moments later the prosecuting attorney learned that the jury had courageously brought in a key decision of guilty as charged. Both in the courtroom and out, W. C. Linden had defeated the San Saba Mob.[181]

Such was the man after whom Lyndon B. Johnson was named: a man who perfectly illustrated the central Texas ethic of self-defense—an upright, honorable man who devoted his life to upholding the law but who was not the least averse to threatening to use violence in a situation—like that in which he defied the Mob leaders face to face—which he viewed as being one in which self-defense was justified, just as President Lyndon B. Johnson would later view the situation in South Vietnam.

Lyndon B. Johnson's own father, Sam Ealy Johnson, Jr., had something of the same allegiance to the self-defense ethic as that of his friend, W. C. Linden. To his great credit, Sam Ealy Johnson, Jr., was an unremitting foe of ethnic and religious bigotry. During the anti-German hysteria of World War I, he had as a state legislator bravely bucked the tide by opposing a repressive bill against German-Americans and, although unable to obtain the defeat of the legislation, he did succeed in gaining the deletion of one of its most oppressive provisions.[182] After the war another threat to civil liberties in Texas emerged with the wild-fire growth of the revived Ku Klux Klan. The Klan was strong and often violent in central Texas,[183] and it was dangerous to defy the Klan, but Sam Ealy Johnson, Jr., did.[184] On one occasion, Sam's hostility to the Klan brought a test of his devotion to the central Texas ethic of self-defense. Like his friend, W. C. Linden, in the case of the San Saba Mob, Sam Ealy Johnson, Jr., rose to the event and was similarly ready to employ violence to defend himself and his family.

The incident has been described by Lyndon B. Johnson's younger brother, Sam Houston Johnson, who recollected that the Ku Klux Klan had threatened to kill Sam Ealy Johnson, Jr., "on numerous occasions" after he made a speech to the state legislature favoring racial tolerance. With his anti-Klan views well reported in the press, Sam received a menacing barrage of anonymous phone calls and letters. One evening, while his brothers George and Tom were visiting Sam and his family, there was another threatening phone call. "Now, listen here, you kukluxsonofabitch," Sam yelled his reply into the phone, "if you and your goddamned gang think you're man enough to shoot me, you come on ahead. My brothers and I will be waiting for you out on the front porch. Just come on ahead, you yellow bastards." The women were then sent down into the cellar as Sam and his brothers armed themselves with shotguns and took up positions on the porch. They kept an all-night guard, remembered Sam Houston Johnson, "occasionally whispering remarks about the yellow bellied Klan and telling us kids to keep out of sight." [185] At the time this occurrence took place, Lyndon Johnson would have been about 13 years old and still at home. The event undoubtedly helped to stamp on Lyndon Johnson's character the self-defense ethic of his home land.

X

The biographers of Lyndon B. Johnson have emphasized the importance of his Hill Country background in central Texas, and the authorities on Johnson's major foreign policy of defending South Vietnam have left no doubt that his position was motivated to an important extent by the lessons and traditions of his ancestral heritage in the violent region of central Texas.[186] Nor is it possible to divide the presidential leadership of Lyndon B. Johnson into two neat compartments of domestic affairs and foreign affairs, for the same nurturing influences brought him acclaim in the former and condemnation in the latter. Although Lyndon B. Johnson's Vietnamese policy can be traced to his central Texas background, it must be acknowledged, briefly, that those same central Texas roots were crucial, too, to his noteworthy progressive achievements in domestic matters. Johnson's own plain upbringing in the depression-plagued region of central Texas and his youthful witness to the unceasing struggle of common farmers and ranchers instilled in him a deep sympathy for the average American, while the example of his father as a dedicated quasi-populist state legislator served as an inspiration for his own career in politics.[187]

On many occasions, and to many listeners, Lyndon B. Johnson clearly related his defense of South Vietnam to the self-defense efforts of his forebears and the people of central Texas against the Indians and outlaws. Lyndon Johnson's consciousness of the self-defense ethic while president was pointedly revealed by the

foreword he wrote in 1965 for a new edition of his friend Dr.
Walter Prescott Webb's classic history, *The Texas Rangers*. The
Rangers had roamed the Hill Country in pursuit of marauding
Indians and white outlaws at just the time in the 1870's that
Lyndon Johnson's pioneering grandparents were carving out a life
for themselves in that dangerous land.[188] The exploits of the
Rangers were minutely described by Webb in his book, and one of
the prominent individuals in the book was the Ranger captain, L.
H. McNelly, who gained fame for his intrepid operations against
frontier bandits.[189] Lyndon Johnson alluded to McNelly in his
foreword as he wrote, "one of the stories Dr. Webb related to me
which I have repeated most often through the years stems from a
figure in this volume, Captain L. H. McNelly. Captain McNelly
was one of the most effective of the Texas Rangers, yet he was thin
as a bed slat, weighing hardly 135 pounds, consumptive, in many
ways the very opposite of the prototype of a Ranger. But Captain
McNelly repeatedly told his men that *'courage is a man who keeps
coming on.'* As Dr. Webb would explain to me, 'you can slow a man
like that, but you can't defeat him—the man who keeps on coming
is either going to get there himself or make it possible for a later
man to reach the goal.' " [190] And then Lyndon Johnson drew the
moral of his story of Captain McNelly: "In the challenging and
perilous times of this century, free men everywhere might profita-
bly consider this motto"—courage is a man who keeps coming on.
Lyndon Johnson wrote this admonition in May, 1965, only a few
months after the beginning of the aerial bombardment of North
Vietnam and about the time of his decision to commit to the
conflict American ground forces on a large scale. "Courage is a
man who keeps coming on"—these were Lyndon Johnson's own
words (*via* L. H. McNelly) to express the I'll-die-before-I'll-run
self-defense ethic of central Texas, and they underscore his
view—often stated—that our mission in South Vietnam was the
defense of an ally (and ultimately ourselves) against outside
aggression.

There are well-authenticated stories, too, of Lyndon Johnson's
many references to the violent past of his central Texas homeland
in explanation of his Vietnam policy. Both Hugh Sidey and Philip
L. Geyelin in their studies of Lyndon Johnson's presidency
emphasized Johnson's motif of "just like the Alamo." "Once when

he explained his Vietnam commitment," wrote Sidey, "he was right back with early Texans. 'Just like the Alamo,' he said, 'somebody damn well needed to go to their aid. Well, by God, I'm going to Vietnam's aid.' " [191] In another passage, Sidey noted the legacy of frontier fierceness that "was a part of every boy's heritage" in the Blanco County of Johnson's youth. "Johnson had a lot of legend to listen to and live up to. He remembered it all"—including stories of cattle drives up to Abilene, Kansas, by his grandfather and great-uncle. Presidential monologues were studded with "pioneer axioms" of central Texas, stressing "the idea that a man must fight in one way or another to get what he wants." One such maxim was "he's a good man to get behind a log with"—an adage going back to Comanche warfare when, in an Indian encounter, one wanted the company of "the stoutest of hearts." [192]

One of Lyndon Johnson's favorite stories—which he told often with gusto—was about the heroism of his frontier grandmother, Eliza Bunton Johnson, the wife of Sam Ealy Johnson, Sr.: One day Sam had joined a group of men in pursuit of raiding Comanches, and Eliza was left at home alone with child and baby. She went to a spring for water, only to see a band of Comanches approaching. Dashing back to the cabin with her children, she bundled them and herself into a fruit cellar out of sight. Lest sounds from the children disclose their refuge, Eliza tied a diaper over the child's mouth and nursed the baby at her breast. Thus, the brave little trio eluded detection while the Indians ravaged the cabin above. The Comanches finally left, but Eliza and her children remained in hiding until her husband returned at last from his own battle with the red men. Quickly disregarding her own ordeal, Eliza fell to the care of the men wounded in the Indian engagement. For Lyndon Johnson, the lesson of this bit of family history was "fight and endure . . . and fight some more." [193] The tale itself was connected with the suffering of the Felps family and the battle of Deer Creek mentioned above.[194] A measure of Eliza's courage and resourcefulness and, hence, the strong impression on her grandson, was what happened to the Felps family on this same Indian raid of 1869. Both Tom Felps and his wife were cruelly massacred by the Comanches. Tom was shot, stripped, and stabbed. His wife took an arrow through the breast, was stripped naked, and scalped alive before she expired.[195]

Whereas the Vietnam war drew Lyndon Johnson's most graphic characterization of the central Texas ethic of violent self-defense, the brief Dominican Republic crisis of April, 1965, in which Johnson decided to send American armed forces to the Caribbean country to protect U. S. citizens and forestall a Communist take over, also gained a presidential application of central Texas wisdom. Again Johnson cited the Alamo and noted the similarity to warfare with the Comanches. "As he later described the moment of decision," wrote Philip L. Geyelin, Johnson "told the National Security Council . . . 'Hell, its just like if you were down at the gate, and you were surrounded, and you damn well needed somebody. Well, by God, I'm going to go—and I thank the Lord that I've got men who want to go with me, from [Defense Secretary] McNamara right on down to the littlest private who's carrying a gun.' " [196]

Lyndon B. Johnson in his memoir of his presidential service stressed his central Texas heritage: "In . . . Johnson City. . . . I was a part of Texas. My roots were its soil. I felt a special identification with its history and its people." [197] He emphasized the self-defense ethic as a key to his foreign policy; as the epigraph for these presidential recollections, he quoted his first address to Congress on November 27, 1963: "This nation will keep its commitments from South Vietnam to West Berlin." [198] Moreover, Johnson was at pains in his book to insist that he had not misled the American people about the Vietnamese conflict and that they had understood his ethic of self-defense. "I made it clear from the day I took office," he wrote, "that I was not a 'peace at any price' man. We would remain strong, prepared at all times to defend ourselves and our friends." [199] In language that echoed the I'll-die-before-I'll-run syndrome of central Texas, he asserted in regard to the presidential campaign of 1964 that when the people re-elected him "they knew that Lyndon Johnson was not going to pull up stakes and run. They knew I was not going to go back on my country's word." [200]

In his memories of crucial decisions on American involvement in the Vietnam war Johnson underscored self-defense and the frontier heritage. Thus, for Lyndon Johnson, the key language in the August, 1964, congressional Gulf of Tonkin Resolution from which he claimed authorization for his intervention in the Vietnam war was Congress's support for the president "to take all necessary measures to repel any armed attack against the forces of the United States and to prevent further aggression." [201] It was this principle of self-defense that Johnson applied in making what was probably his most important decision in regard to the war: his decision, in response to a Vietcong attack on the U. S. Army advisers' barracks at Pleiku, South Vietnam, on February 6, 1965. Johnson decided to meet this blow with an air raid against North Vietnam that initiated the long-term bombing of that country. It was the most significant act of escalation in Lyndon Johnson's administration, for it led inexorably to America's deep involvement in the war. At his decisive meeting with the National Security Council, Johnson employed a central Texas frontier expression to convey his determination to escalate the war: "We have kept our gun over the mantel and our shells in the cupboard for a long time now. And what was the result? They are killing our men while they sleep in the night. I can't ask our American soldiers out there to continue to fight with one hand tied behind their backs." [202] For good or ill, Lyndon B. Johnson was shaped by his origins in the violence-prone region of central Texas.

APPENDIX 1

A Selective Listing of American Colonial Riots, 1641–1759

Year(s)	Colony	Locality	Riot or Riot-Producing Event
1641	R.I.	Providence	Liberty of conscience riot
1654	Md.	Severn R.	"Battle of the Severn"
1654–1655	R.I.		Political factionalism
1663–1750	R.I.		Boundary riots
1663–1750	Conn.		Boundary riots
1663–1750	Mass.		Boundary riots
1682	Va.		Tobacco plant cutters' riots
1690	N.C.		Capt. Gibbs's gubernatorial claim
1699	N.H.	Portsmouth	Sailors' riot
1699–1700	N.J.		Land riots and mob assaults on courts
1703	S.C.	Charleston	Political factionalism
1703–1710	N.Y.	Jamaica	Nonconformist disturbances
1704	Pa.	Philadelphia	Riot of young gentry
1705	N.Y.	N.Y. City	Privateersman's riot
1710	Mass.	Boston	Food riot
1711	N.Y.	Flatbush	Dutch church riot
1711	N.Y.	N.Y. City	Anti-impressment riot
1713	Mass.	Boston	Food riot
1718	N.Y.-Conn.		Boundary riot
1718	N.C.		Riotous seizure of official records
1719–1764	N.Y.-N.J.		Boundary riots
1719	R.I.	Newport	Anticustoms riot
1721–1737	Pa.-Md.		Boundary riots
1722	Conn.	Hartford	Jailbreak riot
1724	Conn.	Hartford Co.	Riot against ship seizure
1734	N.H.	Exeter	Mast-tree riot
1737	Mass.	Boston	Antiprostitution riot
1737	Mass.	Boston	Antimarkethouse riot
1737	N.C.		Antiquitrent riot
1738	Pa.	Schuylkill R.	Fish-dam riot
1742	Pa.	Philadelphia	Election riot
1745–1754	N.J.		Land riots

Year(s)	Colony	Locality	Riot or Riot-Producing Event
1747	Mass.	Boston	Anti-impressment riot
1750	Pa.	York Co.	Election riot
1751–1757	N.Y.	Livingston Manor	Antirent riots by tenants
1751–1757	N.Y.-Mass.		Boundary riots
1754	N.H.	Exeter	Riot against surveyor of woods
1757	N.H.	Brentwoods	Riot against recruiting for royal troops
1757	N.H.	Portsmouth	Mob seizes longboat of H.M.S. *Enterprise*
1759	N.C.		Anti-land-tax riot

Note: For the sources of this list see note 23, Chapter 2.

APPENDIX 2
A Selective Listing of Riots in the Revolutionary Era, 1760–1775

Year(s)	Colony	Locality	Riot or Riot-Producing Event
1760—	N.C.		Regulator riots and disturbances
1760	N.Y.	N.Y. City	Anti-impressment riots (2)
1763–1764	Pa.		Paxton Boys disturbances
1764	N.Y.	N.Y. City	Anti-impressment riot
1764	N.Y.	N.Y. City	"Soldiers Riot and Attempted Rescue"
1764	R.I.	Newport	Anti-impressment riot
1764	Mass.	Dighton	Anticustoms riot
1764	R.I.	Newport	Anticustoms riot
1765	Pa.	Cumberland Co.	Rangers riot against Indian traders
1765	N.C.	Mecklenburg Co.	Riot against land surveyors
1765	R.I.	Newport	Anti-impressment riot
1765–1766	Various	Various	Anti-Stamp Act riots
1766	N.Y.	Hudson R.	Antirent riots
1766	Conn.	New London	Riot vs. Rogerene religious movement
1766	Mass.(Me.)	Falmouth	Anticustoms riot
1766	Conn.	New Haven	Anticustoms riot
1766	Va.	Norfolk	Anticustoms riot
1767	Va.	Norfolk	Anti-impressment riot
1768	Mass.	Boston	Sloop Liberty (anticustoms) riot
1768	Va.	Norfolk	Smallpox riot
1767–1769	S.C.		Regulator riots and disturbances
1769	Conn.	New Haven	Anticustoms riot
1769	Conn.	New London	Anticustoms riot
1769	R.I.	Newport	Anticustoms riot
1769	Pa.	Philadelphia	Anticustoms riot
Late 1760's	R.I.	Newport	Riots against unfaithful husbands
Late 1760's	R.I.	Providence	Riots against unfaithful husbands
Late 1760's	N.Y.	N.Y. City	Riots against unfaithful husbands
1769–1770	N.J.	Monmouth Co.	Antilawyer riot

Year(s)	Colony	Locality	Riot or Riot-Producing Event
1770	R.I.		Anticustoms turmoil
1770	Pa.	Philadelphia	Anticustoms riot
1770	N.Y.	N.Y. City	Liberty pole riot
1770	Mass.	Boston	Boston Massacre
1770–1774	(Vt.)		New Hampshire grant riots
1771	Mass.	Boston	Riot against whorehouse
1771	R.I.	Providence	Riot against tidesman
1771	R.I.		Anticustoms turmoil
1772	R.I.	Providence waters	Burning of the *Gaspee* (anticustoms riot)
1773	Mass.	Boston	Boston Tea Party
1774	R.I.	Providence	Licensing question riot
1774	R.I.	East Green-wich	Antitory riot
1774	R.I.	Newport	Anticustoms riot
1775	Md.	Sassafrass-Bohemia	Anticustoms riot
1775	Ga.		Anticustoms riot

Note: For the sources of this list see notes 23 and 24, Chapter 2.

American Vigilante Movements, 1767–1904

The following list includes only movements that took the law into their own hands. Movements whose purpose was not essentially the usurpation of law enforcement (e.g., the North Carolina Regulators of the late colonial period or the anti-slavery vigilance committees in the North before the Civil War) are omitted. This is a listing, then, of vigilante movements in the classic sense of the term, vigilantism. It is based mainly on the sources cited in the notes to Chapter 4.

Key to Symbols for Type of Movement

L—Large movement or one of particular importance
M—Medium-sized movement or one of medium significance
S—Small movement or one that cannot otherwise be categorized because of lack of adequate information

Place and Movement	Type	Dates	Number Killed	Number of Movement Members
Alabama:				
Chambers and Randolph counties—Slickers	M	1830's		
Cherokee County—Slickers	M	1830's		
Madison and Jackson counties —Slickers	L	1830–1835		500–600
Greensborough—Vigilance Committee	M	1830's		
Montgomery—Regulating Horn	M	*ca.* 1835		
Tuscaloosa—Vigilance Committee	M	1835		
Arizona:				
Holbrook—Vigilantes	S	1885		
Phoenix—Vigilantes, Law and Order Committee	M	1873, 1879	3	
Globe—Vigilantes	S	1882	1	

Place and Movement	Type	Dates	Number Killed	Number of Movement Members
Arizona—Continued				
St. John—Vigilantes	S	1879	2	
Tombstone—Law and Order, Vigilantes	M	1881, 1884	1	
Tucson—Vigilantes	M	1873	4	
Arkansas:				
Cane Hill, Washington County —Committee of 36	L	1839	4	400
Carrollton and Carroll County— Regulators	S	1836		
Little Rock—Regulators	S	1835		
Randolph County—Regulators	S	1897		
California:				
Bakersfield—Vigilantes	L	1897	5	
Bodie—601	M	1881	1	200
Columbia—Vigilance Committee	M	1851–1858	4	
Eureka—Vigilance Committee	M	1853	2	
Grass Valley—Vigilance Committee	M	1851–1857	1	
Hanford—Vigilance Committee, Regulators	M	1880, 1884		
Jackson—Vigilantes	L	1853–1855	10	
Los Angeles:				
Vigilance Committee	L	1852–1858	8	
Vigilantes	L	1863	7	
Vigilance Committee	M	1870	1	500
Mariposa—Vigilance Committee	M	1854	2	
Marysville—Vigilance Committee	M	1851–1858	3	
Modesto area—Regulators	M	1879		
Mokelumne Hill—Vigilance Committee	M	1852–1856	1	
Monterey—Vigilance Committee	M	1851, 1856	5	
Mud Springs—Vigilantes	M	1851–1853	4	
Natchez—Vigilance Committee	S	1851 ff.		
Natividad, Monterey County— Vigilance Committee	M	1854	1	
Nevada City—Vigilance Committee	S	1851	1	

Place and Movement	Type	Dates	Number Killed	Number of Movement Members
California—Continued				
Newton—Vigilantes	M	1851–1852	1	
Ophir—Vigilance Committee	S	1851		
Sacramento—Vigilance Committee	L	1851–1853	1	213
San Diego—Vigilantes	M	1852	3	
San Francisco:				
Regulators	L	1849		100
Law and Order	L	1849		400
Vigilance Committee	L	1851	4	500
Vigilance Committee	L	1856	4	6,000–8,000
San Jose—Vigilance Committee	M	1851–1854	1	
San Juan—Vigilantes	M	1867, 1877	3	
San Louis Obispo—Vigilance Committee	M	1858	*ca.* 4	175
Santa Barbara—Vigilante Movement	L	1857	*ca.* 8	150
Santa Clara—Vigilance Committee	S	1851		
Santa Cruz:				
Vigilance Committee	L	1852–1853	11	
Vigilantes	S	1877	2	
Shasta—Vigilance Committee	S	1851		
Sonora—Vigilance Committee	M	1851, 1854	3	
Stanislaus County—Regulators	S	1880's		
Stockton—Vigilance Committee	M	1851		
Truckee—601	M	1874		
Tulare County—Vigilance Committee	S	1873–1874		
Visalia—Vigilance Committee	S	1865, 1872	1	
Watsonville—Vigilantes	M	1856, 1870	5	
Weaverville—Vigilance Committee	S	1852		
Willits—Vigilantes	M	1879	3	
Colorado:				
Alamosa—Vigilantes	S	Late 1870's–early 1880's	2	
Arkansas Valley (upper)—Vigilantes	S	1870's		
Canon City—Vigilantes	S	1888	1	
Del Norte—Vigilantes	S	Late 1870's–early 1880's	2	40

Place and Movement	Type	Dates	Number Killed	Number of Movement Members
Colorado—Continued				
Denver:				
Vigilantes	L	1859–1861	6	600–800
Vigilantes	M	1868	1	90–100
Durango—Committee of Safety	M	1881	1	300
Elbert County—Vigilantes	S	ca. 1899–1902		
Georgetown—Vigilantes	S	1877	1	
Golden—Vigilantes	M	1879	2	100–150
Leadville—Vigilantes	S	1879		
Meeker—Vigilance Committee	S	1887		
Ouray—Vigilantes	S	1884	2	
Pueblo—Vigilantes	L	1864–1868, 1872	3	
Silverton—Vigilance Committee	M	1881	2	
Rocky Mountain Detective Association (headquarters in Denver: operations in Mountain and Great Plain States)	L	1863–ca. 1898		
Florida:				
Columbia County—Regulators	L	1868–1870		
Hernando County—Regulators	M	1870		
Leon County—Regulators	L	1867–1868		
Madison, Suwanee, Taylor, and Hamilton counties— Regulators	L	1868–1870		
Pine Level, De Soto County— Vigilantes	S	ca. 1900		
Sarasota—Vigilantes	L	1883–1884	7	
Georgia:				
Andersonville Prison Camp— Regulators	M	1864	6	
Carroll County and Carrollton —Regulators	S	ca. 1832		
Northern Georgia—Slickers	L	1830's		
Southern Georgia—Regulators	L	1869–1870		
Idaho:				
Boise—Vigilance Committee	L	1866	3	
Idaho City—Vigilance Committee	L	1865		900

Place and Movement	Type	Dates	Number Killed	Number of Movement Members
Idaho—Continued				
Lewiston—Vigilance Committee	L	1862–1864, 1871	30, 1	
Payette Valley—Vigilance Committee	L	1864, 1874	1	40
Salmon River—Vigilance Committee	M	1862		
Illinois:				
Carlyle—Regulators	S	1822–1823		
Clay County—Regulators	M	Early 1820's	3	100–500
Edgar County—Vigilance Committee	S	1830's		
Gallatin County—Vigilantes	M	*ca.* 1842		
Grafton area, Jersey County—(Vigilantes)	M	1866	5	
Morgan and Scott counties—Regulators	L	1821–1830	(?)	
Northern Illinois (Ogle, Winnebago, DeKalb, Lee, McHenry, and Boone counties)—Regulators	L	1841	2	*ca.* 1,000
Pope County—Regulators	M	1831		
Southern Illinois (Pope, Massac, and Johnson counties)—Regulators	L	1846–1849	*ca.* 20	500
Illinois in general—Regulators	L	1816–17 ff.		
Indiana:				
Harrison and Crawford counties—Regulators	S	1818		
Newton County—Rangers	S	*ca.* 1858		
Northern Indiana (LaGrange and Noble counties)—Regulators	L	1858	1	2,000
Montgomery County—horse-thief detection society	M	*ca.* 1840's–1860's		
Noble County—Regulators	S	1889		
Polk Township, Monroe County—Regulators	M	*ca.* 1850's	2	
Seymour—Vigilance Committee	L	1867–1868	12	
Vincennes—Regulators	S	*ca.* 1820's		

Place and Movement	Type	Dates	Number Killed	Number of Movement Members
Indiana—Continued				
Warren and Benton counties— Vigilantes	S	1819		
White River (Bluffs area)— Regulators	S	1819		
Indiana in general	L	1820's–1830's		
Iowa:				
Bellevue—Regulators	L	1840	*ca.* 6	
Benton County—Regulators	S	1848		
Burlington—Vigilantes	S	1830's		
Cedar County:				
Vigilantes	S	1840–1841		
Vigilantes	M	1857	3	
Comanche and DeWitt— Regulators	M	*ca.* 1840's–1850's		
Dubuque—Miners' Court	M	1834	1	
Eldora—mutual protection society	S	1857–1858		
Emeline—Vigilantes	S	1857		
Fremont County—Vigilantes	M	1866–1869		
Hardin County—Vigilance society	M	1884–1885	2	
Iowa City—Vigilance Committee	M	1844	1	
Iowa City—Committee of 100	M	1858	1	
Iron Hill, Jackson County— Vigilance Committee	L	1857	2	300–400
Keokuk County—Vigilance Committee	S	1857–1858		
Linn County—Vigilantes	M	1840 ff.	1	
Linn Grove—Citizen's Association (including Jones, Cedar, Linn, and Jackson counties)	M	*ca.* 1838–1839		
McGregor—Vigilantes	S	1858		
Monroe County:				
Vigilance Committee	M	1866	1	60–300
Vigilance Committee	M	1883	1	
Polk County—Rangers	S	1848		

Place and Movement	Type	Dates	Number Killed	Number of Movement Members
Iowa—Continued				
Pottawattomie County—Vigilantes	M	1853–1865	4	
Scott, Cedar, and Clinton counties—Vigilantes	L	1857	4	200
Story County—Protective Association	M	Late 1860's		
Van Buren County—Vigilance Committee	S	1848		
Kansas:				
Atchison County—Vigilantes	S	1877		
Butler County—Vigilantes	L	1870–1871	8	798
Cheyenne County—Vigilance Committee	S	1888		
Dodge City:				
Vigilantes	M	1873	4	30–40
Vigilance Committee	S	1883		
Ellsworth—Vigilance Committee	M	1873		
Hays City—Vigilance Committee	S	1868		
Indianola—Vigilance Committee	S	1862		
Labette County—Vigilance Committee	S	1866		
Manhattan—Vigilantes	S	Late 1860's		
Medicine Lodge—Vigilantes	S	1884		
Mound City—Vigilantes	S	Late 1860's		
Neosho—Vigilance Committee	M	*ca.* 1850–1860's		
Rising Sun—Vigilantes	S	Late 1860's		
Sheridan—Vigilance Committee	S	1868	1	
Sumner County—Vigilantes	S	1876	2	
Topeka—Vigilantes	S	Late 1860's		
Wellington—Vigilantes	M	1874	3	
Wichita—secret police force	M	1874		40–50
Kentucky:				
Christian, Muhlenberg, Todd, and Hopkins counties—Regulators	L	1845		
Green River and Little Barren River—Regulators	M	1790's		
Henderson County—Regulators	M	*ca.* 1816–1817		

Place and Movement	Type	Dates	Number Killed	Number of Movement Members
Kentucky—Continued				
Hopkins and Henderson counties—Regulators	S	1820–1822		
Marion, Mercer, Madison, Boyle and Lincoln counties —Regulators	L	1866–1871		
Muhlenberg County—Regulators	S	*ca.* 1825–1850		
Paducah—Regulators	L	1846–1850		
Russellville—Regulators	S	1793		
Union County—Regulators	S	1880–1881		30–40
Western Kentucky—Regulators	M	1798		
Kentucky in general—Regulators	M	*ca.* 1810–1830		
Louisiana:				
Abbeville—Regulators	S	1890's		
Atlanta, Montgomery, and Winnfield—Vigilantes	L	1872	11	
Attakapas—Vigilance Committee (Parishes of Lafayette, Calcasieu, St. Martin, Vermillion, and St. Landry)	L	1859	1	4,000
Cameron—Regulators	S	1874		
New Orleans:				
Vigilance Committee	S	1858		
Vigilantes	L	1891	11	61
Vermillion Parish—Vigilantes	L	1872–1873	12	
Minnesota:				
Balsam Lake—people's court	S	*ca.* 1870's	1	
Duluth—Vigilance Committee	S	1869		
Mississippi				
Madison and Hinds counties— Regulators and Committees of Safety	L	1835	21	
Natchez—Vigilance Committee	S	1835		
Northern Mississippi—Slickers	L	1830's		
Northeast Mississippi— Regulators	L	*ca.* 1865–1866		
Vicksburg—Vigilance Committee	L	1835		

Place and Movement	Type	Dates	Number Killed	Number of Movement Members
Missouri:				
Benton and Hickory counties— Slickers	L	1842	3	
Camden County—Slickers	S	1836 ff.		
Christian and Taney counties— Bald Knobbers	L	1885–1887	3	*ca.* 900
Clark County—Vigilantes	S	1840's–1850's		
Greene County—Regulators	L	1866	3	280
Hickory County—Vigilance Committee	M	Late 1860's	2	
Lees Summit—Vigilance Committee	S	Late 1860's		
Lincoln County—Slickers	S	1843–1845		
St. Louis—Regulators	S	1815		
Saline County—Honest Men's League	S	1866		
Vernon County—Marmaton League, Vigilance Committee	S	*ca.* 1866, 1867		
Warrensburg and Johnson County—Vigilance Committee	L	1867	10	400
Montana:				
Bannack and Virginia City— Vigilantes	L	1863–1865	30	108
Helena—Vigilance Committee	L	1864–1885	10	
Miles City—Vigilantes	M	1883	1	
Northern and Eastern Montana (Judith, Musselshell, and Missouri River areas)— Vigilantes	L	1884	35	
Sun River area—Rangers	M	*ca.* 1870–1884		
Montana in general—Vigilantes	L	*ca.* 1862–1884	25	
Nebraska:				
Cass County—Claim Club	M	1854–1857	4	
Colfax County—Regulators	S	1863		25–40
Columbus—Vigilantes	S	1867	1	
Dixon County—People's Court	S	1870	1	
Fremont area—Regulators	M	1856 ff.		
Nebraska City—Anti-Jayhawk League	S	Early 1860's		

Place and Movement	Type	Dates	Number Killed	Number of Movement Members
Nebraska—Continued				
Nemaha County—Anti-Jayhawk Society	S	1861		
Niobrara region (Brown, Holt, and neighboring counties)—Vigilantes	L	1883–1884	6	250
Omaha—Vigilantes	M	1856–1860	2	
Pawnee County—Regulators	M	1864	3	
Richardson County:				
Vigilantes	M	1858	1	200
Anti-Jayhawk Society	S	1861		
Sidney—Vigilantes	L	1875–1881	2	400
Southeast Nebraska—Anti-Jayhawk Societies	M	1861–1863		
Western Nebraska—Vigilantes	M	1875 ff.		
Nebraska (Eastern) in general—Claim Clubs	M	1850's		
Nevada:				
Aurora—Citizens Protection Committee	L	1864	4	350
Belmont—Vigilance Committee	S	1867, 1874		
Carson Valley and Genoa—Vigilance Committee	S	1855, 1860, 1875		
Cherry Creek—Vigilantes	S	(?)	1	
Egan Canyon (White Pine mine district)—Protection Society	S	1869		
Eureka—601	M	1873	2	
Hamilton—Vigilantes	S	(?)		
Hiko, Lincoln County—601	S	Late 1860's-early 1870's		
Pioche—Vigilantes	S	1871		
Treasure City—Vigilantes	S	(?)		
Truckee Valley—Vigilantes	S	1858		
Virginia City—601 and Vigilantes	M	1860's–1881		
Winnemucca—Vigilance Committee	S	1877		

Place and Movement	Type	Dates	Number Killed	Number of Movement Members
New Mexico:				
Albuquerque—Vigilantes	L	1871–1882		
Colfax County—Vigilance Committee	S	1885		
Deming—Vigilantes	S	1883		
Farmington and San Juan River area—Vigilance Committee	M	1880–1881		
Las Vegas—Vigilantes	L	1880–1882	6	
Lincoln County—Regulators	M	1878		
Los Lunas—Vigilance Committee	S	1880's		
Raton—Vigilantes	M	1881–1882	3	
Rincon—Vigilantes	S	1881		
San Miguel—Vigilantes	S	1882	1	
Socorro—Vigilantes	L	1880–1884	6	
North Dakota:				
Little Missouri River area—Vigilantes	M	1884		
Ohio:				
Ashland County—Black Canes	M	1825–1833		
Cincinnati—Vigilantes	L	1884		
Cleveland—Vigilance Committee	S	1860		
Logan—Regulators	M	1845		
Wood County—Regulators	S	1837–1838		
Oklahoma:				
Beaver County—Vigilance Committee	M	1887	2	
Choctaw County—Vigilantes	S	1873		
Creek Nation—Vigilance Committee	L	1888		100
Okmulgee—Vigilance Committee	S	*ca.* 1901		
South Carolina:				
Back Country (upper Coastal Plain and lower Piedmont area)—Regulators	L	1767–1769	16	*ca.* 5,000–6,000

Place and Movement	Type	Dates	Number Killed	Number of Movement Members
South Dakota:				
Jerauld County—Vigilantes	S	1882		
Northern Black Hills (Deadwood, Spearfish, Sturgis and vicinity)—Vigilantes	L	1877–1879	5	
Pierre—Vigilance Committee	M	1880	1	12–15
Rapid City and vicinity— Vigilantes	L	1877–1878	4	
Tennessee:				
Knoxville vicinity—Regulators	S	*ca.* 1798		
Randolph and Covington— Regulators	S	1830's		
Sevier County—White Caps	L	1892–1897	9	
Stewart County—Regulators	S	1818		
Texas:				
Atascosa and Wilson counties— Citizens Committee	S	1875		
Bell County—Vigilance Committee	M	1866, 1874		
Blanco County—Vigilance Committee	S	1870's–1880's		
Blossom Prairie, Lamar County —Vigilance Committee	S	1877		
Bosque County—Vigilantes	M	1860, 1870	4	
Burnet County—Minute Men and Mob	M	1869–1870's		
Callahan County—Vigilance Committee	S	1870's–1880's		
Clarksville—Regulators	S	1830's–1840's		
Comal County—Vigilance Committee	S	1870's–1880's		
Comanche County—Vigilantes	L	1872–1886	*ca.* 10	
Corpus Christi—Vigilance Committee	S	1860		
Corpus Christi area—Vigilantes	S	1874–1875		
Coryell County—Vigilantes	L	1861–1883, 1893–1894	9	
Decatur—Vigilantes	S	1875		

Place and Movement	Type	Dates	Number Killed	Number of Movement Members
Texas—Continued				
Denton County—Minute Companies	S	1863, 1867		
DeWitt and Gonzales counties —Vigilantes	M	1873		
Eastland County—Mob	S	1887		
El Paso—Vigilance Committee	S	1870's–1880's		
Erath County—Mob	M	1872	3	37
Fort Griffin vicinity—Mob	S	1850's		
Goliad—Vigilantes	M	1858	6	
Hamilton County:				
Vigilantes	M	1860–1862	2	
Mob	M	1870's–1880's	3	
Hardin County—Regulators	S	1850's		
Hays County—Vigilance Committee	S	1870's or 1880's		
Hill County—Vigilantes	S	1873–1878		
Llano and Burnet counties— Vigilance Committee	M	1870's		
McDade area, Bastrop County —Vigilantes	L	1876–1883	13	*ca.* 200
McMullen County—Vigilance Committee	S	1860's–1870's		
Madison County—Vigilance Committee	S	1867–1868		
Mason County—Hoodoos (vigilantes)	L	1875 ff.		
Nueces River (lower) area—Minute Men	S	1875		
Montague County—Law and Order League	M	1872–1875	1	
Navarro County—Vigilantes	M	1840's–1850's		
Neuville—Vigilantes	M	1874–1876	3	
Orange County (and surrounding counties of Jefferson, Newton, and Jasper)—Regulators	L	1856	5	
Palo Pinto County—Vigilance Committee	S	1859		
Rockdale—Vigilantes	S	1875		

Place and Movement	Type	Dates	Number Killed	Number of Movement Members
Texas—Continued				
Rusk County—Vigilance Committee	S	1849		
San Antonio—Vigilance Committee	L	1857–1865	*ca.* 17	
San Saba County—Mob	L	1880–1898	*ca.* 25	
Scurry County—Mob	S	1899		
Shackelford County—Vigilance Committee	L	1876–1878	19	*ca.* 70
Shelby County—Regulators	L	1840–1844	10	
Springtown—Mob	M	1872	6	
Sulphur Springs—Vigilantes	S	1879		
Tarrant County—Regulators	S	1850's		
Trinity County—Law and Order League	M	*ca.* 1904		
Van Zandt County—Vigilantes	S	1876		
Wilbarger County—Vigilance Committee	M	1882	*ca.* 4	
Waco—antihorse thief association	S	1872		
Wrightsboro—Minute Company	S	1877		
Utah:				
Promontory—Vigilance Committee	S	1869		
Virginia:				
Norfolk—Vigilance committee	M	1834		
Richmond—Vigilance Committee	M	1834		
Washington:				
New Dungeness—Vigilance Committee	S	1864		
Pierce County—Vigilance Committee	S	1856		
Pullman and Colfax—Vigilantes	M	1890's	*ca.* 3	
Seattle—Vigilance Committee	L	1882	3	500
Walla Walla—Vigilance Committee	L	1864–1866	*ca.* 5	
Union Gap (then Yakima City)—Vigilantes	S	*ca.* 1885		

Place and Movement	Type	Dates	Number Killed	Number of Movement Members
Wisconsin:				
Prairie du Chien—Regulators	S	1850's		
Wyoming:				
Bear River City—Vigilance Committee	M	1868	3	
Cambria—Vigilantes	S	1890's		
Casper—Vigilance Committee	S	1902	1	*ca.* 24
Cheyenne and Laramie County —Vigilantes	L	1868–1869	16	*ca.* 200
Johnson County—Regulators	L	1892	2	50
Laramie—Vigilance Committee	L	1868	7	300–500
Rawlins—Vigilantes	M	1878, 1881	2	

Black-White Violence, 1663–1970: Slave Insurgencies; Riots; Lynchings

Key to Symbols for Types of Activity
SR—Slave revolt
SC—Conspiracy for slave revolt (but revolt was prevented)
SM—Maroon activity by escaped slaves
R—Riot

Year(s)	Type	State(s)	Place or Description
1663	SC	Va.	Gloucester County
1687	SC	Va.	Westmoreland County
1691	SR	Va.	Rappahannock County
1708	SR	N. Y.	Newton, Long Island
1709–1710	SC	Va.	Surry, James City, and Isle of Wight counties
1711	SR	S. C.	Sebastian's band of rebels
1712	SR	N. Y.	New York City
1713	SC	S. C.	Goose Creek
1720	SC	S. C.	Charleston
1722	SC	Va.	Mouth of Rappahannock River
1723	SC	Va.	Middlesex and Gloucester counties
1727	SM	La.	Maroons of des Natanspallé
1729	SM	Va.	Blue Ridge Mountains
1730	SC	Va.	Princess Anne County and Norfolk
1730	SC	S. C.	Charleston
1730	SC	La.	New Orleans
1738	SM	Md.	Prince Georges County
1739	SC	Md.	Annapolis
1739	SR	S. C.	Stono River
1741	SC	N. Y.	New York City
1765	SM	S. C.	Maroon activity widespread
1767	SC	Va.	Alexandria
1771–1772	SM	Ga.	Savannah and Ebenezer
1774	SR	Ga.	St. Andrew's Parish
1776	SC	N. C.	Beaufort, Pitt, and Craven counties
1780–1786	SM	Ga.	Savannah and elsewhere
1782	SM	Va.	Charles City County
1782–1784	SM	La.	Maroons led by one St. Malo

Year(s)	Type	State(s)	Place or Description
1786	SC	Md.	Cumberland County
1792	SM	Va.	Charles City County
1792	SC	Va.	Northampton County and cities of Norfolk and Portsmouth
1795	SM	N. C.	Wilmington
1795	SC	La.	Pointe Coupée Parish
1799	SR	Va.	Prince William County
1799	SR	Va.	Southampton County
1800	SC	Va.	Gabriel Prosser's conspiracy (Richmond and vicinity from tidewater to Piedmont)
1811	SM	N. C.	Cabarrus County
1811	SR	La.	St. Charles and St. John the Baptist parishes
1812–1813	SM	Fla.	Florida Maroons against the Patriots
1815	SM	Fla.	Florida Maroons at Negro Fort
1816	SC	Va.	Spotsylvania County
1816	SC	S. C.	Camden
1816	SM	S. C.	Ashepoo
1816	SM	Fla.	Appalachicola Bay
1818	SM	Va.	Princess Anne County
1818	SM	N. C.	Wake County
1818	SM	Fla.	Suwanee village
1819	SC	Ga.	Augusta
1819	SM	S. C.	Williamsburg
1820	SM	N. C.	Gates County
1820	SM	N. C.	Onslow, Carteret, and Bladen counties
1822	SC	S. C.	Denmark Vesey's conspiracy (Charleston and environs)
1822	SM	S. C.	Jacksonborough
1823	SM	Va.	Norfolk County
1823	SM	S. C.	Pineville
1824	R	R. I.	Providence (2 riots)
1826	R	Mass.	Boston
1827	SM	Ala.	Mobile County
1827	SM	La.	New Orleans
1829	R	Ohio	Cincinnati
1829	R	Pa.	Philadelphia
1829	SM	S. C.	Christ Church and St. James parishes
1829	SC	S. C.	Georgetown
1830	SM	N. C.	Sampson, Bladen, Onslow, Jones, New Hanover, and Dublin counties and city of New Bern
1831	SR	Va.	Nat Turner's revolt (Southampton County)
1831	R	Conn.	Hartford

Year(s)	Type	State(s)	Place or Description
1831	R	Md.	New Market
1831	R	R. I.	Providence
1831	R	Conn.	New Haven
1833	R	Mich.	Detroit
1834	R	N. Y.	New York City
1834	R	Pa.	Philadelphia (2 riots)
1834	R	N. J.	Newark
1834	R	N. Y.	Palmyra
1834	R	N. J.	Camden
1834	R	N. J.	Trenton
1834	R	Mich.	Detroit
1834	R	Pa.	Columbia
1835	R	Pa.	Philadelphia
1835	R	D. C.	Washington
1835	R	Conn.	Hartford (2 riots)
1835	R	N. Y.	Buffalo
1835	R	N. J.	Burlington
1835	R	Pa.	Pittsburgh
1835–1838	SM	Fla.	Maroons in Second Seminole War
1836	R	Ohio	Cincinnati (2 riots)
1836	R	Ohio	Zanesville
1836	SM	N. C.	Gates County
1836	SM	La.	New Orleans
1837	SC	La.	Alexandria
1837	R	Pa.	Philadelphia (2 riots)
1838	R	Pa.	Philadelphia (2 riots)
1839	R	Pa.	Pittsburgh
1840	SC	La.	Avoyelles, Rapides, St. Landry, Lafayette, Iberville, Vermillion, and St. Martin parishes
1840	R	Ohio	Troy
1840	SC	La.–Miss.	West Feliciana Parish, Louisiana, and Woodville, Mississippi
1841	R	Ind.	Evansville
1841	SC	Ga.	Augusta
1841	R	Ind.	New Albany
1841	R	Ohio	Cincinnati
1841	R	Ky.	Maysville
1841	SM	N. C.	Wilmington
1841	SM	Ala.	Mobile County
1841	SM	La.	Terrebonne Parish
1842	R	Pa.	Philadelphia

Year(s)	Type	State(s)	Place or Description
1842	SM	La.	Concordia, Madison, and Carroll parishes
1843	R	Mass.	Boston
1845	SR	Md.	St. Marys, Charles, and Prince Georges counties
1847	R	Conn.	New London
1848	SR	Ky.	Fayette County
1849	SC	Ga.	St. Mary's
1849	R	Pa.	Philadelphia
1850	SR	Mo.	Lewis County
1851	SR	Tex.	Colorado County
1851	SM	Va.	Grayson County
1856	SM	N. C.	Bladen and Robeson counties
1856	SC	Tex.	Colorado County
1863	R	N. Y.	New York City (anti-draft riot)
1866	R	La.	New Orleans
1866	R	Tenn.	Memphis
1868	L	Southern	Ku Klux Klan lynched 291 blacks
1868	R	La.	New Orleans
1868	R	La.	Opelousas
1869	L	Southern	Ku Klux Klan lynched 31 blacks
1870	R	Miss.	Meridian
1870	L	Southern	Ku Klux Klan lynched 34 blacks
1870	R	S. C.	Laurens
1871	L	Southern	Ku Klux Klan lynched 53 blacks
1871	R	Pa.	Philadelphia
1872–1881	L	Southern	Figures on blacks lynched not available
1873	R	La.	Colfax
1874	R	Miss.	Vicksburg
1874	R	La.	New Orleans
1874	R	La.	Coushatta
1875	R	Miss.	Yazoo City and environs
1876	R	S. C.	Hamburg
1876	R	S. C.	Ellenton
1882	L	U. S.	49 blacks lynched*
1883	L	U. S.	53 blacks lynched*
1883	R	Va.	Danville
1884	L	U. S.	51 blacks lynched*
1885	L	U. S.	74 blacks lynched*
1886	L	U. S.	74 blacks lynched*
1887	L	U. S.	70 blacks lynched*
1887	R	La.	Thibodaux
1888	L	U. S.	69 blacks lynched*

Year(s)	Type	State(s)	Place or Description
1889	L	U. S.	94 blacks lynched*
1889	R	Miss.	LeFlore County
1890	L	U. S.	85 blacks lynched*
1891	L	U. S.	113 blacks lynched*
1892	L	U. S.	161 blacks lynched*
1893	L	U. S.	118 blacks lynched*
1894	L	U. S.	134 blacks lynched*
1895	L	U. S.	113 blacks lynched*
1896	L	U. S.	78 blacks lynched*
1897	L	U. S.	123 blacks lynched*
1898	L	U. S.	101 blacks lynched*
1898	R	N. C.	Wilmington
1899	L	U. S.	85 blacks lynched*
1900	L	U. S.	106 blacks lynched*
1900	R	La.	New Orleans
1900	R	N. Y.	New York City
1900	R	Ohio	Akron
1901	L	U. S.	105 blacks lynched*
1902	L	U. S.	85 blacks lynched*
1903	L	U. S.	84 blacks lynched*
1904	L	U. S.	76 blacks lynched*
1905	L	U. S.	57 blacks lynched*
1906	L	U. S.	62 blacks lynched*
1906	R	Ga.	Atlanta
1907	L	U. S.	58 blacks lynched*
1908	L	U. S.	89 blacks lynched*
1908	R	Ill.	Springfield
1909	L	U. S.	69 blacks lynched*
1910	L	U. S.	67 blacks lynched*
1911	L	U. S.	60 blacks lynched*
1912	L	U. S.	61 blacks lynched*
1913	L	U. S.	51 blacks lynched*
1914	L	U. S.	51 blacks lynched*
1915	L	U. S.	56 blacks lynched*
1916	L	U. S.	50 blacks lynched*
1917	L	U. S.	36 blacks lynched*
1917	R	Ill.	East St. Louis
1917	R	Pa.	Chester
1917	R	Pa.	Philadelphia
1917	R	Tex.	Houston
1918	L	U. S.	60 blacks lynched*
1919	L	U. S.	76 blacks lynched*

Year(s)	Type	State(s)	Place or Description
1919	R	D. C.	Washington
1919	R	Ill.	Chicago
1919	R	Neb.	Omaha
1919	R	S. C.	Charleston
1919	R	Tex.	Longview
1919	R	Tenn.	Knoxville
1919	R	Ark.	Elaine and environs
1920	L	U. S.	53 blacks lynched*
1920	R	Ill.	Chicago
1921	L	U. S.	59 blacks lynched*
1921	R	Okla.	Tulsa
1922	L	U. S.	51 blacks lynched*
1923	L	U. S.	29 blacks lynched*
1924	L	U. S.	16 blacks lynched*
1925	L	U. S.	17 blacks lynched*
1926	L	U. S.	23 blacks lynched*
1927	L	U. S.	16 blacks lynched*
1928	L	U. S.	10 blacks lynched*
1929	L	U. S.	7 blacks lynched*
1930	L	U. S.	20 blacks lynched*
1931	L	U. S.	12 blacks lynched*
1932	L	U. S.	6 blacks lynched*
1933	L	U. S.	24 blacks lynched*
1934	L	U. S.	15 blacks lynched*
1935	L	U. S.	18 blacks lynched*
1935	R	N. Y.	New York City (Harlem)
1936–1970	L	U. S.	During this period the number of blacks lynched was annually less than 10
1943	R	N. Y.	New York City (Harlem)
1943	R	Mich.	Detroit
1946	R	Tenn.	Columbia
1951	R	Ill.	Cicero
1963	R	Ala.	Birmingham
1963	R	Pa.	Philadelphia
1963	R	U. S.	10 lesser riots in 8 cities
1964	R	N. Y.	New York City (Harlem)
1964	R	N. Y.	New York City (Bedford-Stuyvesant)
1964	R	N. Y.	Rochester
1964	R	Pa.	Philadelphia
1964	R	U. S.	12 lesser riots in 12 cities
1965	R	Calif.	Los Angeles (Watts)
1965	R	U. S.	22 lesser riots in 19 cities

Year(s)	Type	State(s)	Place or Description
1966	R	Ill.	Chicago
1966	R	Ohio	Cleveland (Hough)
1966	R	U. S.	51 lesser riots in 42 cities
1967	R	Fla.	Tampa
1967	R	Ohio	Cincinnati
1967	R	N. J.	Newark
1967	R	N. J.	Plainfield
1967	R	Mich.	Detroit
1967	R	N. Y.	Buffalo
1967	R	Wisc.	Milwaukee
1967	R	Minn.	Minneapolis
1967	R	U. S.	156 lesser riots in 122 cities
1968	R	D. C.	Washington
1968	R	Md.	Baltimore
1968	R	Ill.	Chicago
1968	R	Mo.	Kansas City
1968	R	U. S.	approx. 150 lesser riots in 100 cities
1969	R	U. S.	approx. 60 lesser riots in 60 cities
1970	R	U. S.	approx. 75 lesser riots in 75 cities

* Annual lynching statistics are given for the period from 1882 to 1935 that is part of a larger period from 1882 to 1951. During the entire 1882–1951 period a total of 3,437 blacks were lynched in the United States, and all but 109 of the 3,437 were lynched in the former slave states.

Note: The principal sources of this list of black-white violence are as follows: On slave insurgencies the main sources are Herbert Aptheker, *American Negro Slave Revolts* (New York, 1943), and "Maroons within the Present Limits of the United States," *Journal of Negro History*, 24 (1939): 167–84; see, also, Marion D. deB. Kilson, "Towards Freedom: An Analysis of Slave Revolts in the United States," *Phylon*, 25 (1965): 175–87, and the works by Kenneth W. Porter cited in Chapter 7, note 34. On riots the main sources are John M. Werner, "Race Riots in the United States during the Age of Jackson: 1824–1849" (Ph.D. dissertation, Indiana University, 1972); Allen D. Grimshaw, ed., *Racial Violence in the United States* (Chicago, 1969); Arthur I. Waskow, *From Race Riot to Sit-In, 1919 and the 1960s: A Study in the Connections between Conflict and Violence* (Garden City, N. Y., 1966); *Report of the National Advisory Commission on Civil Disorders* (New York, 1968); Bryan T. Downes, "A Critical Reexamination of the Social and Political Characteristics of Riot Cities," *Social Science Quarterly*, 51 (1970–1971): 349–60; and U. S. Department of Commerce, *Pocket Data Book: USA 1971* (Washington, 1971). On lynchings the sources are Allen W. Trelease, *White Terror: The Ku Klux Klan Conspiracy and Southern Reconstruction* (New York, 1971), for the 1868–1871 figures, and Jessie P. Guzman *et al.*, eds., *1952 Negro Year Book: A Review of Events Affecting Negro Life* (New York, 1952), for the 1882–1935 figures.

NOTES

Preface

1. The constructive functions of conflict are explicated in Lewis A. Coser, *The Functions of Social Conflict* (Glencoe, 1956).
2. On Watergate: the *New York Times, The End of a Presidency* (New York, 1974). On the C. I. A.: Victor Marchetti and John Marks, *The CIA and the Cult of Intelligence* (New York, 1974): Philip Agee, *Inside the Company: CIA Diary* (London, 1974); and *Newsweek*, Jan. 27, 1975, pp. 29–30.
3. A related question, Does violence succeed?, is thoughtfully treated by Hugh Davis Graham and Ted Robert Gurr in *The History of Violence in America* (New York, 1969), pp. 809–14.
4. Mihailo Marković, "Violence and Human Self-Realization," p. 234, in Philip P. Wiener and John Fisher, eds., *Violence and Aggression in the History of Ideas* (New Brunswick, 1974). Marković's statement about violence in history suggests a larger question—Is man innately aggressive?—that has been the subject of a lively debate touched off by the writings of Konrad Lorenz and Robert Ardrey. Lorenz and Ardrey are vigorously criticized by M. F. Ashley Montagu, ed., in *Man and Aggression*, 2nd ed. (New York, 1973); see, also, the sources in Chap. 1, note 57, this book. Rollo May, in *Power and Innocence: A Search for the Sources of Violence* (New York, 1972), emphasizes the drive for power. The behavioral and philosophical treatment of violence has produced a scholarly literature that is too extensive for citation here, but among many such works see (in addition to those mentioned here) Hans Toch, *Violent Men: An Inquiry into the Psychology of Violence* (Chicago, 1969); Hannah Arendt, *On Violence* (New York, 1969); and J. Glenn Gray, *The Warriors* (New York, 1967).
5. *To Establish Justice, to Insure Domestic Tranquility: The Final Report of the National Commission on the Causes and Prevention of Violence* (New York, 1970), pp. 229–37. The commission was headed by Milton S. Eisenhower.
6. Contemporary factors of economic stress—inflation, depression, and energy shortages—imply that in future years and decades economic discontent may reappear as a major source of American violence. In this regard, the violent strike of independent truckers in 1974 is suggestive; see Chap. 1, this book. A demographic factor that may affect future American violence is · found in current population projections which indicate that the under-25 age group (which produces about 75 per cent of the serious crimes) will continue to make up nearly one-half the population into the 1990's.

Chapter 1

1. Among general works on American violence are the following: Richard Maxwell Brown, ed., *American Violence* (Englewood Cliffs, N. J., 1970); Richard Hofstadter and Michael Wallaces, eds., *American Violence: A Documentary History* (New York, 1970); and Thomas Rose, ed., *Violence in America: A Historical and Contemporary Reader* (New York, 1970), are three documentary collections. A notable interdisciplinary volume is by Hugh Davis Graham and Ted Robert Gurr, eds., *The History of Violence in America* (New York, 1969), originally published (Washington, 1969) under the title of *Violence in America: Historical and Comparative Perspectives* as a task force report of the National

Commission on the Causes and Prevention of Violence; see, also, James F. Short, Jr., and Marvin E. Wolfgang, eds., *Collective Violence* (Chicago, 1972). Two studies of American protest and violence are Jerome H. Skolnick, *The Politics of Protest* (New York, 1969), and Richard Rubenstein, *Rebels in Eden: Mass Political Violence in the United States* (Boston, 1970); two treatments of political violence are by H. L. Nieburg, *Political Violence: The Behavioral Process* (New York, 1969), and Ted Robert Gurr, *Why Men Rebel* (Princeton, 1970). Hugh Davis Graham *et al., Violence: The Crisis of American Confidence* (Baltimore, 1971), presented a spectrum of recent American opinion on violence.

2. See Chap. 2.
3. See, for example, Ivor Noël Hume, *1775: Another Part of the Field* (New York, 1966), pp. 32–34, 125–30, 284–88.
4. See Chap. 2.
5. Adrian C. Leiby, *The Revolutionary War in the Hackensack Valley* (New Brunswick, 1962).
6. Miles R. Feinstein, "The Origins of the Pineys of New Jersey" (B. A. thesis, Rutgers University, 1963), pp. 56–73.
7. See Chap. 3.
8. On the sense of foreboding see Francis Grierson's *Valley of the Shadows*, ed. Bernard De Voto (New York, 1966). Of the many writings on John Brown, see Stephen B. Oates' *To Purge This Land with Blood: A Biography of John Brown* (New York, 1970).
9. Allan Nevins, *The Emergence of Lincoln*, vol. II, *Prologue to Civil War, 1859–1861* (New York, 1950), pp. 306–8.
10. On Texas, see Chap. 8. For a less violent example of the same mania, see Steven A. Channing's *Crisis of Fear: Secession in South Carolina* (New York, 1970).
11. George Lefebvre, *The Great Fear of 1789: Rural Panic in Revolutionary France*, trans. Joan White (New York, 1973).
12. The newest treatment is by Adrian Cook, *The Armies of the Streets: The New York Draft Riots of 1863* (Lexington, 1974), the first extended scholarly study.
13. Frank L. Klement, *The Copperheads in the Middle West* (Chicago, 1960).
14. Richard S. Brownlee, *Gray Ghosts of the Confederacy: Guerrilla Warfare in the West, 1861–1865* (Baton Rouge, 1958).
15. E. Merton Coulter, *The Civil War and Readjustment in Kentucky* (Chapel Hill, 1926).
16. Georgia L. Tatum, *Disloyalty in the Confederacy* (Chapel Hill, 1934), pp. 36–44, 54–72, 143–55.
17. Tatum, *Disloyalty in the Confederacy*, pp. 97–98.
18. *Ibid.,* pp. 44–53. See, also, Chap. 8, this book.
19. See the discussion, this chapter, on vigilantism and agrarian violence.
20. Virgil C. Jones, *The Hatfields and the McCoys* (Chapel Hill, 1948).
21. Meriel D. Harris, "Two Famous Kentucky Feuds and Their Causes" (M.A. thesis, University of Kentucky, 1940).
22. Rufus L. Gardner, *The Courthouse Tragedy, Hillsville, Va.* (Mt. Airy, N. C., 1962).
23. On "Devil Anse" Hatfield: Jones, *Hatfields and McCoys*, pp. 2–3 and *passim*. On Judge James Hargis: Harris, "Two Famous Kentucky Feuds," pp. 100, 104, and *passim*.
24. C. L. Sonnichsen, *I'll Die before I'll Run: The Story of the Great Feuds of Texas* (New York, 1962) and *Ten Texas Feuds* (Albuquerque, 1957). See, also, Chap. 8, this book.
25. Sonnichsen, *I'll Die before I'll Run*, pp. 35–115.

26. *Ibid.,* pp. 125–49, 232–81, 299–315.
27. One of the most spectacular of the family-factional feuds in New Mexico was the Lincoln County War, 1878 and later, from which Billy the Kid emerged to fame. See Maurice G. Fulton, *History of the Lincoln County War,* ed. Robert N. Mullin (Tucson, 1968).
28. See the discussion of political assassination, this chapter.
29. Earle R. Forrest, *Arizona's Dark and Bloody Ground* (Caldwell, Idaho, 1936); Zane Grey, *To the Last Man* (New York, 1922).
30. William O. Stevens, *Pistols at Ten Paces: The Story of the Code of Honor in America* (Boston, 1940), pp. 84–86, 147–85, 228–44, 260–61, 280–81.
31. Charles E. Rosenberg, *The Trial of the Assassin Guiteau* (Chicago, 1968).
32. Walter Channing, "The Mental Status of Czolgosz, the Assassin of President McKinley," *American Journal of Insanity,* 49 (1902–1903): 233–78.
33. *Report of the Warren Commission on the Assassination of President Kennedy* (New York, 1964), pp. 350–99, 596–659. For studies of the psychology of the assassins of leading public figures, with emphasis upon presidential assassins, that stress the factor of individual abnormality, see the articles by Lawrence Z. Freedman, David A. Rothstein, and Thomas Greening in William J. Crotty ed., *Assassinations and the Political Order* (New York, 1971). Also emphasizing the factor of individual abnormality is the book by James F. Kirkham, Sheldon G. Levy, and William J. Crotty, *Assassination and Political Violence: A Report to the National Commission on the Causes and Prevention of Violence* (Washington, 1969), pp. 62–69, which also contains the most complete quantitative data on assassinations in America to date.
34. This is a generally held view supported by, among others, William J. Crotty, p. 3, and Lawrence Z. Freedman, p. 144, in Crotty, *Assassinations and the Political Order,* and by Kirkham, Levy, and Crotty in *Assassination and Political Violence,* pp. xvii–xviii, 110. A dissent is registered by Richard E. Rubenstein, pp. 415–17, in Crotty, *Assassinations and the Political Order.*
35. Allen W. Trelease, *White Terror: The Ku Klux Klan Conspiracy and Southern Reconstruction* (New York, 1971), pp. 212–15. Albion W. Tourgee incorporated Stephens's assassination into his best-selling novel, *A Fool's Errand* (New York, 1969).
36. Daniel W. Crofts, "The Blair Bill and the Elections Bill: The Congressional Aftermath to Reconstruction" (Ph.D. dissertation, Yale University, 1968), pp. 244–45.
37. On Kennedy: Robert B. Kaiser, *"R. F. K. Must Die"* (New York, 1970), and Thomas C. Greening in Crotty, *Assassinations and the Political Order.* On Wallace: Arthur H. Bremer, *An Assassin's Diary* (New York, 1973), which reveals that Wallace was a surrogate for Bremer's original intended victim, President Richard M. Nixon, whose shooting Bremer failed to carry out. The assassinations of King, Malcolm X, Evers, Rockwell, and Yablonski await further study. On the Long assassination: T. Harry Williams, *Huey Long* (New York, 1969), and "Louisiana Mystery—An Essay Review" in *Louisiana History,* 6 (1965), which surveys the numerous works on the event, including books by Hermann R. Deutsch and David Zinman.
38. Goebel's election as governor was vociferously contested by Republicans who claimed that their candidate had really been elected.
39. Thomas D. Clark, "The People, William Goebel, and the Kentucky Railroads," *Journal of Southern History,* 5 (1939): 34–48. See, also, Woodson Urey, *The First New Dealer* (Louisville, 1939), a biography of Goebel.
40. Fountain and his young son disappeared and were never found. Contemporaries—and later, historians—were sure Fountain had been assassinated.

41. Howard R. Lamar, *The Far Southwest, 1846–1912: A Territorial History* (New Haven, 1966), pp. 192–95.
42. In the 1890's Fall was still a Democrat. He did not switch to the Republican party until after the turn of the century. Today Fall is chiefly remembered for his connection with the unsavory Teapot Dome scandal as Harding's Secretary of the Interior, but Arrell M. Gibson in *The Life and Death of Colonel Albert Jennings Fountain* (Norman, 1965) branded Fall as the leading plotter against Fountain. A milder treatment of Fall's role in the Fountain case appears in C. L. Sonnichsen, *Tularosa: Last of the Frontier West* (New York, 1960).
43. Two leading authorities attest assassination as a political weapon in territorial New Mexico: Lamar, *Far Southwest*, pp. 192–95, and Warren A. Beck, *New Mexico: A History of Four Centuries* (Norman, 1962). See, also, Crotty, *Assassinations and the Political Order*, pp. 25–26.
44. See statements by Joseph Satten, Amitai Etzioni, and other social scientists reported in the *New York Times*, June 9, 1968, sec. I, p. 64, cols. 1–3, and see also Ladd Wheeler's "Toward a Theory of Behavioral Contagion," *Psychological Review*, 73 (1966): 179–92, and Ladd Wheeler and Anthony R. Caggiula's "The Contagion of Aggression," *Journal of Experimental Social Psychology*, 2 (1966): 1–10.
45. Eric J. Hobsbawm, *Social Bandits and Primitive Rebels* (Glencoe, 1959).
46. William A. Settle, *Jesse James Was His Name or Fact and Fiction Concerning the Careers of the Notorious James Brothers of Missouri* (Columbia, Mo., 1966). A recent novel that gives a social-bandit image to certain fictional Mafia leaders is Mario Puzo's *The Godfather* (New York, 1969), and the later film version of the book conveys the same image.
47. W. McKee Evans, *To Die Game: The Story of the Lowry Band, Indian Guerrillas of Reconstruction* (Baton Rouge, 1971). For the enormous literature on Billy the Kid, see Ramon F. Adams's *A Fitting Death for Billy the Kid* (Norman, 1960).
48. Paul I. Wellman, *A Dynasty of Western Outlaws* (New York, 1961), Chap. 12. This provocative book traces a southwestern criminal dynasty from Civil War guerrilla William C. Quantrill through the Jameses to Pretty Boy Floyd.
49. John Toland, *The Dillinger Days* (New York, 1963), and William Schnurr, *Johnnie Death* (New York, 1974), a novel based on Dillinger's career. The popular movie, *Bonnie and Clyde*, depicts Clyde Barrow and Bonnie Parker as social bandits as does, more realistically, Jan I. Fortune, *The True Story of Bonnie & Clyde: As Told by Bonnie's Mother and Clyde's Sister* (New York, 1968).
50. Herbert Asbury, *The Gangs of New York: An Informal History of the Underworld* (New York, 1928). A significant study of the general level of urban criminal violence is Roger Lane's "Urbanization and Criminal Violence in the Nineteenth Century: Massachusetts as a Test Case," in Graham and Gurr, *History of Violence in America*, pp. 468–84.
51. Leo Katcher, *The Big Bankroll: The Life and Times of Arnold Rothstein* (New York, 1959).
52. Donald R. Cressey, *Theft of the Nation: The Structure and Operations of Organized Crime in America* (New York, 1969), pp. 8ff.
53. Estes Kefauver, *Crime in America*, ed. Sidney Shalett (Garden City, N. Y., 1951). See also John Kobler, *Capone* (New York, 1971). An important new study is William H. Moore, "The Kefauver Committee and the Politics of Crime, 1950–1952" (Ph.D. dissertation, University of Texas at Austin, 1971).
54. *The Challenge of Crime in a Free Society: A Report of the President's Commission on Law Enforcement and Administration of Justice* (Washington, 1967),

pp. 187–200. See also President's Commission on Law Enforcement and Administration of Justice, *Task Force Report: Organized Crime* (Washington, 1967); Peter Maas, *The Valachi Papers* (New York, 1968); Hank Messick, *Lansky* (New York, 1971); and on the Bonanno family, Gay Talese, *Honor Thy Father* (New York, 1971). The leading scholarly studies are Cressey's *Theft of the Nation* and two books that ably attack many standard conceptions about the Mafia: Joseph L. Albini, *The American Mafia: Genesis of a Legend* (New York, 1971), and Francis A. J. Ianni, *A Family Business: Kinship and Social Control in Organized Crime* (New York, 1972). See, also, Jay R. Nash, *Bloodletters and Badmen: An Encyclopedia of American Criminals from the Pilgrims to the Present* (New York, 1973).

55. Jack Altman and Marvin C. Ziporyn, *Born to Raise Hell* (New York, 1967).

56. On Whitman: *Time*, Aug. 12, 1966, pp. 19ff. Another alleged freelance mass murderer, most recently, is Dean Allen Corll—see Chap. 8, below. For some other noted freelance mass murderers see Nash, *Bloodletters and Badmen*.

57. On the biological factor: Donald J. Mulvihill and Melvin M. Tumin with Lynn A. Curtis, *Crimes of Violence: A Staff Report to the National Commission on the Causes and Prevention of Violence* (Washington, 1969), vol. II, pp. 420–23; Gerald E. McClearn, "Biological Bases of Social Behavior with Specific Reference to Violent Behavior," *ibid.*, vol. III, pp. 997–1003; Frank Ervin, "The Biology of Individual Violence: An Overview," *ibid.*, vol. III, pp. 1020–21, 1032–33. A study that examines the relationship between the anxieties and neuroses of the 1890's and local violence and disorder is Michael Lesy's *Wisconsin Death Trip* (New York, 1973).

58. Otto A. Rothert, *The Outlaws of Cave-In-Rock* (Cleveland, 1924), pp. 55–156, 241–66. See also Robert M. Coates, *The Outlaw Years . . .* (New York, 1930).

59. John T. James, *The Benders of Kansas* (Wichita, 1913).

60. Frank P. Geyer, *The Holmes-Pitezel Case . . .* (Philadelphia, 1896). Colin Wilson and Patricia Pitman, *Encyclopedia of Murder* (New York, 1962), pp. 286–89. For other freelance multiple murderers see, also, Nash, *Bloodletters and Badmen*.

61. Pioneering treatments in this direction are Lesy's *Wisconsin Death Trip* and Sheldon Hackney's "Southern Violence," in Graham and Gurr, *History of Violence in America*, pp. 505–27. Useful to the study of murder in American history is Thomas McDade's *The Annals of Murder: A Bibliography of Books and Pamphlets on American Murders from Colonial Times to 1900* (Norman, 1961) in which the 1,126 bibliographical entries are heavily annotated. A relevant literary study is by David B. Davis, *Homicide in American Fiction, 1798–1860: A Study in Social Values* (Ithaca, 1957).

62. Walter Prescott Webb, *The Texas Rangers* (Austin, 1965); Ben H. Procter, "The Modern Texas Rangers: A Law Enforcement Dilemma in the Rio Grande Valley," in John A. Carroll, ed., *Reflections of Western Historians* (Tucson, 1969); Frank R. Prassel, *The Western Peace Officer: A Legacy of Law and Order* (Norman, 1972). Philip D. Jordan deals primarily with the Mississippi Valley in *Frontier Law and Order* (Lincoln, 1970).

63. George A. Ketcham, "Municipal Police Reform: A Comparative Study of Law Enforcement in Cincinnati, Chicago, New Orleans, New York, and St. Louis, 1844–1877" (Ph.D. dissertation, University of Missouri, Columbia, 1967); Selden D. Bacon, "The Early Development of American Municipal Police: A Study of the Evolution of Formal Controls in a Changing Society" (Ph.D. dissertation, Yale University, 1939). James F. Richardson, *The New York Police: Colonial Times to 1901* (New York, 1970). William R. Miller, "The Legitimation

of the London and New York City Police, 1830–1870" (Ph.D. dissertation, Columbia University, 1973). Roger Lane, *Policing the City: Boston, 1822–1885* (Cambridge, Mass., 1967).

64. Martha Derthick, *The National Guard in Politics* (Cambridge, Mass., 1965), pp. 16–17. Joseph L. Holmes, "The National Guard of Pennsylvania: Policeman of Industry, 1865–1905" (Ph.D. dissertation, University of Connecticut, 1971).

65. Derthick, *National Guard*, pp. 16–17.

66. James D. Horan, *The Pinkertons: The Detective Dynasty that Made History* (New York, 1968).

67. Anthony S. Nicolosi, "The Rise and Fall of the New Jersey Vigilant Societies," *New Jersey History*, 86 (1968): 29–32; Hugh C. Gresham, *The Story of Major David McKee, Founder of the Anti-Horse Thief Association* (Cheney, Kan., 1937); Patrick B. Nolan, "Vigilantes on the Middle Border: A Study of Self-Appointed Law Enforcement in the States of the Upper Mississippi from 1840 to 1880" (Ph.D. dissertation, University of Minnesota, 1971). See, also, Chap. 4, this book.

68. J. P. Shalloo, *Private Police: With Special Reference to Pennsylvania* (Philadelphia, 1933), pp. 58–134.

69. Jurgen Thorwald, *The Century of the Detective*, trans. Richard and Clara Winston (New York, 1965).

70. On the third-degree problem see the study by the Wickersham Commission: National Commission on Law Observance and Enforcement, *Report on Lawlessness in Law Enforcement* (Washington, 1931), pp. 13–261. On police brutality since World War II see, for example, Albert J. Reiss, "Police Brutality—Answers to Key Questions," *Trans-Action*, 5 (1968): 10–19, and William A. Westley, *Violence and the Police: A Sociological Study of Law, Custom, and Morality* (Cambridge, Mass., 1970).

71. Two older historical studies are Harry E. Barnes's *The Story of Punishment* (Boston, 1930) and Blake McKelvey's *American Prisons* (Chicago, 1936). Recent studies are W. David Lewis, *From Newgate to Dannemora: The Rise of the Penitentiary, 1796–1848* (Ithaca, 1965); Karl A. Menninger, *The Crime of Punishment* (New York, 1968); Norman Johnston, Leonard Savitz, and Marvin E. Wolfgang, *The Sociology of Punishment and Correction* (New York, 1970).

72. Rodney Stark, *Police Riots: Collective Violence and Law Enforcement* (Belmont, Calif., 1972); Daniel Walker, *Rights in Conflict: The Violent Confrontation of Demonstrators and Police in the Parks and Streets of Chicago during the Week of the Democratic National Convention of 1968* (New York, 1968).

73. Mitford M. Mathews, ed., *A Dictionary of Americanisms on Historical Principles* (Chicago, 1956), p. 1010; Richard Maxwell Brown, *The South Carolina Regulators* (Cambridge, Mass., 1963), pp. 38–39ff.

74. James E. Cutler, *Lynch-Law: An Investigation into the History of Lynching in the United States* (New York, 1905), pp. 24–31.

75. *Ibid.,* p. 177.

76. *Ibid.*

77. In addition to Cutler, *Lynch-Law*, see Walter White, *Rope & Faggot: A Biography of Judge Lynch* (New York, 1929), and Arthur F. Raper, *The Tragedy of Lynching* (Chapel Hill, 1938).

78. Cutler, *Lynch-Law*, pp. 180–81 and *passim.* See, also, Chap. 4, this book.

79. For a fuller treatment of vigilantism see Chaps. 4–6.

80. See Chaps. 4–5.

81. Lucile Morris, *Bald Knobbers* (Caldwell, Idaho, 1939).

82. For an expanded treatment of elite participation in vigilantism see Chap. 6.

83. Eliphalet Price, "The Trial and Execution of Patrick O'Conner," *Palimpsest*, 1 (1920): 86–97.
84. Granville Stuart, *Forty Years on the Frontier*, ed. Paul C. Phillips (Cleveland, 1925), vol. II, pp. 196–97. See, also, Chap. 6, this book.
85. Episodes of neovigilantism appear in John W. Caughey, ed., *Their Majesties the Mob* (Chicago, 1960). See, also, Chaps. 4–5, this book.
86. See this chapter, previous discussion, and Chap. 4.
87. Mathews, *Dictionary of Americanisms*, p. 1865, defines White Caps as "a voluntary group formed ostensibly for punishing offenders not adequately dealt with by law."
88. The *Chicago Tribune*, Jan. 23, 1887, p. 3, col. 7, and the *New York Times*, Oct. 12, 1887, p. 2, col. 1, record the outbreak of white capping in Crawford, Orange, and Harrison counties of southern Indiana in 1887. It is possible, however, that white capping occurred earlier, in late 1886. Within the year White Cap activity had spread to Ohio; it is described in the *Ohio State Journal* (Columbus), Nov. 26, 29, Dec. 1, 3, 5–7, 10, 12, 21, 1888. The *New York Times* story of Oct. 12, 1887, is reprinted in Brown, *American Violence*, pp. 96–99. On the Indiana origins of white capping see Madeleine M. Noble, "The White Caps of Harrison and Crawford County, Indiana: A Study in the Violent Enforcement of Morality" (Ph.D. dissertation, University of Michigan, 1973). Sally L. James, "American Violent Moral Regulation and the White Caps" (senior honors essay, College of William and Mary, 1969), treats the movement nationally as well as in its Indiana beginnings.
89. Samuel L. Evans, "Texas Agriculture, 1880–1930" (Ph.D. dissertation, University of Texas, 1960), pp. 320–21. *Texas Farm and Ranch* (Dallas), Oct. 1, 8, 1898. William F. Holmes, "Whitecapping: Agrarian Violence in Mississippi, 1902–1906," *Journal of Southern History*, 35 (1969): 165–85.
90. Sheriff A. M. Avant, Atascosa County, Sept. 20, 1898, to Governor C. A. Culberson in Letters to Governor C. A. Culberson (manuscripts in Texas State Archives, Austin).
91. "The 'White Caps,' 1890–1893" (file of manuscripts and clippings in L. Bradford Prince papers in the New Mexico State Records Center, Santa Fe). See especially the August 12, 1890, memorandum of Governor Prince to John W. Noble, federal Secretary of the Interior. Secondary sources on the White Caps include Andrew Bancroft Schlesinger's "Las Gorras Blancas, 1889–1891," *Journal of Mexican-American History*, 1 (1971) and Robert W. Larsen's "The 'White Caps' of New Mexico: The Political and Ethnic Origins of Western Violence" (unpublished paper, Organization of American Historians, Washington, 1972). On Tijerina's *Alianza* movement and its violent activities, see Peter Nabokov, *Tijerina & the Courthouse Raid* (Albuquerque, 1969); Michael Jenkinson, *Tijerina* (Albuquerque, 1968); and Richard Gardner, *Grito!: Reies Tijerina and the New Mexico Land Grant War of 1967* (Indianapolis, 1972).
92. For example, Robert E. Cunningham, *Trial by Mob* (Stillwater, 1957), pp. 12–13.
93. For example, Ethelred W. Crozier, *The White-Caps: A History of the Organization in Sevier County* (Knoxville, 1899), pp. 10–11, 87ff., 180ff.
94. Booth Tarkington, *The Gentleman from Indiana* (New York, 1899).
95. Douglas E. Leach, *The Northern Colonial Frontier, 1607–1763* (New York, 1966). See, also, Alden T. Vaughan, *New England Frontier: Puritans and Indians, 1620–1675* (Boston, 1965).
96. Douglas E. Leach, *Flintlock and Tomahawk: New England in King Philip's War* (New York, 1966).

97. Leach, *Northern Colonial Frontier*, pp. 12–13.
98. *Encyclopaedia Britannica* (11th edition; New York, 1910–1911), vol. XXIV, pp. 286–87. Leach, *Northern Colonial Frontier*, p. 112. Major Indian wars are treated in William T. Hagan, *American Indians* (Chicago, 1961); William Brandon, *The American Heritage Book of Indians* (New York, 1961); and Dee Brown, *Bury My Heart at Wounded Knee: An Indian History of the American West* (New York, 1970). See, also, Wilbur R. Jacobs, *Dispossessing the American Indian: Indians and Whites on the Colonial Frontier* (New York, 1972).
99. See Chap. 7.
100. *Ibid.*
101. *Ibid.*
102. *Ibid.*
103. *Ibid.*
104. *Ibid.*
105. Trelease, *White Terror.*
106. On violent aspects of the second Ku Klux Klan, see David M. Chalmers, *Hooded Americanism: The First Century of the Ku Klux Klan, 1865–1965* (Garden City, N. Y., 1965), and Charles C. Alexander, *The Ku Klux Klan in the Southwest* (Lexington, 1965).
107. Ray A. Billington, *The Protestant Crusade, 1800–1860: A Study of the Origins of American Nativism* (New York, 1938).
108. Robert E. Wynne, "Reaction to the Chinese in the Pacific Northwest and British Columbia: 1850 to 1910" (Ph.D. dissertation, University of Washington, 1964).
109. See Chap. 6.
110. Donald L. Kinzer, *An Episode in Anti-Catholicism: The American Protective Association* (Seattle, 1964).
111. See, for example, David Brody, *Steelworkers in America: The Nonunion Era* (Cambridge, Mass., 1960).
112. Important comparative studies of violence in eighteenth-century America and Great Britain are Lloyd I. Rudolph's "The Eighteenth-Century Mob in America and Europe," *American Quarterly*, 11 (1959): 447–69; William Ander Smith's "Anglo-Colonial Society and the Mob, 1740–1775" (Ph.D. dissertation, Claremont Graduate School, 1965); and Pauline Maier's "Popular Uprisings and Civil Authority in Eighteenth-Century America," *William and Mary Quarterly*, 3d Ser., 27 (1970): 3–35.
113. Jesse Lemisch, "Jack Tar in the Streets: Merchant Seamen in the Politics of Revolutionary America," *William and Mary Quarterly*, 3d Ser., 25 (1968): 387–93.
114. See Chap. 2.
115. Asbury, *Gangs of New York*, pp. 1–45.
116. J. Thomas Scharf, *The Chronicles of Baltimore* . . . (Baltimore, 1874), pp. 468–69, 476–79, 523, 528, 548–52, 555, 565, 570–74. The twelve riots were (1) 1834, political riot; (2) 1835, bank riot; (3) 1847, firemen's riots; (4) 1848, election riot; (5) 1855, firemen's riot; (6) 1856, club riot; (7–8) 1856, two election riots; (9) 1857, labor riot; (10) 1858, anti-German riot; (11) 1858, election riot; and (12) 1859, election riot. In addition, Baltimore had three riots in 1861–1862; they arose from Civil War tensions. *Ibid.,* pp. 588–94ff., 622–24, 627.
117. Ellis P. Oberholtzer, *Philadelphia: A History of the City* (Philadelphia, 1912), vol. II, pp. 283, 285–89, 291, 293–96. J. Thomas Scharf and Thompson Westcott, *History of Philadelphia, 1609–1884* (Philadelphia, 1884), vol. III,

p. 2184. The eleven riots were: (1) 1834, anti-Negro riot; (2) 1834, election riot; (3) 1835, anti-Negro riot; (4) 1838, Penn Hall (antiabolitionist) riot; (5) 1838, anti-Negro riot; (6) 1840, antirailroad riot; (7) 1842, anti-Negro riot; (8) 1843, labor (weavers' strike) riot; (9) 1844, anti-Irish Catholic riot, May; (10) 1844, anti-Irish Catholic riot, July; (11) 1849, California House (election and anti-Negro riot) riot. Scharf and Westcott are the source for the 1840 antirailroad riot. Oberholtzer is the source for all the other riots. In addition, there were riots in 1828 (a weavers' riot that was a conflict between pro-Irish and anti-Irish elements) and in 1871 (an anti-Negro riot). Oberholtzer, *Philadelphia*, vol. II, p. 291. Joseph Jackson, *Encyclopedia of Philadelphia* (Harrisburg, 1931–33), vol. I, p. 87. Sam Bass Warner, Jr., *The Private City: Philadelphia in Three Periods of Its Growth* (Philadelphia, 1968), pp. 125–57, interprets the Philadelphia riots of the 1830's and 1840's as representing "the interaction of most of the important elements of the big-city era: industrialization, immigration, mixed patterns of settlement, changing styles of leadership, weakness of municipal institutions, and shifting orientations of politics." Michael J. Feldberg, "The Philadelphia Riots of 1844: A Social History" (Ph.D. dissertation, University of Rochester, 1970), emphasizes religious-ethnic conflict between native Protestants and Irish-Catholic immigrants.

118. J. T. Headley, *The Great Riots of New York, 1712 to 1783 . . .* (New York, 1873), pp. 66–135. The eight riots were: (1) 1834, election riots; (2) 1834, antiabolitionist riots; (3) 1835, antiabolitionist riots; (4) 1835, labor (stone cutters') riot; (5) 1837, food (flour) riot; (6) 1849, Astor Place (theatrical factions) riots; (7) 1857, police (Mayor's police vs. Metropolitan police) riot; (8) 1857, Dead Rabbits' riot (gang conflict). In addition to these riots and the great draft riots of 1863 there were two "Orange" riots (Irish Catholics vs. Irish Protestants) in 1870–1871. On the Orange riots see Headley, *Great Riots of New York*, Chap. 21.

119. Lane, *Policing the City*, pp. 26–33; Ketcham, "Municipal Police Reform," p. 54. The four riots were: (1) 1834, anti-Catholic (Charlestown convent burning) riot; (2) 1835, antiabolitionist ("Broadcloth Mob" assault on William Lloyd Garrison) riot; (3) 1837, Broad Street riot; (4) 1843, anti-Negro riot. Boston also had draft riots in 1861 and 1863. Lane, *Policing the City*, pp. 118–34.

120. The four Cincinnati riots were: (1) 1836, proslavery riot in April; (2) 1836, proslavery riot in July; (3) 1842, bank riots; and (4) 1853, Bedini (nativist vs. Catholic) riots. Ketcham, "Municipal Police Reform," pp. 50, 53, 153. For the cities of 20,000 or more: John C. Schneider, "Mob Violence and Public Order in the American City" (Ph.D. dissertation, University of Minnesota, 1971). A perceptive study dealing with rural as well as urban rioting is David Grimsted, "Rioting in Its Jacksonian Setting," *American Historical Review*, 77 (1972): 361–97.

121. Labor riots occurred in New York, 1835; Philadelphia, 1843; and Baltimore, 1857.

122. There were election riots in Baltimore in 1848, 1856 (2), 1858, and 1859; in Philadelphia, 1834, 1849; and in New York, 1834.

123. There were antiabolitionist riots in New York, 1834, 1835; Boston, 1835; Cincinnati, 1836; and Philadelphia, 1838. A significant study is Leonard L. Richards, *"Gentlemen of Property and Standing": Anti-Abolition Mobs in Jacksonian America* (New York, 1970).

124. Anti-Negro riots occurred in Philadelphia in 1834, 1835, 1838, 1842, and 1849 and in Boston in 1843. These are only some of the leading race riots of the

period; according to John M. Werner, "Race Riots in the United States during the Age of Jackson: 1824–1849" (Ph.D. dissertation, Indiana University, 1972), there were a total of forty-two.

125. Among the anti-Catholic riots were two in Philadelphia (1844) and one in Boston (1834); anti-Catholic feeling was basic to Cincinnati's Bedini riot of 1853. The epigraph to this chapter is from Abraham Lincoln's 1837 address dealing with mob violence in the period discussed here. Lincoln's address is cited in full in Chap. 4, note 121, below.

126. See, for example, Andrew H. Neilly, "The Violent Volunteers: A History of the Volunteer Fire Department of Philadelphia, 1736–1871" (Ph.D. dissertation, University of Pennsylvania, 1959).

127. Robert V. Bruce, *1877: Year of Violence* (Indianapolis, 1959), a most important study.

128. See previous discussion, this chapter.

129. See Chaps. 4–5.

130. See Chap. 7.

131. *Ibid.*

132. *Ibid.*

133. On Bacon's Rebellion: Wilcomb E. Washburn, *The Governor and the Rebel: A History of Bacon's Rebellion in Virginia* (Chapel Hill, 1957); Thomas J. Wertenbaker, *Torchbearer of the Revolution: The Story of Bacon's Rebellion and Its Leader* (Princeton, 1940). On the New Jersey land rioters: Gary S. Horowitz, "New Jersey Land Riots, 1745–1755" (Ph.D. dissertation, Ohio State University, 1966). On the Paxton Boys: Brooke Hindle, "The March of the Paxton Boys," *William and Mary Quarterly*, 3d Ser., 3 (1946): 461–86; Wilbur R. Jacobs, ed., *The Paxton Riots and the Frontier Theory* (Chicago, 1967); and David Sloan, "The Paxton Riots" (Ph.D. dissertation, University of California at Santa Barbara, 1968).

134. John S. Bassett, "The Regulators of North Carolina (1765–1771)," American Historical Association, *Annual Report for the Year 1894*, pp. 141–212. On the background of the North Carolina Regulators: Marvin L. M. Kay, "The Payment of Provincial and Local Taxes in North Carolina, 1748–1771," *William and Mary Quarterly*, 3d Ser., 26 (1969): 218–40. A collection of historical sources is William S. Powell, James K. Huhta, and Thomas J. Farnham, eds., *The Regulators in North Carolina: A Documentary History, 1759–1776* (Raleigh, 1971). The best general study remains Elmer Douglas Johnson's "The War of the Regulation: Its Place in History" (M.A. thesis, University of North Carolina at Chapel Hill, 1942).

135. Irving Mark, *Agrarian Conflicts in Colonial New York, 1711–1775* (New York, 1940); Patricia U. Bonomi, *A Factious People: Politics and Society in Colonial New York* (New York, 1971); David M. Ellis, *Landlords and Farmers in the Hudson-Mohawk Region, 1790–1850* (Ithaca, 1946); Henry Christman, *Tin Horns and Calico* (New York, 1945); Sung Bok Kim, "The Manor of Cortlandt and Its Tenants: New York, 1697–1783" (Ph.D. dissertation, Michigan State University, 1966).

136. Maron L. Starkey, *A Little Rebellion* (New York, 1955); Robert A. Feer, "Shays's Rebellion" (Ph.D. dissertation, Harvard University, 1958); Van Beck Hall, *Politics without Parties, 1780–1791* (Pittsburgh, 1972).

137. Leland D. Baldwin, *Whiskey Rebels* (Pittsburgh, 1939).

138. William W. H. Davis, *The Fries Rebellion, 1798–1799* . . . (Doylestown, Pa., 1899). Peter Levine, "The Fries Rebellion: Social Violence and the Politics of the New Nation," *Pennsylvania History*, 15 (1973): 241–58.

139. Allan G. Bogue, "The Iowa Claim Clubs: Symbol and Substance," *Mississippi Valley Historical Review*, 45 (1958): 231–53.
140. Robert Lee Hunt, *A History of Farmer Movements in the Southwest: 1873–1925* (n. p., n. d.), pp. 28–29.
141. Still the most complete account of the Populist movement is John D. Hicks' *The Populist Revolt* (Minneapolis, 1931). For the violent suppression of a local interracial white-black Populist movement: Lawrence C. Goodwyn, "Populist Dreams and Negro Rights: East Texas as a Case Study," *American Historical Review*, 76 (1971): 1435–56.
142. James L. Brown, in *The Mussel Slough Tragedy* (n. p., 1958), deals with the settlers' land league in the Hanford vicinity and its night-riding activities, which came to a climax in the Mussel Slough gun battle, an episode that Frank Norris used as the basis of his novel, *The Octopus: A Story of California* (New York, 1901).
143. James O. Nall, *The Tobacco Night Riders of Kentucky and Tennessee, 1905–1909* (Louisville, 1939). See also Robert Penn Warren's brilliant novel, *Night Rider* (Boston, 1939). Paul J. Vanderwood, in *Night Riders of Reelfoot Lake* (Memphis, 1969), studies another night-rider movement—that along Reelfoot Lake in northwest Tennessee in 1908.
144. John Womack, Jr., "Oklahoma's Green Corn Rebellion" (B.A. thesis, Harvard College, 1959); H. C. Peterson and Gilbert C. Fite, *Opponents of War, 1917–1918* (Madison, 1957), pp. 40–42, 171–76.
145. Robert L. Morlan, *Political Prairie Fire: The Nonpartisan League, 1915–1922* (Minneapolis, 1955).
146. John L. Shover, *Cornbelt Rebellion: The Farmers' Holiday Association* (Urbana, 1965).
147. Lemisch, "Jack Tar in the Streets," pp. 381–400.
148. Smith, "Anglo-Colonial Society and the Mob," pp. 175–79.
149. "Molly Maguire" was an anti-British persona in Irish folklore whom the Irish miners of Pennsylvania adopted as a symbol of their resistance to the authority of the mine owners and bosses.
150. Wayne G. Broehl, Jr., *The Molly Maguires* (Cambridge, Mass., 1964), is an outstanding study that treats in depth the European roots, as well as the American substance, of a violent movement.
151. Henry David, *The History of the Haymarket Affair* (New York, 1936).
152. Leon Wolff, *Lockout . . .* (New York, 1965).
153. Louis Adamic, *Dynamite: The Story of Class Violence in America* (New York, 1934), pp. 179–253. Another old but still useful work is by Samuel Yellen, *American Labor Struggles* (New York, 1936). An excellent newer study is by Graham Adams, Jr., *Age of Industrial Violence, 1910–1915: The Activities and Findings of the United States Commission on Industrial Relations* (New York, 1966). The most systematic and comprehensive treatment is by Philip Taft and Philip Ross, "American Labor Violence: Its Causes, Character, and Outcome," in Graham and Gurr, *History of Violence in America*, pp. 281–395.
154. George S. McGovern, "The Colorado Coal Strike, 1913–1914" (Ph.D. dissertation, Northwestern University, 1953), pp. 81–111. A revised and expanded version of Senator McGovern's dissertation is George S. McGovern and Leonard F. Guttridge, *The Great Coalfield War* (Boston, 1972).
155. McGovern and Guttridge, *Great Coalfield War*. Brown, *American Violence*, pp. 122–26.
156. Jack London, *The Iron Heel* (New York, 1907).
157. *Newsweek*, Feb. 18, 1974, pp. 19–22.

158. This is the import of a meticulous quantitative study—Monica D. Blumenthal, Robert C. Kahn, Frank M. Andrews, and Kendra B. Head, *Justifying Violence: Attitudes of American Men* (Ann Arbor, [1972])—that, on the basis of in-depth interviews in 1969 with 1,374 men, found "that half to two-thirds of American men . . . justify shooting in the situations described as requiring social control" (p. 243).

Chapter 2

1. Herbert Butterfield, *The Whig Interpretation of History* (London, 1931), p. 19.
2. Brooke Hindle, "The March of the Paxton Boys," *William and Mary Quarterly*, 3d Ser., 3 (1946): 461–86; James H. Hutson, *Pennsylvania Politics, 1746–1770: The Movement for Royal Government and Its Consequences* (Princeton, 1972), pp. 84ff.; John S. Bassett, "The Regulators of North Carolina (1765–1771)," American Historical Association, *Annual Report for the Year 1894*, pp. 141–212. Richard Maxwell Brown, *The South Carolina Regulators* (Cambridge, Mass., 1963).
3. Brown, *South Carolina Regulators*, p. 184.
4. James E. Cutler, *Lynch-Law: An Investigation into the History of Lynching in the United States* (New York, 1905), pp. 24–30.
5. Pontiac's Rebellion (1763), Lord Dunmore's War against the Shawnees (1775), and Indian wars connected with the Revolutionary War (1776–1782) are briefly treated by Ray Allen Billington in *Westward Expansion: A History of the American Frontier* (New York, 1967), pp. 137–39, 165–68, 175–91. For the Cherokee War in South Carolina (1760–1761) see Brown, *South Carolina Regulators*, pp. 1–12. On the warfare of the colonists with the French and the Indians the most recent general treatments are by Howard H. Peckham, *The Colonial Wars, 1689–1762* (Chicago, 1964), and Douglas Edward Leach, *Arms for Empire: A Military History of the British Colonies in North America, 1607–1763* (New York, 1973). See, also, Wilbur R. Jacobs, *Dispossessing the American Indian: Indians and Whites on the Colonial Frontier* (New York, 1972).
6. For the problem of the causes of the American Revolution, see the essays by Bernard Bailyn, Jack P. Greene, Rowland Berthoff and John M. Murrin, and Edmund S. Morgan in Stephen G. Kurtz and James H. Hutson, eds., *Essays on the American Revolution* (Chapel Hill, 1973).
7. Wilcomb E. Washburn, *The Governor and the Rebel: A History of Bacon's Rebellion in Virginia* (Chapel Hill, 1957); Jerome R. Reich, *Leisler's Rebellion: A Study of Democracy in New York, 1664–1720* (Chicago, 1953); William H. Whitmore, ed., *The Andros Tracts* (Boston, 1868), vol. I, pp. 11–12 and *passim*; Michael G. Hall, Lawrence H. Leder, and Michael G. Kammen, eds., *The Glorious Revolution in America: Documents on the Colonial Crisis* (Chapel Hill, 1964), pp. 9–79, 143–211; M. Eugene Sirmans, *Colonial South Carolina: A Political History, 1663–1763* (Chapel Hill, 1966), pp. 126–28.
8. Wesley Frank Craven, *The Southern Colonies in the Seventeenth Century* (Baton Rouge, 1949), pp. 233–34, 297–99; Richard P. McCormick, *New Jersey from Colony to State, 1609–1789* (Princeton, 1964), pp. 26–27; Craven, *Southern Colonies*, pp. 409–10; Samuel A'Court Ashe, *History of North Carolina* (Greensboro, N.C., 1908–1925), vol. I, pp. 160–78; Sirmans, *Colonial South Carolina*, pp. 47–48.
9. Craven, *Southern Colonies*, pp. 411–12; Everett S. Stackpole, *History of New*

Hampshire (New York, 1916), vol. I, pp. 133–36; Thomas F. Waters, *Ipswich in the Massachusetts Bay Colony* (Ipswich, Mass., 1905), vol. I, pp. 238–67; Edwin P. Tanner, *The Province of New Jersey: 1664–1738* (New York, 1908), pp. 95–96; Hutson, *Pennsylvania Politics,* pp. 25–26.

10. The six violent rebellions were Ingle-Claiborne, Gove's, anti-Hamilton, Cary's, South Carolina antiproprietary, and Bacon's. The seven nonviolent armed uprisings were Culpeper's, Leisler's, Coode's, anti-Andros, anti-Sothel, anti-Colleton, and Hambright's. The five nonforceful uprisings were Fendall's first and second, New Jersey antiquitrent, Davyes-Pate, and Essex County.

11. The six successful insurgencies were Culpeper's, anti-Andros, Coode's, anti-Colleton, anti-Sothel, and South Carolina antiproprietary. The six temporarily successful rebellions were Ingle-Claiborne, Fendall's first, New Jersey antiquitrent, Bacon's, Leisler's, and Cary's. The six failed rebellions were Davyes-Pate, Fendall's second, Gove's, Essex County, anti-Hamilton, and Hambright's.

12. The other uprisings that took place in the period from 1670 to 1700 were Gove's, New Jersey antiquitrent, Davyes-Pate, Fendall's second, Essex County, anti-Sothel, anti-Colleton, and anti-Hamilton.

13. Clarence L. Ver Steeg, *The Formative Years, 1607–1763* (New York, 1964), Chap. 6, quoting from pp. 129, 149. Four uprisings occurred in 1689: anti-Sothel in North Carolina, Coode's in Maryland, Leisler's in New York, and anti-Andros in Massachusetts. These rebellions were all connected with the Glorious Revolution in England, which seemed to elicit the outbreaks in America, although the latter sprang from deep-seated, indigenous American grievances. Hall, Leder, and Kammen, eds., *Glorious Revolution in America*; David S. Lovejoy, *The Glorious Revolution in America* (New York, 1972).

14. See Chap. 7.

15. *Ibid.*

16. The exception was the overthrow of the proprietary government in South Carolina in 1719.

17. See Chap. 7.

18. George Rudé, *The Crowd in History: A Study of Popular Disturbances in France and England, 1730–1848* (New York, 1964); Gustave Le Bon, *The Crowd: A Study of the Popular Mind* (New York, 1896).

19. Arthur M. Schlesinger, Sr., "Political Mobs and the American Revolution, 1765–1776," American Philosophical Society, *Proceedings,* 79 (1955): 244–50; Edmund S. and Helen M. Morgan, *The Stamp Act Crisis: Prologue to Revolution* (New York, 1963); Lloyd I. Rudolph, "The Eighteenth-Century Mob in America and Europe," *American Quarterly,* 11 (1959): 447–69; Bernard Bailyn, ed., *Pamphlets of the American Revolution, 1750–1776* (Cambridge, Mass., 1965), vol. I, pp. 581–84; Gordon S. Wood, "A Note on Mobs in the American Revolution," *William and Mary Quarterly,* 3d Ser., 23 (1966): 635–42; Jesse Lemisch, "Jack Tar in the Streets: Merchant Seamen in the Politics of Revolutionary America," *ibid.,* 3d Ser., 25 (1968): 371–407; William Ander Smith, "Anglo-Colonial Society and the Mob: 1740–1775" (Ph.D. dissertation, Claremont Graduate School, 1965); G. B. Warden, *Boston: 1689–1776* (Boston, 1970); Pauline Maier, "Popular Uprisings and Civil Authority in Eighteenth-Century America," *William and Mary Quarterly,* 3d Ser., 27 (1970): 3–35. All of these scholars reject the dominant view of a generation ago [e.g., Philip G. Davidson, *Propaganda and the American Revolution, 1763–1783* (Chapel Hill, 1941)] that eighteenth-century mobs in revolutionary America were not purposively pursuing their own aims but were manipulated by the propaganda of such calculating leaders as Samuel Adams. The older, manipulated-mob

interpretation has been held in recent years by Clifford K. Shipton in biographical sketches of Harvard alumni (Samuel Adams, James Bowdoin, and others who took part in the patriotic movement) in Shipton's volumes of *Sibley's Harvard Graduates: Biographical Sketches of Those Who Attended Harvard College* . . . (Cambridge, Mass., and Boston, 1933–), vols. IX–XV, and in Hiller B. Zobel, *The Boston Massacre* (New York, 1970). Lengthy critiques of Zobel's book have been published by Jesse Lemisch in the *Harvard Law Review*, 84 (1970): 485–504, and by Pauline Maier in *The Journal of Interdisciplinary History*, 2 (1971): 119–35. Rudolph, writing before Rudé's work on European mobs had made its full impact, attributed purposive action to American mobs while denying it to those of Europe.

20. Maier, "Popular Uprisings," p. 4. See, also, Maier's subsequent book, *From Resistance to Revolution: Colonial Radicals and the Development of American Opposition to Britain, 1765–1776* (New York, 1972).
21. Smith, "Anglo-Colonial Society and the Mob," p. 1.
22. *Ibid.*, pp. 31–32.
23. The listing in Appendix 1 is based almost entirely upon the riots cited in Maier, "Popular Uprisings," pp. 3–35, and David M. Matteson, "Riots in the United States," MS, David Maydole Matteson Papers, Library of Congress. I am indebted to Prof. Robert V. Bruce for calling Matteson's manuscript to my attention.
24. The number 44 is an understatement for the total of riots in the period from 1760 to 1775, since it is based on the same approach as that used for Appendix 1.
25. Smith, "Anglo-Colonial Society and the Mob," p. 68, quoting from Harry A. Cushing, ed., *The Writings of Samuel Adams* (New York, 1904), vol. I, p. 237. For the reporting of British riots in American colonial newspapers see Smith, p. 89.
26. Smith, "Anglo-Colonial Society and the Mob," pp. 31–32.
27. *Ibid.* A recent work emphasizing the "stunningly rapid transformation" of the British economy in the mid-eighteenth century and citing relevant authorities in the literature of economic history is Michael G. Kammen's *Empire and Interest: The American Colonies and the Politics of Mercantilism* (Philadelphia, 1970), p. vi, Chap. 4. Smith, in "Anglo-Colonial Society and the Mob," sees British mob activity within the context of an economy of scarcity and American mob activity in the context of an economy of abundance.
28. Smith, "Anglo-Colonial Society and the Mob," pp. 92–93, 99.
29. *Ibid.*, pp. 94–99.
30. Zobel, *Boston Massacre*, pp. 216, 236, 266.
31. Smith, "Anglo-Colonial Society and the Mob," p. 91.
32. *Ibid.*, pp. 103–8. In an important article, "The Charleston Mob and the Evolution of Popular Politics in Revolutionary South Carolina, 1765–1784," *Perspectives in American History*, 4 (1970): 173–98, that also documents the current image of the purposive, controlled character of revolutionary era mobs, Pauline Maier concisely notes that "throughout the eighteenth century the mob had played an important role in British politics. It had forced Walpole's abandonment of his excise scheme in 1733, defeated the Jew Bill two decades later, caused the repeal of the cider tax in 1766, and, again in 1780, the year of the bloody Gordon riots, the mob opposed legislative concessions to Irish Catholics," and "the Americans understood this process" (p. 181).
33. The 11 economic riots were Virginia tobacco (1682), New Jersey land (1699–1700, 1745–1754), Massachusetts food (1710, 1713), Massachusetts anti-

markethouse (1737), Connecticut ship (1724), North Carolina quitrent (1737), Pennsylvania fish-dam (1738), New York antirent (1751–1757), and North Carolina land tax (1759).

34. The seven intercolonial boundary disputes were Rhode Island (1663–1750), Connecticut (1663–1750), Massachusetts (1663–1750), New York-Connecticut (1718), New York-New Jersey (1719–1764), Pennsylvania-Maryland (1721–1737), and New York-Massachusetts (1751–1757).

35. The six political or economic-political riots were Rhode Island (1654–1655), North Carolina Capt. Gibbs (1690), South Carolina (1703), North Carolina (1718), New Hampshire mast-tree (1734), and New Hampshire surveyor of woods (1754).

36. The three religious riots were in Rhode Island (1641), New York (1703–1710), and in Flatbush, N.Y. (1711). The three maritime riots were in New Hampshire (1699), New York (1705), and Portsmouth, N.H. (1757).

37. The two election riots were in Pennsylvania (1742, 1750). The two impressment riots were in New York (1711) and Massachusetts (1747). The two riots caused by social factors were in Pennsylvania (1704) and Connecticut (1722).

38. The customs riot was in Rhode Island (1719).

39. Riots of a miscellaneous nature were in Maryland (1654), Massachusetts (1737), and Brentwoods, N.H. (1757).

40. The seven anti-British riots were in New York City (1711), Rhode Island (1719), New Hampshire (1734), Massachusetts (1747), and New Hampshire (1754 and two in 1757).

41. The colony-by-colony total adds up to forty-four rather than forty, because boundary-dispute riots always involved two colonies.

42. The decade-by-decade total is seventy-five rather than forty, because many of the riots—e.g., the New Jersey land riots—spanned more than one decade.

43. Thomas J. Wertenbaker, *Virginia Under the Stuarts: 1607–1688* (Princeton, 1914), pp. 232–38.

44. On a twentieth-century violent movement organized to restrict the growth of tobacco, see James O. Nall, *The Tobacco Night Riders of Kentucky and Tennessee: 1905–1909* (Louisville, 1939).

45. McCormick, *New Jersey*, 77–78. See also Gary S. Horowitz, "New Jersey Land Riots, 1745–1755" (Ph.D. dissertation, Ohio State University, 1966).

46. Thomas Hutchinson, *The History of Massachusetts-Bay, from the Charter of King William and Queen Mary, in 1691, Until the Year 1750* (Boston, 1767), pp. 330–33. See also Carl Bridenbaugh, *Cities in Revolt: Urban Life in America, 1743–1776* (New York, 1964), pp. 114–17, and Warden, *Boston*, pp. 135–38.

47. Edmund S. Morgan, *The Birth of the Republic, 1763–89* (Chicago, 1956), p. 20.

48. Warden, *Boston*, p. 93. This entire paragraph is based on Warden's valuable book. It has been customary for historians [e.g., John C. Miller, *Sam Adams: Pioneer in Propaganda* (Boston, 1936)] to cite the link between the Cooke tradition and Samuel Adams, but it has remained for Warden to give us—in this long-needed study of the politics of colonial Boston—the first comprehensive treatment of the connection. Warden's Ph.D. dissertation, "Boston Politics, 1692–1765" (Yale University, 1966), is helpful too, for it contains a valuable unpublished analysis of the era of Elisha Cooke, Sr.

49. The following sketch of the patriot infrastructure in Boston is based on the standard authorities among whom the following have been most helpful: Charles W. Akers, *Called Unto Liberty: A Life of Jonathan Mayhew, 1720–1766* (Cambridge, Mass., 1964); George P. Anderson, "Ebenezer Mackintosh: Stamp Act Rioter and Patriot," Colonial Society of Massachusetts, *Transactions*, 26

(1927): 15–64, 348–61; Bernard Bailyn, "Religion and Revolution: Three Biographical Studies," *Perspectives*, 4 (1970): 85–169; Bridenbaugh, *Cities in Revolt*; Alice M. Baldwin, *The New England Clergy and the American Revolution* (Durham, N.C., 1928); John Cary, *Joseph Warren: Physician, Politician, Patriot* (Urbana, 1961); Alan and Katherine Day, "Another Look at the Boston 'Caucus,' " *Journal of American Studies*, 5 (1971): 19–42; Benjamin W. Labaree, *The Boston Tea Party* (New York, 1964); R. S. Longley, "Mob Activities in Revolutionary Massachusetts," *New England Quarterly*, 6 (1933): 98–130; Miller, *Sam Adams*; Morgan and Morgan, *Stamp Act Crisis*; Arthur M. Schlesinger, Sr., *Prelude to Independence: The Newspaper War on Britain, 1764–1776* (New York, 1958); John Shy, *Toward Lexington: The Role of the British Army in the Coming of the American Revolution* (Princeton, 1965); Page Smith, *John Adams* (Garden City, N.Y., 1962); Smith, "Anglo-Colonial Society and the Mob"; Warden, *Boston*; Zobel, *Boston Massacre*. Very valuable are Shipton's biographical sketches of the following Harvard graduates (graduating class indicated) in *Sibley's Harvard Graduates*, vols. IX–XV: Samuel Adams '40, Samuel Cooper '43, James Otis '43, Thomas Cushing '44, James Bowdoin '45, Benjamin Church '54, John Hancock '54, John Avery '59, Joseph Warren '59, and Josiah Quincy, Jr., '63.

50. James Otis, a member of the Saint John's lodge, is the exception that proves the rule, for Otis, in economic and social status, did conform to the Saint John's type and had joined it before the Saint Andrew's lodge was founded.

51. For example, 4 of the 14 revolutionary pamphlets reprinted in Bailyn, ed., *Pamphlets*, vol. I, were originally printed in the shop of Edes and Gill.

52. Until the appearance of Zobel, *Boston Massacre*, in 1970, all authorities had named Samuel Swift, Boston lawyer and Harvard graduate of 1735, as the "Swift" cited in contemporary sources as the leader of the North End Mob. But Zobel, p. 321, notes that Samuel Swift lived on Pleasant Street in the South End and thinks it "more likely" that the North End Mob leader was one "Henry Swift, Shipwright," who was indicted for the 1764 Pope's Day riot—a surmise that I find persuasive.

53. The origins of the popular sovereignty concept in the revolutionary period are discussed in this chapter.

54. *Boston Evening-Post*, Nov. 6, 1769, p. 3.

55. Cutler, *Lynch-Law*, pp. 61–72.

56. Peter Oliver, *Origin & Progress of the American Rebellion*, eds. Douglass Adair and John A. Schutz (San Marino, Calif., 1961), p. 157.

57. Laurence Veysey, ed., *Law and Resistance: American Attitudes toward Authority* (New York, 1970), pp. 208–34.

58. Mitford M. Mathews, *A Dictionary of Americanisms on Historical Principles* (Chicago, 1951), p. 1706.

59. Cutler, *Lynch-Law*, p. 1.

60. See Chap. 4. See also Gary T. Marx and Dane Archer, "Citizen Involvement in the Law Enforcement Process: The Case of Community Patrols," *American Behavioral Scientist*, 15 (1971–1972): 52–72. Among the black community patrol organizations have been the "Deacons" in a Deep South belt from Louisiana to the Carolinas and "Operation Interruption," a Harlem association. Seventeen of the twenty-eight self-defense patrol groups studied by Marx and Archer were black.

61. Chap. 4.

62. *Ibid.* Brown, *South Carolina Regulators*.

63. Brown, *South Carolina Regulators*, pp. 123–126.

64. Cutler, *Lynch-Law*, pp. 24–30. See, also, William Waller Hening, ed., *The Statutes at Large . . . of Virginia . . .* (Richmond and Philadelphia, 1809–1823), vol. X, p. 195; vol. XI, pp. 134–35.

65. Gordon S. Wood, *The Creation of the American Republic, 1776–1787* (Chapel Hill, 1969), pp. 319–21.

66. *Ibid.,* p. 383.

67. *Ibid.,* p. 371.

68. *Ibid.,* p. 599.

69. *Ibid.,* p. 600.

70. Alexis de Tocqueville, *Democracy in America* (New York, 1948), vol. I, p. 56.

71. Michael Zuckerman, *Peaceable Kingdoms: New England Towns in the Eighteenth Century* (New York, 1970), pp. vii, 154, and *passim*.

72. Warden, *Boston*, pp. 218–19.

73. Chap. 6.

74. Chap. 4.

75. S. E. Morison, ed., *Sources and Documents Illustrating the American Revolution, 1764–1788, and the Formation of the Federal Constitution* (New York, 1920), p. 124.

76. Ivor Noël Hume, *1775: Another Part of the Field* (New York, 1966), pp. 287–88; see, also, pp. 32–33, 285–86. On coercion of the Tories, see, also, William H. Nelson's *The American Tory* (New York, 1961), pp. 193–96; Robert M. Calhoon, *The Loyalists in Revolutionary America: 1760–1781* (New York, 1973), Chaps. 23, 35, 41–42, and *passim*. For a study of a leading target of patriot animosity, see Bernard Bailyn, *The Ordeal of Thomas Hutchinson* (Cambridge, Mass., 1974). On the political process of resistance to the British that paralleled the violent opposition, see Richard D. Brown, *Revolutionary Politics in Massachusetts: The Boston Committee of Correspondence and the Towns, 1772–1774* (Cambridge, Mass., 1970).

77. Leland D. Baldwin, *Whiskey Rebels* (Pittsburgh, 1939), p. 103.

78. *Albany Argus,* Aug. 11, 1845, p. 2, reprinted in Richard Maxwell Brown, ed., *American Violence* (Englewood Cliffs, N.J., 1970), pp. 53–55. See also Henry Christman, *Tin Horns and Calico* (New York, 1945), and David M. Ellis, *Landlords and Farmers in the Hudson-Mohawk Region, 1790–1850* (Ithaca, N.Y., 1946).

79. Charles P. Roland, *The Confederacy* (Chicago, 1960), pp. 40–41.

80. Laura A. White, *Robert Barnwell Rhett: Father of Secession* (Gloucester, Mass., 1965), pp. 14–15, 17, 24, 121. See, also Chap. 3, in this book.

81. Avery O. Craven, *The Growth of Southern Nationalism: 1848–1861* (Baton Rouge, 1953), p. 327.

82. Harold S. Schultz, *Nationalism and Sectionalism in South Carolina: 1852–1860* (New York, 1969), pp. 226, 229.

83. Henry T. Shanks, *The Secession Movement in Virginia: 1847–1861* (Richmond, 1934), p. 125.

84. Frank L. Klement, *The Copperheads in the Middle West* (Chicago, 1960), pp. 165–66ff.

85. John L. Shover, *Cornbelt Rebellion: The Farmers' Holiday Association* (Urbana, 1965), pp. 46, 59–65, 97, and *passim*.

86. Jerome H. Skolnick, *The Politics of Protest* (New York, 1969), pp. 232–38. See, also, J. Harry Jones, *The Minutemen* (New York, 1968).

87. An exception is the radical historian Staughton Lynd, an advocate of thoroughgoing but nonviolent reform, who, in his *Intellectual Origins of American Radicalism* (New York, 1968), seeks to connect the radical reform

movement of the present with an American radical tradition represented in the eighteenth century, so he argues, by the American Revolution.

Chapter 3

1. John G. Van Deusen, *Economic Bases of Disunion in South Carolina* (New York, 1928); David Duncan Wallace, *South Carolina: A Short History: 1520–1948* (Chapel Hill, 1951), pp. 385–86; and Charles S. Sydnor, *The Development of Southern Sectionalism, 1819–1848* (Baton Rouge, 1948), pp. 250–52, 258.
2. Wallace, *South Carolina*, pp. 384–86; John Hope Franklin, *The Militant South* (Cambridge, Mass., 1956), pp. vii–viii, x, 65–80, 193, 214, and *passim*; William W. Freehling, *Prelude to Civil War: The Nullification Controversy in South Carolina, 1816–1836* (New York, 1966), emphasizes extreme fears of a slave uprising aroused by the aborted Denmark Vesey plot of 1822; on the latter see Chap. 7, this book. Steven A. Channing, *Crisis of Fear: Secession in South Carolina* (New York, 1970), stresses similar forebodings following the John Brown uprising. Although I deal here only with South Carolina and southern extremism, the North, too, was afflicted with militant passions: see Michael B. Chesson, "The Militant North: 1800–1861" (senior honors essay, College of William and Mary, 1969).
3. On Calhoun, in addition to the sources in note 13, below: Richard N. Current, "John C. Calhoun, Philosopher of Reaction," *Antioch Review*, 3 (1943): 223–34; Richard Hofstadter, *The American Political Tradition: And the Men Who Made It* (New York, 1960), Chap. 4; and Charles M. Wiltse, *John C. Calhoun* (Indianapolis, 1944–1951).
4. On Fitzhugh: Eugene D. Genovese, *The World the Slaveholders Made: Two Essays in Interpretation* (New York, 1969), part 2; George Fitzhugh, *Cannibals All! Or, Slaves without Masters* [1857], ed. C. Vann Woodward (Cambridge, Mass., 1960); Harvey Wish, *George Fitzhugh: Propagandist of the Old South* (Baton Rouge, 1943). Two lesser but still notable extremist Virginia defenders of slavery in the post-Jeffersonian generation were Thomas R. Dew and Edmund Ruffin. In Jefferson's own time the Virginian, John Taylor of Caroline, was a skilled proponent of slavery.
5. This is not to suggest that there were no moderates in the ante-bellum Up Country. For example, the leading Unionist politician in the state was Benjamin F. Perry of Greenville County in the Piedmont. Nor did the Low Country escape extremism; Robert Barnwell Rhett, the fiery editor of the Charleston *Mercury*, came from the Low Country district of Beaufort. And Charleston of the Low Country has had a long history of turmoil highlighted by Christopher Gadsden and the Sons of Liberty in the 1760's, the demagogic Alexander Gillon in the 1780's, and Mayor John P. Grace who bitterly attacked both the Charleston aristocracy and America's entry into World War I. Yet the point remains that moderation was overwhelmed by extremism in the Up Country and that the extremism of Charleston was less important than that of the Up Country. On these matters see Lillian A. Kibler's *Benjamin F. Perry: South Carolina Unionist* (Durham, N. C., 1946); Richard Walsh's *Charleston's Sons of Liberty: A Study of the Artisans, 1763–1789* (Columbia, S. C., 1959); and, on Grace, see John J. Duffy's "Charleston Politics in the Progressive Era," (Ph.D. dissertation, University of South Carolina, 1963).
6. See, for example, M. Eugene Sirmans, *Colonial South Carolina: A Political*

History, 1663–1763 (Chapel Hill, 1966), and George C. Rogers, Jr., *Charleston in the Age of the Pinckneys* (Norman, 1969).

7. William R. Taylor, *Cavalier and Yankee* (New York, 1961), pp. 55, 58, 63. George C. Rogers, Jr., *Evolution of a Federalist: William Loughton Smith of Charleston (1758–1812)* (Columbia, S. C., 1962), pp. 363–64, 369–72, 392–96.

8. Taylor, *Cavalier and Yankee*, p. 58.

9. *Ibid.*, p. 63.

10. *Ibid.*, p. 55.

11. *Historical Collections of the Joseph Habersham Chapter (Atlanta, Ga.)*, Daughters of the American Revolution, 3 (1910): letter from John C. Calhoun to Charles H. Allen, Nov. 21, 1847, in John H. Logan, "From manuscript of Dr. John H. Logan, collected with a view of writing a second volume of His History of the Upper Country of South Carolina (collected by Lyman C. Draper)." [John C. Calhoun], *Life of John C. Calhoun* (New York, 1843), pp. 3–4. Richard Maxwell Brown, *The South Carolina Regulators* (Cambridge, Mass., 1963), pp. 97, 103–4, 134, 208.

12. Brown, *South Carolina Regulators*, pp. 4–5.

13. Allen Johnson, Dumas Malone, *et al.*, eds. *Dictionary of American Biography* (New York, 1928–1958), vol. III, pp. 411–19; Gerald M. Capers, *John C. Calhoun—Opportunist: A Reappraisal* (Gainesville, 1960), pp. 3–6; Margaret L. Coit, *John C. Calhoun: An American Portrait* (Boston, 1950), pp. 2–4.

14. Brown, *South Carolina Regulators*, Chap. 1.

15. *Ibid.*, pp. 27–37.

16. *Ibid.*, p. 49.

17. *Ibid.*, pp. 90, 92–111.

18. Edward B. McCrady, *The History of South Carolina in the Revolution, 1775–1780* (New York, 1901), pp. 36–38, 41–52, 86–87, 95–97.

19. *Ibid.*, pp. 192–99.

20. *Royal Gazette* (Charleston), Apr. 6, 1782. According to "Letters from John Lewis Gervais to Henry Laurens, 1777–1778," ed. Raymond Starr, *South Carolina Historical Magazine*, 66 (1965): 32, Judge Pendleton may not have been so strongly anti-Tory earlier in the war.

21. McCrady, *South Carolina, 1775–1780*, p. 86.

22. Robert Woodward Barnwell, Jr., "Loyalism in South Carolina, 1765–1785" (Ph.D. dissertation, Duke University, 1941), p. 196.

23. *Gazette of the State of South Carolina* (Charleston), Sept. 9, 1778.

24. Paul H. Smith, *Loyalists and Redcoats: A Study in British Revolutionary Policy* (Chapel Hill, 1964), pp. 131–32. See, also, Wallace, *South Carolina*, p. 296, and Don Higginbotham, *The War of American Independence: Military Attitudes, Policies, and Practice, 1763–1789* (New York, 1971), pp. 360–64.

25. Edward B. McCrady, *The History of South Carolina in the Revolution, 1780–1783* (New York, 1902), pp. 744–53. A brief treatment of the Back Country conflict is Russell F. Weigley's *The Partisan War: The South Carolina Campaign of 1780–1782* (Columbia, S. C., 1970).

26. McCrady, *South Carolina, 1775–1780*, pp. 852–53, and *South Carolina, 1780–1783*, pp. 744–47. There were 3,718 casualties in Buford's Defeat, Camden, and King's Mountain.

27. McCrady, *South Carolina, 1780–1783*, pp. 744–53.

28. Leah Townsend, *South Carolina Baptists: 1670–1805* (Florence, S. C., 1935), pp. 139, 278.

29. *South-Carolina and American General Gazette* (Charleston), Aug. 23, 1780.

30. *Ibid.*, Sept. 20, 1780.

31. McCrady, *South Carolina, 1780–1783*, pp. 144–48. In 1784 the state legislature legalized the system, retroactively, for both Sumter and Pickens—hence, the term "Sumter's Law." Wallace, *South Carolina*, p. 314.
32. *Ibid.*
33. McCrady, *South Carolina, 1780–1783*, pp. 425–26.
34. *Royal Gazette*, Apr. 17, 27, 1782.
35. *Ibid.*, Apr. 13, 1782.
36. *Ibid.*, Apr. 17, 1782.
37. *Ibid.*, Apr. 27, 1782.
38. McCrady, *South Carolina, 1775–1780*, pp. 524–25.
39. *Ibid.*, pp. 610–11.
40. McCrady, *South Carolina, 1780–1783*, pp. 19–20.
41. *Ibid.*, p. 638.
42. Brown, *South Carolina Regulators*, pp. 203–4.
43. McCrady, *South Carolina, 1780–1783*, p. 469.
44. *Royal Gazette*, Sept. 12, 1781. McCrady, *South Carolina, 1780–1783*, pp. 470, 748–49.
45. *Royal Gazette*, Nov. 28, 1781; McCrady, *South Carolina, 1780–1783*, pp. 627–30; John A. Chapman, *History of Edgefield County from the Earliest Settlements to 1897* (Newberry, S. C., 1897), pp. 30–46. The Tory-supporting *Royal Gazette* in a straightforward account, understandably making no mention of any atrocity, said that Cunningham's party killed 21 Whigs. McCrady, *South Carolina, 1780–1783*, says that 28 of 30 men were killed.
46. *Royal Gazette*, Dec. 8, 1781; McCrady, *South Carolina, 1780–1783*, pp. 471–75; David Ramsay, *The History of the Revolution of South-Carolina from a British Province to an Independent State* (Trenton, 1785), vol. II, pp. 272–73.
47. Joseph Johnson, *Traditions and Reminiscences of the American Revolution in the South* (Charleston, 1851), pp. 427–28; Wallace, *South Carolina*, p. 325.
48. Wallace, *South Carolina*, p. 325.
49. *Ibid.*, pp. 491–92.
50. Chapman, *Edgefield County*, pp. 30–46.
51. *Ibid.*, pp. 67, 72, 265.
52. David Donald, *Charles Sumner and the Coming of the Civil War* (New York, 1960), pp. 294–95. In his account Donald correctly notes that Brooks was not a "fire-eater" but that under his placid exterior there burned a smoldering hatred of abolitionists, proud devotion to the South and South Carolina, loyalty to family (Butler was his second cousin), and allegiance to the code of the gentleman.
53. See Hampton M. Jarrell, *Wade Hampton and the Negro: The Road Not Taken* (Columbia, S. C., 1950).
54. McCrady, *South Carolina, 1775–1780*, pp. 192–99.
55. *Royal Gazette*, Apr. 17, 24, 1782.
56. McCrady, *South Carolina, 1780–1783*, pp. 144–48.
57. William Watts Ball, *The State that Forgot: South Carolina's Surrender to Democracy* (Indianapolis, 1932), p. 22 (emphasis mine).
58. Chapman, *Edgefield County*, pp. 66–67, 72.
59. *Ibid.*, p. 72.
60. M. L. Weems, *The Devil in Petticoats or God's Revenge against Husband Killing* (reprinted Saluda, S. C., 1935), p. 3.
61. Chapman, *Edgefield County*, p. 84.
62. In the red hot context of South Carolina politics of the 1850's such Edgefieldians as Butler and Brooks in addition to the influential *Edgefield*

Advertiser (edited by Arthur Simkins) were actually mild. There were two wings of the dominant Democratic party, an extremist wing and a moderate wing. Both wings, however, were mainly secessionist in sentiment. The extremist wing of "fire-eaters" led by Rhett and Lawrence M. Keitt was for immediate secession. The more moderate wing of "Cooperationists" or "National Democrats" were inclined to secession but with the cooperation of other Southern states, and they fought shy of a complete break with Northern Democrats. James L. Orr led the Cooperationists, a group that included Butler, Brooks, Francis W. Pickens, and Simkins. There was also a third or "swing" group of in-betweeners that was not formally organized but of whom James H. Hammond was representative. The important point, however, is that all of these groups were really quite extreme in their views on sectional issues—hence, I call them extremists. Of the leading members of the Cooperationist bloc only Benjamin F. Perry was a genuine Unionist. See Harold S. Schultz, *Nationalism and Sectionalism in South Carolina, 1852–1860: A Study of the Movement for Southern Independence* (Durham, N. C., 1950). See, also, Channing, *Crisis of Fear*, p. 182, for the contention that the more moderate and Union-minded South Carolinians could not escape the imperatives of ante-bellum South Carolina society and politics that drove so many toward the extremist stance.

63. Chapman, *Edgefield County*, p. 171.
64. *Ibid.*, pp. 184–85.
65. On Pickens and the secession crisis: John B. Edmunds, Jr., "Francis W. Pickens and the War Begins" (unpublished paper, South Carolina Historical Association, Charleston, 1970), pp. 1–3. The phrase "radical persuasion" used in regard to secession is the title of Chap. 8 in Channing, *Crisis of Fear*. On Pickens's family background: Chapman, *Edgefield County*, pp. 143–45; *Dictionary of American Biography*, vol. XIV, pp. 559–61; Alice N. Waring, *The Fighting Elder: Andrew Pickens (1739–1817)* (Columbia, S. C., 1962).
66. Elizabeth Merritt, *James Henry Hammond, 1807–1865* (Baltimore, 1923). *Dictionary of American Biography*, vol. VIII, pp. 207–8.
67. Wallace, *South Carolina*, p. 423. Two other notable ante-bellum Edgefield extremists were Louis T. Wigfall, "one of the most incendiary of secessionists, who, when he left Edgefield to represent Texas in the Senate, carried Edgefield's traditions with him," and Chancellor Francis H. Wardlaw, author of South Carolina's secession ordinance. James G. Banks, "Strom Thurmond and the Revolt against Modernity" (Ph.D. dissertation, Kent State University, 1970), pp. 14–15.
68. Francis Butler Simkins, *Pitchfork Ben Tillman: South Carolinian* (Baton Rouge, 1944), p. 57.
69. Ball, *State that Forgot*, pp. 22, 211. Simkins, *Pitchfork Ben Tillman*, pp. 57, 64–66.
70. Rayford W. Logan, *The Negro in American Life and Thought: The Nadir, 1877–1901* (New York, 1954).
71. Simkins, *Pitchfork Ben Tillman*, p. 407. Simkins's remarkable biography of Tillman is unusually well informed on the nuances and Edgefield aspects of Tillman's career, because Simkins—one of the leading Southern historians of recent times—was himself a native Edgefieldian descended from an elite local family of revolutionary era vintage.
72. Simkins, *Pitchfork Ben Tillman*, Chaps. 6–15; William J. Cooper, Jr., *The Conservative Regime: South Carolina, 1877–1890* (Baltimore, 1968), Chaps. 5–6.
73. Simkins, *Pitchfork Ben Tillman*, pp. 8, 396. Jack S. Mullins, "Lynching in South Carolina, 1900–1914" (M.A. thesis, University of South Carolina, 1961), pp. 4,

7–9. See, also, George B. Tindall, *South Carolina Negroes: 1877–1900* (Columbia, S. C., 1952), pp. 256–58, for a mass white attack on blacks in Edgefield and other counties in 1898 as a response to a race riot in the village of Phoenix.

74. Simkins, *Pitchfork Ben Tillman*, p. 551.
75. *Ibid.,* p. 315.
76. *Ibid.,* p. 85.
77. *Ibid.,* pp. 38, 40.
78. *Ibid.,*p. 58.
79. *Ibid.,* pp. 58–61. A brief account of the 1874–1876 role of the white activists of Edgefield County appears in Joel Williamson's *After Slavery: The Negro in South Carolina during Reconstruction, 1861–1877* (Chapel Hill, 1965), pp. 266–72. On Reconstruction, generally: Francis B. Simkins and Robert H. Woody, *South Carolina during Reconstruction* (Chapel Hill, 1932).
80. Simkins, *Pitchfork Ben Tillman*, pp. 58–61.
81. *Ibid.,* pp. 64–67.
82. *Ibid.,* pp. 531–34.
83. Banks, "Strom Thurmond," pp. 26, 29–30.
84. *Ibid.,* p. 1. An enthusiastic treatment of Thurmond's extreme conservatism is Alberta Lachicotte's *Rebel Senator: Strom Thurmond of South Carolina* (New York, 1966).
85. This is not to imply that Thurmond is unaggressive personally. He is a physical culture enthusiast and not averse to scuffles at the man-to-man level.
86. Banks, "Strom Thurmond," pp. 1, 214, 387, and *passim.*
87. *Ibid.,* pp. 6, 29.
88. *Ibid.,* p. 9.
89. South Carolina's only major outbreak of violence in race relations in the post-World War II period occurred in Orangeburg on Feb. 8, 1968, when a civil rights controversy involving South Carolina State College students culminated in the killing of 3 black students and the wounding of 27 other blacks by white state highway patrolmen. Jack Nelson and Jack Bass, *The Orangeburg Massacre* (New York, 1970). In contrast to other Deep South states, South Carolina desegregated its public secondary schools and colleges and universities without violence and with little strain.
90. Banks, "Strom Thurmond," pp. 60–73 and *passim.*
91. The decades-long leader of the Barnwell Ring was state senator Edgar A. Brown of Barnwell County. On the Barnwell Ring: W. D. Workman, Jr., *The Bishop from Barnwell: The Political Life and Times of Senator Edgar A. Brown* (Columbia, S. C., 1963), and a pointed early account, V. O. Key, Jr., *Southern Politics in State and Nation* (New York, 1949). Although dominant within the state legislature, Brown three times lost primary bids to serve in the U. S. Senate in 1926, 1938, and 1954, the last time to Strom Thurmond.

Introduction
III Vigilantism: The Conservative Mob

1. The term "mob" is not used here in any pejorative sense as a purposeless, chaotic crowd but, rather, symbolically, in the modern scholarly meaning of "mob" as a crowd motivated, explicitly or implicitly, by a purposive rationality. See Chap. 2 (and note 19 of Chap. 2) on the riotous mob of the eighteenth

century and Chap. 7 on riotous black ghetto mobs of the 1960's. Vigilante movements were, as a rule, well organized.

2. In addition to Nixon, Mitchell, Haldeman, and Ehrlichman, the remaining nine are John W. Dean III, Charles W. Colson, Jeb Stuart Magruder, Gordon C. Strachan, Robert C. Mardian, Egil Krogh, Jr., G. Gordon Liddy, Dwight L. Chapin, and Frederick C. LaRue. Also involved was President Nixon's personal lawyer, Herbert W. Kalmbach. "Watergate Prosecution Status," *Washington Post*, Jan. 3, 1975, p. A-22. For a concise description of the Watergate and related matters, see the *New York Times, The End of a Presidency* (New York, 1974).

Chapter 4

1. Many small vigilante movements undoubtedly left no traces; this seems to have been especially true in the Old Northwest and Old Southwest in the first 20 or 30 years of the nineteenth century. The 326 movements, presently known, are listed in Appendix 3.

2. [Charles Hitchin], *The Regulator* . . . (London, 1718); Christopher Hibbert, *The Road to Tyburn* . . . (Cleveland, 1957).

3. Hubert Howe Bancroft, *Popular Tribunals* (San Francisco, 1887), vol. I, pp. 2–6.

4. James G. Leyburn, *Frontier Folkways* (New Haven, 1935), p. 219.

5. There have indeed been urban as well as rural vigilante movements. The greatest of all American vigilante movements—the San Francisco vigilance committee of 1856—was urban. Vigilantism has been by no means restricted to the frontier, although most typically it has been a frontier phenomenon.

6. Richard Maxwell Brown, *The South Carolina Regulators* (Cambridge, Mass., 1963). See, also, Chap. 3, this book.

7. Aside from the South Carolina Regulators there was little vigilante activity in the original 13 states of the Atlantic seaboard. The North Carolina Regulators (1768–1771) did not constitute a vigilante movement but, rather, embodied a violent agrarian protest against corrupt and galling local officials and indifferent provincial authorities.

8. The 96th meridian coincides, approximately, with both physiographic and state boundaries. Physiographically it roughly separates the humid prairies of the East from the semiarid Great Plains of the West. The states of Minnesota, Iowa, Missouri, Arkansas, and Louisiana fall into the province of Eastern vigilantism. The states of North and South Dakota, Nebraska, Kansas, and Oklahoma mainly fall into the area of Western vigilantism. In Texas the 96th meridian separates east Texas from central and west Texas, but for the sake of convenience all Texas vigilantism (along with that of the Dakotas, Nebraska, Kansas, and Oklahoma) has been included under the heading of Western vigilantism.

9. Lynn Glaser, *Counterfeiting in America* . . . (New York, 1968), Chap. 5. On the relationship between counterfeiting and the frontier money shortage, see Ruth A. Gallaher, "Money in Pioneer Iowa, 1838–1865," *Iowa Journal of History and Politics*, 31 (1934): 42–45. The use of counterfeit money for public land purchases is revealed in *Counties of Warren, Benton, Jasper and Newton, Indiana: Historical and Biographical* (Chicago, 1883), p. 458.

10. See, for example, Randall Parrish, *Historic Illinois* . . . (Chicago, 1906),

pp. 405–6; Charles Edward Pancoast, *A Quaker Forty-Niner* . . . , ed. Anna P. Hannum (Philadelphia, 1930), pp. 103–4.

11. William Faux, *Memorable Days in America* . . . [1823] (*Early Western Travels*, ed. Reuben G. Thwaites, vols. XI–XII; Cleveland, 1905), vol. XI, pp. 293–94; John L. McConnel, *Western Characters* (New York, 1853), pp. 171–75; William N. Blane, *An Excursion through the United States and Canada during the Years 1822–23* (London, 1824), pp. 233–35; Robert M. Coates, *The Outlaw Years* . . . (New York, 1930).

12. James W. Bragg, "Captain Slick, Arbiter of Early Alabama Morals," *Alabama Review*, 11 (1958): 125–34; Jack K. Williams, "Crime and Punishment in Alabama, 1819–1840," *ibid.*, 6 (1953): 14–30.

13. Williams, "Crime and Punishment in Alabama," p. 27; James E. Cutler, *Lynch-Law: An Investigation into the History of Lynching in the United States* (New York, 1905), p. 99; H. R. Howard, comp., *The History of Virgil A. Stewart* (New York, 1836); Edwin A. Miles, "The Mississippi Slave Insurrection Scare of 1835," *Journal of Negro History*, 42 (1957): 48–60; David Grimsted, "The Mississippi Slave Insurrection Panic, 1835" (unpublished paper, Southern Historical Association, Atlanta, 1973).

14. John E. Briggs, "Pioneer Gangsters," *Palimpsest*, 21 (1940): 73–90; John C. Parish, "White Beans for Hanging," *ibid.*, 1 (1920): 9–28; Harvey Reid, *Thomas Cox* (Iowa City, 1909), pp. 126, 154–55, 165–67; Jackson County Historical Society, *Annals of Jackson County, Iowa*, 2 (1906): 51–96.

15. C. L. Sonnichsen, *Ten Texas Feuds* (Albuquerque, 1957), Chap. 1; Lela R. Neill, "Episodes in the Early History of Shelby County" (M.A. thesis, Stephen F. Austin State College, 1950), pp. 77–153 and *passim.*

16. On the northern Illinois Regulators, see Alice L. Brumbaugh, "The Regulator Movement in Illinois" (M.A. thesis, University of Illinois, 1927), pp. 3, 5–27, and William Cullen Bryant, *Letters of a Traveller* . . . (New York, 1850), pp. 55–68. Two of the most important sources on the southern Illinois Regulators are Brumbaugh, "Regulator Movement," pp. 29–65, and James A. Rose, comp., Papers Relating to the Regulator and Flathead Trouble in Southern Illinois (bound typescript in Illinois State Historical Society, Springfield).

17. James H. Lay, *A Sketch of the History of Benton County, Missouri* (Hannibal, Mo., 1876), pp. 46–61. Pancoast, *Quaker Forty-Niner*, pp. 101–21. J. W. Vincent, "The 'Slicker War' and Its Consequences," *Missouri Historical Review*, 7 (1912–1913): 138–45.

18. *The Iowan*, 6 (1958): 4–11, 50–51. Jackson County Hist. Soc., *Annals*, 1 (1905): 29–34; *The History of Clinton County, Iowa* (Chicago, 1879), pp. 437ff.; Paul W. Black, "Lynchings in Iowa," *Iowa Journal of History and Politics*, 10 (1912): 151–209; Orville F. Graham, "The Vigilance Committees," *Palimpsest*, 6 (1925): 359–70.

19. M. H. Mott, *History of the Regulators of Northern Indiana* (Indianapolis, 1859); Weston A. Goodspeed and Charles Blanchard, eds., *Counties of Whitley and Noble, Indiana: Historical and Biographical* (Chicago, 1882), pp. 33–37, 63–73.

20. Among many sources, see Dorothy K. Gibson, "Social Life in San Antonio, 1855–1860" (M.A. thesis, University of Texas, 1937), pp. 122–31.

21. George A. Ketcham, "Municipal Police Reform: A Comparative Study of Law Enforcement in Cincinnati, Chicago, New Orleans, New York, and St. Louis, 1844–1877" (Ph.D. dissertation, University of Missouri, 1967), pp. 148–50.

22. Harry L. Griffin, "The Vigilance Committees of the Attakapas Country; or Early Louisiana Justice," Mississippi Valley Historical Association, *Proceedings*, 8 (1914–1915): 146–59; Alexander Barde, *History of the Committees of Vigilance*

in the Attakapas Country [1861], trans. and ed., Henrietta G. Rogers (M.A. thesis, Louisiana State University, 1936).

23. Chap. 5, this book, deals with the San Francisco vigilantes of 1856. An earlier important vigilante movement in San Francisco was that of 1851; see Mary Floyd Williams' *History of the San Francisco Committee of Vigilance of 1851: A Study of Social Control on the California Frontier in the Days of the Gold Rush* (Berkeley, 1921); George R. Stewart, *Committee of Vigilance: Revolution in San Francisco, 1851* (Boston, 1964); Bancroft, *Popular Tribunals*, vol. I, pp. 201–428.

24. *The History of Johnson County, Missouri* (Kansas City, 1881), Chap. 15; *History of Vernon County, Missouri* (St. Louis, 1887), pp. 348–49; *History of Greene County, Missouri* (St. Louis, 1883), pp. 497–501.

25. Lewis and Richard H. Collins, *History of Kentucky* (Louisville, 1924), vol. I, pp. 198–209; E. Merton Coulter, *The Civil War and Readjustment in Kentucky* (Chapel Hill, 1926), p. 359.

26. Wayne G. Broehl, *The Molly Maguires* (Cambridge, Mass., 1965), pp. 239–40, describes the Seymour, Indiana, vigilance committee of 1867–1868.

27. Ralph L. Peek, "Lawlessness and the Restoration of Order in Florida" (Ph.D. dissertation, University of Florida, 1964), pp. 91, 105–8, 111, 125–26, 149–50, 216–20.

28. See, especially, Bancroft, *Popular Tribunals*, vol. I, pp. 441ff., and the California listing in Appendix 3.

29. Thomas J. Dimsdale, *The Vigilantes of Montana* . . . (Virginia City, Mont., 1866); Nathaniel Pitt Langford, *Vigilante Days and Ways* (Boston, 1890); Hoffman Birney, *Vigilantes* (Philadelphia, 1929).

30. Granville Stuart, *Forty Years on the Frontier*, ed. Paul C. Phillips (Cleveland, 1925), vol. II, pp. 195–210; Michael A. Leeson, *History of Montana: 1739–1885* (Chicago, 1885), pp. 315–16.

31. Montana Territory Vigilance Committee, *Notice!* (broadside, Helena, Mont., Sept. 19, 1865). Leeson, *History of Montana*, pp. 303–16.

32. See Chap. 8.

33. Among many sources, see Jerome C. Smiley, *History of Denver* . . . (Denver, 1901), pp. 338–50.

34. Albuquerque *Republican Review*, Feb. 18, 1871. *Santa Fe Weekly New Mexican*, Nov. 13, 22, 1879; Victor Westphal, "History of Albuquerque: 1870–1880" (M.A. thesis, University of New Mexico, 1947), pp. 64–65; Bernice A. Rebord, "A Social History of Albuquerque: 1880–1885" (M.A. thesis, University of New Mexico, 1947), p. 34.

35. Miguel A. Otero, *My Life on the Frontier* (New York and Albuquerque, 1935–1939), vol. I, pp. 181–206; vol. II, pp. 2–3; *Santa Fe Daily New Mexican*, Mar. 12, 25–26, Apr. 13, 1881.

36. Erna B. Fergusson, *Murder & Mystery in New Mexico* (Albuquerque, 1948), pp. 15–32; Chester D. Potter, "Reminiscences of the Socorro Vigilantes," ed. Paige W. Christiansen, *New Mexico Historical Review*, 40 (1965): 23–54.

37. On the Butler County vigilantes, see A. T. Andreas, *History of the State of Kansas* . . . (Chicago, 1883), pp. 1431–32, and Correspondence of Governor J. M. Harvey, File on County Affairs, 1869–1872 (MSS in Archives Department of Kansas State Historical Society, Topeka). Materials on Kansas vigilantism are also to be found in Nyle H. Miller and Joseph W. Snell, *Why the West Was Wild* . . . (Topeka, 1963), and Genevieve Yost, "History of Lynching in Kansas," *Kansas Historical Quarterly*, 2 (1933): 182–219. See, also, Robert R. Dykstra, *The Cattle Towns* (New York, 1968).

38. On the Sidney vigilantes, see Grant L. Shumway, ed., *History of Western*

Nebraska . . . (Lincoln, 1921), vol. II, pp. 152–57, and Bryan T. Parker, "Extra-Legal Law Enforcement on the Nebraska Frontier" (M.A. thesis, University of Nebraska, 1931), pp. 53–54, 62–63. On the Niobrara region vigilantes, see Parker, "Extra-Legal Law Enforcement," pp. 63–65, and, among extensive newspaper coverage: O'Neill (Neb.) *Frontier*, Nov. 15, 1883, p. 2, c. 3; Nov. 22, 1883, p. 3, c. 4; Nov. 29, 1883, p. 2, c. 3; Dec. 13, 1883, p. 3, c. 5; Dec. 27, 1883, p. 4, c. 5; Jan. 10, 1884, p. 3, c. 5; Jan. 24, 1884, p. 3, c. 4; Feb. 14, 1884, p. 2, c. 3, and p. 3, c. 4 and *Holt County Banner* (O'Neill, Neb.), Feb. 5, 1884, p. 1, c. 5.

39. J. H. Triggs, *History of Cheyenne and Northern Wyoming* . . . (Omaha, 1876), pp. 14, 17–18, 21, 23–27; J. H. Triggs, *History and Directory of Laramie City* . . . (Laramie, 1875), pp. 3–15. The classic (but far from flawless) contemporary account of the Johnson County War by the anti-Regulator Asa Shinn Mercer was *The Banditti of the Plains* . . . (Cheyenne, 1894). Outstanding is Helena H. Smith's *The War on Powder River* (New York, 1966). General treatments of Western vigilantism are found in Bancroft's *Popular Tribunals*, vol. I, pp. 593–743; Wayne Gard's *Frontier Justice* (Norman, 1949), Chap. 14; Carl Coke Rister's "Outlaws and Vigilantes of the Southern Plains," *Mississippi Valley Historical Review*, 19 (1933): 537ff.

40. The state-by-state detail in Appendix 3 in regard to Eastern and Western vigilantism is summarized in Table 5-2 in Richard Maxwell Brown, "The American Vigilante Tradition," p. 164, in Hugh Davis Graham and Ted Robert Gurr, eds., *The History of Violence in America* (New York, 1969). The decade-by-decade chronological statistics on vigilante movements and the number of their victims (also drawn from Appendix 3) appear in Tables 5-3a, 5-3b, and 5-6d in *ibid.*, pp. 165 and 175.

41. For regular vigilante killings in California, see Appendix 3. The instant vigilantism toll of 79 men was gained from an analysis of Bancroft's narrative in *Popular Tribunals*, vol. I, pp. 515–76.

42. The distinction between "colonized" and "cumulative" new communities was formulated by Page Smith in *As a City upon the Hill: The Town in American History* (New York, 1966), pp. 17–36.

43. The following sketch of the three-level American community structure is based upon my own research and recent studies of American society. Among the latter are Jackson Turner Main's *The Social Structure of Revolutionary America* (Princeton, 1965) and, for the nineteenth century, Stephan Thernstrom's *Poverty and Progress: Social Mobility in a Nineteenth Century City* (Cambridge, Mass., 1964); Ray A. Billington's *America's Frontier Heritage* (New York, 1966), Chap. 5; Merle Curti's *The Making of an American Community* (Stanford, 1959), pp. 56–63, 78, 107–11ff., 126, 417ff., 448.

44. On the marginal "lower people" of the South (where they have been labeled "poor whites," "crackers," and so on), see Brown, *South Carolina Regulators*, pp. 27–29, and Shields McIlwaine, *The Southern Poor White from Lubberland to Tobacco Road* (Norman, 1939), a literary study. For lower people in the North, see Bernard De Voto, *Mark Twain's America* (Boston, 1932), pp. 54–58, and George F. Parker, *Iowa Pioneer Foundations* (Iowa City, 1940), vol. II, pp. 37–48.

45. Kai Erikson, *Wayward Puritans: A Study in the Sociology of Deviance* (New York, 1966), Chap. 1.

46. J. Milton Yinger, "Contraculture and Subculture," *American Sociological Review*, 25 (1960): 629, holds that a contraculture occurs "wherever the normative system of a group contains, as a primary element, a theme of conflict with the values of the total society . . . ." See, also, David M. Downes, *The*

Delinquent Solution: A Study in Subcultural Theory (New York, 1966), pp. 10–11.

47. See, for example, De Voto, *Mark Twain's America*, pp. 58–62; Parker, *Iowa Pioneer Foundations*, vol. II, pp. 37–48, 247–65.

48. See Howard, *History of Virgil A. Stewart*; Miles, "Mississippi Slave Insurrection Scare"; Grimsted, "Mississippi Slave Insurrection Panic," on the alleged Murrell plot. On the Flatheads, see Brumbaugh, "Regulator Movement," pp. 28–65; Rose, Papers Relating to Regulator and Flathead Trouble; Charles Neely, *Tales and Songs of Southern Illinois* (Menasha, Wis., 1938), pp. 7, 35, 41; Norman W. Caldwell, "Shawneetown: A Chapter in the Indian History of Illinois," *Journal of the Illinois State Historical Society*, 32 (1939): 199–200.

49. See note 101, below, for sources.

50. See note 91, below, for sources.

51. Brown, *South Carolina Regulators*, pp. 27–37.

52. Langford, *Vigilante Days*, vol. I, pp. 320–24. Howard A. Johnson, "Pioneer Law and Justice in Montana," Chicago Corral of the Westerners, *Brand Book*, 5 (1948–1949): 10.

53. About frontier Masons in Texas, the late Walter Prescott Webb wrote that "they believed in the law and aided in preserving order, often in ways best known to themselves." James D. Carter, *Masonry in Texas . . . to 1846* (Waco, 1955), p. xviii.

54. Thomas and Augustus Wildman, Letters, 1858–1865 (MSS in Western Collection, Beinecke Rare Book and Manuscript Library, Yale University, New Haven).

55. *Cowley County Censor* (Winfield, Kan.), Jan. 7, 1871.

56. David Donald, ed., "The Autobiography of James Hall, Western Literary Pioneer," *Ohio State Archaeological and Historical Quarterly*, 56 (1947): 297–98.

57. Mott, *Regulators of Northern Indiana*, pp. 6–7 and *passim*.

58. Dimsdale, *Vigilantes of Montana*, p. 116.

59. Fred M. Mazulla, "Undue Process of Law—Here and There," *Brand Book of the Denver Westerners*, 20 (1964): 273–79. Dr. Osborne became governor of Wyoming in 1893. On the vigilante taking of bodily trophies see, also, Chap. 6, this book.

60. Membership figures are drawn from Appendix 3 and are cumulated in Tables 5-4 and 5-5 in Brown, "American Vigilante Tradition," p. 172.

61. The source for the lynch-mob total of 4,730 is Jessie P. Guzman *et al.*, eds., *1952 Negro Year Book: A Review of Events Affecting Negro Life* (New York, 1952), p. 277. The grand total of 5,459 represents some double counting of victims, but this is more than offset, undoubtedly, by unknown (and thus uncounted) victims. Like the grand total, the total of documented vigilante victims (729) understates the actual undocumented total, which may be as high as 1,000. For the excess of annual lynchings over annual legal executions, 1883–1898, see Cutler, *Lynch-Law*, chart 1, opposite p. 162.

62. The statistics on vigilante killings in this and preceding paragraphs are taken from Appendix 3. They are cumulated, also, in Tables 5-6a through 5-6d in Brown, "American Vigilante Tradition," pp. 174–75.

63. Allen Johnson, Dumas Malone *et al.*, eds., *Dictionary of American Biography* (New York, 1928–1958), vol. IV, pp. 295–96; A. B. Scherer, *"The Lion of the Vigilantes": William T. Coleman and the Life of Old San Francisco* (Indianapolis, 1939). On Sanders: *Dictionary of American Biography*, vol. XVI, pp. 336–37.

64. See, for example, Anthony S. Nicolosi, "The Rise and Fall of the New Jersey Vigilant Societies," *New Jersey History*, 86 (1968): 29–32.

65. "Uses and Abuses of Lynch Law," *American Whig Review*, May, 1850, p. 461.

Pancoast, *Quaker Forty-Niner*, pp. 103–4. Brumbaugh, "Regulator Movement," pp. 9–11.

66. Dwyn M. Mounger, "Lynching in Mississippi, 1830–1930" (M.A. thesis, Mississippi State University, 1961), p. 9.

67. Brumbaugh, "Regulator Movement," pp. 10–11.

68. James Stuart, *Three Years in North America* (Edinburgh, 1833), vol. II, pp. 212–13; Williams, "Crime and Punishment in Alabama," p. 26.

69. Smiley, *History of Denver*, p. 349. (Emphasis mine.)

70. "The Vigilance Committee: Richmond during the War of 1812," *Virginia Magazine of History and Biography*, 7 (1899–1900): 225–41.

71. Harris G. Warren, "Pensacola and the Filibusters, 1816–1817," *Louisiana Historical Quarterly*, 21 (1938): 816.

72. See, for example, Documents relating to the Committee of Vigilance and Safety of Nacogdoches, Texas, Jan. 3, 1835, to Dec. 5, 1937 (transcripts in University of Texas Archives, File Box B 15/40).

73. *Hardesty's Historical and Geographical Encyclopedia . . . of Meigs County, Ohio* (Chicago, 1883), pp. 273–75.

74. Wilbur H. Siebert, *The Underground Railroad from Slavery to Freedom* (New York, 1898), pp. 71ff., 326ff., 436–39. See, also, Larry Gara, *The Liberty Line: The Legend of the Underground Railroad* (Lexington, 1961), pp. 99, 104–9.

75. John Hope Franklin, *The Militant South* (Cambridge, Mass., 1956), pp. 87–90; Gara, *Liberty Line*, pp. 157–58.

76. *National Police Gazette*, Sept. 17, 1845, p. 5.

77. Pierce County, Washington Territory, Vigilance Committee, Draft of Compact, June 1, 1856 (MS in Western Collection, Beinecke Rare Book and Manuscript Library, Yale University, New Haven).

78. Griffin, "Vigilance Committees of Attakapas," pp. 153–55.

79. Dimsdale, *Vigilantes of Montana*, p. 107.

80. *History of Johnson County*, pp. 372–73.

81. Thomas Ford, *A History of Illinois from Its Commencement as a State in 1818 to 1847* [1854], ed. Milo M. Quaife (Chicago, 1945–1946), vol. 1, pp. 10–11.

82. Griffin, "Vigilance Committees of Attakapas," pp. 153–55.

83. Barde, *History of the Committees*, pp. 26–27.

84. Mott, *Regulators of Northern Indiana*, pp. 15–18.

85. Alfred J. Mokler, *History of Natrona County, Wyoming 1888–1922 . . .* (Chicago, 1923).

86. *History of Johnson County*, pp. 372–73.

87. Mott, *Regulators of Northern Indiana*, p. 17.

88. *Denver Tribune*, Dec. 30, 1879, cited in John W. Cook, *Hands Up . . .* (Denver, 1897), p. 103.

89. Otero, *My Life*, vol. II, p. 2–3.

90. Pamphlet No. 342, Document No. 37 (typescript, State Historical Society of Colorado, Denver), pp. 118–19.

91. Brumbaugh, "Regulator Movement," pp. 3, 5–27. Bryant, *Letters of a Traveller*, pp. 55–68. Of the leading vigilante movements, all but the following seem to have been socially constructive: Madison and Hinds counties movements, Mississippi, 1835; east Texas Regulators, Shelby County, 1840–1844; southwest Missouri Slickers, Benton and Hickory counties, 1842; southern Illinois Regulators, 1846–1849; San Saba County Mob, Texas, 1880–1896; Johnson County, Wyoming, cattlemen Regulators, 1892; and the Sevier County, Tennessee, White Caps, 1892–1897. The evidence is ambiguous about the following movements: central Kentucky Regulators, Marion and other

counties, 1866–1871; northern Florida Regulators, Madison and other counties, 1868–1870; Los Angeles Vigilance Committee, 1852–1858; San Francisco Vigilance Committee, 1856; Socorro, New Mexico, Vigilantes, 1880–1884; and New Orleans vigilantes, 1891. Although the Los Angeles, San Francisco, Socorro, and New Orleans movements produced at least temporary stability, they did so by attacking Mexican, Irish, Mexican, and Italian ethnic groups, respectively, and, in the long run, they may have exacerbated rather than reduced tensions.

92. For example, the Turk family (Slickers) vs. the Jones family (anti-Slickers) in southwest Missouri. Lay, *History of Benton County*, pp. 46–61.

93. For example, in the southwest Missouri Slicker conflict the Slickers were mostly Whigs, and the anti-Slickers were mostly Democrats. Pancoast, *Quaker Forty-Niner*, p. 104. In the southern Illinois Regulator-Flathead struggle, the factor of local political rivalry was important. Parker B. Pillow, Elijah Smith, and Charles A. Shelby, Regulators and political "outs," were in conflict with a Flathead "in" faction led by Sheriff John W. Read. Report of Governor Augustus C. French, Jan. 11, 1847, and *Sangamo Journal*, Jan. 28, 1847—both in Rose, Papers Relating to Regulator and Flathead Trouble. See, also, Brumbaugh, "Regulator Movement," pp. 66, 69. Political factionalism also contributed to the Regulator-Moderator strife in Shelby County of east Texas where a political "in" faction of old pre-Texas Revolution settlers (Moderators) was opposed by a political "out" faction of post-revolutionary newcomers (Regulators). Neill, "Shelby County," pp. 75–77.

94. For example, in later years San Francisco's 1856 vigilance committee leader, William T. Coleman, criticized Charles Doane (the grand marshal of the vigilantes) for running for sheriff on the People's party ticket. Coleman felt that vigilante leaders, such as Doane, should not run for office. William T. Coleman, Vigilance Committee, 1856 (MS, ca. 1880, in Bancroft Library, University of California, Berkeley), p. 139.

95. In New Mexico's Lincoln County War of 1878–1879, the McSween-Tunstall-Brewer mercantile faction organized (unsuccessfully) as Regulators against the dominant Murphy-Dolan mercantile faction. William A. Keleher, *Violence in Lincoln County: 1869–1881* (Albuquerque, 1957), pp. 152–54. Maurice G. Fulton, *History of the Lincoln County War*, ed. Robert N. Mullin (Tucson, 1968), pp. 137–42ff.

96. In addition to the east Texas Regulators (see below), other movements that fell into sadism and extremism were, most notably, the southern Illinois Regulators and the southwest Missouri Slickers. There were other movements of this stripe; even in well-controlled movements, the elements of sadism and extremism often crept in in a minor way. The problem was inherent in vigilantism.

97. The east Texas Regulators are discussed later. For the southern Illinois Regulators see *passim* and note 16, this chapter, and for the southwest Missouri slickers see passim and note 17, this chapter.

98. See San Francisco *Daily Town Talk*, Aug. 8–9, 1856. Political factionalism was a factor in the 1856 San Francisco vigilante troubles. By and large, the vigilante leaders were composed of old Whigs and Know-Nothings who were in the process of becoming Republicans. The political "ins" who controlled San Francisco and whom the vigilantes attacked were the Irish-Catholic Democrats led by David C. Broderick. The "Law and Order" antivigilante faction tended to draw its strength from the southern-oriented wing of the California Democratic party. Unlike most San Francisco vigilante leaders, William T. Coleman was a Democrat, but as a Kentuckian he maintained a life-

long devotion to the principles of Henry Clay and, hence, had much in common with the many vigilante leaders who were also oriented to Henry Clay nationalism as Whigs, Know-Nothings, or Republicans. See Chap. 5, this book.

99. Brown, *South Carolina Regulators*, Chap. 6. Down to about the 1850's opponents of regulators and vigilantes were often called "moderators."

100. For a nineteenth-century paradigm of vigilante movements gone bad, see "Uses and Abuses of Lynch Law," pp. 462–63.

101. Sonnichsen, *Ten Texas Feuds*, Chap. 1; Neill, "Shelby County," pp. 77–153 and *passim*.

102. Robert B. David, *Malcolm Campbell, Sheriff* (Casper, Wyo., 1932), pp. 18–21.

103. See Chap. 5.

104. For a treatment of collusion between vigilantes and public officials see Chap. 6, this book, where examples from Illinois, Louisiana, Missouri, Nebraska, Tennessee, and Texas are given.

105. On the anti-horse thief movement in the Northeast and in New Jersey, see Nicolosi, "New Jersey Vigilante Societies," pp. 29–53.

106. On the National Horse Thief Detective Association of Indiana and neighboring states, see J. D. Thomas, "History and Origin of the National Horse Thief Detective Association" in *Journal of the National Horse Thief Detective Association*, 50th annual session (Union City, Ind., 1910), pp. 19–20, and Ted Gronert, *Sugar Creek Saga . . .* (Crawfordsville, Ind., 1958), pp. 140, 256–57.

107. On the Anti-Horse Thief Association of the trans-Mississippi Midwest and Southwest, see Hugh C. Gresham, *The Story of Major David McKee, Founder of the Anti-Horse Thief Association* (Cheney, Kan., 1937), and, especially, the Association's newspaper, the *A. H. T. A. Weekly News* (with variant titles) for 1902–1943, on file in the Kansas State Historical Society, Topeka. A recent study is that of Patrick B. Nolan, "Vigilantes on the Middle Border: A Study of Self-Appointed Law Enforcement in the States of the Upper Mississippi from 1840 to 1880" (Ph.D. dissertation, University of Minnesota, 1971). The A. H. T. A.'s membership was largest in Kansas with the Indian Territory (now eastern Oklahoma) also heavily represented. There were also substantial memberships in Oklahoma Territory, Missouri, and Arkansas. A number of other states had smaller enrollments. Late in the history of the organization, long after it had passed its peak, Illinois had a large membership.

108. For an extended discussion of the vigilante participation (or support of vigilantism) by these men, see Chap. 6.

109. Chap. 6.

110. *The Vigilantes* (New York, 1918), pp. 5, 8–14. This pamphlet was probably written and compiled by the Vigilantes' managing editor, Charles J. Rosebault. The Vigilantes were aided by leading American capitalists who served as "underwriters" or associate members; among them were George F. Baker, Jr., Cleveland H. Dodge, Coleman Dupont, Jacob H. Schiff, Vincent Astor, Elbert H. Gary, Simon Guggenheim, Dwight Morrow, and George W. Perkins.

111. The following interpretation of the San Francisco vigilante movement of 1856 is based on Chap. 5.

112. On the first Ku Klux Klan: Allen W. Trelease, *White Terror: The Ku Klux Klan Conspiracy and Southern Reconstruction* (New York, 1971). On the second Klan: David M. Chalmers, *Hooded Americanism* (Garden City, N. Y., 1965); Charles C. Alexander, *The Ku Klux Klan in the Southwest* (Lexington, 1965) and *Crusade for Conformity: The Ku Klux Klan in Texas, 1920–1930* (Houston,

1962); Kenneth T. Jackson, *The Ku Klux Klan in the City: 1915–1930* (New York, 1967).

113. See, especially, Chalmers, *Hooded Americanism*, and Alexander, *Ku Klux Klan*, and *Crusade for Conformity*.

114. The White Cap movement is discussed in Chap. 1.

115. In one sense the mass lynching was a classic vigilante response to a crime problem (the Italians had apparently been members of the Mafia and involved in the killing of the New Orleans chief of police), but the element of strong anti-Italian ethnic prejudice was crucial to the episode and typical of neovigilantism. See Chap. 6 and, also, Joseph L. Albini, *The American Mafia: Genesis of a Legend* (New York, 1971).

116. For example, in 1917 in Tulsa, Oklahoma, vigilantes attacked 17 I. W. W. members who were attempting to organize oil field workers. *The "Knights of Liberty" Mob and the I. W. W. Prisoners at Tulsa, Okla. (November 9, 1917* (New York, 1918). In this incident the police apparently connived with the vigilantes.

117. See William Preston, *Aliens and Dissenters* (Cambridge, Mass., 1963), which contains examples of neovigilante attacks on workers, immigrants, and radicals. See, also, John W. Caughey, ed., *Their Majesties the Mob* (Chicago, 1960), pp. 1–25, 100–205.

118. Brown, "American Vigilante Tradition," pp. 201–8; Harold A. Nelson, "The Defenders: A Case Study of an Informal Police Organization," *Social Problems*, 15 (1967–1968): 127–47; Gary T. Marx and Dane Archer, "Citizen Involvement in the Law Enforcement Process: The Case of Community Police Patrols," *American Behavioral Scientist*, 15 (1971–1972): 52–72. Contemporary vigilantism world wide is treated by H. Jon Rosenbaum and Peter C. Sederberg in "Vigilantism: An Analysis of Establishment Violence," *Comparative Politics*, 6 (1973–1974): 541–70, and in a forthcoming interdisciplinary collection edited by H. Jon Rosenbaum and Peter C. Sederberg, *Vigilante Politics: Pro-Establishment Violence in the Contemporary World*, to which I have contributed "The History of Vigilantism in America," a synthesis of the themes elaborated in Chaps. 4–6 of this book. I have also plumbed, much more briefly, contemporary American violence and vigilantism in historical context in "The History of Extralegal Violence in Support of Community Values" (a publication of my testimony before the National Commission on the Causes and Prevention of Violence in 1968), pp. 86–95, in Thomas Rose, ed., *Violence in America: A Historical and Contemporary Reader* (New York, 1970), and "An Escape from Paranoia," *American West*, Jan., 1970, p. 48.

119. Editorial in the New York *National Democrat* quoted in Bancroft, *Popular Tribunals*, vol. II, pp. 554–55; *Illinois State Register* (Springfield), Jan. 1, 1847 (transcript in Rose, Papers Relating to Regulator and Flathead Trouble).

120. William Anderson Scott, *A Discourse for the Times Delivered in Calvary Church, July 27, 1856* (San Francisco, 1856). On Scott: Clifford M. Drury, *William Anderson Scott: "No Ordinary Man"* (Glendale, Calif., 1967).

121. John G. Nicolay and John Hay, eds., *Complete Works of Abraham Lincoln* (New York, 1905), vol. I, pp. 35–50. In his address Lincoln dwelled on the ubiquity of "mob law" in the 1830's and specifically cited the Mississippi vigilante actions in 1835 in Madison and Hinds counties and Vicksburg as well as a case of lynch law in St. Louis.

122. James Truslow Adams, "Our Lawless Heritage," *Atlantic Monthly*, 42 (1928): 736. In recent years a prime example of arbitrary disregard of the law has been

the idealistic tactic of civil disobedience. See Abe Fortas, *Concerning Dissent and Civil Disobedience* (New York, 1968), Chaps. 4–5.

Chapter 5

1. See Chap. 4.
2. *Ibid.*
3. *Ibid.* For some examples of the new vigilantism, see, also, John W. Caughey, ed., *Their Majesties the Mob* (Chicago, 1960), pp. 1–25, 100–205.
4. See Hubert Howe Bancroft, *Popular Tribunals* (San Francisco, 1887), vol. II, pp. 548–59, where many eastern and European editorials appear, most of which (including such journals as the *Tribune, Herald,* and *Times* of New York and the Boston *Journal*) favored the vigilance committee. This second volume of Bancroft's massive two-volume *Popular Tribunals* is devoted entirely to the vigilance committee of 1856. Its 748-page text amounts to practically a primary source on the movement because of Bancroft's friendship with, and access to, many old vigilante leaders, including the greatest of them all, William T. Coleman. Despite Bancroft's strong and open bias in favor of the vigilantes, the book remains not only the largest but the best published treatment of the 1856 vigilance committee. A useful newly published collection of three important primary sources with an able bibliographic survey by the editor is edited by Doyce B. Nunis, *The San Francisco Vigilance Committee of 1856: Three Views* [by] *William T. Coleman, William T. Sherman* [and] *James O'Meara* (Los Angeles, 1971). The most recent studies of San Francisco vigilantism in the 1850's are Roger W. Lotchin, *San Francisco, 1846–1856: From Hamlet to City* (New York, 1974), Chaps. 8–9 and *passim,* and Robert Michael Senkewicz, "Business and Politics in Gold Rush San Francisco, 1851–1856" (Ph.D. dissertation, Stanford University, 1974).
5. Perhaps the most notable of the vigilante movements outside California following the San Francisco model were those of Bannack and Virginia City, Montana, 1863–1864. See Chap. 4, this book.
6. In San Francisco in the 1850's the contrast between the old and the new vigilantism is graphically revealed. The San Francisco vigilance committee of 1851 arose mainly in response to an orthodox crime problem stemming from Australian ex-convicts and other ne'er-do-wells. The vigilante movement of 1856 was in its objectives much more typical of the new vigilantism. On the 1851 affair: Chap. 4, note 23, this book.
7. Harris, Bogardus, and Labatt (comps.), *San Francisco City Directory for the year commencing October, 1856 . . .* (San Francisco, 1856), pp. 129–32.
8. *The Daily Town Talk* (San Francisco), Sept. 13, 1856. The four French newspapers were *Bibliotheque Populaire, Echo du Pacifique, Le Phare,* and *De La Chapelle.* Harris, *Directory,* 127; *Town Talk,* May 22, 1856. The *Town Talk* was founded in the spring of 1856 shortly before the vigilante movement got underway. Contrary to the implication of its title, the *Town Talk* was not a scandal or gossip sheet. Instead, it was a regular four-page daily, similar to the other leading dailies of San Francisco of the era. The *Town Talk* gave excellent coverage to the vigilante movement. Its editorial policy, like that of all the dailies of the city except the *Herald,* favored the vigilance committee.
9. The vigilance committee itself gave lip-service to the ideal of brotherhood. Thus its motto was: "No creed. No party. No sectional issues." Bancroft was

technically correct when he said that the vigilance committee was "composed of all classes and conditions of men" with every nationality, political and religious sentiment, trade, occupation, and profession represented. *Popular Tribunals*, Vol. II, pp. 84–85, 110. This was true, not surprisingly, in a movement of from 6,000 to 8,000 members; but the important point is that the movement was strongly dominated by merchants and old-stock Americans of Northern origin and of Whig, Know Nothing, or Republican politics with relatively few Irish or Catholics among the membership.

10. John Myers Myers, *San Francisco's Reign of Terror* (New York, 1966), pp. 25–36, 68–69.

11. Bancroft, *Popular Tribunals*, vol. II, pp. 1–21. Note, however, that two recent authorities, Roger W. Lotchin and Robert Michael Senkewicz (see note 4, above), hold that vigilante charges of election malpractices were exaggerated. A sympathetic biography of Broderick is David A. Williams, *David C. Broderick: A Political Portrait* (San Marino, Calif., 1969). Despite the crudity of his ward tactics, Broderick seems to have had a good deal of social consciousness in regard to his Irish-Catholic and lower-class adherents in San Francisco.

12. Myers, *San Francisco's Reign of Terror*, 80. J. P. Young, *San Francisco: A History of the Pacific Metropolis* (San Francisco, [1913]), vol. I, p. 216.

13. See the exposé in the form of a front-page, three-column report from the executive committee of the vigilantes: "Official Corruption," San Francisco *Daily Evening Bulletin*, July 14, 1856. This is one of the key documents in the vigilante episode. See also Young, *San Francisco*, vol. I, p. 216.

14. The Huntington Library has a complete file of the *Bulletin* for the years 1855–1856, which I used. The *Bulletin*, especially the editorials of King, are crucial for an understanding of the fears and anxieties that gave rise to the vigilance committee of 1856. Had his newspaper career not been cut short before it had fairly gotten started, I am confident that King would have become one of the famous journalists in American history. King had been a failure in business but had found his metier in journalism. He was a remarkably trenchant, even demagogic, editor, and he took San Francisco by storm in the months before his death. Although it is a favorable treatment, *Villains and Vigilantes: The Story of James King of William and Pioneer Justice in California* (New York, 1961) by Stanton A. Coblentz does not adequately explain the martyred editor. Originally from the District of Columbia, King early acquired the distinctive name, James King of William (after his father, William King), to distinguish him from other James Kings.

15. For examples, see especially these issues of the *Bulletin*: Oct. 13, 16, and Dec. 27, 1855; Jan. 4, 8, 22, Feb. 2, and Apr. 1, 3, 1856.

16. *Bulletin*, Nov. 19, 1855.

17. See, for example, the *Bulletin*, Nov. 20, 22, 24, and Dec. 12, 1855.

18. *Bulletin*, Jan. 8, 17, 1856.

19. On Casey's background, see the *Bulletin*, Nov. 5, 1855.

20. Bancroft, *Popular Tribunals*, vol. II, pp. 69ff.; *Bulletin* and *Town Talk*, May 15, 1856. Cora remained in jail, awaiting the possibility of a new trial, until the vigilantes took him out and hanged him. On July 29, 1856, two relatively obscure murderers, Philander Brace and Joseph Hetherington, were hanged after vigilante trials. *Town Talk*, July 30, 1856.

21. In the *Century Magazine* of November, 1891, Coleman put the membership at about 8,000 (p. 145). The 1856 sources on the vigilance committee estimated its military force as being about 6,000. The file of applications for membership documents the frequent contemporary assertion that each vigilante was assigned

a number. The highest number that I have seen in the Committee of Vigilance Papers in the Huntington Library is 5,757.

22. Bancroft, *Popular Tribunals*, vol. II, pp. 80–81, 117–18, 121, 125–26, 418. Letter from "Cosmos" in *Bulletin*, June 6, 1856. All contemporary sources attest mercantile domination.

23. Bancroft, *Popular Tribunals*, vol. II, pp. 86–87 and *passim*. See, also, James A. B. Scherer, *"The Lion of the Vigilantes": William T. Coleman and the Life of Old San Francisco* (Indianapolis, 1939).

24. Box labeled "Applications for Membership, 1856," Committee of Vigilance Papers, Huntington Library.

25. These generalizations are made upon the basis of my analysis of each one of the approximately 2,500 applications. Internal evidence indicates that virtually all of the applications were accepted. Only one was marked as rejected. It is likely that most of the rejected applications were not retained in this file. Thus the approximately 2,500 applications represent the same number of members or from about 30% to 40% of the entire membership, depending upon whether 6,000 or 8,000 is accepted as the figure for the total membership. For statistical purposes, the 2,500 applications represent a more than adequate sample of the vigilante membership.

26. For the anxieties this could cause, see the article, "Steamer Day," in *Town Talk*, Oct. 5, 1856. Steamers left San Francisco every two weeks for the East with remittances for Eastern creditors. The attempt of San Francisco businessmen to raise money for the Steamer Day sailings had economic reverberations throughout the entire city.

27. Following the executions of Casey and Cora, the effects of further vigilante actions were anticipated in *Town Talk*, May 28, 1856: "The 'reign of terror' is working our redemption, and California stocks will rise in the market when this news reaches the Atlantic."

28. Extensive testimony and evidence are in "Papers relating to Ballot Box Stuffing and Fraudulent Elections, 1854–1856," a box of 112 pieces in Committee of Vigilance Papers. An account of dishonest election practices in nineteenth-century San Francisco is Richard Reinhardt's "Tape Worms and Shoulder Strikers," *American West*, Nov., 1966, pp. 34–41, 85–88.

29. [James O'Meara], *The Vigilance Committee of 1856* (San Francisco, 1887), pp. 46, 56.

30. *Town Talk*, Oct. 5, 1856; Bancroft, *Popular Tribunals*, vol. II, pp. 590–609. Anti-Irish feeling was very strong in nineteenth-century America. See, for example, Adrian Cook, *The Armies of the Streets: The New York City Draft Riots of 1863* (Lexington, 1974), pp. 22, 66, 129, 189, 197–98, and *passim*.

31. The colorful story of Ned McGowan is told by Myers in *San Francisco's Reign of Terror*. Despite the deceptive title, this book is really a biography of McGowan with a heavy emphasis on the vigilante period.

32. A prominent "shoulder striker" and election manipulator, Yankee Sullivan, would have undoubtedly been banished had he not died, allegedly by suicide, while in vigilante custody. *Town Talk*, May 31, 1856. Bancroft, *Popular Tribunals*, vol. II, p. 649, states that it was "roughly estimated" that eight hundred of the "worst characters" voluntarily left San Francisco because of the vigilante action. Included were "thieves, murderers, corrupters of public morals, gamblers, prize-fighters, ballot-box stuffers, loafers, and vagabonds."

33. *Town Talk*, Aug. 9, 12, 1856.

34. *Bulletin*, Aug. 18, 19, 1856.

35. *Town Talk*, Aug. 9, 12, 1856.

36. *Daily Alta California* (San Francisco), Aug. 9, 1856; *Town Talk*, Aug. 12, Sept. 16, 1856.
37. *Town Talk*, Sept. 16, Nov. 4, 1856.
38. *Bulletin*, Oct. 9, 11, 1856.
39. *Ibid.*, Nov. 25, 1856.
40. Young, *San Francisco*, vol. I, p. 216.
41. *Ibid.*, vol. I, p. 104.
42. *Century Magazine*, 43 (Nov., 1891): 145. See, also, W[illiam] T. Coleman, Vigilance Committee, 1856 (manuscript, Bancroft Library, University of California at Berkeley), from which the epigraph to this chapter is taken. Also to be found in the Bancroft Library manuscript collection are statements by the following leading vigilantes of 1856: C. J. Dempster, John L. Durkee, James D. Farwell, and Thomas J. Smiley.
43. Despite King's fulminations in the editorial columns, my survey of the police news columns in the *Bulletin* and *Town Talk* during the fall, winter, and spring of 1855–1856 has convinced me that the San Francisco crime problem was under control. King was outraged at the hung jury in the murder trial of Charles Cora, but the circumstances surrounding Cora's killing of Richardson leave the real possibility that it could have been in self-defense. That Cora went free does not seem to be a reflection on San Francisco justice. At another level, King's crusade against wide-open houses of prostitution in San Francisco showed a commendable regard on his part for the general conditions of morality in the city, but the news of arrests and convictions indicate that any overt crime stemming from the latitude of life in a wide-open city was kept well under control. Vigilante leaders had sufficient confidence in the regular system that in the summer of 1856, while the vigilance committee had an iron grip on the city, they allowed the police officers and courts to enforce law in a regular way. The vigilance committee restricted itself to four hangings, investigation of the Broderick machine, and banishment of its leading operatives. For some examples of regular law enforcement in San Francisco during the height of the vigilante period, see *Town Talk*, May 28, 29, 30, 31, 1856. See also Joseph L. King, "The Vigilance Committee of '56," *Overland Monthly*, 68 (July-Dec., 1918): 519.
44. *Town Talk*, June 10, 15, 1856. The vigilantes made much of their discovery of a ballot box with a false bottom that had been used for stuffing purposes by Yankee Sullivan in the interest of Ned McGowan, Charles Duane, and other Broderick stalwarts. See Bancroft, *Popular Tribunals*, vol. II, pp. 6–8 where the false ballot box is described and sketched.
45. *Town Talk*, June 4, 5, 1856.
46. Bancroft, *Popular Tribunals*, vol. II, pp. 87–111. The names of vigilante officers were printed in the newspapers. A convenient listing of the officers, down to the level of the captains who commanded the companies, is in Samuel Colville's *Colville's 1856–1857 San Francisco Directory: Volume I: for the year commencing October, 1856* . . . (San Francisco, 1856), pp. 226–27.
47. Bancroft, *Popular Tribunals*, vol. II, p. 113.
48. *Colville's Directory for 1856*, pp. 226–27.
49. Bancroft, *Popular Tribunals*, vol. II, pp. 109–13; *Town Talk*, Aug. 8, 1856.
50. Seymour J. Mandelbaum in *Boss Tweed's New York* (New York, [1965]), pp. 46–47, has pointed out that this was a major problem in New York City after the Civil War. The similarities between the problems of San Francisco in the 1850's and New York after the Civil War are striking. The Tammany machine in New York, like the Broderick machine in San Francisco, produced

similar reactions although in New York incipient vigilante movements never got to the point of taking the law into their own hands.

51. This problem has been of major concern in important studies by Oscar Handlin, John Higham, Barbara Miller Solomon, Stephan Thernstrom, Moses Rischin, David Brody, Gunther Barth, and others.

Chapter 6

1. See Chap. 4.
2. Herbert L. Packer, "Two Models of the Criminal Process," *University of Pennsylvania Law Review*, 113 (1964): 1–68, reprinted in revised form in Herbert L. Packer, *The Limits of Criminal Sanction* (Stanford, 1968), pp. 149–173.
3. Packer, *Limits of Criminal Sanction*, p. 158.
4. Charles C. Butler, "Lynching," *American Law Review*, 44 (1910): 208–9. Butler was a leading Colorado lawyer and judge who finished his career on the Colorado Supreme Court, 1927–1937. *Who Was Who in America* [1897–1968] (Chicago, 1943–1968), vol. II, p. 94.
5. Granville Stuart, *Forty Years on the Frontier*, ed. Paul C. Phillips (Cleveland, 1925), vol. II, pp. 195–210; Michael A. Leeson, *History of Montana: 1739–1885* (Chicago, 1885), pp. 315–16.
6. See Chap. 8.
7. Chap. 4.
8. *Ibid.*, note 35.
9. *Ibid.*, note 36.
10. *Omaha Weekly Bee*, Feb. 1, 1882, p. 6.
11. See Chap. 4.
12. Lucile Morris, *Bald Knobbers* (Caldwell, Idaho, 1939).
13. *Ohio State Journal* (Columbus), Nov. 12, 1888, p. 1.
14. See following discussion, this chapter.
15. Ethelred W. Crozier, *The White-Caps: A History of the Organization in Sevier County* (Knoxville, 1899). This particular White Cap group behaved like a classic, large-scale vigilante movement.
16. Helena H. Smith, *The War on Powder River* (New York, 1966).
17. For sources on the White Caps see notes 87–94, Chap. 1, above.
18. For an example of economic white capping: William F. Holmes, "Whitecapping: Agrarian Violence in Mississippi," *Journal of Southern History*, 35 (1969): 165–85.
19. James E. Cutler, *Lynch-Law: An Investigation into the History of Lynching in the United States* (New York, 1905), Chap. 6 and *passim.*
20. On the nature of Southern Negro lynchings: Walter White, *Rope & Faggot* (New York, 1929) and Arthur F. Raper, *The Tragedy of Lynching* (Chapel Hill, 1938). An example appears in the *New York Times*, Dec. 7, 1899, p. 1, reprinted in Brown, *American Violence*, pp. 107–109. See, also, Chap. 7, this book.
21. Roscoe Pound, *Criminal Justice in America* (New York, 1930), p. 64. Although not published until 1930, Pound's *Criminal Justice in America* was an outgrowth of his classic critique of 24 years earlier, "The Causes of Popular Dissatisfaction with the Administration of Justice," *Reports of American Bar Association*, 29 (1906), part 1, pp. 395–417. *Criminal Justice in America* applies specifically to criminal law many of the themes developed in the earlier work. On Nebraska vigilantism, see Chap. 4, this book.

22. O. F. Hershey, "Lynch Law," *Green Bag*, 12 (1900): 466–69. O[mer] F. Hershey was a Harvard graduate (1891) with an LL.B. from the University of Maryland (1892). He became a leading Baltimore lawyer, president of the Baltimore Bar Association, a member of various state legislative and judicial commissions, and a writer on state and legal problems. *Who Was Who in America*, vol. IV, p. 433.
23. "John G. Jury," "Lynch Law in California," *Green Bag*, 14 (1902): 291–94.
24. M. H. Mott, *History of the Regulators of Northern Indiana* (Indianapolis, 1859), pp. 15–18. The La Grange and Noble Regulators, numbering about 2,000 members, executed one person and expelled many others. See Mott, *ibid.*, and Chap. 4, this book.
25. John S. Kendall, "Who Killa De Chief?," *Louisiana Historical Quarterly*, 22 (1939): 520. The New Orleans vigilante movement of 1891 is discussed later in this chapter. Walter D. Denègre (1858–1934) was a Harvard graduate (1879) and a Tulane law student before being admitted to the bar in 1881. He became a leading New Orleans attorney with a heavy practice in corporation law. He was a leader of the reform faction of the Democratic Party in New Orleans politics in the 1880's and 1890's, and barely missed election to the U.S. Senate in 1896. He was an active club man in New Orleans (where he was king of the Mardi Gras), New York City (Harvard and University clubs), and Massachusetts (Myopia Hunt and Essex County clubs). Far from being ashamed of his role in the lynching of the 11 Italians, he seemed to view it as of a piece with his political reform activities in New Orleans, and indirectly but proudly referred to it in his *Who's Who* sketch with the item: "Helped suppress the 'Mafia' and 'black hand' in New Orleans, in 1889 [*sic*]." *The National Cyclopaedia of American Biography* (New York, 1892–1969), vol. X, p. 354. *Who Was Who in America*, vol. I, p. 314. On the perfection of the American concept of the "sovereignty of the people" in the Revolutionary period see Gordon S. Wood, *The Creation of the American Republic, 1776–1787* (Chapel Hill, 1969), pp. 319–21, 371, 383, 599, 600, and *passim*. See, also, Chap. 2, this book.
26. James Willard Hurst, *The Growth of American Law: The Law Makers* (Boston, 1950), pp. 39, 92–93.
27. See Chap. 4, this book, which emphasizes the community character of vigilantism.
28. James Willard Hurst, *Law and Social Process in United States History* (Ann Arbor, 1960), p. 287.
29. The quotations in this sentence are from Hurst, *Growth of American Law*, p. 4.
30. Pound, "Causes of Popular Dissatisfaction," p. 397.
31. Henry M. Hart, Jr., "The Aims of the Criminal Law," *Law and Contemporary Problems*, 23 (1958): 404–5.
32. Quoted in *ibid.*, citing Gardner in *Boston University Law Review*, 33 (1953): 176, 193.
33. Hart, "Aims of Criminal Law," pp. 404–5.
34. Thomas J. Dimsdale, *The Vigilantes of Montana* . . . (Virginia City, Mont., 1866), p. 116.
35. Robert M. Coates, *The Outlaw Years* . . . (New York, 1930), pp. 59–67.
36. Fred M. Mazzulla, "Undue Process of Law—Here and There," *Brandbook of the Denver Westerners*, 20 (1964): 273–79. See, also, Chap. 4, above.
37. *American Law Review*, 26 (1892): 248–49.
38. J[oseph] S. Tunison, *The Cincinnati Riot: Its Causes and Results* (Cincinnati, 1886), pp. 27–28. In 1886 Tunison was on the staff of the New York *Tribune*, but from 1874 to 1883 he had worked on Cincinnati newspapers. He later resumed his career in Ohio journalism. *Who Was Who in America*, vol. IV, p. 956.

39. Mott, *Regulators of Northern Indiana*, p. 17.
40. *Denver Tribune*, Dec. 30, 1879, quoted in John W. Cook, *Hands Up* . . . (Denver, 1897), p. 103.
41. Miguel A. Otero, *My Life on the Frontier* (New York and Albuquerque, 1935–1939), vol. II, pp. 2–3.
42. *Meeker Herald*, Sept. 3, 1887. These examples are also cited in Chap. 4, this book.
43. James Stuart, *Three Years in North America* (Edinburgh, 1833), vol. II, pp. 212–13; Jack K. Williams, "Crime and Punishment in Alabama, 1819–1840," *Alabama Review*, 6 (1953): 26; Hurst, *Growth of American Law*, pp. 92–93; James Bryce, *The American Commonwealth* (London, 1891), vol. II, p. 453, which is quoted as an epigraph to this chapter. See also Chap. 4, this book.
44. Pound, "Causes of Popular Dissatisfaction," pp. 395–417.
45. *Ibid.*, p. 408. See, also, Bryce, *American Commonwealth*, vol. II, pp. 452–53 (quoted in the epigraph), which stresses procedural defects.
46. Henry Bischoff, "The Law's Delay No Excuse for Lynching," *Albany Law Journal*, 65 (1903–1904): 337–41. An 1871 graduate of Columbia Law School, Bischoff was judge of the New York Court of Common Pleas from 1890 to 1895. From 1896 to 1917 he was justice of the New York State Supreme Court. *Who Was Who in America*, vol. I, p. 97. David J. Brewer, "The Right of Appeal," *The Independent*, Oct. 29, 1903, pp. 2547–50, wrote in condemnation of the law's delay; see following discussion, this chapter.
47. Henry A. Forster, "Why the United States Leads the World in the Relative Proportion of Murders, Lynchings and Other Felonies, and Why the Anglo-Saxon Countries Not Under the American Flag Have the Least Proportion of Murders and Felonies and Know No Lynchings," *Central Law Journal*, 85 (1917): 299–304.
48. Charles J. Bonaparte, "Lynch Law and Its Remedy," *Yale Law Journal*, 8 (1898–1899): 335–43. In effect, Bonaparte would have adapted vigilantism to the legal system, and Brewer would have eliminated the right of appeal. See following discussion, this chapter.
49. Pound, "Causes of Popular Dissatisfaction," pp. 402–6.
50. *Ibid.* Walter Clark, "The True Remedy for Lynch Law," *American Law Review*, 28 (1894): 801–7; on Clark see below. Bonaparte, "Lynch Law," p. 342.
51. Pound, "Causes of Popular Dissatisfaction," pp. 408–10.
52. Bonaparte, "Lynch Law," p. 342.
53. Clark, "True Remedy for Lynch Law"; Bonaparte, "Lynch Law," p. 342; F. L. Oswald, "Lynch Epidemics," *North American Review*, 165 (1897): 119–21; various references to Darwinian concepts in this article point to the conclusion that the author was the writer and naturalist, Felix L. Oswald (1845–1906) of Grand Rapids, Michigan. *Who Was Who in America*, vol. I, p. 923.
54. Oswald, "Lynch Epidemics"; Bonaparte, "Lynch Law," p. 342.
55. Alice L. Brumbaugh, "The Regulator Movement in Illinois" (M.A. thesis, University of Illinois, 1927), pp. 10–11.
56. "Uses and Abuses of Lynch Law," *American Whig Review*, May, 1850, p. 461.
57. Quoted in James C. Smiley's *History of Denver* (Denver, 1901), p. 349. See, also, Chap. 4, this book.
58. United States v. Shipp, 29 S. Ct. 636 (1908). Justices Rufus W. Peckham, Edward D. White, and Joseph McKenna dissented from the decision in their finding that Shipp had not participated in the conspiracy against the law. It may be noted that White (Louisiana) and McKenna (California) came from states with strong vigilante and lynch law traditions. (See Chap. 4, this book.) There is

no evidence that Edward D. White took part in the 1891 lynching of the 11 Italians in New Orleans, but he was a leading resident of the city at the time, and the New Orleans "establishment" of which he was a member supported the lynching with some of its members—for example, W. S. Parkerson and Walter D. Denègre (see preceding discussion)—taking part in it. Governor Francis T. Nicholls of Louisiana, who was in New Orleans at the time of the lynching, and who made no effort to prevent it, had been the "political mentor" of White in the latter's younger days and was still close to him in 1891. Late in 1891 White was appointed to the U.S. Senate and in 1894 to the Supreme Court which he served as chief justice from 1911 to 1921. Although he was an Irish Catholic, Joseph McKenna became a leading California Republican after the Civil War; he was a political protégé of the powerful Leland Stanford who had been a member of the San Francisco vigilance committee of 1856. James F. Watts, Jr., "Edward Douglas White," pp. 1636–37, and "Joseph McKenna," pp. 1721–25, in Leon Friedman and Fred L. Israel, eds., *The Justices of the United States Supreme Court, 1789–1969* (New York, 1969), vol. III. On Governor Nicholls and the 1891 lynching and Leland Stanford see following discussions.

59. A. T. Andreas, *History of the State of Nebraska* (Chicago, 1882), vol. II, pp. 1265–66.

60. *History of Vernon County, Missouri* (St. Louis, 1887), pp. 348–49.

61. *Report of the Adjutant-General of the State of Texas*, 1872, pp. 22, 121–23; Billy B. Lightfoot, "The History of Comanche County, Texas, to 1920" (M.A. thesis, University of Texas, 1949), Chap. 5; John Wesley Hardin, *The Life of John Wesley Hardin as Written by Himself* (Seguin, Tex., 1896).

62. Torrence B. Wilson, Jr., "A History of Wilbarger County, Texas" (M.A. thesis, University of Texas, 1938), p. 97.

63. Thomas Ford, *A History of Illinois from Its Commencement as a State in 1818 to 1847*, ed. Milo M. Quaife (Chicago, 1945–1946), vol. II, pp. 10–11.

64. Nicholls was an 1855 graduate of West Point and a Confederate brigadier general. After the Civil War he became a lawyer, served two terms as governor of Louisiana (1877–1880 and 1888–1892), and, in 1893–94—two years after the lynching which he had done nothing to prevent—was the chief justice of the Louisiana Supreme Court. *Who Was Who in America*, vol. I, p. 896.

65. In addition to W. S. Parkerson and Walter D. Denègre other leaders in the lynching of the 11 Italians were James D. Houston, "a prominent political leader," and John C. Wickliffe. The latter was "a West Pointer" and an editor of the New Orleans *New Delta. New York Times*, Mar. 15, 1891, p. 1.

66. *Ibid.* See, also, Kendall, "Who Killa De Chief?," pp. 492–530, and John E. Coxe "The New Orleans Mafia Incident," *Louisiana Historical Quarterly*, 20 (1937): 1067–1110, as well as Joseph L. Albini, *The American Mafia: Genesis of a Legend* (New York, 1971), pp. 159–67. Although New Orleans strongly approved the lynching, the event was condemned elsewhere in the nation, and the Italian government expressed its outrage.

67. Butler, "Lynching," pp. 217–19.

68. People *ex rel.* Davis v. Nellis, 94 N.E. 165 (Ill., 1911), for the decision of the Illinois Supreme Court, which related the facts of the case and upheld the removal of the sheriff. The county seat of Alexander County, Cairo, where the 1909 lynching took place has been the scene in recent years of racial violence. Collusion between officials and vigilantes has again been charged. J. Anthony Lukas, "Bad Day at Cairo, Ill.," *New York Times Magazine*, Feb. 21, 1971, pp. 22–23ff.

69. Butler, "Lynching," pp. 217–19.

70. Francis W. Coker, "Lynching," in Edwin R. A. Seligman, and Alvin Johnson, eds., *Encyclopaedia of the Social Sciences* (New York, 1930–1935), vol. IX, pp. 639–43. Cutler, *Lynch-Law*, pp. 231–45. See, also, James H. Chadbourn, *Lynching and the Law* (Chapel Hill, 1933).
71. The following account of notable American vigilantes expands that in Chap. 4, this book.
72. Eliphalet Price, "The Trial and Execution of Patrick O'Conner," *Palimpsest*, 1 (1920): 86–97.
73. Stuart, *Forty Years on the Frontier*, vol. II, pp. 195–210; Ray H. Mattison, "Roosevelt and the Stockmen's Association," *North Dakota History*, 17 (1950): 81–85; Leeson, *History of Montana*, pp. 315–16; and Chap. 4, this book, all deal with the Montana vigilante movement of 1884. For Roosevelt's lifelong admiration for vigilantism, see *The Letters of Theodore Roosevelt*, ed. Elting E. Morison *et al.* (Cambridge, Mass., 1951–1954), vol. VIII, p. 946; *The Works of Theodore Roosevelt*, ed. Hermann Hagedorn (New York, 1926), vol. I, pp. 383–84; *Presidential Addresses and State Papers of Theodore Roosevelt*, [1902–1905] (New York, n.d.), vol. II, pp. 523–28; and Carleton Putnam, *Theodore Roosevelt: The Formative Years, 1858–1886* (New York, 1958), pp. 460–61. Roosevelt's figure of "sixty odd" for the number of executions by the Montana vigilantes of 1884 is excessive.
74. Allen Johnson, Dumas Malone *et al.*, eds., *Dictionary of American Biography* (New York, 1928–1958), vol. IV, pp. 295–96. On the San Francisco vigilantes of 1856 see Chap. 5, this book.
75. *Dictionary of American Biography*, vol. XVII, pp. 501–6. For Stanford's vigilante membership see his application in Applications for Membership, San Francisco Committee of Vigilance Papers, 1856 (MS, Huntington Library, San Marino, Calif.).
76. *Dictionary of American Biography*, vol. IV, pp. 257–58; *The History of Johnson County, Missouri* (Kansas City, 1881), pp. 372–73.
77. *Dictionary of American Biography*, vol. XIII, p. 295; Alexander Barde, *History of the Committees of Vigilance in the Attakapas Country* [1861], trans. and ed. Henrietta G. Rogers (M.A. thesis, Louisiana State University, 1936), pp. 43, 347.
78. *Dictionary of American Biography*, vol. X, pp. 305–6. See Houston (Tex.) *Telegraph*, Oct. 3, 1872, for Kellogg's encouragement of the vigilantes.
79. *National Cyclopaedia of American Biography*, vol. XI, pp. 46–47; *The History of Edgar County, Illinois* (Chicago, 1879), pp. 332, 396–97, 590.
80. *Dictionary of American Biography*, vol. XVIII, pp. 168–69; Stuart, *Forty Years on the Frontier.*
81. *Dictionary of American Biography*, vol. XVI, pp. 336–37; [John Xavier Beidler], *X. Beidler: Vigilante*, ed. Helen Fitzgerald Sanders and William H. Bertsche (Norman, 1957), pp. 40–46.
82. *Who Was Who in America*, vol. I, p. 803; William J. McConnell (with the collaboration of Howard R. Driggs), *Frontier Law: A Story of Vigilante Days* (Yonkers, N. Y., 1924. On Borah: *Dictionary of American Biography*, vol. XXII, pp. 49–53.
83. Mazzulla, "Undue Process of Law," pp. 273–79.
84. *Ibid. Who Was Who in America*, vol. III, p. 152.
85. Otero, *My Life on the Frontier*, vol. I, pp. 181–206; *Who Was Who in America*, vol. II, pp. 407–8. Among his many distinctions the senior Otero was New Mexico's territorial delegate to Congress and had the honor of declining Lincoln's appointment as American minister to Spain.
86. George Curry, *George Curry, 1861–1947: An Autobiography*, ed. H. B. Henning

(Albuquerque, 1958), pp. 50–52 and *passim.*; *Who Was Who in America*, vol. II, p. 140.

87. Hubert Howe Bancroft, *Popular Tribunals* (San Francisco, 1887), vols. I–II; John W. Caughey, *Hubert Howe Bancroft* (Berkeley, 1946).

88. Thomas J. Dimsdale, *The Vigilantes of Montana . . .* (Virginia City, Mont., 1866; ed. and reprinted by A. J. Noyes, Helena, Mont., 1940?); pp. 5–8 of the Noyes edition has information on Dimsdale's background. Nathaniel Pitt Langford, *Vigilante Days and Ways* (Boston, 1890), vols. I–II. *Dictionary of American Biography*, vol. X, pp. 592–93, has a biographical sketch of Langford, who was a vigilante.

89. Owen Wister, *The Virginian* (New York, 1902), especially pp. 433–36. Fanny K. Wister, ed., *Owen Wister Out West* (Chicago, 1958); like his friend, Theodore Roosevelt, Wister had law training but did not practice. Among the many lesser nineteenth-century and early twentieth-century novelists who portrayed vigilantism favorably were James Weir, *Lonz Powers: or, the Regulators: A Romance of Kentucky* (Philadelphia, 1850), and Harris Dickson, *The House of Luck* (Boston, 1916). The enthusiastic reception of Walter Van Tilburg Clark's anti-vigilante *The Ox-Bow Incident* (New York, 1940)—the best novel ever written about American vigilantism (upon which a classic film was based)—marked an important shift in public attitudes, from favoring to condemning vigilantism.

90. Quoted in Emerson Hough, *The Story of the Outlaw* (New York, 1907), pp. 399ff. On White's life: *Dictionary of American Biography*, vol. XX, pp. 88–93.

91. *National Cyclopaedia of American Biography*, vol. IV, p. 147.

92. Locke was a New Englander and a Republican. The Civil War brought him to Florida where he remained after the war to become a lawyer, a county judge, and a member of the Florida State Senate (1870–1872). From 1872 to 1912 he was federal judge for the southern district of Florida. *Who Was Who in America*, vol. I, p. 739. Although as a Democrat Wall may have had no love lost for the Republican "carpetbagger" Locke, politics do not seem to have been a factor in this affair. Although the lynching of John was supported by almost the whole community of Tampa, it was opposed by the sheriff and the mayor both of whom, presumably, were Democrats.

93. This account of the lynching and Wall's role in it is from *Ex Parte* Wall, 107 U.S. 265 (1882); and *In re* Wall, 13 F. 814 (Cir. S.D. 1882). The record does not disclose the last name of the victim, John. He was accused of attempted rape.

94. *National Cyclopaedia of American Biography*, vol. IV, p. 147.

95. The myth that the rape of white women by Negroes was the overwhelming cause of late nineteenth-century Southern lynching was convincingly refuted by James E. Cutler in 1905. Cutler found that for 1882–1903 only 34% of the Negroes lynched in the South met their fate for rape; 38% were lynched for murder, and the remaining 28% were lynched for other reasons. Cutler, *Lynch-Law*, p. 176.

96. Henry T. Lewis was an associate justice of the Georgia Supreme Court from 1897 to 1903; before that he had practiced law in Greensboro, Georgia. He was a member of the Democratic national conventions of 1884 and 1896 and placed William Jennings Bryan in nomination in the 1896 meeting. *Who Was Who in America*, vol. I, pp. 726. Burton Smith was one of Georgia's distinguished lawyers. A graduate of the University of Georgia in 1882, he practiced law in Atlanta, was vice-president of the American Bar Association in 1900, and was president of the Georgia Bar Association, 1902–1903. *Who Was Who in America*, vol. II, pp. 493. Lewis Thomas was from Atlanta, and G. P. Munro was from Buena Vista, Georgia.

97. "Is Lynch Law Due to Defects in the Criminal Law, or Its Administration?,"
    Georgia Bar Association, *Report*, 1897, pp. 164–97.

98. Born in 1846, Clark was a graduate of the University of North Carolina and
    Columbia Law School. He became a leading North Carolina lawyer and
    newspaper editor and from 1885 to 1889 was a state Superior Court judge. He
    served for 35 years (1889–1924) on the Supreme Court of North Carolina, and
    from 1902 to his death in 1924 he was its chief justice. One of the leading
    progressive Democrats in North Carolina politics, he also found time to edit
    for publication 16 volumes of the *State Records of North Carolina, 1777–1790*
    (Winston and Goldsboro, N.C., 1895–1905). *Dictionary of American Biography*,
    vol. IV, pp. 140–41.

99. Clark, "True Remedy for Lynch Law," pp. 801–7. Clark's true remedy was a
    suggestion for rigorous procedural reform.

100. [Hezekiah L. Hosmer], *Charge of Chief Justice Hosmer to the Grand Jury of the
     First Judicial District, M. T., delivered, December 5th, 1864* (broadside, Virginia
     City, Mont., 1864). Born in 1814, Hosmer was an Ohio lawyer, editor, and
     author who served in 1861–1864 as secretary of the U.S. House of Representa-
     tives committee on territories from which post in 1864 he was appointed chief
     justice of Montana Territory, a position he held until 1868. In 1869 he became
     Virginia City postmaster and held office until going to San Francisco in 1872
     where he served as a customs official and state mining functionary until his
     death in 1893. *National Cyclopaedia of American Biography*, vol. XIII, pp. 237.

101. See Chap. 4.

102. *Ex Parte* Wall, 107 U.S. 265 (1882) at 274, which is also the source of the
     epigraph for this chapter quoting Bradley on the responsibility of the lawyer to
     uphold the law.

103. William Gillette, "Samuel Miller," *Justices of the Supreme Court*, vol. II,
     pp. 1011–24. For Iowa vigilantism in the 1850's see Chap. 4, this book.

104. Robert McCloskey, "Stephen J. Field," *Justices of the Supreme Court*, vol. II,
     pp. 1069–89. Field dissented from Bradley's opinion in *Ex Parte* Wall
     (290–318) on points of law; he made no objection to Bradley's general
     statements on lynch law. On California vigilantism see Chaps. 4–5, this book.

105. Pound, *Criminal Justice in America*, p. 123.

106. Francis J. Grund, *The Americans in Their Moral, Social, and Political Relations*
     (London, 1837), vol. II, pp. 320–23.

107. Stephen J. Field, *Personal Reminiscences of Early Days in California* (reprinted
     New York, 1968), pp. 2–17.

108. *Ibid.*, pp. 22, 25–28.

109. An 1873 graduate of Washington and Lee, Kernan studied law under his father
     and became a leading Baton Rouge lawyer and politician. He served as a
     presidential elector in 1892 and as a member of the state constitutional
     convention of 1898 and of the state legislature. *Who Was Who in America*, vol.
     IV, p. 524.

110. Thomas J. Kernan, "The Jurisprudence of Lawlessness," *Reports of American
     Bar Association*, 29 (1906), part 1, pp. 450–67.

111. Quoted in Richard Maxwell Brown, ed., *American Violence* (Englewood Cliffs,
     N. J.(, p. 137.

112. Ernest J. Hopkins, *Our Lawless Police: A Study of the Unlawful Enforcement of
     Law* (New York, 1931), Chap. 2 and pp. 27, 47, 60.

113. Eric F. Goldman, *Charles J. Bonaparte: Patrician Reformer: His Earlier Career*
     (Baltimore, 1943). *Dictionary of American Biography*, vol. II, pp. 427–28.

114. Quoted in Goldman, *Charles J. Bonaparte*, p. 32.

115. Bonaparte, "Lynch Law," p. 336.
116. *Ibid.,* pp. 338–41.
117. *Ibid.,* p. 342.
118. See the preceding discussion of Theodore Roosevelt, this chapter.
119. Goldman, *Charles J. Bonaparte,* pp. 130–31; *Dictionary of American Biography,* vol. II, pp. 427–28.
120. Arnold M. Paul, "David J. Brewer," *Justices of the Supreme Court,* vol. II, pp. 1515–33. On Kansas vigilantism see Chap. 4, this book.
121. Brewer, "Right of Appeal," p. 2548; see, also, *Leslie's Weekly,* Aug. 20, 1903.
122. Brewer, "Right of Appeal," p. 2549.
123. *Dictionary of American Biography,* vol. I, pp. 544–47.
124. Originally from Massachusetts, Daniel H. Chamberlain was a Yale graduate, a Harvard law student, and an officer of black troops in the Civil War. A Republican and the last Reconstruction governor of South Carolina, in 1883 he was appointed nonresidential professor of constitutional law at Cornell. *Dictionary of American Biography,* vol. III, p. 595.
125. A prominent St. Louis lawyer, Henry Hitchcock was a Yale graduate, an officer on Sherman's staff in the Civil War, and the first dean of the law school of Washington University of St. Louis. He became president of the American Bar Association, 1889–1890. *Dictionary of American Biography,* vol. IX, pp. 75–76.
126. *Reports of American Bar Association,* 9 (1886): 286–93; 10 (1887): 55–78. In voting to table, the Association seems to have been influenced by the argument that, in regard to the basic cause—drunkenness—of the petty offenses for which they were considering whipping, temperance would be a more effective remedy.
127. On the link between white capping and the movement to legalize whipping, see Sally L. James, "American Violent Moral Regulation and the White Caps" (senior honors essay, College of William and Mary, 1969), pp. 52–53. On the campaign for legalized whipping, see: "Whipping Not a Cruel and Unusual Punishment," *Criminal Law Magazine,* 4 (1883): 401–10; "Whipping as a Punishment," *Green Bag,* 2 (1890): 400–01; Francis B. Lee, "The Whipping Post and Some of Its Uses," *New Jersey Law Journal,* 15 (1892): 356–60. President Theodore Roosevelt probably had whipping in mind when on December 6, 1904, in regard to the District of Columbia, he asked that Congress consider "some form of corporal punishment" for those—such as wife beaters—"whose criminality takes the shape of brutality and cruelty toward the weak." *Presidential Addresses and State Papers of Theodore Roosevelt,* vol. II, pp. 523–28. Roosevelt may possibly have been influenced in this by the views of Simeon E. Baldwin as well as by his own long standing pro-vigilante feelings.
128. Simeon E. Baldwin, "Whipping and Castration as Punishments for Crime," *Yale Law Journal,* 8 (1898–1899): 371–79, 383. The two articles in 1899 in the *Yale Law Journal* by Bonaparte and Baldwin, Baldwin's long connection with the Yale Law School, and Bonaparte's pro-lynch law speech to the Yale Law School graduating class in 1890 might seem to suggest that a lynch law-oriented Draconian attitude to the law was dominant in the Yale Law School. Whether or not this was true, it should be emphasized that one of the most powerful intellectual blows against lynch law was struck from Yale in this very same period, although it came not from the lawyers but from the sociologists. James E. Cutler's important book, *Lynch-Law* (1905) was a product of the Sumnerian tradition of sociology at Yale. It seems to have been

Cutler's doctoral dissertation (or a revision of it), and it was sponsored by Yale's distinguished sociologist, Albert G. Keller, as well as by William Graham Sumner who wrote a strong anti-lynch law foreword for the book. Cutler's book was the first monographic study of lynching, a subject that had been distorted by mythology and impressionism, which Cutler did much to dispel. Unlike the legal illuminati who tended to find the cure for lynch law in drastic procedural reform of the law, Cutler, who, as a good Sumnerian, was concerned with a folkway—lynching—placed his hopes in developing "public sentiment" against lynching and obviously conceived of his book as a step in that direction. See Cutler, *Lynch-Law*, Chap. 9, especially p. 279. On Cutler: *National Cyclopaedia of American Biography*, vol. XLV, p. 119.

129. This appears to have been another popular myth of the day. For a pointed statistical refutation of this argument see the authoritative study of Delaware's legal system of whipping, Robert G. Caldwell, *Red Hannah: Delaware's Whipping Post* (Philadelphia, 1947), pp. 76–79, 87.

130. See Mark H. Haller, Jr., *Eugenics: Hereditarian Attitudes in American Thought* (New Brunswick, 1963), pp. 42, 46–49, and *passim.*

131. Baldwin, "Whipping and Castration," pp. 380–82. In 1901 Baldwin renewed his plea for whipping (but not castration) in "The Restoration of Whipping as a Punishment for Crime," *Green Bag*, 13 (1901): 65–67. As late as 1925—two years before his death—Baldwin continued to advocate legalized whipping. See pp. 245–46 of his book, *The American Judiciary* (New York, 1925), a study in "The American State Series" that was first published in 1905.

Chapter 7

1. *Newsweek*, Oct. 21, 1974, pp. 37–39.

2. See note 119, Chap. 1, this book, for a nineteenth-century anti-Negro riot in Boston.

3. The enduring although beleaguered quality of black life in America during its two bleakest periods—ante-bellum slavery and the late nineteenth century—is, among many books, treated in John W. Blassingame, *The Slave Community: Plantation Life in the Antebellum South* (New York, 1972); Eugene D. Genovese, *Roll, Jordan, Roll: The World the Slaves Made* (New York, 1974); Rayford W. Logan, *The Negro in American Life and Thought: The Nadir, 1877–1901* (New York, 1954).

4. Winthrop D. Jordan, *White over Black: American Attitudes toward the Negro, 1550–1812* (Chapel Hill, 1968), pp. 102–3, 141; Orlando Patterson, *The Sociology of Slavery: An Analysis of the Origins, Development and Structure of Negro Slave Society in Jamaica* (Rutherford, N. J., 1969), pp. 274–75; Genovese, *Roll, Jordan, Roll*, pp. 586–97. See, also, Carl N. Degler, *Neither Black nor White: Slavery and Race Relations in Brazil and the United States* (New York, 1971), pp. 47–52.

5. Arthur Ramos, *The Negro in Brazil*, trans. Richard Pattee (Washington, 1951), Chaps. 3–4.

6. Melville J. and Francis Herskovits, *Rebel Destiny* (New York, 1934).

7. Genovese, *Roll, Jordan, Roll*, pp. 589–90.

8. Patterson, *Sociology of Slavery*, Chap. 9.

9. Thomas O. Ott, *The Haitian Revolution: 1789–1804* (Knoxville, 1973).

10. Ott, *Haitian Revolution*, p. 9.

11. Harry Hoetink, "Race Relations in Curaçao and Surinam," p. 182, in Laura Foner and Eugene D. Genovese, eds., *Slavery in the New World* (Englewood Cliffs, N. J., 1969).

12. Patterson, *Sociology of Slavery*, Chap. 9.

13. *Ibid.*, p. 274, citing Kenneth M. Stampp, *The Peculiar Institution: Slavery in the Ante-Bellum South* (New York, 1963), p. 41.

14. This I document in an unpublished paper, "White and Black in Eighteenth-Century South Carolina" (South Carolina Historical Association, Charleston, 1970). On agriculture: Peter H. Wood, *Black Majority: Negroes in Colonial South Carolina from 1670 through the Stono Rebellion* (New York, 1974), Chap. 2.

15. Genovese, *Roll, Jordan, Roll*, pp. 597–98. In this significant book, Genovese emphasizes slave religion, seeing it as providing "simultaneous accommodation and resistance to slavery" and contributing to black "cohesion and strength . . . threatened by disintegration and demoralization." Genovese concludes that "the slaves' religion developed into the organizing center of their resistance within accommodation; it reflected the hegemony of the master class but also set firm limits to that hegemony." *Ibid.*, pp. 597–98, 659.

16. Stampp, *Peculiar Institution*, pp. 97–109. For the eighteenth century: Gerald W. Mullin, *Flight and Rebellion: Slave Resistance in Eighteenth-Century Virginia* (New York, 1972), pp. 53–55, 60; Wood, *Black Majority*, pp. 287–88.

17. Blassingame, *Slave Community*, p. 107. See, also, Mullin, *Flight and Rebellion*, p. 59; Wood, *Black Majority*, pp. 286, 288–98; Stampp, *Peculiar Institution*, pp. 124–32. Genovese, *Roll, Jordan, Roll*, pp. 599–657, deals with slave stealing, arson, poisoning, murder, malingering, malpractice on the job, generally bad behavior, and runaway activity.

18. For Mississippi in 1835, see note 12, Chap. 8, this book.

19. Allan Nevins, *The Emergence of Lincoln*, vol. II, *Prologue to Civil War, 1859–1861* (New York, 1950), pp. 306–8. The anxiety of the summer of 1860 in Texas is discussed in Chap. 8, this book.

20. The listing of 44 slave revolts and conspiracies in Appendix 4 is based on the most complete work on the subject by Herbert Aptheker, *American Negro Slave Revolts* (New York, 1943), and a pointed work of analysis by Marion D. deB. Kilson, "Towards Freedom: An Analysis of Slave Revolts in the United States," *Phylon*, 25 (1965): 175–87.

21. On the New York City events of 1712 and 1741: Gary B. Nash, *Red, White, and Black: The Peoples of Early America* (Englewood Cliffs, N. J., 1974), pp. 198–200.

22. Wood, *Black Majority*, Chap. 12.

23. Genovese, *Roll, Jordan, Roll*, p. 588.

24. Aptheker, *American Negro Slave Revolts*, pp. 249–51.

25. Mullin, *Flight and Rebellion*, Chap. 5.

26. John Lofton, *Insurrection in South Carolina: The Turbulent World of Denmark Vesey* (Yellow Springs, 1964); Robert S. Starobin, ed., *Denmark Vesey: The Slave Conspiracy of 1822* (Englewood Cliffs, N. J., 1970). Richard Wade, "The Vesey Plot: A Reconsideration," *Journal of Southern History*, 30 (1964): 148–61, contends that there was no substantial plot, a view that has been attacked by Sterling Stuckey, "Remembering Denmark Vesey," *Negro Digest*, 15 (1966): 28–41, and William W. Freehling, *Prelude to Civil War* (New York, 1966), pp. 53–61.

27. Mullin, *Flight and Rebellion*, p. 160. Genovese, in *Roll, Jordan, Roll*, pp. 593–94, while agreeing generally with Mullin's classification of the three rebellious movements, puts a higher valuation on Vesey's leadership: "Vesey seems to

have come closest to formulating a flexible religious appeal based on the folk religion and both African and classical Christian ideas and appeals; Nat Turner assumed a messianic stance among a people not prone to following messiahs; Denmark Vesey most creatively captured the complex tradition of the people he sought to lead."

28. The remarkable documentary collection by Henry I. Tragle, ed., *The Southampton Slave Revolt of 1831: A Compilation of Source Material* (New York, 1973), is the leading work on the revolt. Also helpful are Eric Foner, ed., *Nat Turner* (Englewood Cliffs, N. J., 1971); John B. Duff and Peter M. Mitchell, eds., *The Nat Turner Rebellion: The Historical Event and the Modern Controversy* (New York, 1971), which includes a treatment of the attack by black scholars on William Styron's novel, *The Confessions of Nat Turner* (New York, 1967); and Herbert Aptheker, *Nat Turner's Slave Rebellion* (New York, 1966). Badly out of date in important particulars but still worth consulting is William S. Drewry, *The Southampton Insurrection* (Washington, 1900).

29. Degler, *Neither Black nor White*, pp. 47–52.

30. The following section on American Maroons is based on Herbert Aptheker, *American Negro Slave Revolts*, and "Maroons within the Present Limits of the United States," *Journal of Negro History*, 24 (1939): 167–84, which are the sources for the Maroon movements listed in Appendix 4.

31. Aptheker, "Maroons," p. 178.

32. *Ibid.*, p. 179.

33. *Ibid.*

34. On the basis of six outstanding articles that are, in effect, a monograph, Kenneth W. Porter is the leading authority on the Florida Maroons. His climactic study, "Negroes and the Seminole War, 1835–1842," *Journal of Southern History*, 30 (1964): 427–50, was preceded by "Florida Slaves and Free Negroes in the Seminole War, 1835–1842," *Journal of Negro History*, 28 (1943): 390–421; "Three Fighters for Freedom," *ibid.*, 51–72; "Negroes and the East Florida Annexation Plot, 1811–1813," *Journal of Negro History*, 30 (1945): 9–29; "Negroes on the Southern Frontier, 1670–1763," *Journal of Negro History*, 33 (1948): 58–78; "Negroes and the Seminole War, 1817–1818," *Journal of Negro History*, 36 (1951): 249–80. Also important is John K. Mahon's *History of the Second Seminole War: 1835–1842* (Gainesville, 1967), the leading study of the military conflict. Porter, "Negroes and East Florida Annexation Plot," pp. 15–16, is the source for the quotation on the Maroon way of life.

35. Major authorities on American slavery who emphasize the Florida Maroons (with varying degrees of emphasis) are Aptheker, "Maroons," p. 180; Blassingame, *Slave Community*, pp. 119–24; Degler, *Neither Black nor White*, p. 52; Genovese, *Roll, Jordan, Roll*, p. 591; and Stampp, *Peculiar Institution*, p. 138.

36. Foreman is quoted in Aptheker, "Maroons," p. 180.

37. Mahon, *History of Second Seminole War*, p. 20.

38. On Osceola's band: Porter, "Florida Slaves," p. 407.

39. For the Florida Maroons with the Seminoles in their new homes in what is now Oklahoma, see Edwin C. McReynolds, *The Seminoles* (Norman, 1957).

40. Allen D. Grimshaw, ed., *Racial Violence in the United States* (Chicago, 1969), pp. 254–55. There were also three riots below the Mason-Dixon line: New Market, Maryland (1831); Washington, D. C. (1835); and Maysville, Kentucky (1841).

41. John M. Werner, "Race Riots in the United States during the Age of Jackson: 1824–1849" (Ph.D. dissertation, Indiana University, 1972), pp. 4, 273ff.

42. Jordan, *White over Black*, and the revised and abridged edition of it: *The White Man's Burden: Historical Origins of Racism in the United States* (New York, 1974).

43. Werner, "Race Riots," pp. 78–79 and pp. 257–58, in which the preceding passage from the Boston *Emancipator and Free American*, Sept. 1, 1842, is quoted.

44. William Frederic Warner, "The Columbia Race Riots," *Lancaster County Historical Society Papers*, 26 (1922): 175–87. In 1842, Smith moved to Philadelphia where in time he became the nation's wealthiest black.

45. Werner, "Race Riots," pp. 83–84, 156–70, 229, 231, and Chap. 6. Sam Bass Warner, Jr., *The Private City: Philadelphia in Three Periods of Its Growth* (Philadelphia, 1968), Chap. 7.

46. Werner, "Race Riots," Chap. 6. Warner, *Private City*, Chap. 7.

47. The following sketch of the Wilmington race riot and its background is based on Helen G. Edmonds' *The Negro and Fusion Politics in North Carolina: 1894–1901* (Chapel Hill, 1951), Chap. 11. See, also, the remarkable novel based on the riot by the black writer, Charles W. Chesnutt, *The Marrow of Tradition*, ed. Robert M. Farnsworth (1901; reprinted Ann Arbor, 1969).

48. Charles Crowe, "Racial Violence and Social Reform—Origins of the Atlanta Riot of 1906," *Journal of Negro History*, 53 (1968): 234–56. On the riot itself: "Racial Massacre in Atlanta: September 22, 1906," *ibid.*, 54 (1969): 150–73.

49. Richard D. Lambert, "Hindu-Moslem Riots" (Ph.D. dissertation, University of Pennsylvania, 1951), pp. 220–21, quoted in Allen D. Grimshaw, "A Study in Social Violence: Urban Race Riots in the United States" (Ph.D. dissertation, University of Pennsylvania, 1959), p. 217. Lambert noted that a pogrom could also occur "when the minority community was a very small part of the population but had political and economic control . . . ."

50. Grimshaw, *Racial Violence*, pp. 46–55.

51. *Ibid.*, pp. 92–94. Arthur I. Waskow, *From Race Riot to Sit-In, 1919 and the 1960s: A Study in the Connections between Conflict and Violence* (Garden City, N. Y., 1966), pp. 110–20.

52. Grimshaw, *Racial Violence*, pp. 153–61.

53. *Ibid.*, pp. 170–83.

54. Elliott M. Rudwick, *Race Riot at East St. Louis: July 2, 1917* (Carbondale, 1964).

55. Waskow, *Race Riot to Sit-In*, Chaps. 7–8.

56. Richard Hofstadter and Michael Wallace, eds., *American Violence: A Documentary History* (New York, 1970), pp. 249–53.

57. Lambert, "Hindu-Moslem Riots," p. 218, quoted in Grimshaw, "Study in Social Violence," p. 216. The term "communal riots" is from Morris Janowitz's "Patterns of Collective Racial Violence," pp. 412–44, in Hugh Davis Graham and Ted Robert Gurr, eds., *The History of Violence in America* (New York, 1969). Grimshaw, who has successfully applied Lambert's categories in regard to Hindu-Moslem riots in India to U. S. race riots, *ca.* 1917–1951, uses the terms "contested area" (originally employed by the Chicago Commission on Race Relations—see note 63, this chapter) and "communal violence." Grimshaw, Study in Social Violence," p. 202 and *passim*.

58. Grimshaw, *Racial Violence*, pp. 73–87.

59. Waskow, *Race Riot to Sit-In*, pp. 105–10.

60. For Washington, Chicago, and Detroit see following discussions.

61. Grimshaw, *Racial Violence*, p. 385.

62. Waskow, *Race Riot to Sit-In*, Chap. 3.

63. William M. Tuttle, Jr., *Race Riot: Chicago in the Red Summer of 1919* (New York, 1970); Chicago Commission on Race Relations, *The Negro in Chicago: A Study of Race Relations and a Race Riot* (Chicago, 1922); Waskow, *Race Riot to Sit-In*, Chaps. 4–5; Richard Maxwell Brown, ed., *American Violence* (Englewood Cliffs, N. J., 1970), pp. 126–36.

64. Hofstadter and Wallace, *American Violence*, pp. 253–58; Robert Shogan and Tom Craig, *The Detroit Race Riot: A Study in Violence* (Philadelphia, 1964); Alfred McClung Lee and Norman D. Humphrey, *Race Riot* (New York, 1943).

65. Jessie P. Guzman *et al.*, eds., *1952 Negro Year Book: A Review of Events Affecting Negro Life* (New York, 1952), p. 278. See Appendix 4 for the number of blacks lynched annually in the U. S., 1882–1935.

66. National Association for the Advancement of Colored People, *Thirty Years of Lynching in the United States, 1889–1918* (New York, 1969), pp. 31–32.

67. *Ibid.*, p. 36 and *passim*.

68. William Warren Rogers and Robert David Ward, *August Reckoning: Jack Turner and Racism in Post-Civil War Alabama* (Baton Rouge, 1973).

69. National Association for Advancement of Colored People, *Thirty Years of Lynching*, pp. 50, 54, 60, 88, 98.

70. David M. Tucker, "Miss Ida B. Wells and Memphis Lynching," *Phylon*, 32 (1971): 112–22. In Chicago, Ida B. Wells eventually married Ferdinand Barnett and as Mrs. Wells-Barnett continued to spearhead the national anti-lynching movement down to the time of World War I. Ida B. Wells-Barnett, *On Lynching*, ed. August Meier (New York, 1969).

71. On the anti-lynching movement: Donald L. Grant, "The Development of the Anti-Lynching Reform Movement in the United States, 1883–1932" (Ph.D. dissertation, University of Missouri—Columbia, 1972); Robert L. Zangrando, "The Efforts of the National Association for the Advancement of Colored People to Secure Passage of a Federal Anti-Lynching Law, 1920–1940" (Ph.D. dissertation, University of Pennsylvania, 1963).

72. For the many cases of lynch law that illustrate the lynching ritual: Arthur F. Raper, *The Tragedy of Lynching* (Chapel Hill, 1933); Ralph Ginsburg, ed., *100 Years of Lynching* (New York, 1962); Brown, *American Violence*, pp. 107–9. There is no definitive study of post-Civil War Southern lynching of blacks, but the most acute treatment is by Raper's *Tragedy of Lynching*, followed by Walter White's *Rope & Faggot: A Biography of Judge Lynch* (New York, 1929), and the pioneering scholarly work on the subject by James E. Cutler, *Lynch-Law: An Investigation into the History of Lynching in the United States* (New York, 1905). A legal study is James H. Chadbourn's *Lynching and the Law* (Chapel Hill, 1933). Although lynching was predominantly in the rural South, the large cities were by no means immune. The story of one notable lynching that had its genesis in a great city, Atlanta, is ably told in Leonard Dinnerstein, *The Leo Frank Case* (New York, 1968), a sensational event of the World War I era. Frank, a young Jewish factory manager, was lynched for the alleged murder of Mary Phagan, a youthful worker in his plant—a lynching in which anti-Semitism was a factor.

73. Richard B. Sherman, ed., *The Negro and the City* (Englewood Cliffs, N. J., 1970), p. 5.

74. Hollis R. Lynch, ed., *The Black Urban Condition: A Documentary History, 1866–1971* (New York, 1973), pp. 421–32.

75. *Ibid.*

76. *Ibid.*

77. August Meier and Elliott Rudwick, *From Plantation to Ghetto* (New York, 1970), p. 215.

78. *Ibid.*, p. 216.

79. Sherman, *Negro and the City*, p. 5.

80. On transportation to the Northeastern cities see, for example, Dwayne W. Walls, *Chickenbone Special* (New York, 1973).

81. On the move to Chicago: Allan H. Spear, *Black Chicago: The Making of a Negro Ghetto, 1890–1920* (Chicago, 1967), p. 140 and *passim;* Richard Wright, *Black Boy: A Record of Childhood and Youth* (New York, 1945), pp. 223–26. On the Northern ghetto life of Southern-born black children see Robert Coles, *The South Goes North* (Boston, 1971).

82. Willaim E. B. DuBois, quoted in William M. Tuttle, ed., *W. E. B. DuBois* (Englewood Cliffs, N. J., 1973), p. 7.

83. Brief biographical sketches of these persons, with the exception of Fard, are found in Edgar A. Toppin, *A Biographical History of Blacks in America since 1528* (New York, 1971). On Fard: C. Eric Lincoln, *The Black Muslims in America* (Boston, 1969), pp. 10–15.

84. On the growth of the Harlem ghetto: Seth M. Scheiner, *Negro Mecca: A History of the Negro in New York City, 1865–1920* (New York, 1965); Gilbert Osofsky, *Harlem: The Making of a Ghetto, Negro New York, 1890–1930* (New York, 1966).

85. Alain Locke, ed., *The New Negro: An Interpretation* (New York, 1925), a rich sampler containing contributions by such leading figures of the Harlem Renaissance as Zora Neale Hurston, Countee Cullen, Jessie Fauset, Claude McKay, James Weldon Johnson, Langston Hughes, Arthur A. Schomburg, Walter White, and Locke himself as well as excerpts from the fictional volume, *Cane* (New York, 1923) by Jean Toomer, with *Cane* being a "conscious exploration of Negro identity" in terms of the link between modern black life in the urban North and its primal roots in the deep South. Nathan Irvin Huggins, *Harlem Renaissance* (New York, 1971), pp. 179–87 (from whence comes the phrase in the preceding sentence), salutes *Cane* as the outstanding literary achievement of the Harlem Renaissance—a well-deserved tribute.

86. Huggins, *Harlem Renaissance*, is a brilliant probe in depth of these issues as well as being the best work on the movement.

87. The leading study is Edmund David Cronon, *Black Moses: The Story of Marcus Garvey and the Universal Negro Improvement Association* (Madison, 1966).

88. Adam Clayton Powell, Jr. (1945), quoted in Cronon, *Black Moses*, p. 172. On the impact of Garvey and his movement see, in addition to Cronon's *Black Moses*: John Hope Franklin, *From Slavery to Freedom: A History of Negro Americans* (New York, 1967), pp. 489–92; Meier and Rudwick, *Plantation to Ghetto*, pp. 226–28; Toppin, *Biographical History of Blacks*, pp. 180–84, 302–4; Sherman, *Negro and the City*, pp. 153–57; Malcolm X, with the assistance of Alex Haley, *The Autobiography of Malcolm X* (New York, 1966), pp. 1–2, 4–7.

89. Ralph Ellison, *Invisible Man* (New York, 1947). James Baldwin, *Go Tell It on the Mountain* (New York, 1953). For the appraisal of *Invisible Man* as the best piece of American writing since World War II, see Toppin, *Biographical History of Blacks*, p. 292, who cites a 1965 poll of leading experts.

90. Richard Wright, *Native Son* (New York, 1940); Wright, *Black Boy*; Wright's introduction to St. Clair Drake and Horace R. Cayton, *Black Metropolis: A Study of Negro Life in a Northern City* (New York, 1945), pp. xvii–xviii.

91. Wright's introduction to Drake and Cayton, *Black Metropolis*, pp. xvii–xviii.

92. For facts of publication see note 90, above.

93. Drake and Cayton, *Black Metropolis*, pp. 391–92 and *passim*.
94. *Ibid.*, p. 753.
95. On the Black Muslim movement: E. U. Essien-Udom, *Black Nationalism: A Search for an Identity in America* (Chicago, 1962); Lincoln, *Black Muslims*; Malcolm X, *Autobiography*.
96. Toppin, *Biographical History of Blacks*, p. 375.
97. See, for example, Charles Keil, *Urban Blues* (Chicago, 1966), pp. 186, 192.
98. Keil, *Urban Blues*. Among the other scholars and their works are: (1) on music (including jazz and blues as well as Soul music)—LeRoi Jones (now Immamu Amiri Baraka), *Blues People: Negro Music in White America* (New York, 1963) and *Black Music* (New York, 1967); Frank Kofsky, *Black Nationalism and the Revolution in Music* (New York, 1970); Ben Sidran, *Black Talk* (New York, 1971); Ortiz Walton, *Music: Black, White & Blue: A Sociological Survey of the Use and Misuse of Afro-American Music* (New York, 1972); Marien Tally Brown, "Soul Music . . ." (cited in full in note 100, below); (2) on humor—Roger D. Abrahams, *Deep Down in the Jungle: Negro Narrative Folklore from the Streets of Philadelphia* (Hatboro, Pa., 1964); (3) on speech—J. L. Dillard, *Black English: Its History and Usage in the United States* (New York, 1972), which, pp. xiii and 345, emphasizes the scholarship of William A. Stewart; Arthur L. Smith, ed., *Language, Communication, and Rhetoric in Black America* (New York, 1972); and the salient collection, Thomas Kochman, ed., *Rappin' and Stylin' Out: Communication in Urban Black America* (Urbana, 1972); (4) on nonverbal expressiveness—Benjamin G. Cooke, "Nonverbal Communication among Afro-Americans: An Initial Classification," pp. 32–64, and Herbert Kohl and James Hinton, "Names, Graffiti, and Culture," pp. 109–33, both in Kochman, *Rappin' and Stylin' Out*.
99. Keil, *Urban Blues*.
100. Marien Tally Brown, "Soul Music: The Voice of a New Black Assertiveness" (unpublished paper, Association for the Study of Afro-American History and Life, Philadelphia, Oct. 26, 1974), reported and quoted in the *Washington Post*, Oct. 28, 1974, p. B-14, c. 4–5.
101. Kenneth B. Clark, *Dark Ghetto: Dilemmas of Social Power* (New York, 1965); Elliott Liebow, *Tally's Corner* (Boston, 1967); Ulf Hannerz, *Soulside: Inquiries into Ghetto Culture and Community* (New York, 1969).
102. Ulf Hannerz, "The Significance of Soul," p. 164, in August Meier, ed., *The Transformation of Activism: Black Experience* (Chicago, 1970).
103. *Ibid.*, p. 172.
104. Richard B. Gregg, A. Jackson McCormack, and Douglas J. Pedersen, "The Rhetoric of Black Power: A Street-Level Interpretation," pp. 267–83, in Smith, *Language, Communication, and Rhetoric*. See, also, Robert D. Brooks, "Black Power: The Dimensions of a Slogan," pp. 339–46, in the same work, and the general treatise by Stokely Carmichael and Charles V. Hamilton, *Black Power: The Politics of Liberation in America* (New York, 1967).
105. The following seven-stage prototype is my own formulation but one based on standard conclusions by leading authorities, especially Joe R. Feagin and Harlan Hahn in *Ghetto Revolts: The Politics of Violence in American Cities* (New York, 1973), pp. 160, 179; Hans W. Mattick in "The Form and Content of Recent Riots," *University of Chicago Law Review*, 35 (1968): 660–85; *Report of the National Advisory Commission on Civil Disorders* (New York, 1968), pp. 116–27.
106. Feagin and Hahn, *Ghetto Revolts*, p. 160.
107. *Ibid.*

108. *Ibid.,* p. 179.

109. From a huge bibliography on the Watts riot, see Robert Conot, *Rivers of Blood, Years of Darkness* (New York, 1967), and the book edited by Nathan Cohen that is cited in note 120, below.

110. From works dealing with the Detroit riot, see *Report on Civil Disorders*, pp. 84–108, and the remarkable study by John Hersey, *The Algiers Motel Incident* (New York, 1968).

111. The following sketch of Newark and its riot is based on *Report on Civil Disorders*, pp. 56–69.

112. Janowitz, "Patterns of Collective Racial Violence," p. 418.

113. Feagin and Hahn, *Ghetto Revolts*, pp. 280–81.

114. *Report on Civil Disorders*, pp. 128–29.

115. T. M. Tomlinson, "The Development of a Riot Ideology among Urban Negroes," p. 229, in Grimshaw, *Racial Violence.*

116. Nathan Caplan, "The New Ghetto Man: A Review of Recent Empirical Studies," pp. 343–59, in David Boesel and Peter H. Rossi, eds., *Cities under Siege: An Anatomy of the Ghetto Riots, 1964–1968* (New York, 1971). Feagin and Hahn, *Ghetto Revolts*, pp. 300–1, adopt Caplan's conceptualization of the New Ghetto Man.

117. Feagin and Hahn, *Ghetto Revolts*, p. 301.

118. *Ibid.,* pp. 300–1.

119. *Ibid.,* pp. 268–69.

120. T. M. Tomlinson and David O. Sears, "Negro Attitudes toward the Riot," p. 304, in Nathan Cohen, ed., *The Los Angeles Riots: A Socio-Psychological Study* (New York, 1970).

121. Feagin and Hahn, *Ghetto Revolts*, pp. 268–69.

122. Tomlinson and Sears, "Negro Attitudes," p. 301.

123. *Ibid.*

124. Feagin and Hahn, *Ghetto Revolts*, pp. 268–69.

125. *Ibid.,* p. 271.

126. Tomlinson and Sears, "Negro Attitudes," p. 302.

127. Tomlinson, "Development of a Riot Ideology," pp. 230–31.

128. Feagin and Hahn, *Ghetto Revolts*, p. 329.

129. *Ibid.,* p. 26.

130. This point has been elaborated at great length by those specialists who explain the ghetto riots of the 1960's by the concept of "relative deprivation" according to which blacks, feeling relatively deprived when they compare their living standard to the rapidly rising living standard of American whites, reacted by rioting. Exponents of the "relative deprivation" interpretation have not, ordinarily, restricted this interpretation to black ghetto riots but have applied it, generally, to rebellious activity. See James C. Davies, "The *J*-Curve of Rising and Declining Satisfactions as a Cause of Some Great Revolutions and a Contained Rebellion," pp. 690–730, in Graham and Gurr, *History of Violence in America*, and Ted R. Gurr, *Why Men Rebel* (Princeton, 1970) and "Urban Disorder: Perspectives from the Comparative Study of Civil Strife," pp. 51–67, in Louis H. Masotti and Don R. Bowen, eds., *Riots and Rebellion* (Beverly Hills, 1968).

131. Feagin and Hahn, *Ghetto Revolts*, p. 329.

132. *Ibid.,* pp. 53–54. See, also, Chap. 2, this book.

133. Feagin and Hahn, *Ghetto Revolts*, p. 54.

Chapter 8

1. See Chap. 3.
2. See Chap. 1.
3. See Chap. 4.
4. See Chap. 1.
5. Paul M. Angle, *Bloody Williamson: A Chapter in American Lawlessness* (New York, 1952).
6. See Chap. 6, note 68.
7. D. W. Meinig, *Imperial Texas: An Interpretive Essay in Cultural Geography* (Austin, 1969), p. 108.
8. *Ibid.,* map 1. Writers' Program of the Work Projects Administration in the State of Texas, *Texas: A Guide to the Lone Star State* (New York, 1940).
9. Meinig, *Imperial Texas,* pp. 10–23; map 17.
10. *Ibid.,* pp. 108 and 122; map 16.
11. For a recent treatment of Texas violence, see W. Eugene Hollon, *Frontier Violence* (New York, 1974), Chap. 3, from which (p. 36) the epigraph to this chapter is taken.
12. Edwin A. Miles, "The Mississippi Slave Insurrection Scare of 1835," *Journal of Negro History,* 42 (1957): 48–60. David Grimsted, "The Mississippi Slave Insurrection Panic, 1835" (unpublished paper, Southern Historical Association, Atlanta, 1973). See, also, Chap. 1, this book.
13. See Chap. 1.
14. See Appendix 4.
15. *Texas State Gazette* (Austin), Oct. 14, 1854, p. 5, c. 1; Oct. 21, 1854, p. 5, c. 1–2; Oct. 28, 1854, p. 4, c. 3.
16. Frank H. Smyrl, "Unionism, Abolitionism, and Vigilantism in Texas, 1856–1865" (M.A. thesis, University of Texas, 1961), pp. 28–30.
17. *Ibid.,* pp. 49ff.
18. *Ibid.,* pp. 37–38, 50.
19. *Ibid.,* pp. 57–59.
20. *Ibid.,* pp. 59–61, 63–64, 65, 72.
21. *Ibid.,* pp. 67–70.
22. *Ibid.,* pp. 66–67; Grimsted, "Mississippi Slave Insurrection Panic."
23. Smyrl, "Unionism," pp. 124–32; Thomas Barrett, *The Great Hanging at Gainesville, Cook County, Texas: October, A.D. 1862* (Austin, 1961); Writers' Program, *Texas,* p. 425.
24. Corinne Cameron, "Haenger Bande," *Junior Historian,* 15 (1955): 28–29, 32.
25. C. L. Sonnichsen, *Ten Texas Feuds* (Albuquerque, 1971), p. 68.
26. *Ibid.,* p. 68, quoting James Hatch.
27. *Ibid.,* p. 68.
28. *Ibid.,* pp. 69–77.
29. Ernest Wallace and E. Adamson Hoebel, *The Comanches: Lords of the South Plains* (Norman, 1952), pp. 257, 301. See, also, Rupert N. Richardson, *The Comanche Barrier to South Plains Settlement* (Glendale, Calif., 1933). On the Kiowas, specifically, see Mildred P. Mayhall, *The Kiowas* (Norman, 1962), and James Mooney, "Calendar History of the Kiowa Indians," Bureau of American Ethnology, *Seventeenth Annual Report* (1895–96), part 1, pp. 188–89 and *passim.*
30. W. C. Nunn, *Texas under the Carpetbaggers* (Austin, 1962), pp. 191–97.
31. *Ibid.,* pp. 198–202. From northeast to southwest the 27 counties were Cooke, Montague, Wise, Jack, Young, Parker, Palo Pinto, Erath, Callahan, Comanche, Hamilton, Brown, Coleman, Lampasas, San Saba, McCulloch, Burnet, Llano,

Mason, Menard, Blanco, Gillespie, Kimble, Kendall, Kerr, Bandera, and Medina.
32. Walter Prescott Webb, *The Texas Rangers* (Austin, 1965), pp. 312–18.
33. Wallace and Hoebel, *Comanches*, pp. 255–59.
34. Webb, *Texas Rangers*, pp. 313–18.
35. Nunn, *Texas under the Carpetbaggers*, p. 211.
36. The raid on the Buckmeyers took place only about 45 miles from the ranch of the grandparents of Lyndon B. Johnson and was similar to the attacks undergone by the Johnsons and their neighbors. See following discussions this chapter.
37. Nunn, *Texas under the Carpetbaggers*, p. 211.
38. *Ibid.,* p. 212.
39. Austin *Daily State Journal*, Aug. 24, 1870, quoted in Nunn, *Texas under the Carpetbaggers*, p. 212.
40. *Galveston Weekly Civilian*, June 23, 1870, quoted in Nunn, *Texas under the Carpetbaggers*, p. 213.
41. Austin *Daily State Journal*, Aug. 20, 1870, quoted in Nunn, *Texas under the Carpetbaggers*, p. 213.
42. *Ibid.*
43. Austin *Daily Republican*, Dec. 14, 1870, quoted in Nunn, *Texas under the Carpetbaggers*, pp. 213–15.
44. Webb, *Texas Rangers*, pp. 312–18.
45. *Ibid.,* p. 319.
46. *Ibid.,* pp. 319–20.
47. George W. Tyler, *The History of Bell County*, ed. Charles W. Ramsdell (San Antonio, 1936), pp. 301ff.
48. James Verdo Hill, "A History of Hill County, Texas to 1873" (M.A. thesis, University of Texas, 1961), pp. 143–45.
49. William C. Holden, "Law and Lawlessness on the Texas Frontier, 1875–1890," *The Cattleman*, Jan., 1942, p. 95 (reprinted from the *Southwestern Historical Quarterly*, Oct., 1940).
50. Felix Burton to Maj. John B. Jones, Kimble Co., Tex., Feb. 22, 1877. H. B. Waddill, Co. C, Frontier Battalion of Texas Rangers, to Maj. John B. Jones, Ft. Mason, Tex., Feb. 27, 1877. Judge W. A. Blackburn to Maj. John B. Jones, Lampasas, Tex., Mar. 30, 1877. Gen. Order No. 15 of Frontier Battalion of Texas Rangers by Maj. John B. Jones, Austin, Tex., Mar. 20, 1877. Maj. John B. Jones to Judge W. A. Blackburn, Austin, Tex., Apr. 2, 1877. A. McFarland to Maj. John B. Jones, Kerrville, Tex., Mar. 27, 1877. Maj. John B. Jones to Adj.-Gen. William Steele, Ft. McKavett, Tex., May 6, 1877. All of these letters and documents are in Transcripts from the Office of the Adjutant-General of Texas, 1838–1889 (9 vols., University of Texas Archives, File B-13, Boxes 131–33), cited hereafter as Adj.-Gen. Transcripts. See, also, Webb, *Texas Rangers*, pp. 328–33, and James B. Gillett, *Six Years with the Texas Rangers: 1875 to 1881*, ed. M. M. Quaife (New Haven, 1925), pp. 69–70.
51. These 27 vigilante movements are listed in Appendix 3. Evidence for these vigilante movements and central Texas vigilantism in general was gained mainly from research in the following: (1) the rich book and periodical collection of the Barker Texas History Center of the University of Texas; (2) the outstanding manuscript collection of the University of Texas Archives; (3) county histories of Texas in the form of M.A. theses done under the supervision of the late Walter Prescott Webb and other members of the history department of the University of Texas; and (4) Sonnichsen papers (extracts from Texas newspa-

pers and notes on Texas feuds and violence in the personal possession of C. L. Sonnichsen; grateful acknowledgment is made to Dr. Sonnichsen for allowing me to examine his valuable collection). In the notes below, documentation is given for the vigilante movements specifically mentioned in this chapter.

52. Some vigilante movements spanned more than one county, therefore 27 movements spread over 38 counties. In addition to the counties named in the text, those that had vigilante movements were Bexar, Blanco, Bosque, Callahan, Comal, Denton, DeWitt, Eastland, Gillespie, Goliad, Gonzales, Hays, Jack, Knox, McLennan, Milam, Palo Pinto, Parker, Wilbarger, Wilson, Wise, and Young.

53. On the San Saba Mob, see following discussions, this chapter.

54. Vallie Eoff, "A History of Erath County, Texas" (M.A. thesis, University of Texas, 1937), p. 101; *Report of the Adjutant-General of the State of Texas*, 1872, pp. 21–25; Billy Bob Lightfoot, "The History of Comanche County, Texas, to 1920" (M.A. thesis, University of Texas, 1949), pp. 121–23.

55. For Comanche County vigilantism and violence, see following discussions, this chapter.

56. *Flake's Semi-Weekly Bulletin* (Galveston), Apr. 20, 1872, p. 7, c. 4; Guy R. Donnell, "The History of Montague County, Texas" (M.A. thesis, University of Texas, 1940), pp. 6–63; Ed. F. Bates, *History and Reminiscences of Denton County* (Denton, 1919), p. 147; *Austin Daily Statesman*, Oct. 9, 1874, p. 1, c. 6; San Antonio *Express*, Apr. 19, 1872, p. 2, c. 4 (transcripts in Sonnichsen Papers).

57. Sonnichsen, *Ten Texas Feuds*, pp. 65–78; Bertha Atkinson, "The History of Bell County, Texas" (M.A. thesis, University of Texas, 1929), pp. 131–33; Tyler, *Bell County*, pp. 135, 186–91, 240, 301ff.; Adj.-Gen. Transcripts, 1838–69 volume, p. 143; Austin *Weekly Statesman*, Jan. 11, Mar. 8, 1877; W. H. Estill to Maj. John B. Jones, June 10, 1878 (transcripts in Sonnichsen Papers).

58. Sonnichsen, *Ten Texas Feuds*, pp. 87–107.

59. M. G. Bowden, "History of Burnet County" (M.A. thesis, University of Texas, 1940), pp. 63, 74–79; *Report of the Adjutant-General of the State of Texas*, 1872, pp. 21–25; Miles Barler, *Early Days in Llano* (n. p., n. d.)—although this publication is undated, Barler wrote these reminiscences in 1898.

60. C. L. Sonnichsen, *I'll Die before I'll Run: The Story of the Great Feuds of Texas* (New York, 1962), pp. 167–87, 244–46; Luckett P. Bishop, "Shoot-Out on Christmas Day," *Frontier Times*, June–July, 1965, pp. 6–11, 59–63.

61. Adj.-Gen. Transcripts, 1878 volume, pp. 68–69, 116, 166–70, 175, 248; 1879–80 volume, pp. 5–17, 274–75; Sonnichsen, *I'll Die before I'll Run*, pp. 149–66, 341–43; Holden, "Law and Lawlessness," p. 97; James K. Greer, *Bois d'Arc to Barb'd Wire: Ken Cary: Southwest Frontier Born* (Dallas, 1936), p. 331.

62. Hervey Chesley, More Hamilton County Notes: Recollections of Felix Williams as told to Hervey Chesley, Sept. 11, 1941 (typescript, Earl Vandale, Collection, University of Texas Archives, File Box A 21/7), pp. 1–2.

63. Zelma M. Scott, *A History of Coryell County, Texas* (Austin, 1965), Chap. 5 and pp. 135, 143, and "The History of Coryell County to 1920" (M.A. thesis, University of Texas, 1946), pp. 122, 141, 144–56; Frank E. Simmons, *History of Coryell County* (Belton, 1965), pp. 29–30; Mildred W. Mears, *Coryell County Scrapbook* (Waco, 1963), pp. 188–89; Austin *Weekly Statesman*, Sept. 27, 1877, p. 2, c. 5; *Galveston Daily News*, July 29, 1883; *Austin Daily Statesman*, July 20, 1875, p. 2, c. 2–3, Aug. 25, 1875, p. 2, c. 7, Sept. 8, 1875, p. 4, c. 1 (transcripts in Sonnichsen Papers).

64. Sonnichsen, *I'll Die before I'll Run*, pp. 206–31, 348–51. District Attorney W. C. Linden is discussed later in this chapter.

65. On Barry: Diary of James Buckner Barry, 1855–1862 (MSS, University of Texas Archives, File Box B 13/167); James Buckner Barry, *A Texas Ranger and Frontiersman: The Days of Buck Barry in Texas, 1845—1906*, ed. James K. Greer (Dallas, 1932); William C. Pool, *Bosque Territory* . . . (Kyle, Tex., 1964); Greer, *Bois d'Arc to Barb'd Wire*.
66. Quoted in Sonnichsen, *Ten Texas Feuds*, p. 7.
67. Unless otherwise indicated, the following analysis of central Texas community feuds is based upon the historical sketches of feuds in Sonnichsen, *I'll Die before I'll Run* and *Ten Texas Feuds*.
68. For the Truitt-Mitchell feud, see the following sketch of Bill Mitchell, this chapter.
69. The Baylor-Brann feud is discussed later in this chapter.
70. The following account of the DeWitt County feud is based on C. L. Sonnichsen's chapter, "Thirty Years A-Feuding: The Sutton-Taylor Feud," in *I'll Die before I'll Run*, pp. 35–115, 330–37.
71. Jack Hays Day, *The Sutton-Taylor Feud* (San Antonio, 1937), pp. 14–15, quoted in Sonnichsen, *I'll Die before I'll Run*, p. 63.
72. The following account of the Jaybird-Woodpecker feud is based on Sonnichsen, *I'll Die before I'll Run*, pp. 232–77, 351–55.
73. In social attitudes toward blacks the Woodpeckers appeared to have been every bit as racist as their Jaybird enemies, and their main stance to Negroes seems to have been the manipulative one of exploiting their votes to maintain political power. But there was a *quid pro quo*, for blacks did vote, hold office, and exercise a greater control over their own destiny than they were able to do, later, under the Jaybird regime. For a similar conflict in east Texas, which resulted in the violent suppression of Negro voting in Grimes County in 1900, see Lawrence C. Goodwyn, "Populist Dreams and Negro Rights: East Texas as a Case Study," *American Historical Review*, 76 (1971): 1435–56. As in Ft. Bend County, the Grimes County struggle was climaxed by a murderous gun battle before the courthouse, which may well have been inspired by the example of Ft. Bend County ten years earlier.
74. Quoted in Sonnichsen, *I'll Die before I'll Run*, p. 279. The straight-laced, holier-than-thou attitudes of Carrie Nation and her husband, David, were an affront to the hard-drinking libertines of both the Jaybirds and Woodpeckers. After the young hellions of Richmond administered a bad beating to David in the spring of 1889 the Nations packed up and left for Kansas where Carrie gained fame as a militant temperance advocate.
75. "Lunar Caustic" in Galveston *News*, Oct. 11, 1867, quoted in Sonnichsen, *Ten Texas Feuds*, pp. 210–11.
76. J. B. Cranfill, *Dr. J. B. Cranfill's Chronicle* (New York, 1916), p. 316, quoted in Sonnichsen, *Ten Texas Feuds*, p. 211.
77. The following sketch of John Wesley Hardin is based on: John Wesley Hardin, *The Life of John Wesley Hardin as Written by Himself* (Seguin, Tex., 1896); Lewis Nordyke, *John Wesley Hardin: Texas Gunman* (New York, 1957); C[harles] L. Sonnichsen, *Pass of the North: Four Centuries on the Rio Grande* (El Paso, 1968), Chap. 22; John Wesley Hardin Papers (1½ boxes of letters, University of Texas Archives).
78. For example, in his autobiography Hardin proudly tells how, much later in Florida, he led a mob that burned to death a Negro accused of rape. Hardin, *Life*, p. 111.
79. Hardin, *Life*, pp. 88–106. For the Comanche County background and aftermath of the Hardin-Webb gunfight see following discussions, this chapter.

80. The following sketch of Bill Mitchell is based on C. L. Sonnichsen's remarkable biography, *Outlaw: Bill Mitchell alias Baldy Russell: His Life and Times* (Denver, 1965). This book revises an earlier version of the Truitt-Mitchell feud that Sonnichsen published in *Ten Texas Feuds*, Chap. 9.

81. Sonnichsen, *Outlaw*, p. 35.

82. *Ibid.,* p. 29 and *passim.*

83. *Ibid.,* p. 70. Nelson Mitchell considered his hanging to be judicial murder, incited by the Truitts.

84. Sonnichsen, *Outlaw*, p. 74.

85. *Ibid.,* p. 80.

86. Meinig, *Imperial Texas*, pp. 66–68; Ray A. Billington, *Westward Expansion: A History of the American Frontier* (New York, 1967), p. 676.

87. Andy Adams, *The Log of a Cowboy: A Narrative of the Old Trail Days* (Lincoln, 1964), Chaps. 3–9; Billington, *Westward Expansion*, p. 676; Writers' Program, *Texas*, p. 461.

88. The following account of Print Olive and his kin is based on Harry E. Chrisman, *The Ladder of Rivers: The Story of I. P. (Print) Olive* (Denver, 1965). Olive's full name was Isom Prentice with "Print," by which he was best known, being a corruption of his middle name.

89. Chrisman, *Ladder of Rivers*, pp. 10–11.

90. *Ibid.,* pp. 254–55.

91. To be noted, too, is that Print Olive's eldest son, Billy, killed his best friend in a drunken rage, only to fall victim, later, to vigilantes while still a youth. Chrisman, *Ladder of Rivers*, Chap. 21.

92. On Comanche's reputation: Boyce House to Billy Bob Lightfoot in Comanche County Scrapbooks (clippings and manuscripts, University of Texas Archives, File Boxes B 35/65–66). On Comanche's topography: Writers' Program, *Texas*, pp. 540–41; Meinig, *Imperial Texas*, maps 1, 2.

93. Wallace and Hoebel, *Comanches*, pp. 257, 301; Nunn, *Texas under the Carpetbaggers*, pp. 198–202.

94. Meinig, *Imperial Texas*, map 12.

95. Statement of L. F. Elkins, Comanche, Tex., Jan. 28, 1949, in Comanche Scrapbooks.

96. *Comanche Chief*, Golden Anniversary Edition, June 26, 1924, in Comanche Scrapbooks.

97. J. R. Eanes, "Hazel Dell," *Comanche Chief*, Apr. 19, 1940, in Comanche Scrapbooks.

98. Eanes, "Hazel Dell." Lightfoot, "Comanche County," p. 176.

99. Eanes, "Hazel Dell."

100. Lightfoot, "Comanche County," p. 177.

101. Eanes, "Hazel Dell."

102. Lightfoot, "Comanche County," pp. 120–21.

103. Noble Hardin was no relation to Joe Hardin of Comanche County or John Wesley Hardin (Joe's brother).

104. Lightfoot, "Comanche County," pp. 120–21.

105. The slaying of Webb is described earlier in this chapter.

106. Statement by G. W. White, Oct., 1932, in Felix Williams and Hervey Chesley, Hamilton County, Texas, Notes on as Told by Early Settlers to Felix Williams and Hervey Chesley (typescripts, University of Texas Archives, Earl Vandale Collection, File Box A 21/20).

107. Statement of Mrs. Aaron Little, Jan. 29, 1949, in Comanche Scrapbooks.

108. Hardin, *Life*, pp. 94–106. Lightfoot, "Comanche County," Chap. 5 and pp. 134, 138, 146.
109. Lightfoot, "Comanche County," pp. 173–84.
110. The following account of the expulsion of the blacks from Comanche County is based on Lightfoot, "Comanche County," pp. 173–85, and Billy Bob Lightfoot, "The Negro Exodus from Comanche County, Texas," *Southwestern Historical Quarterly*, 56 (1952–1953); 407–16.
111. Lightfoot, "Comanche County," pp. 173–85.
112. On the relationship between the Farmers' Alliance and the Populist movement see, among many authorities, C. Vann Woodward, *Origins of the New South: 1877–1913* (Baton Rouge, 1951), Chaps. 7, 9.
113. Robert Lee Hunt, *A History of Farmer Movements in the Southwest: 1873–1875* (n. p., n. d.), pp. 28–29. See, also, Woodward, *Origins of the New South*, pp. 188–89.
114. C. W. Macune, "The Farmers Alliance" (1920; manuscript, University of Texas Archives). This manuscript was brought to my attention by Mr. Charles W. Macune, Jr., the great-grandson of the great Alliance leader; Charles W. Macune, Jr., also allowed me to read his unpublished "Biographical Sketch of C. W. Macune" (1964), and I gratefully acknowledge his assistance.
115. Macune, "Farmers Alliance," p. 3. In objective and manner of operation the original Farmers' Alliance as described by Macune had much in common with the Anti-horse Thief Association movement of the Midwest and Southwest. See Chap. 4, preceding discussions.
116. Henry D. and Frances T. McCallum, *The Wire that Fenced the West* (Norman, 1965), pp. 156–57, 162–66; Webb, *Texas Rangers*, pp. 426–37.
117. The following account of Brann's involvement in central Texas violence is based upon Charles Carver, *Brann and the "Iconoclast"* (Austin, 1957); a brief account is in Sonnichsen, *I'll Die before I'll Run*, pp. 285–87.
118. Carver, *Brann*, pp. 31–32.
119. Brann got into journalism in St. Louis and then moved on to Texas where he worked for newspapers in Houston and San Antonio before going to Waco to accept an attractive position as editor of the *Daily News*. But not long after arriving in Waco, Brann revived his *Iconoclast* (which he had published with little success in Austin from 1891 to 1894) and soon devoted himself entirely to the thriving *Iconoclast*. Carver, *Brann*, Chap. 2 and *passim*.
120. Although the Antonia Teixeira affair was certainly grist for Brann's anti-Baptist mill, his ardent defense of Antonia was quite possibly, in part, a conscience-stricken compensation for Brann's role in a family tragedy: in 1890 the Branns' pretty 13-year-old daughter, Dottie, took her own life in remorse over Brann's harsh scolding of her flirtatious activity, an activity that appears in retrospect to have been completely innocent. Dottie took an overdose of morphine and left a note for her mother, declaring, "I don't want to live. I could never be as good as you want me to. I was born for a rowdy and you would be ashamed of me." Later Brann wrote, "I killed her." Carver, *Brann*, pp. 22–24.
121. Antonia's child died. In the spring of 1897 a hung jury in the trial of Steen Morris put the case over to the next term of court for rehearing. Then, in late summer, 1897, Antonia retracted her accusation of Morris, and the case, apparently, was dismissed. But Brann was unconvinced by the retraction and charged, with circumstantial evidence to back him, that Morris and his attorney had purchased Antonia's retraction in return for the payment of her fare back to Brazil. Carver, *Brann*, pp. 110–11.

122. *Iconoclast*, Dec., 1897, quoted in Carver, *Brann*, p. 171.
123. W. A. Harris was killed instantly; J. W. Harris died several hours later.
124. Carver, *Brann*, p. 168.
125. Most notable were the Colorado County (1890–1906) and Waller County (1905) feuds, this chapter, preceding discussions. See, also, C. L. Sonnichsen's brief mention of the Black-Johnson-Echols feud in Coahoma (1910), the Johnson-Sims feud in Snyder (1916), and the 1943 feud in Victoria, all of which took place on the margins of central Texas. *I'll Die before I'll Run*, pp. 288–89.
126. Carl Coke Rister, *Oil!: Titan of the Southwest* (Norman, 1949), Chaps. 9, 11, 17, esp. pp. 154–57.
127. A. C. Greene, *The Santa Claus Bank Robbery* (New York, 1972), Chaps. 12–13. I am indebted to Prof. William H. Goetzmann for calling my attention to Greene's book, one of the best works on latter-day central Texas violence.
128. Charles C. Alexander, *The Ku Klux Klan in the Southwest* (Lexington, 1965), p. 19. See, also, Alexander's earlier study, *Crusade for Conformity: The Ku Klux Klan in Texas, 1920—1930* (Houston, 1962). On the nation-wide Klan movement in the 1920's, see Chap. 1, this book.
129. Alexander, *Ku Klux Klan*, pp. 28–29.
130. *Ibid.*, pp. 41, 79.
131. *Ibid.*, p. 41.
132. *Ibid.*, p. 50.
133. John Bainbridge, *The Super-Americans,* (Garden City, N. Y., 1961), p. 243.
134. *Ibid.*, p. 243.
135. *Ibid.*, p. 244.
136. *Ibid.*, Chap. 14.
137. *Ibid.*, pp. 238–39, 245–47.
138. U. S. Federal Bureau of Investigation, *Uniform Crime Reports—1970* (Washington, 1971)), pp. 66–71.
139. *Ibid.*
140. *Ibid.*, pp. 82–97.
141. Bainbridge, *Super-Americans*, pp. 242–43.
142. *Ibid.*, pp. 256–57.
143. Sonnichsen, *I'll Die before I'll Run*, pp. 288–89.
144. Bainbridge, *Super-Americans*, pp. 239, 248–50.
145. Sonnichsen, *I'll Die before I'll Run*, pp. 8–9, the source, also, for the epigraph to this chapter.
146. *Report of the Warren Commission on the Assassination of President Kennedy* (New York, 1964), pp. 54–56.
147. *Ibid.*, pp. 350–58, 399.
148. *Ibid.*, p. 331.
149. See Chap. 1.
150. *Newsweek*, Aug. 20, 1973, p. 32; Aug. 27, 1973, pp. 22, 25. Corll was assisted, allegedly, by two young henchmen, Elmer Wayne Henley, Jr., and David Owen Brooks.
151. *Report of the Warren Commission on the Assassination of President Kennedy* (New York, 1964).
152. *The Challenge of Crime in a Free Society: A Report of the President's Commission on Law Enforcement and Administration of Justice* (Washington, 1967).
153. *Report of the National Advisory Commission on Civil Disorders* (Washington, 1968).

154. *To Establish Justice, To Insure Domestic Tranquility: Final Report of the National Commission on the Causes and Prevention of Violence* (Washington, 1969).

155. Among the many books on the war itself, see Frances FitzGerald's *Fire in the Lake: The Vietnamese and the Americans in Vietnam* (Boston, 1972).

156. David Halberstam, *The Best and the Brightest* (New York, 1972), p. 41.

157. *Ibid.*, pp. 47–56. See, also, C. Wright Mills, *The Power Elite* (New York, 1956), Chaps. 3, 10, 12, and *passim.*

158. Baltimore, 1956.

159. See note 156, above, for facts of publication.

160. Halberstam, *Best and Brightest*, Chap. 4. Aside from his crucial role in the Kennedy and Johnson administrations, McGeorge Bundy is the prototype of the Eastern elite adherent of the policy of paternalistic military intervention-ism. Franklin D. Roosevelt, in background and foreign policy, too, was an exemplar of the type described here, although Roosevelt did not share the conservatism in domestic affairs that has characterized the typical Eastern elite interventionist since the turn of the century. It should be noted, however, that by no means all elite Easterners have been proponents of paternalistic military intervention, as the case of Chester Bowles shows. On Bowles, see Halberstam, *Best and Brightest*, pp. 11–21.

161. Halberstam, *Best and Brightest*, pp. 94–99, 169–80, 200.

162. On this long-term process, 1961–1965, see Halberstam, *Best and Brightest*, and Neil Sheehan, Hedrick Smith, E. W. Kenworthy, and Fox Butterfield, *The Pentagon Papers* (New York, 1971), Chaps. 3–7.

163. Alfred Steinberg, *Sam Johnson's Boy: A Close-Up of the President from Texas* (New York, 1968), pp. 838–39, the source, also, for the epigraph to this chapter.

164. *Ibid.*, p. 173. See, also, pp. 233–34, 243, 307–12, 355–56, 373–75, 399–403, 566–67, 753, and *passim;* Philip L. Geyelin, *Lyndon B. Johnson and the World* (New York, 1966), pp. 30–35.

165. Steinberg, *Sam Johnson's Boy*, p. 771; see, also, p. 747.

166. See following discussions, this chapter.

167. Webb, *Texas Rangers*, pp. 386–90, for the end of Sam Bass. Other episodes of central Texas violence mentioned in this paragraph appear earlier in this chapter.

168. William C. Pool, Emmie Craddock, and David E. Conrad, *Lyndon Baines Johnson: The Formative Years* (San Marcos, 1965), pp. 12–13.

169. *Ibid.*, pp. 19–20.

170. *Ibid.*, pp. 12–13.

171. *Ibid.*, pp. 13, 15.

172. *Ibid.*, p. 15. Rebekah Baines Johnson, *A Family Album*, ed. John S. Moursund (New York, 1965), pp. 72–74.

173. See following discussions, this chapter.

174. Johnson, *Family Album*, pp. 70–71.

175. Pool *et al.*, *Lyndon Baines Johnson*, pp. 21–47.

176. Johnson, *Family Album*, pp. 75–80.

177. The quotations in the conversation between Sam and Rebekah are exactly as Rebekah gave them in her reminiscence in *Family Album*, p. 18, except for my emphasis of the words, "he will still be named for my friend Linden."

178. Pool *et al.*, *Lyndon Baines Johnson*, p. 24.

179. The account of the San Saba Mob and W. C. Linden's prosecution of it is based upon Sonnichsen, *I'll Die before I'll Run*, pp. 206–31, 348–51.

180. *Ibid.*, p. 229.

181. *Ibid.*, pp. 229–30.
182. Pool *et al.*, *Lyndon Baines Johnson*, p. 37.
183. For an account of the Ku Klux Klan in central Texas, see preceding discussion, this chapter.
184. Steinberg, *Sam Johnson's Boy*, p. 28.
185. Sam Houston Johnson, *My Brother Lyndon*, ed. Enrique H. Lopez (New York, 1970), pp. 30–31.
186. Although at this time most Americans look back upon the Vietnam War as having been a mistake, there are some who still feel that Johnson's Vietnamese policy was correct. Quite possibly such supporters of Johnson's Vietnamese policy would be thankful for the shaping impact of the central Texas tradition of violence upon Johnson's statesmanship.
187. Eric F. Goldman, *The Tragedy of Lyndon Johnson* (New York, 1969), pp. 43–46; Hugh Sidey, *A Very Personal Presidency: Lyndon Johnson in the White House* (London, 1968); Pool *et al.*, *Lyndon Baines Johnson*, pp. 21–48, 174–81; Lyndon Baines Johnson, *The Vantage Point: Perspectives of the Presidency, 1963–1969* (New York, 1971), pp. 154–55.
188. See preceding discussion, this chapter.
189. Webb, *Texas Rangers*, Chaps. 12–13.
190. *Ibid.*, p. x. (Emphasis mine.)
191. Sidey, *Very Personal Presidency*, pp. 211–12. See, also, Geyelin, *Lyndon B. Johnson*, Chap. 10 and *passim.*
192. Sidey, *Very Personal Presidency*, pp. 20–21.
193. *Ibid.*, pp. 21–22.
194. See preceding discussion, this chapter.
195. Pool *et al.*, *Lyndon Baines Johnson*, pp. 14–15. Bill Porterfield, *LBJ Country* (Garden City, N. Y. 1965), p. 39.
196. Geyelin, *Lyndon B. Johnson*, p. 237; Goldman, *Tragedy of Lyndon Johnson*, p. 395, also tells this story.
197. Johnson, *Vantage Point*, p. 155. In addition to the writers cited in the note above, the following writers refer to the importance of Johnson's Hill Country background in central Texas: Rowland Evans and Robert Novak, *Lyndon B. Johnson: The Exercise of Power: A Political Biography* (New York, 1966), pp. 6–7 and *passim;* William S. White, *The Professional: Lyndon B. Johnson* (Boston, 1964), Chap. 6; Tom Wicker, *JFK and LBJ: The Influence of Personality upon Politics* (New York, 1968), pp. 234, 252; Richard Harwood and Haynes Johnson, *Lyndon* (New York, 1973), pp. 22–23; and Jack R. Maguire, ed., *A President's Country: A Guide to the Hill Country of Texas* (Austin, 1964). Two Texas writers extensively treat Johnson's role in Texas politics and life but do not particularly stress his Hill Country origins; both works are strongly critical of Johnson and, despite being written from almost diametrically opposed ideological viewpoints (ultra-conservative vs. progressive), stress alleged flaws in Johnson's ethical character that more sympathetic writers have viewed as examples of pragmatism: J. Evetts Haley, *A Texan Looks at Lyndon: A Study in Illegitimate Power* (Canyon, Tex., 1964); Robert Sherrill, *The Accidental President* (New York, 1967).
198. Johnson, *Vantage Point*, p. xi.
199. *Ibid.*, p. 68.
200. *Ibid.*
201. *Ibid.*, p. 118.
202. *Ibid.*, pp. 124–25.